# THE PERCEPTION OF POVERTY

# CONTRIBUTIONS TO ECONOMIC ANALYSIS

156

*Honorary Editor*
J. TINBERGEN

*Editors*
D. W. JORGENSON
J. WAELBROECK

NORTH-HOLLAND
AMSTERDAM · NEW YORK · OXFORD

# THE PERCEPTION OF POVERTY

Aldi J. M. HAGENAARS
*Center for Research in Public Economics*
*Leyden University*
*The Netherlands*

1986

NORTH-HOLLAND
AMSTERDAM · NEW YORK · OXFORD

© ELSEVIER SCIENCE PUBLISHERS B.V., 1986

All rights reserved. No part of this publication may be reproduced, stored in a retrieval system, or transmitted, in any form or by any means, electronic, mechanical, photocopying, recording or otherwise, without the prior permission of the copyright owner.

ISBN: 0 444 87898 x

*Publishers:*
ELSEVIER SCIENCE PUBLISHERS B.V.
P.O. Box 1991
1000 BZ Amsterdam
The Netherlands

*Sole distributors for the U.S.A. and Canada:*
ELSEVIER SCIENCE PUBLISHING COMPANY, INC.
52 Vanderbilt Avenue
New York, N.Y. 10017
U.S.A.

PRINTED IN THE NETHERLANDS

# Introduction to the series

This series consists of a number of hitherto unpublished studies, which are introduced by the editors in the belief that they represent fresh contributions to economic science.

The term 'economic analysis' as used in the title of the series has been adopted because it covers both the activities of the theoretical economist and the research worker.

Although the analytical methods used by the various contributors are not the same, they are nevertheless conditioned by the common origin of their studies, namely theoretical problems encountered in practical research. Since for this reason, business cycle research and national accounting, research work on behalf of economic policy, and problems of planning are the main sources of the subjects dealt with, they necessarily determine the manner of approach adopted by the authors. Their methods tend to be 'practical' in the sense of not being too far remote from application to actual economic conditions. In addition they are quantitative.

It is the hope of the editors that the publication of these studies will help to stimulate the exchange of scientific information and to reinforce international cooperation in the field of economics.

*The Editors*

"In fact, poverty studies never risk going out of business even in rich, industrial societies, but they do face an awkward problem of definition"
[Mary Douglas and Baron Isherwood, The World of Goods, p.17]

## PREFACE

After a long post-war period in which the attention of economists in western countries was mainly focused on economic growth, in recent times renewed attention is given to poverty and income distribution.

Galbraith (1958) was among the first to notice that "with the transition of the very poor from a majority to a comparative minority position, they ceased to be automatically an object of interest to the politician. (...) But in the United States the survival of poverty is remarkable. We ignore it because we share with all societies at all times the capacity for not seeing what we do not wish to see. (...) But while our failure to notice can be explained, it cannot be excused."

This reappraisal of poverty as an economic and social problem in affluent countries may appear ironic, while the differences between these countries and developing countries are still striking. Is one justified in studying poverty in European societies, where GNP per head is on average about 10 times as high as in developing countries [United Nations (1979)]?

We think the answer should be affirmative: we cannot abstain from noticing deprivation in western societies, because of even stronger deprivation elsewhere. The differences in the kind of deprivation in both areas, however, show that the concept "poverty" may have two meanings; the first being a situation in which means are not or hardly sufficient to stay alive; the second being a situation in which means are not sufficient to live a life that is considered normal in society.

These two different interpretations of the concept of poverty have important consequences for measurement, analysis and reduction of poverty.

Poverty measurement is an important first step in a program aimed at reducing poverty; however, the choice of the definition of poverty as a relative or an absolute concept may result in different measurement methods and hence different values of indices that represent the extent of poverty. A definition of poverty hence is essential for the results of poverty measurement.

In analysing poverty determinants, the same problem arises; depending on the definition of poverty chosen one may find different groups in society to be at a high poverty risk. The implication of these problems in measurement and analysis of poverty for any social policy program aimed at reducing poverty is obvious; the choice of a specific program will in the

end always depend on the definition of poverty chosen.
In this book a number of well-known poverty definitions are reviewed, and one definition is chosen to be the basis of empirical research. This poverty line definition is based on direct measurement of welfare by means of survey questions. The poverty line is defined as the income level at which households say their income is just between sufficient and insufficient. This (empirical) poverty line definition is applied to a dataset on eight European countries (Belgium, Denmark, France, (West) Germany, Ireland, Italy, the Netherlands, and the United Kingdom) that was collected in 1979 with financial support from the European Communities.
Once the definition is chosen, our interest is in measurement of poverty and analysis of poverty determinants, from which policies for the reduction of poverty may be derived.

In order to measure poverty, indices have to be chosen that reflect the extent of poverty. Again, however, the index to be used depends on the definition of what one wishes to measure - is it the number of poor (either as a percentage of the total population, or as an absolute number)? Is it the extent to which people in poverty on average fall short of the income that is defined to be minimal? Is a possible income inequality amongst the poor relevant to the measurement of poverty? Do we look at the poor as a separate group in society, or do we relate their conditions to those of others in society? All these questions have to be answered before an index of poverty can be chosen. In this book, we develop a social welfare framework that enables us to choose a poverty index on the basis of social welfare arguments. This framework provides us with a class of poverty indices that meets a set of requirements. One index out of this class of poverty indices is chosen to measure the extent of poverty.

Given the poverty line definition adapted, the analysis of determinants of poverty consists of two parts. On the one hand, we have to assess how the income level households consider to be between sufficient and insufficient varies with socio-economic characteristics, and on the other hand we have to estimate the effect of these characteristics on actual household income. By confrontation of these effects on actual income and income perceived to be just sufficient we may derive poverty probabilities for various socio-economic types, for instance, the probability of being poor for households where no income is earned because of unemployment or retirement. This analysis yields information on the characteristics that make people poverty prone.

Finally, some conclusions for social policy are drawn; it is described to what extent economic growth will eliminate poverty, and what alternative general measures are available. It is also described which groups are at especially high poverty risk, and therefore need more specific policies. We end by discussing some recent trends in income and poverty, and give some suggestions for further research.

The structure of this book is as follows. In chapter 1 a review of poverty line definitions is given. In chapter 2 the Leyden poverty line that is applied throughout the book is formally derived, and compared to the other main poverty line definitions. In chapter 3 the determinants of income are discussed, and in chapter 4 the determinants of welfare. Chapter 5 combines these two in the derivation of some hypotheses on poverty for special subgroups. In chapter 6 indices that measure the extent of poverty are reviewed and a new class of poverty indices is derived. Chapter 7 gives a description of the data. In chapter 8 the first empirical results are presented: a review of average welfare levels for different household types in different countries is given, that gives a first insight into the determinants and the extent of poverty. Chapter 9 describes the empirical estimation of the determinants of income, while chapter 10 describes the empirical results for the welfare parameters. In chapter 11 these two are combined to yield poverty lines and poverty determinants. In chapter 12 a new poverty index, developed in chapter 6, is calculated for the eight different countries. Within each country, the index is decomposed to assess the extent of poverty in various subgroups in the population. Chapter 13 concludes.
Throughout the book, the words "he" and "she", "his" and "her" are used indiscriminately.

## ACKNOWLEDGEMENTS

This book has served as my Ph.D. thesis at Leyden University in June 1985. Bernard van Praag has contributed to this book not only as supervisor of the thesis and co-author of one of the articles it is based on, but also by his general help and inspiration in the production of the book. Bob Haveman, the referee of the Ph.D. thesis, was of enormous help in structuring and organizing the book.

Previous drafts of this book have been commented upon by Paul van Batenburg, Eitel Homan, Philip de Jong, Arie Kapteyn, and Teun Kloek. Their suggestions are gratefully acknowledged. The research in this book is part of the Leyden Income Evaluation Project which is supervised by Bernard van Praag.

The data have been collected as part of the "Struggle Against Poverty" of the European Communities, and with their financial support. The Central Bureau of Statistics has kindly given us permission to use the Dutch data. The questionnaire used in this survey has been designed by Bernard van Praag and the present author. The willingness of my co-designer to let me use the data is gratefully acknowledged. In the collection, screening and preparation of this dataset the assistance of Onno de Jong and Hans van Weeren has been invaluable.

Also, I should like to express my appreciation to Ed van Duin and Onno de Jong who did the computer programming for the results presented.

This book has benefited from a discussion paper by Michael O'Higgins in which he commented upon earlier research. Part of chapter 2 has been published in the Review of Income and Wealth [Hagenaars and Van Praag (1985)].

Finally, I should like to mention that it was a pleasure to cooperate with Saskia ten Asbroek, who skilfully typed and retyped numerous drafts of this monograph.

TABLE OF CONTENTS

Preface / ix

Acknowledgements / xii

Table of contents / xiii

1. The poverty concept / 1

    1.1 What is poverty? / 1
    1.2 A review of poverty line definitions / 15
    1.3 Conclusion / 37

    Notes / 41

2. The derivation of the poverty line / 43

    2.1 A welfare definition of poverty / 44
    2.2 Comparison with other poverty line definitions / 55
    2.3 Evaluation of different definitions / 59

    Notes / 65

3. Determinants of income / 67

    3.1 The income concept used / 67
    3.2 Determinants of individual income / 71
    3.3 Participation of the partner in the labour force / 79

    Notes / 82

    Appendix / 83

4. Determinants of welfare parameters / 86

    4.1 Determinants of the individual welfare function of income / 86
    4.2 Hypotheses on the effects of socio-economic variables on $\mu$ / 95
    4.3 Hypotheses on the effects of socio-economic variables on $\sigma$ / 100

    Notes / 102

    Appendix / 103

5. Determinants of poverty / 105

    5.1 Derivation of the poverty line / 106
    5.2 Poverty determinants / 109
    5.3 Poverty determinants for other household types / 112
    5.4 Hypotheses on determinants of poverty / 114

6. The extent of poverty / 119
    6.1 Introduction / 119
    6.2 Axiomatic requirements / 121
    6.3 Performance of various poverty indices / 125
    6.4 Generalization of CHU's index / 128
    6.5 Special cases of the general class of poverty indices / 132
    6.6 Extensions / 136
    6.7 Poverty measurement and the individual welfare function of income / 138

    Notes / 141

    Appendix / 142

7. Description of the data / 149
    7.1 Organization / 149
    7.2 Sampling methods / 150
    7.3 Written questionnaires versus oral interviews / 150
    7.4 Differences in questionnaires / 151
    7.5 The interview / 151
    7.6 Analysis of response / 152
    7.7 Representativeness of the sample / 153
    7.8 The use of weights in regression analysis / 156
    7.9 Missing observations / 158
    7.10 Measurement errors / 159

    Notes / 160

    Appendix / 161

8. Empirical results: differences in welfare / 167

    Notes / 174

    Appendix / 175

9. Empirical results: determinants of income / 180
    9.1 Individual income functions for working men / 180
    9.2 Individual income functions for working women / 196
    9.3 Income of non-working households / 204

    Notes / 211

    Appendix / 212

10. Empirical results: determinants of welfare / 216
    10.1 Determinants of $\mu$ / 216
    10.2 Determinants of $\sigma$ / 227

    Notes / 231

    Appendix / 232

11. Empirical results: poverty lines and poverty determinants / 240

    11.1 Poverty lines, differentiated according to household type / 240
    11.2 Poverty lines in different countries / 243
    11.3 The effect of children / 245
    11.4 Comparison of one- and two-earner families / 247
    11.5 The probability of being poor / 249

    Notes / 259

    Appendix / 260

12. Empirical results: the extent of poverty / 264

    12.1 The poverty index for concave utility functions / 264
    12.2 The poverty index with the welfare function of income / 267

13. Conclusions / 271

    13.1 Derivation of poverty lines / 271
    13.2 Poverty characteristics / 274
    13.3 The extent of poverty / 275
    13.4 Recent developments / 276

    Notes / 279

Bibliography / 280

Author index / 293

Subject index / 297

Chapter 1

THE POVERTY CONCEPT

1.1 What is poverty?

Poverty might in general be defined as a situation in which needs are not sufficiently satisfied [see e.g. Drewnowski, (1976)]. This general definition must be further specified. What needs are considered? What is meant by "sufficiently"?

To provide a specification of this poverty definition is the objective of most of this first chapter. Before turning to the problems involved in such a definition we first try to assess the place of a poverty study like this in the general framework of economic theory. Is there an economic theory of poverty? As mentioned in the introduction, poverty has been relatively neglected in both economic science and in economic policy in a long post-war period of economic growth, because "economists and sociologists had lost confidence in their ability to specify why one income distribution was better than another" [Lampman (1971), p.16]. The confidence needed to make statements involving interpersonal comparison was, however, once felt strongly enough by Pigou to conclude that social welfare would increase by an income transfer of a rich person to someone who is poorer, and by Bernoulli to recommend a progressive income tax. These scholars of the "material welfare school"[1] have later, when the cardinal utility theory on which their statements were based was replaced by ordinalism, been accused of "a tendency to draw facile welfare conclusions (...), ignoring the difficulties in making meaningful interpersonal comparisons" [Blaug (1968), p.357]. However, the same critic admits that "... very little survives once the taboo on interpersonal comparisons is imposed" [Blaug (1968), p.596].

As in this monograph on poverty necessarily some assumptions on interpersonal comparisons are made, it is useful to restate briefly the basic assumptions on utility, made by the material welfare school, and the main points of criticism on these assumptions. We hope to show that without making the same errors, the confidence to be able to make statements on income distribution and poverty may to some extent be restored to economists.

The name of the material welfare school is based on the definition of economics that was current in the nineteenth century when Jevons (1871), Marshall (1874), and Menger (1871) wrote their pioneering works. Economics was "the study of the causes of material welfare". Two aspects of this definition deserve special attention. Firstly, the restriction of the realm of economics to "material" matters obviously excludes many subject matters that are nowadays included in economics. This criticism was made by Robbins (1932) who proposed a more general definition of economics, viz. "the study of human behaviour as a relationship between ends and scarce means which have alternative uses". The restriction to "material" causes of welfare had major consequences for the utility concept adapted in the material welfare school. Utility was defined to be a property of goods that causes a certain feeling, that we call satisfaction; or, in Bentham's words:

> "By utility is meant that property in any object whereby it tends to produce benefit, advantage, pleasure, good, or happiness (all this in the present case comes to the same thing) or, (what comes again to the same thing) to prevent the happening of mischief, pain, evil, or unhappiness to the party whose interest is considered".
> [Bentham (1823), quoted in Page (1968)]

It may be noted that in this definition the restriction to "material" is only found in the objects that provide utility, and not in the feelings these objects are defined to produce, which are as immaterial as "happiness" can be. However, by studying material objects only, the assumption of measurability was facilitated. We return to this assumption shortly.

The second point to make on the material welfare definition is that it is explicitly concerned with welfare, which includes both individual and social welfare. In the material welfare school, poverty is hence an integrated part of welfare economics: poverty is a situation of low welfare, and to study the determinants of poverty is to study the determinants of welfare. This concern with welfare sometimes took the form of a moral obligation: Bentham's "Principle of utility", for example, dictates that every action is to be approved that promotes welfare [Bentham (1823)]. Although such normative prescriptions are nowadays no longer accepted as scientific statements, most economists do in fact agree upon the desirability of maximizing social welfare. They disagree, however, about the definition of social welfare and, moreover, about the question whether it can be defined at all. Again, this was easier in the restrictive definition of economics used in the material welfare school.

Given this definition of economics, how did the material welfare school set out to study and improve material welfare? Two general ways of improving welfare may be distinguished: by increasing the total number of commodities that provide utility ("economic growth") or by distributing these commodities differently over society ("income redistribution").
If one wishes to evaluate the effect of either of these changes on welfare, one needs a measure of welfare that reflects increases or decreases in the satisfaction felt. In deriving such a measure, a number of problems have to be solved:
(1) Is it possible for a person to compare the utility provided by different commodities?
(2) Is it possible to observe and measure the extent to which needs are satisfied? What is the unit of measurement?
(3) Is it possible to compare and add one person's satisfaction to that of another?

The answers of the materialists to these questions were affirmative: satisfaction or utility could in principle be measured, observed and compared over persons. From the utility of commodities the utility of all commodities taken together could hence be derived for each individual, yielding the utility of total "command over resources" or income. The utility of income for different persons could be measured (at least in principle), compared and added, leading to an index for total welfare in society.
The further assumption of decreasing marginal utility, first stated by Gossen[2] in 1854 on intuitive grounds, and argued by Jevons (1871) on the basis of the Weber/Fechner law, enabled conclusions on the effect of income redistribution on total welfare in society to be drawn: social welfare would increase if a transfer of income was made from a rich person to a poor person [Pigou (1932)].
Hence the welfare conclusions drawn by Pigou and others depend upon the assumptions that utility may be measured,[3] compared over persons, and has the property of decreasing marginal returns. For these assumptions no "proofs" could be given by the materialists, which was not necessary ac-

cording to Bentham:

> "... though each of these propositions may prove false or inexact in a given individual case, that will furnish no argument against their speculative truth and practical utility. It is enough for the justification of these propositions, (...), if they approach nearer the truth than any others which can be substituted for them".
> [Bentham, quoted by Stigler (1950)]

This truth by assumption did not satisfy the critics of the materialist school who stated that utility, as it could not be observed, was outside positivist science.
Pareto (1906) threw doubt on the ability of the consumer to rank utility differences; an ability that is required for cardinal measurement. Moreover, Pareto argued that an ordinal utility concept, reflected by indifference curves, suffices as well for the derivation of demand curves. Slutsky (1915) followed in an attempt to make economics "completely independent of psychological assumptions and philosophical hypothesis". Although the leading economists of the day were gradually convinced cardinal utility was not essential to the derivation of demand curves they were reluctant to dismiss the concept completely because of its uses for welfare analysis.

The new definition of economics in terms of scarce means for many ends by Robbins in 1932, was followed by a change in emphasis from welfare economics, stained by the denounced welfare definitions of economics, to scarcity of commodities and equilibrium analysis. For this aim ordinal utility provided answers requiring less assumptions than the cardinalist utility theory of the material welfare school. Occam's razor hence declared the new ordinalist approach an improvement, and it soon gained a strong position in economics, that still lasts.

However, one may doubt whether the supposed improvement was indeed a progress of science. Cooter and Rappoport (1984) conclude their valuable review of both schools in saying that "one can talk unequivocally about the progress of science only when it continues to address the same questions". Ordinalists address different questions and use a different definition of utility than the cardinalists of the material welfare school. Hence, one cannot declare one approach to be better than the other; one should ask which approach is most fitted for the specific questions that one addresses.

A synthesis of the theories of ordinal and cardinal utility is found in the formulation of a social welfare function [Bergson (1938), Samuelson (1953)] that leads to the same conclusions on the subjects of production and exchange as the theory of ordinal utility, without requiring more assumptions, but leads in addition to explicit statements on income distributional issues once one is willing to accept an additional assumption, which concerns interpersonal comparability of utility.

The recent revival of attention for problems of poverty and income distribution has led to a reappraisal of cardinalism. Such a reappraisal may be even more welcomed in a period of economic recession, when the Paretian solution of economic growth fails for the purpose of increasing social welfare and the only instrument left is redistribution.

Van Praag (1968) restores a cardinal welfare concept as a possible solution for problems the ordinalists cannot easily solve, like uncertainty and dynamics in consumer behaviour. He considers utility to be a "primitive concept" that "cannot be defined in terms of other concepts without eliciting a lot of questions on the definition of those allegedly more basic questions" [Van Praag (1968), p.1]. Utility is in fact defined by means of a measurement method, in the same way as temperature is defined by a score on a thermometer. As thermometers give a temperature score which is unique up to a linear transformation, so is the utility score defined by the measurement method.

Kapteyn (1977), following the cardinal approach laid out by Van Praag, concludes that cardinality of utility enables more hypotheses to be tested, and that measures of social welfare may be derived directly from the theoretical utility concept.

Sen (1970) argues that the discussion between ordinalists and cardinalists is one between two extreme points of view: either no interpersonal comparison, or complete interpersonal comparison is believed to be possible. He suggests that such "pure" systems for collective choice should be replaced by "impure" systems, where the possibility of partial interpersonal comparability is analysed. His notion of partial comparability is beautifully illustrated in the following quotation:

"Suppose we are debating the consequence on the aggregate welfare of Romans of the act of Rome being burnt while Nero played his fiddle. We recognize that Nero was delighted while the other Romans suffered, but suppose we still say that the sum total of welfare went down as a consequence. What type of interpersonal comparability are we assuming? If there is no comparability at all, we can change the utility units of different individuals differently, and by multiplying Nero's utility measures by a suitably large number, it should be possible to make Nero's gain larger in size than the loss of others. Hence we are not assuming noncomparability. But are we assuming that every Roman's welfare units can be put into one-to-one correspondence with the welfare units of every other Roman? Not necessarily. We might not be sure what precise correspondence to take, and we might admit some possible variability, but we could still be able to assert that no matter which of the various possible combinations we take, the sum total went down in any case. This is a case intermediate between noncomparability and full comparability of units."
[Sen (1970), p.99]

In order to be able to use such partial comparability we have to assume, however, that some agreement will be found in society as to the increase or decrease in total welfare in less extreme situations as the one described here. The less extreme the situations are that we consider, the more interpersonal comparability is needed for a judgement of changes in overall welfare. In one of Sen's applications a poverty index is developed on the basis of axiomatic requirements including the Pigou-Dalton requirement that a transfer from rich to poor decreases poverty. By imposing this axiom implicit statements on marginal utility are made. However, one may believe with Stigler (1950) that this approach is more honest, in that it starts by the value judgements that are otherwise hidden in the assumptions on utility functions. On the other hand some of the results following Sen's approach will be shown to be opposed to some intuitive notions on utility. The value of an axiomatic approach hence depends on the extent to which the implicit notions on individual utility functions correspond to the actual "facts", however difficult it may be to obtain information on these facts. The welfare concept developed by Van Praag, which is based on a method to measure utility directly, essentially rests upon one assumption of interpersonal comparability, i.e. that the meaning of words like "good" and "insufficient" is in one language area understood by different persons as referring to one specific identical utility level. When one accepts this axiom (upon which most of human communication rests), the method enables us to compare utility over persons on an ordinal scale. For some purposes, like the calculation of the number of people below a certain welfare level, this will be sufficient. For other purposes an additional assumption will provide us with cardinal welfare functions of individuals, from which an index of the extent of poverty may be derived.

These assumptions will be further discussed in chapter 2, when the measurement method is formally introduced. Before concluding this review, it should be noted that although the material welfare school is recognized in this revival of the belief that utility is to some extent measurable, no sole attention to "material" needs and objects is given in the works of Van Praag and Kapteyn c.s.; on the contrary, much attention is given to "immaterial" matters that may influence welfare. Not only do they therefore avoid the mistake that disreputed their predecessors, but they are also able to test empirically a number of hypotheses that the ordinalists could not, like interdependence of utility.

We will now describe some specific problems encountered in the definition of poverty, after having concluded that
- a situation of poverty is a situation of low welfare;
- in order to solve distributional problems involved in a poverty analysis a welfare concept is needed that allows some degree of comparability of persons.

Returning to the problem of defining poverty, we have to specify further the "needs" that are said not to be sufficiently satisfied.
The first question to be answered then is whether we should be concerned with some specific ("basic") needs, or with all needs of an individual, whether basic or not. The question reminds us of the discussion on the nature of economics summarized above; are "material" needs more worthy of attention by economists than "immaterial" needs? We believe that Robbins's answer to this question is still valid:

> "The economist is not concerned with ends as such. He is concerned with the way in which the attainment of ends is limited. The ends may be noble or they may be base. They may be "material" or "immaterial" if ends can be so described. But if the attainment of one set of ends involves the sacrifice of others, then it has an economic aspect".
> [Robbins (1933), p.25]

The implications of this point of view for poverty analysis are stated clearly by Watts (1968). Suppose a household has a choice between two categories of consumer goods: necessities and luxuries. The household's preferences among these goods are reflected by a set of indifference curves as illustrated in figure 1.1.

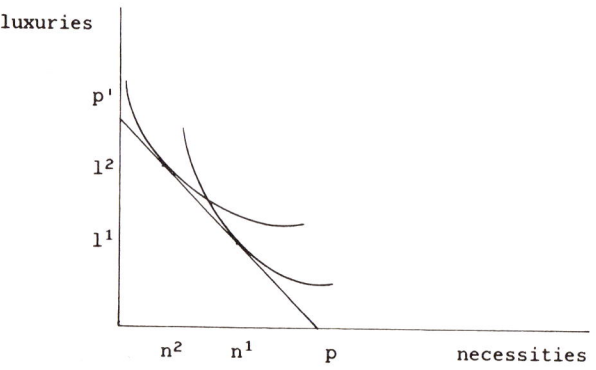

Figure 1.1  Definition of command over resources

Given a set of fixed prices and income the line p'p denotes the budget restriction. The utility maximizing household described here will choose the combination $(n^1, l^1)$. Suppose, however, that another household, facing the same budget restriction, chooses to buy a combination $(n^2, l^2)$ with less necessities and more luxuries, because it happens to have another preference ordering between the two. Can we conclude this second household to be poorer, because it spends less on necessities, say, food and housing? Watts argues that a positive answer would impose a restriction on the norms and values of individual decision makers. Instead, we might argue that everyone who has sufficient command over goods and services (reflected by the budget restriction) to consume a certain combination of luxuries and necessities is at least as well off if he actually chooses some other combination [Watts (1968), pp.321-322]. This respect for the diversity of tastes and values (an economist's value judgement, according to Watts) will be maintained in this monograph. We therefore adapt this part of Watts's definition of poverty: it is the command over resources to satisfy needs that a poverty definition should be concerned with, rather than the actual consumption of some specific goods.

The definition and operationalization of "command over resources" has over the last two decades improved from current money income to composite indicators of economic status. Morgan et al. (1962) take account of non-money income like home production, and deduct taxes from current pre-tax money income. In later work the value of leisure is also included [Morgan (1969)]. Both the inclusion of leisure and of home production neutralizes the index of command over resources for the household's preferences with respect to cash income, income in kind, and leisure. To current net income an annuitized value of net worth is added by Weisbrod and Hansen (1968), whereby they render the index of economic status neutral for differences in tastes between consumption and saving. A further improvement is the inclusion of non-cash transfers like subsidized food, housing or medical care [Taussig (1973), Smeeding (1975), Moon (1977)].

The concept of "full income" or "full wealth", developed by Becker (1965), may be seen as the theoretical basis for this generalization of command over resources; his "full wealth" reflects the present value of the maximum money income achievable over lifetime by devoting all the time and resources of a household to earning income. Garfinkel and Haveman (1978, p.8) describe a procedure to estimate the "earnings capacity" of a household, which they define as "the income stream that would be generated if a household unit employed its human and physical assets to capacity". Their index also includes human capital, and is one of the most comprehensive measures of economic status presently available. However, their generalized definition of command over resources as well as the others reviewed here reflect economic status, and not necessarily utility or welfare of a household. This discrepancy between economic status and utility is mentioned by Garfinkel and Haveman with respect to the way the presence of children should be taken into account: "In most cases, the presence of children conveys utility to the parents; an ideal measure of economic welfare would reflect this value. In an ideal framework, the net benefit of children would equal the gross flow of satisfaction they convey, less the cost required for their care". As they lack a measure of utility, however, they have to proceed by ignoring the utility conveyed by the presence of children. A similar problem arises if one considers permanent income as an index of economic status rather than current income, in order to smooth out year-to-year fluctuations in income; evidence is given by Mirer (1974) that income variability itself probably affects well-being of families.

More examples of the possible discrepancy between economic status and welfare can be found,[4] of which the determination of equivalence scales for households of different size is for our purpose the most relevant. How can the welfare of households with different size and composition be compared, when an index of economic status rather than welfare is used? In most studies described above one proceeds to use an equivalence scale developed elsewhere, e.g. for the poverty index of the Social Security Administration [see Orshansky (1965)], which does not necessarily give the appropriate standardization factors for more comprehensive measures of economic status.[5]

It appears that the improved measures of economic status, however valuable in refining the definition of "command over resources", are not equivalent to measures of economic welfare, and that the lack of a measure of welfare impairs welfare neutral comparison of households.

Ideally, in a study of poverty one wishes to relate the (generalized) command over resources to utility, and define poverty in terms of welfare, rather than in terms of command over resources:

> Poverty is a situation in which the welfare, derived from the command over resources of a household falls below a certain minimum welfare level, called the poverty threshold.

This definition has several advantages. It shares with the measures of economic status the property of not imposing a norm on a household's preference between goods, services and leisure. Moreover, it allows for differentiation according to household size and composition, as well as (in principle) other aspects that influence welfare from a certain command over resources, like income stability and health. A disadvantage is that it requires knowledge of the relationship between command over resources and welfare, and that it requires the choice of a certain poverty threshold in terms of welfare. If a one-to-one correspondence between command over resources and welfare exists and can be measured, the poverty definition given above provides us with a definition of a poverty line in terms of command over resources:

> The poverty line for a household is the command over resources that this household needs to have a certain welfare level that is chosen to be the poverty threshold.

We will review the various poverty line definitions that have been proposed in poverty research, and discuss to what extent they conform with

our "ideal" definition. One property that all these poverty lines share is that the command over resources is defined in terms of current money income.[6] If one wishes to take account of other, non-cash components of command over resources one may calculate for each household an index of economic status (e.g. the earnings capacity) that represents its generalized command over resources, before comparing it with the poverty line. As indices of economic status are not necessarily equivalent to indices of welfare, however, the differences in welfare that various household types derive from a certain money income should be reflected by equivalence scales that neutralize these differences. Although many poverty researchers start by saying that "ideally, the distribution of welfare should be studied instead of the distribution of income" [Thurow (1969), p.13], few actually use an explicit welfare concept in the derivation of the poverty line. Implicitly, however, every poverty line definition can be seen to be based on a definition of welfare. On the relationship between welfare and poverty different hypotheses are found in the literature. Some authors[7] argue that poverty is not a discrete condition, but that the constriction of choice becomes progressively more damaging in a continuous manner. This leads to the notion of a "welfare ratio" that reflects the extent to which a household's command over resources exceeds or falls short of the poverty line. Others consider the poverty line to be a line with "some absolute justification of its own" [Sen (1983), p.167] below which "one cannot participate adequately in communal activities, or be free of public shame from failure to satisfy conventions". In this absolutist view, the poverty line represents some kink in the utility function. The distinction between these two points of view will appear to be especially important in the measurement of poverty, to be discussed in chapter 6. Here we discuss the welfare concepts used in all poverty line definitions, and their merits. They are compared with respect to the following aspects:
(a) whether an absolute or relative poverty concept is used;
(b) which equivalence scales are used;
(c) whether they are subjective or objective.
Let us first see why these aspects of a poverty line definition deserve special attention.

ad (a): Absolute versus relative
An absolute poverty line is not meant to change with the standard of liv-

ing in society. People are defined as poor when some absolute needs are not sufficiently satisfied, i.e., needs that are not related to the consumption pattern of other people in society. A relative poverty line is in some way related to the general standard of living in society; a completely relative poverty line will increase or decrease with the same percentage as the decrease or increase in the standard of living. In other words, a completely absolute poverty line has an elasticity of 0 with respect to changes in the general standard of living in society, while a completely relative poverty line has an elasticity of 1 [see Kilpatrick (1973), Van Praag (1984), Hagenaars and Van Praag (1985)]. The concept "general standard of living" is operationalized by median income in society in this monograph.

The question whether poverty should be seen as an absolute condition of deprivation, or as a situation of relative deprivation has dominated the discussion on poverty line definitions.[8] The arguments pro and con each point of view, with the appropriate references, will be summarized when the various definitions are introduced.

The reason that this aspect of poverty line definitions is so important is that it also partly determines the policy that might reduce poverty. Poverty as measured by an absolute line may be abolished by economic growth. Poverty as measured by some relative lines can only be reduced by a decrease in income inequality. In other relative poverty definitions (percentile definitions) poverty can never be abolished or reduced as long as a certain extent of inequality is present.

### ad (b): Equivalence scales

Hardly anybody will promote one income level as a poverty line for all families, independent of family composition. Even the crudest poverty line definition usually makes some differentiation according to family size, if only by defining a separate line for families and for unrelated individuals, like the $3000 and $1500 poverty lines that have been used in the United States for a few years.[9] However, the way in which differentiation for family size and composition is made differs considerably between different poverty line definitions. We will discuss the assumptions made in such a differentiation for each definition.

In fact equivalence scales may be desirable that differentiate according to other variables that influence the welfare of a family. Cost of living may for example be influenced by health or region, and may be different for farm and non-farm households; this may be an argument to differentiate poverty lines accordingly. A desirable property of a poverty line definition would hence be the possibility of differentiation according to factors influencing welfare. The choice of characteristics in an equivalence scale to be used in social policy is, however, in the end a political problem that has to be solved outside science.

ad (c): Objective versus subjective

Another important difference between poverty line definitions is found in the criteria used to identify somebody as poor. These criteria may be either objective, that is, based on objective aspects of somebody's situation, or subjective, that is, based on the opinion and feeling of the person concerned. One may associate the subjective evaluation by the welfare or utility that people experience, and the objective aspects by the command over resources. In general the subjective opinion of individuals whether they consider themselves to be poor will be correlated with objective circumstances like income, family size, et cetera. If this correlation would be perfect, and all variables concerned are included in the objective line, people would be classified in the same way by the subjective and the objective poverty line. If the correlation is not perfect, two incongruities may occur. First, a certain number of people may be classified as poor on the basis of some objective criteria like income and family size, but do not consider themselves poor. Secondly, a number of people may be classified as non-poor according to income and family size, but poor according to their own evaluation. All possible situations are summarized in table 1.

Table 1

|  |  | objective classification: | |
|---|---|---|---|
|  |  | poor | non-poor |
| subjective classification | poor | consensus | type II error |
|  | non-poor | type I error | consensus |

We may call these two situations type I and type II errors, respectively.

In fact the errors are made because the evaluation of one's situation depends on more circumstances than income, family size, and the few other differentiating characteristics that are usually chosen. These circumstances may be, e.g., health, expectations on the future, leisure, and various other individual characteristics. These are not, however, any less "objective" than income and family size. If we would devise methods of observing these characteristics as well, they might be included in an objective poverty line, if society judges differentiation according to these characteristics to be desirable. It is this last "if" that is crucial: some of the characteristics that cause the differences between an objective poverty evaluation and a subjective poverty evaluation will be generally accepted as valid, e.g. health, while others will not, like "greed".

Hence the ideal way of solving the incongruities discussed above is to measure both someone's subjective evaluation, and as many objective characteristics as possible, and to describe the relationship between them. Once a (sub)set of characteristics is chosen to be the basis for differentiation, the other characteristics may be "averaged out".

In this procedure the choice of characteristics for differentiation of the poverty line should be the result of a democratic decision making process.

In our "ideal" definition of poverty we follow Watts in his emphasis on the command over resources as an indicator of economic status, rather than the actual consumption pattern of a household. For each of the poverty lines reviewed we will discuss whether it satisfies this requirement of respect for a household's preferences.

We mention two more aspects of a poverty line definition that deserve our attention. The first is that no proper definition of whatever phenomenon we study is allowed to be a circular definition: by defining poverty as "the situation of those people who are poor" we have merely used different words to denote the same; no more meaning is given to the phenomenon. It appears that, although this seems to be an obvious requirement, a number of poverty line definitions violate it seriously.

A second requirement to a poverty line definition is that, in order to be practicable, it should be relatively simple: if the poverty status would be described by so many different dimensions that no empirical study, within the usual financial restrictions, can measure them all, we have overreached ourselves.

Finally a last remark is in order. The choice of a poverty line is a social choice to be made; the place for social choices of this type is in politics, not in science. Although we do not shrink from assumptions on welfare comparison, and may use these to give an economist's view of the advantages and disadvantages of a certain choice, the final balance should be made in a democratic process where the choice we are discussing here may be set against other social choices to be made, as varied as the social desirability of a specific income distribution to the undesirability of decreasing national income. Although in the analysis to follow some definitions are evaluated to be better than others, this is no guarantee that in a final balance of choices to be made these definitions will (or should) be adapted in social policy.

## 1.2 A review of poverty line definitions

We will distinguish the following categories of definitions:
 basic needs approaches (to be described in subsection 1.2.1),
 food ratio methods (1.2.2),
 percentage of mean or median income (1.2.3),
 percentile of income distribution (1.2.4),
 official definitions (1.2.5),
 subjective definitions, based on survey data (1.2.6),
 other definitions (1.2.7).

### 1.2.1 Basic needs approaches

The first poverty lines to be used in poverty research were based on cost for "basic needs", usually defined as food, housing and clothing [Booth (1892), Rowntree (1901)]. These basic needs have the same connotation as the "material needs" that used to be the subject of material welfare economics. Their approach has been the basis of many poverty line definitions, among which the Social Security Administration (SSA) poverty index in the United States.

The usual procedure is to estimate first the cost of minimum food requirements, and to use this cost of food as the basis for the poverty line in income terms. Three separate problems have to be solved in a definition of

this kind:
I   Is it possible to distinguish "basic needs" from other needs?
II  If we consider food to be the most basic need, how is "food" to be defined, and how are the cost of food to be calculated?
III How are the cost of food to be transformed into an income level, that is to be the poverty line?

ad I   The distinction between "basic needs" and other needs
Basic needs may be seen as the material needs on the lowest end of the hierarchical ordering of needs proposed by, e.g., Marshall (1920). However, in an interesting attempt to start the "anthropology of consumption" Douglas and Isherwood (1979, p.72) propose to "put an end to the widespread and misleading distinction between goods that sustain life and health and others that service the mind and heart". The counter argument proposed is that goods are bought and consumed because they carry meaning in the social environment of men, and that food and drink are no less or more carriers of meaning than ballet or poetry. Food hence serves many purposes besides "sustaining life"; people may derive status out of the meals they provide to friends, and the kind of food one can afford is an important determinant of one's position in society. Certain goods may not be used as food because in the culture one is living in they are not considered edible, although the goods might be perfect for the purpose of "sustaining life" (pork, beef). On the other hand, people may spend their little money on goods that do not meet a direct life sustaining purpose, because it serves a social purpose: expensive burial services are an example. Hence it is a misconception that basic needs may be defined as goods that "sustain life and health". One may, however, still distinguish a hierarchy of some sort in the consumption pattern of people. Douglas and Isherwood distinguish three stadia in which a society may find itself, and in describing these a close analogy with the old hierarchy of needs is found. In the first sector, where the poor live, people spend most of their time in production and preparation of food. In the second sector people are gradually getting provided with (time-saving) durables, like washing-machines. In the third sector, finally, people maximize social interaction and adapt their consumption pattern to enable these information flows by buying, e.g., telephone, car, theatre tickets.
The relevance of this analysis to our study is that goods cannot be con-

sidered separately, but only in relation to each other and with regard to the services they provide. Furthermore, their analysis suggests that one cannot solve poverty by getting people enough to eat and drink but by including people in the secondary and tertiary sectors. This would imply that no "basic needs" may be derived for once and for all: the opinion on basic needs of a society changes when society is gradually moving into other sectors.

In defence of some element of subsistence or basic needs Sen quotes Marx in saying that

> "nevertheless, in a given country, at a given period, the average quantity of the means of subsistence necessary for the labourer is practically known".
> [Sen (1979), p.286; Marx (1887), p.150]

If one would find agreement on the definition of basic needs, at a certain time in a certain country, they may provide an acceptable definition of the poverty line. However, the usual approach is to call food, shelter and clothing the basic needs, without further reference to society. If this approach is adapted, one has first to decide how to estimate the cost of basic needs, starting with food.

## ad II  Estimation of the cost of food

Calculation of the cost of food usually starts with an estimate of the calories that are needed to maintain "physical efficiency". This estimate is provided by nutritional experts, who decide upon an economic diet which is just sufficient to subsist.

Rowntree used estimates by Atwater, an American physiologist, and estimates by Dunlop, who studied the dietaries of prisoners in Scotland. For the SSA poverty index in the U.S. estimates were (and still are) given by the Agricultural Department.

The various estimates have been criticized for two reasons. The first criticism concerns the definition of "nutritional need". Townsend (1962, 1979) argues that the nutritional needs of individuals vary considerably with age, sex, occupation, physical activity, housing, climate, and leisure activities. Estimates of needs, even of nutritional needs, cannot be absolute: they must be relative to the kind of society in which one is living. In fact, this very argument is used by Atwater, in defending his nutritional standards against lower estimates made by some of his European colleagues:

> "My own belief is that the American standard is a much more desirable one. The scale of living or "standard of life" here is much higher than it is in Europe. (...) While it is not absolutely proven, it seems in the highest degree probable that the higher standard of living, the better nutrition, the larger product of labour, and the higher wages go together. It is in view of such considerations as these that I have ventured to suggest more liberal standards for dietaries than those which have been proposed by the European authorities above quoted."
> [Atwater, quoted in Rowntree (1901), pp.93-94]

The professional debate continues with Dunlop's justification of his caloric estimate, which in turn is higher than Atwater's:

> It might be urged that these studies contradict Atwater's standard. He states 3500 calories as sufficient food for moderate labour, these prison studies show that for convict labour 3500 was insufficient, while 3700 was necessary. But this I consider does not amount to a contradiction, because the term moderate or middle labour is ambiguous".
> [Dunlop, quoted in Rowntree (1901), p.96]

These quotations illustrate that "the issue of level of physical activity does highlight value problems by undermining the nutritionist claim for objectivity and by dramatizing the difficulties of measurement" [Rein (1974), p.58].

The second problem in determining the ingredients of a minimum food basket is the conflict between expert advice and actual behaviour. If the dietary allowances are estimated without reference to the actual consumption pattern in society, these allowances will in practice seldom be used in the economical way that nutritionists have prescribed. The actual consumption pattern of people will be influenced both by individual habits and by customary social consumption behaviour [see, e.g., Townsend (1962), Rein (1974)]. This is acknowledged by most advocates of the basic needs approach. Their solutions, however, vary considerably. Rowntree (1901) solved the problem by introducing two different definitions of poverty: primary poverty is the situation in which means are not sufficient to buy the prescribed minimum; secondary poverty is the situation in which a family does have enough means to meet its basic needs, but fails to spend it in the prescribed, economical way. The SSA tried to incorporate social customs into the minimum food basket, for which purpose budget surveys are carried out. Nutritional experts decide upon an economy food plan, which is adapted to the pattern of food expenditures of families in the lower income categories. In estimating these cost, however, two new difficulties arise. Firstly, by using budget surveys amongst low income families in defining their nutritional needs, a circularity in the definition is introduced: the needs of the poor are defined by the actual spending of the alleged poor, i.e. those people we try to identify with the definition of a poverty line. Secondly, in defining an economy food plan as a compromise between actual behaviour and expert estimates of basic needs, assumptions are made with respect to cost minimizing behaviour of consumers, without taking account of the fact that the poor are usually less informed consumers, and can, moreover, often not afford to buy the "optimal" cheap bulk quantities that such behaviour would imply. Hence, even if one would agree to adapt the poverty line to the customary pattern of food consumption in society, the problem of how to reconcile these customs with the nutritional expert advice still remains. If poverty is defined in terms of restriction to the command over resources of a household, the discrepancy between actual and prescribed behaviour is not a problem: if people have enough resources to be able to buy the prescribed nutritional diet, they are considered to be at least as well off if they actually buy another combination of goods [see Watts (1968), and the summary of his arguments described above].

## ad III  Transformation of cost of food into a poverty line

When a certain estimate of the cost of food is chosen, a method has to be found to relate these cost to an overall income level, that is considered to be the poverty line. We will discuss three ways in which this can be done.

### (i) The cost of other basic needs are estimated separately

This method was used by Rowntree. The other basic needs he considered consisted of clothing, housing, fuel and light. As the cost for housing he used the actual sums paid for rent, "in view of the difficulty of forming an estimate of a reliable standard of accommodation, required to maintain families of different size in health" [Rowntree (1901), p.106].

In order to obtain an estimate for the minimum cost of clothing, in a survey of working men the following question was asked:

"What in your opinion is the very lowest sum upon which a man can keep himself in clothing for a year? The clothing should be adequate to keep the man in health, and should not be so shabby as to injure his chances of obtaining respectable employment. Apart from these two conditions, the clothing to be the most economical obtainable."
[Rowntree (1901), p.107]

In addition, extra details on cost of women's and children's clothing, as well as on fuel, light, soap, et cetera were obtained by similar questions. The objections described above to the assessment of the minimum cost of food do not hold as strongly here, as the way in which these other cost are obtained allows them, at least in principle, to vary according to region, climate, and social custom. However, the choice of the other necessary items is certainly questionable: why not include travelling cost? Cost for education of children? Apparently the opinion on which needs are basic is not fixed, independent of time and place; in later research Rowntree did add newspapers, union subscription, travel expenses and some other items he called "personal sundries" to his list of basic needs [Rowntree (1941)]. In his last study Rowntree, together with Lavers (1951) used a list of "household sundries" which includes sheets, pillow cases and toothbrushes; articles that were not mentioned in earlier research. The very problem of choosing items besides food that are considered to be necessary has prevented many authors from attempts to estimate other cost separately. They use an estimate of food expenditures only, as, in the words of Orshansky (1965), "there is no generally acceptable standard of adequacy for essentials of living except food". As the discussion mentioned above shows, even this latter assertion is questionable.

(ii) Cost of food are multiplied by the inverse of the average Engel coefficient in society

An Engel coefficient is a number, indicating the proportion of total income spent on food. The rationale of its use in poverty line definitions is that there is a systematical empirical relationship between consumption of food and total income: when income increases, the expenditures on food increase less than proportionally [Engel (1883)].
If the cost of food are multiplied by the inverse of the average Engel coefficient, a poverty line in terms of income is found. This method has been used by Orshansky in the construction of the SSA poverty index; as

the average proportion spent on food in the US was 1/3, her estimate of food expenditures was multiplied by 3 to cover all other items. A problem with this method is that the level of the poverty line is extremely sensitive to the exact value of the coefficient used. Studies of the Engel function of food expenditures show that the estimated coefficients may vary considerably over different surveys. Orshansky found values of 0.25 and 0.33 in different surveys; if the former would have been used instead of the latter, the poverty line would have increased by one third. Moreover, the estimated coefficients may vary according to season [Brown (1954)]. An advantage of the method, on the other hand, is that no choice has to be made of the items to be included; no fixed consumption pattern is imposed, apart from the initial diet. In choosing the average proportion in society to be the appropriate Engel coefficient, a relationship between the poverty line and the average standard of living is established. If the general standard of living increases, the average proportion of income spent on food decreases, and the multiplier of food expenditures will therefore increase. A poverty line defined in this way, periodically adapted according to the most recent estimate of the multiplier, will hence be at least partly relative. This is not, however, the practice with the poverty line definition proposed by Orshansky; although the cost of food are regularly adapted to changes in the consumer price index, the multiplier is not adapted to changes in the average proportion spent on food. The resulting poverty line is hence, in spite of its theoretical relativity, in practice an absolute poverty line. An argumentation for this practice is given among others by Lampman:

> "While income poverty is a relative matter, I do not think we should engage in frequent changes of the poverty lines, other than to adjust for price changes. As I see it, the elimination of income poverty is usefully thought of as a one-time operation in pursuit of a goal unique to this generation. That goal should be achieved before 1980, at which time the next generation will have set new economic and social goals, perhaps including a new distributional goal for themselves."
> [Lampman (1971)]

Although unfortunately this goal has not been achieved in terms of the official poverty line definition,[10] one may question whether this goal in terms of an absolute poverty line is appropriate, even for one generation; if this goal would have been achieved the next generation might discover that in spite of this said elimination of poverty the welfare of the households who used to be called poor has decreased over the years, even though their incomes have increased. This would be found if welfare of households does depend at least partly on their relative position in society; by using an absolute poverty line definition one implicitly assumes either that welfare does not depend on the general standard of living in society, or that poverty should be measured in terms of income rather than welfare.

## (iii) Cost of food are multiplied with the inverse of the Engel coefficient of the poor

As in the former method, in this approach the relationship between food expenditures and income is used. Instead of choosing the average ratio of food expenditures to income, the ratio of the poor themselves is used. Rose Friedman (1965) argues that the fraction of the income spent on food at low levels of income is about 0.60, instead of the 0.33 that Orshansky used. Using this Engel coefficient of the poor, she arrives at a poverty line of about 55 % of the line Orshansky used. However, the result is a circular definition: if one wishes to use the Engel coefficient of the poor, one has to identify the poor first. Another choice of "low levels of income" might result in another Engel coefficient, and hence in another poverty line. Such a definition is not very helpful.

Summarizing the different poverty lines within the basic needs approach, we see that :

a. Absolute or relative

The poverty line will be absolute if in defining the minimum nutritional needs and the Engel coefficient only the behaviour and consumption pattern of the poor are taken into account. If in the definition of basic needs or the Engel coefficient an estimate of average behaviour in society is used, which is changed when average income in society changes, the resulting line will be at least partly relative. In case of an estimate of the average Engel coefficient this relativity can be made explicit in terms of coefficients of the Engel function. If this Engel coefficient is not periodically revised, an absolute poverty line results.

b. Equivalence scales

In the estimation of cost of food, differences in family size are taken into account by assessing the necessary caloric intake for family members according to sex and age, and assessing the total cost of a diet providing them all with this minimum. If other cost are estimated separately, a similar procedure is used for clothing, and other items. In arriving at a final poverty line, however, some allowance is usually made for "economies of scale" especially in rent and household sundries. Hence, equivalence scales can be arrived at, even though to their "objectivity" the same objections can be made as before.

The Engel coefficient methods might in theory be extended to account for different family sizes: one might multiply the food expenditures of a specific family size with the average coefficient found for that specific family size. Analogously, if the Engel coefficient of the poor is used, different coefficients for different families might be obtained. However, there is an objection to be made to this procedure in either method. If the Engel coefficient of the poor only is used, the coefficient of large families will usually be larger: this would imply that the food expenditure of a large family will be multiplied with a smaller multiplier than the food expenditures of a small family, reflecting larger economies of scales for expenditures, other than food. If the difference in Engel coefficients is very large, this might even offset the effect of larger food expenditures, causing large families to have lower poverty lines than small families.

A similar problem may arise for poverty lines using average Engel coefficients if large families have on average lower incomes, and hence higher average Engel coefficients than small families. Hence the choice of one average Engel coefficient for all family size, and different estimates of the cost of food for different family sizes is to be preferred.

In practice the actual equivalence scale used is often an ad hoc estimate, instead of being based on the procedure described above [see, e.g., Orshansky (1965)].

c. Objective versus subjective

The poverty lines based on the basic needs approach are all meant to be objective, especially with regard to the estimate of cost of food. However, even their objectivity is questionable, as the discussion between the nutritional experts cited above shows. Both in the definition of food and in the calculation of the corresponding cost, value judgements are made, either by the "expert" or by the politicians deciding on a certain definition or method.

Evaluation

In the poverty lines described, no attempt is made to define poverty in terms of individual or household welfare. Basically, poverty is considered to be a situation where physical efficiency cannot be maintained. One might say that welfare in these definitions is defined as the fulfilment of these basic needs. If the basic needs are assumed to be independent of the standard of living in society, welfare is assumed to be independent of the standard of living in society. If, on the other hand, basic needs are related to the living style in society, welfare depends on the fulfilment of needs, compared to the general fulfilment of needs in society.

## 1.2.2 Food ratio method

This method, proposed by Watts (1967), applied by, e.g., Love and Oja (1975) and discussed by, e.g., Rosenthal (1969), Deaton and Muelbauer (1980), Grootaerts (1981), and Van Praag, Spit and Van de Stadt (1982), is also based on the relationship between expenditures on food and total income. A certain food-income ratio is taken to be the poverty threshold: families with an actual food-income ratio higher than this threshold are considered to be poor, and families with a lower food-income ratio are considered to be non-poor.

The method has certain advantages to the basic needs approach. The first of these is that the problem of defining minimum nutritional needs is avoided, although the definition of "food" remains a problem. Secondly, the method explicitly allows actual expenditure patterns to be determinants of the poverty line, instead of a prescribed economical diet.[11] A third advantage is that in choosing the percentage spent on food as a poverty threshold equivalence scales for families of different size can be easily derived by including family size as an explanatory variable in the Engel function used to derive the relationship between food expenditures and income in society. A disadvantage of such an equivalence scale, however, is that it depends on the choice of food, rather than other "basic needs", because both family size elasticity and income elasticity of food differs from the elasticity of non-food expenditures (housing, clothing).[12] The one (arbitrary) choice to be made in every poverty line definition is for this method the choice of the poverty threshold, the ratio between food expenditures and income, which serves as a cut-off point. If the actual Engel coefficient of the poor is chosen to be the poverty threshold, the method results in a poverty line equal to the Rose Friedman line, with the same circularity in definition. On the other hand, in choosing for instance a percentage of the median Engel coefficient in society to be the poverty threshold, a relative poverty line definition is found if the poverty line is updated periodically with changing average income in society. Hence the poverty line definition may be absolute or relative, depending on the choice of an absolute or relative poverty threshold.

The food ratio method is objective in the sense that it does not depend on feelings or opinions of people. The welfare concept used is the ratio of income to the expenditures on food.

Evaluation

The food ratio method assumes that the welfare of two households that spend the same proportion of their income on food is equal. The resulting equivalence scales depend on the family size elasticity and income elasticity of food expenditures. The poverty line is hence defined in terms of prescribed behaviour, not in terms of a restriction to the choice set of a household.

1.2.3  Percentage of mean or median income

Definitions of this type are based on the idea that poverty is a situation of relative deprivation, instead of absolute deprivation, and that the poverty line should therefore be linked to some indicator of the standard of living in society. The concept of relative deprivation, introduced by Stouffer et al. (1949) in his study on the life of American soldiers, has been described in a more general context by Runciman (1966). Townsend (1962) advocates the application of the concept of relative deprivation to poverty research: he criticizes the existing standards of absolute poverty for having restricted the attention to the preservation of physical efficiency, without acknowledging that (p.219):

> "Poverty is a dynamic, not a static concept. Man is not a Robinson Crusoe living on a desert island. He is a social animal entangled in a web of relationships at work and in family and community which exert complex and changing pressures to which he must respond, as much in his consumption of goods and services as in any other aspect of his behaviour."

He proposes to replace the concept of subsistence by the concept of relative deprivation (p.225):

> "Our general theory, then, should be that individuals and families, whose resources over time fall seriously short of the resources commanded by the average individual or family in the community in which they live, whether that community is a local, national or international one, are in poverty".

His first application of the concept was the study he carried out with Abel-Smith (1965), where in addition to official poverty lines, poverty line definitions of 50 and 66 % of mean incomes of certain family types were used. Numerous scholars followed this change in emphasis from absolute poverty lines to relative poverty lines. Fuchs (1967), Rainwater (1969), Rein (1974), Lansley (1980), they all propose that poverty lines should be linked to an indicator of the standard of living in society.

Among the authors in the relative deprivation approach, both the choice of the indicator (mean or median income) and the choice of the percentage of this indicator to be used varies. Fuchs, Lansley and Rainwater use median income in society; Fuchs and Lansley use percentages of about 50. As mentioned above, Abel-Smith and Townsend use the mean income; Townsend argues that the mean is a more stable point of reference for comparing different countries or different years [Townsend (1979)]. His preference for the mean is a result of his emphasis on income inequality: he argues that using the median, two countries might have the same percentage of poor whereas the percentage of people with an income between the median and the mean may be very different. The authors using the median, however, reply that it is only the lower part of the income distribution that one is concerned with in studying poverty. Townsend uses percentages of 50 (very low poverty line) and 80 (low poverty line) of the mean income. The choice for mean income has also been made in a study by Sawyer (1975) for the OECD (1976), where a percentage of 66 is chosen.

Whether the mean or the median is chosen, and whatever percentage is chosen, the resulting poverty line will always be completely relative with respect to the indicator chosen: if the indicator increases with one percent, the poverty line will also increase with one percent.

One of the problems of definitions of this kind is the way in which equivalence scales are calculated. The OECD uses ad hoc fractions of the standard two-person family. Lansley (1980) changes the focus of attention from families to individuals, by converting household income into income per "equivalent adult" couple; however, in the conversion procedure ad hoc equivalence scales are used. Townsend (1979) calculates the mean income for various family types; the poverty line for a specific family type is a percentage of the mean income of that family type. A problem with this approach is, however, that family size and income may be correlated: for example, large families might be found more often in lower income classes. If the mean of these large family incomes is calculated, their poverty line may even be lower than that of a small family. The concept of relative deprivation itself is lost in the procedure: why should large families be expected to refer only to other large families? However, no other solution has as yet been found to the problem of defining equivalence scales within this approach. The poverty line definitions in this category are all objective definitions, in the sense that they do not depend on the perception of people themselves.

Evaluation

In this type of poverty line definition it is assumed that people's welfare depends on the ratio of their own income to the mean or median income in society, as an indicator of the general standard of living. Equivalence scales used in this approach are adapted ad hoc, and not based on any specific assumption on welfare.

1.2.4 Percentile definitions

A fourth group of poverty line definitions is completely based on income inequality; poverty is considered to be found in a certain lowest percentile of the income distribution, e.g. the lowest 10 or 20 percent. Miller and Roby (1974) argue that this choice is the logical result of a discussion of poverty in terms of relative deprivation and social stratification; they see the poor as "those who lag behind the rest of society in terms of one or more dimensions of life". As the percentage of the poor is fixed in this definition, the attention is mainly given to the share of aggregate income accruing to the bottom decile or quintile chosen, and to the composition of this lowest percentile. By definition, the resulting poverty line is completely relative: an increase in the standard of living of all individuals in society will increase the poverty line with the same percentage. A result of the definition is also that a decrease in income inequality shifts the poverty line upwards. This may be explained by a larger sensitivity for remaining income differences [see e.g. Kapteyn (1977)].

A problem with this approach is the determination of family equivalence scales. Miller and Roby (1970) do not try to derive differentiated poverty lines: family size is one of the variables they consider in the study of the characteristics of people in the lowest percentile. In theory, an approach similar to the one Townsend used to get equivalence scales might be used, by calculating the bottom percentile of income distributions for each family type separately. However, the same anomaly of decreasing poverty lines with increasing family size might result. Poverty line definitions of the percentile type are objective according to our criterion.

Evaluation

In percentile definitions of poverty it is assumed that the welfare of a household depends on the ranking of one's position in the income distribution. Being worse off than others makes people feel poor, at whatever absolute income level they find themselves. No equivalence scale for households of different types results from this approach.

### 1.2.5 Official definitions

A fifth category of poverty line definitions is the group of so-called "official" definitions. These are the poverty lines that one has agreed upon in a certain country at a certain time; it is in most EC countries the income level below which one can apply for social assistance.

Such official poverty lines have been used in numerous poverty studies, among which Abel-Smith and Townsend (1965), Wedderburn (1962), Thurow (1969), Lampman (1971), and Plotnick and Skidmore (1975). Most of these authors use the official poverty line because to their knowledge no good alternative is available, and often they use it in addition to other (usually relative) poverty lines. Thurow, however, states that a poverty line should be defined as the "adequate standards of living as seen by the majority of the population" [Thurow (1969), p.21]. In the long run, this amounts in his view to a poverty line as a percentage of median income; in the short run, he chooses the official SSA poverty index "... since the political process has opted for this definition, it must be accepted for the time being as the social definition of poverty" (Thurow, id., p.23). Plotnick and Skidmore (1975, p.42) use the SSA poverty index because "... the political and historical importance of this definition argues strongly for its use". Assuming that official poverty lines reflect a democratic decision on the level of the poverty line, the use of official poverty lines may well be defended. However, official poverty lines have often been introduced in a distant past, and their adaptation to rising prices and standards of living is not always decided upon in a clear and democratic procedure. Moreover, their scientific basis is not always very strong: Kapteyn and Halberstadt (1980, p.40) in studying official poverty line definitions in EC countries conclude that:

> "Nowhere an explicit theoretical framework seems to have been formulated upon which anti poverty policy has been built. As a consequence, the design of the anti poverty policies appears to be strongly affected by the political situation in the member-countries and the picture of regulations is therefore chaotic".

If one wants poverty to be defined as a reflection of the views on the adequate standards of living as seen by a majority of the population, the official definition may not be the best choice available. The equivalence scales used in official poverty lines vary widely, but are usually defined in an *ad hoc* way. The official poverty lines often claim to be objective, in the sense that they are not based on survey data; implicitly, however, they are supposed to be a reflection of the opinions and perceptions of people in society. The actual decision on the level of a poverty line is usually taken in the government and agreed upon in parliament: the politicians making this decision may not always have intimate knowledge of the standard of living implied by such a poverty line. To some extent, official poverty lines hence do reflect subjective views, namely, those of political decision makers; this may not always be equivalent to the opinion of their constituency.

Evaluation

Official poverty line definitions vary widely over countries, both in their conceptual basis and in their actual level, equivalence scales and updating practice. On the assumption that concept and operationalization are decided upon in a democratic procedure, and are periodically reexamined, they may represent the majority view on adequate standards of living in society. This majority view does not necessarily reflect scientific evidence on welfare.

## 1.2.6 Subjective definitions, based on survey data

As poverty concerns well-being of individuals, the perception people have of their own situation is considered to be of crucial importance in this approach. If one wants the poverty line to be a reflection of the opinions in society, why not ask for these opinions, and use them in the definition of a poverty line? The method, used to get information on people's perception of poverty is direct questioning: in oral or written interviews people are asked to give their opinion. The relevance of direct questioning on this kind of subjective aspects of life is more and more recognized. As the OECD Working Party on Social Indicators has stated:

> "The well-being of individuals in many goal areas cannot be readily detected without recourse to the account of individuals themselves. This may be particularly true of working conditions and health. In several other areas as well where there is, for example, a mixture of individual and collective ways of meeting needs, asking the individual himself is in some instance the only way to obtain relevant information".
> [OECD (1973)]

In this approach to the definition of poverty lines two types of questions are used. In the first, people are asked to give the minimum income necessary to get along for a representative family, e.g., two adults with two children. This question has been asked in a number of Gallup Polls [see Kilpatrick (1973) and Rainwater (1974)].

A poverty line for a family of four can now be found as the average of all answers. Rainwater (1974, p.56) implicitly found that the poverty line thus defined has an elasticity of 1 with respect to mean income; Kilpatrick, however, found an elasticity of 0.60 (using partly different data). An advantage of the method is that the place of the poverty line between absolute and relative is not determined by the researcher or by the politician: it is an empirical finding, based on the perception of what a minimum income should be in society. Family equivalence scales can be found by asking the minimum income to get along for varying family types. One difficulty with this kind of question where the minimum income is asked for somebody else, is that people may forget or ignore various cost increasing or decreasing factors when evaluating other people's situation, while they would include these factors when they evaluate their own situation [according to Withey (1974)].

This observation has led to a second type of question, in which people are asked to give the minimum income necessary to get along for their own situation. This is called the minimum income question. This approach has been used by Goedhart et al. (1977) and at the Centre for Social Policy in Belgium [Deleeck (1977)].[13] Goedhart et al. developed a method of defining a poverty line from the answers given. The resulting definition is called the Leyden poverty line definition, after its place of origination. The method is based on the relationship between the answer of an individual to the minimum income question, and the actual income of the individual. If the amount individuals consider to be their minimum income is an increasing function of income, with an elasticity $\alpha$ between 0 and 1,[13] this function can be drawn like in figure 1.2, where $y_{min} = cy^{\alpha}$.

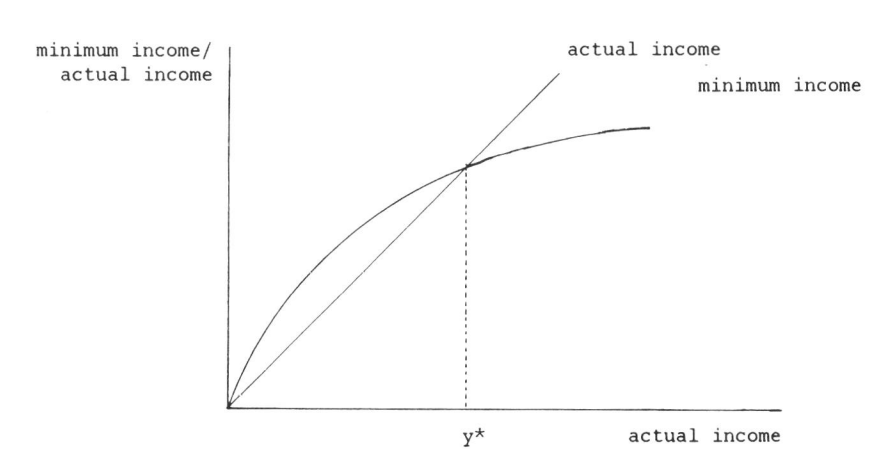

Figure 1.2 Determination of the poverty line

The higher someone's actual income, the higher the income he considers minimal. If in the same figure the 45° line is drawn, which represents the line at which the individual minimum income is equal to the actual income, a "natural solution" to the aggregation problem is found: the lines intersect at $y = y^*$. On the right hand side of $y^*$, people have actual incomes which are higher than the incomes they consider to be minimal; on the left hand side people have incomes that are lower than the income level they consider to be minimal. Hence the point of intersection divides those who do get along from those who do not, according to their own standards. Hence $y^*$ is a poverty line, dividing the poor from the non-poor.

Deleeck (1977) used the same question, but a different aggregation procedure: a selective sample of individuals, likely to be in the lower income classes, was chosen instead of a representative sample. The poverty line is then found by simple averaging of all answers. However, in this procedure the level of the poverty line depends on the choice of the sample. In later research [Deleeck et al. (1984)] this method is improved by the choice of a representative sample as a point of departure. All households in this sample are asked to evaluate their own income as "good", "bad", "minimal", et cetera. Those households who answer that their own income is absolutely minimal to get along are considered to be at the poverty line. In order to assess the level of the poverty line their incomes are averaged. This procedure yields in principle the same poverty line as the one found by Goedhart et al.

Poverty line definitions using these questions can be easily extended to different family sizes; the effect of the actual family size on the income level said to be minimal can be estimated, and the point of intersection (or straightforward average, in the Deleeck method) can be calculated for each family size. Moreover, other characteristics for which equivalence scales are desired may be included in the same way as family size (e.g. urban/rural, good health/bad health).

The place of the resulting poverty line on the scale between absolute and relative depends on the way in which people's needs shift with the general standard of living; the elasticity of this poverty line with respect to the standard of living can be calculated if data on more periods or more countries are available. Whether the poverty line is absolute or relative is hence an empirical fact, not an a priori opinion of the researchers. The poverty line is defined on the basis of the subjective feelings of individuals: the actual level of the poverty line is an average of the incomes of people who feel they can just get along. The basic assumption in this poverty line definition is that people give a certain common interpretation in terms of welfare to the verbal qualification "minimum income to get along", or "minimum income to make ends meet", and are able to assess for their specific situation the income level they associate with this welfare level. This assumption is in fact based on the notion that words, by means of which a large part of human communication takes place, will have roughly speaking the same meaning to everybody. That does not imply that everybody will use this qualification for the same income level; we have already seen that people with a higher income level will adapt their needs, in terms of minimum income necessary to get along, to this higher level. By estimating the relationship between actual income and minimum income, still a unique income level can be found, below which most people feel that they need more than they have to "get along", and above which most people feel that they have more than necessary to "get along".

The relationship between actual income and stated minimum income may be quantitatively different for different categories of respondents. For instance, a family of four will need a higher amount of money income throughout to "get along", under ceteris paribus conditions, than a single person. If we assume that the words "necessary to get along" convey the same welfare feeling to families of both types, this can be used to derive welfare neutral equivalence scales, where different points of intersection are calculated for different household types. The same holds for differences in, say, human wealth: a student will give another (lower) answer to this question than someone of his age who has chosen to work, rather than to invest in human capital. By calculating different points of intersection for students and others, their difference in human wealth will be taken into account. The same applies to differences in health, non-cash income, instability of income, and all other variables that are part of the generalized command over resources, but are also felt to have a separate effect on welfare. Hence, the one basic assumption that people associate a certain common, interpersonally comparable feeling of welfare with a certain verbal description, enables us to calculate a poverty line in terms of monetary income for different household types. Whether the resulting poverty line is absolute or relative depends on the way in which welfare, defined in this way, is related to the general standard of living in society. It is an empirical result, rather than an <u>a priori</u> assumption.

Evaluation

The subjective poverty line definition described here depends on the basic assumption that people associate roughly the same welfare feeling to certain verbal qualifications, like for instance "enough to get along". Once this assumption has been accepted, income levels may be derived that provide just that welfare level to households of different size and type; this procedure yields at the same time welfare neutral equivalence scales for the welfare level under consideration.

1.2.7  Other poverty line definitions

A new conceptual definition of poverty has been given by Townsend (1979, p.249), based on the notion of relative deprivation. Townsend hypothesizes that, as resources of an individual or family are diminished, there is a point at which a sudden withdrawal from participation in the customs and activities that are usual in the individual's community occurs. The point at which the withdrawal escalates disproportionately when resources fall may be defined as the poverty line. Hence, people are poor if they cannot participate in the "style of living" in society.

A list of sixty indicators is designed to summarize "style of living". If one does not participate with respect to any of these indicators, one gets a certain deprivation score. For each family or individual a score on the deprivation index is calculated. By relating these scores on the deprivation index to a (broad) income concept, the hypothesis of more than proportional deprivation below a certain income level can be tested. If it exists, this income level is considered to be the poverty line.

deprivation index score

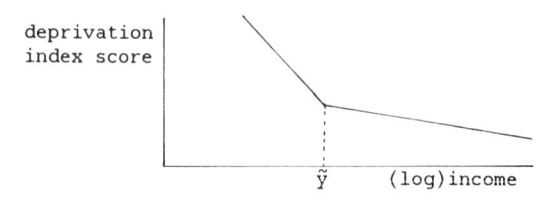

$\tilde{y}$    (log) income

Figure 1.3  The relation between income and deprivation

By drawing such figures for different family sizes, equivalence scales may be obtained. However, Townsend himself calls the evidence for the existence of such a poverty threshold, resulting from his huge study on poverty in the UK, "inconclusive" [Townsend (1979), p.255]. Even though his overall figures may suggest the existence of a breakdown point, the figures for different household types are certainly not convincing. There are, moreover, several theoretical drawbacks to the method. Firstly, the definition of a poverty line depends on the hypothesis that at a certain income level deprivation increases more than proportionally. This assumption is crucial - if it does not hold, the poverty line is not defined - but it is rather hard to defend. Why should the decrease in deprivation not be part of a smooth, continuous process? One might assume that the marginal deprivation score is a decreasing function of income, in line with standard assumptions on the utility function of income. If that is true, Townsend's method does not yield a unique poverty line. As mentioned, his data do not really support the hypothesis of a breakdown point. Townsend does not report whether the hypothesis has been tested against the alternative of a continuously decreasing function; however, figures like figure 1.4 suggest that such a test may be worthwhile.

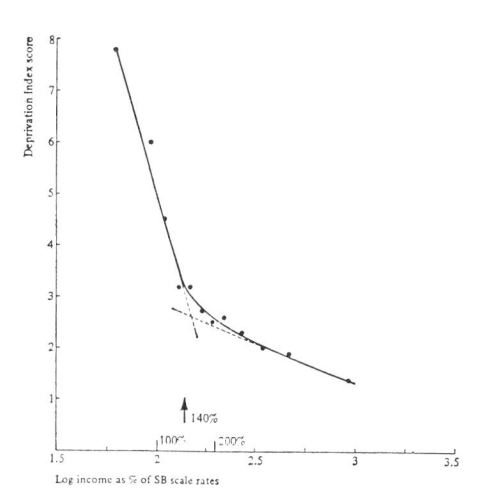

Figure 1.4  Modal deprivation by logarithm of income as a percentage of supplementary benefit scale rates
[Reproduced from Townsend (1979), p.261]

A second objection may be made against his choice of indicators that are supposed to represent a lack of participation in the general style of living in society. With respect to three out of his twelve main characteristics a deprivation score is found for more than half of his sample of individuals. A deprivation score for "not having a cooked breakfast most days of the week" was even found in more than two-thirds of the sample. It does not appear to be very meaningful to define a "general style of living in society" by aspects of life that are only enjoyed by a minority. Moreover, the correlation between some of the items and income is very low (less than 0.07 for six out of twelve items). This would not be a problem if it represents the fact that this specific form of deprivation is only found in lower income classes; it does present a problem, however, if it is the result of different ways of living of families due to sociological or psychological differences, independent of income. The item "has not been out in the last four weeks to a relative or friend for a meal or snack" may have only a correlation of 0.05 with income because the question whether people have an active social life outdoors depends on their tastes and preferences, rather than on their income.

Thirdly, the method used to derive equivalence scales may be questioned. Is it reasonable to use the same indicators for general style of living for each household type? Indicators for social activity, like having a friend or relative to the home for a meal may have a different meaning for individuals living alone, who depend for their social life on these activities, than for families. The same may apply to going out for entertainment, and to having holidays away from home. Having a refrigerator may be more necessary for large families, and for families where both husband and wife are working; it may be less necessary for unemployed or retired persons, or for families where one of the parents is staying at home.

These examples show that it may be more reasonable to define "style of living" for each household type separately, by selecting items that are typical for that household type, and to apply the procedure described above with such a household differentiated set of indicators. Still, it would be difficult to define what is meant by "equivalence" for different household types. In Townsend's results, the poverty line is not only different in terms of income for different families, but also in terms of deprivation score. In his figures, the deprivation index is about three at the poverty threshold for two- or more-person families; it is four for

single individuals and for couples over sixty. It seems again hard to defend poverty lines as equivalent, if they result in higher deprivation for some household types than for others.
Although the study contains valuable information on the incidence and determinants of poverty, the conceptual basis of its poverty line definition is weak.

Evaluation

The poverty line defined by Townsend depends on the assumption that there is a certain income level, below which welfare as a function of income decreases abruptly. This point reflects an income threshold below which people cannot participate in the general style of living in society. Both theoretically and empirically Townsend's hypothesis is hard to defend. Without that assumption, however, no poverty line is defined. Equivalence scales are derived by applying the method to different household types; the resulting poverty lines are not, however, equivalent in terms of degree of deprivation. Finally, we note that the procedure rests upon the choice of a number of indicators, that are supposed to reflect (lack of) deprivation. This choice does not take account of the fact that households may have different consumption patterns according to their preferences and tastes, even if they have the same household income.

1.3  Conclusion

We have described a variety of poverty line definitions. The essential difference between them is found in the assumptions on welfare that are implicit in the definitions. We might say that three major points of view may be distinguished in the way poverty is defined:
(1)  Being poor is lacking some basic necessities.
(2)  Being poor is having less than others in society.
(3)  Being poor is feeling you do not have enough to get along.
In the first category, poverty as absolute deprivation, definitions derived from basic needs and the food ratio are found; in the second class, we find the fraction of mean income, percentile definitions and Townsend's deprivation index and in the last category, poverty as a subjective condition, the subjective definitions are found. As we have seen, in each of these definitions certain assumptions on the welfare concept have to be

made. The assumption implicit in the first category is that welfare depends on the extent to which some basic needs are met. This definition does not allow for variations in a household's tastes and preferences. The assumption implicit in the second category is that welfare depends on your relative position in the income distribution. Hence, both in the first and the second category, assumptions on welfare are made on which the poverty line definition rests, that are not tested empirically, but based on a priori notions of the researcher. The third category assumes that we can find out whether people can or cannot "get along" by asking them. The question which variables influence welfare is to be answered by the empirical results, and not by the researcher beforehand. As we have also seen that the subjective definitions allow for welfare neutral differentiation according to family size and other factors influencing welfare, derived from command over resources, they resemble our "ideal" definition of poverty more than the other poverty line definitions discussed.

We have therefore adapted in this monograph a particular subjective poverty line definition, that will be further developed in the next chapter. So far we have discussed the differences between various poverty line definitions. We will end this chapter by noting some of their conformities. In fact, the poverty concepts underlying the various definitions are not as dissimilar as it might appear from the preceding discussion. Almost all scholars of the basic needs approach acknowledge that the definition of basic needs depends on the society with which one is concerned, and may therefore be subject to change. Sen (1982), in a reappraisal of absolute deprivation, quotes both Adam Smith and Karl Marx to show that the concept of minimum necessities or means of subsistence has always been defined in relation to the particular place and time of the society concerned. This can also be found in the work of the two pioneers in poverty research: Rowntree implicitly acknowledged it by allowing in his later poverty line definitions for a larger increase than merely changing prices would allow for, and Booth by stating that:

> "The poor are those whose means may be sufficient, but are barely sufficient for decent independent living; the very poor those whose means are insufficient for this according to the usual standard of living in this country".
> [Booth (1892), p.5]

The main difference between the various poverty line definitions is hence found in the formulation of the relationship with the standard of living in society. The basic needs approaches vary implicitly with changing standards of living, by allowing more needs to be basic, or by increasing the existing standards for food, clothing, etc.

The relative deprivation definitions, on the other hand, define a proportional relationship between the poverty line and the standard of living. It is in fact this proportional relationship that scholars of the absolute approach object to: by defining poverty as a percentage of mean or median, or as a percentile of the income distribution, poverty is seen as an issue of inequality only. Especially in international comparisons this yields results that may be considered undesirable: two countries may have the same extent of income inequality, while one has a median income that is twice as high as the other. Moreover, as Sen puts it:

> "There is an irreducable core of absolute deprivation in our idea of poverty, which translates reports of starvation, malnutrition and hardship into a diagnosis of poverty without having to ascertain first the relative picture."
> [Sen (1982), p.17]

On the other hand, the choice of an absolute poverty line cannot be made without reference to the general standard of living. Fields (1980, p.140) distinguishes these two approaches in saying that:

> "recognizing that the definition of poverty within a country is chosen relative to that country's economic level is very different from using a relative poverty measure for that country."

He argues that the exact dollar figure of a poverty line is not of major importance "provided that the poverty line is appropriate to living standards in the country under investigation". By holding the poverty line constant in real terms over time, however, a possible change in living standards is not allowed to affect the absolute poverty line. In fact, Fields uses the same poverty lines for all (developing) countries he examines; his allowance for changing poverty lines with changing standards of living apparently only applies to large changes, like those between developing countries and industrialized countries. This does not give a solution to the problem of how to define a poverty line in European countries or the U.S. Sen reconciles the absolute and relative aspects of poverty by choosing a fixed poverty line, and developing a summary index for poverty in which more weight is attached to poor people if their relative rank in the income distribution of the poor is lower [Sen (1976, 1982)]. However, the problem of where to fix the poverty line remains. A possible approach to redefine absolute poverty lines, without the disadvantages of the basic needs approaches, might be to get information on what are considered to be "basic needs" in a particular country at a particular time, and to ask people the minimum amount they would need to meet all these needs, like Rowntree did for clothing. The sum of all these amounts would result in a poverty line according to the basic needs approach, where the needs themselves are, however, defined by the contemporaneous standards in society.

The poverty line used in this research is in fact based on this method: by asking people to tell us the income level they think "sufficient", "insufficient", et cetera, we ask for the sum of all the amounts needed to meet the needs that they perceive to be basic without imposing a specific consumption pattern. Whether the resulting poverty line is completely relative or completely absolute is an empirical question: we will try to make explicit the relationship between the poverty line and median income, as an indicator of the standard of living in society, and use this relation to assess empirically the relativity of our poverty line definition.

Summarizing the main results of this chapter, we see that all poverty line definitions implicitly or explicitly define "welfare" in some way. The income level at which the poverty line is set may be seen to provide some basic welfare level. A number of requirements to a poverty line definition are discussed: it should not be circular, it should allow for differentiation according to various characteristics, it should enable us to relate the subjective evaluation of someone's situation to the objective circumstances causing it, and it should reflect the extent to which the perception of welfare in society is relative. The Leyden poverty line definition, that will be used in this research, meets all these requirements. The formal derivation of this poverty line will be given in the next chapter.

## NOTES TO CHAPTER 1

[1] This name, that will be explained later in this chapter, was used by Cooter and Rappoport in their recent JEL article (1984).

[2] Bentham implicitly formulated the same law as early as 1823 in saying "The excess of happiness of the richer (of two individuals with unequal fortunes) will not be so great as the excess of his wealth" [Bentham (1823), p.103, quoted by Stigler (1950), p.311].

[3] Although the predecessors of the material welfare school had doubts on the measurability of utility, most leading economists in the period following had not; see Stigler (1950) for references.

[4] See, e.g., the discussion on the inclusion of net worth by Projector and Weiss (1969), and the discussion on the way in which disability and unemployment should be incorporated in the estimate of earnings capacity by Garfinkel and Haveman (1977).

[5] If non-cash income like Medicare and food stamps yields additional welfare to, e.g., larger families, the equivalence scales for different household types, that do not take account of these non-cash components may not be appropriate to compare welfare between households, benefiting from such income in kind.

[6] Some definitions are in pre-tax, others are in after-tax income.

[7] See, e.g., Morgan (1962), Watts (1968), Garfinkel and Haveman (1977).

[8] See, e.g., Lampman (1971) and Fields (1980) for arguments in favour of an absolute poverty line; Rein (1974), Townsend (1962), Rainwater (1974) and Miller and Roby (1974) for a relativist point of view.
Sen (1984) takes an intermediate position; he states that one should define a line in terms of absolute capabilities (to meet nutritional requirements, to escape avoidable disease, to be sheltered, to be clothed, to be able to travel, and to be educated), but that changes in the structure of society will result in changing commodities, required to meet these needs. However, as no operationalization of a poverty line defined in terms of capabilities is yet available, this suggested definition is not included in our survey.

[9] After the call for the elimination of poverty by President Johnson in 1964.

[10] See, e.g., Danziger et al. (1984).

[11] This is not an unambiguous advantage, however, as it violates our requirement that the poverty line should be defined in terms of command over resources, and not in terms of actual behaviour. Moon and Smolensky (1969, p.3), for instance, write on this matter: "categorizing families as equals on the basis of their behaviour (e.g. food consumption) is inappropriate if the similarity in behaviour results from differences in tastes rather than similarities in resource constraints".

[12] The family size elasticity Watts found for food was about twice as high as the family size elasticity found for "all necessities" [Watts (1967)].

[13] Later applications of the method are described by Van Praag, Goedhart, and Kapteyn (1980), Van Praag, Hagenaars, and Van Weeren (1982), Van Praag, Spit, and Van de Stadt (1982), Danziger et al. (1984), Colasanto, Kapteyn, and Van der Gaag (1984).

[14] In analogy to the aggregate relationships found by Kilpatrick (1973) and Rainwater (1974).

Chapter 2
THE DERIVATION OF THE POVERTY LINE

We have discussed various poverty line definitions and concluded that only subjective definitions do not require a priori assumptions on the nature or the form of the relationship between income and welfare derived from it.[1] Subjective definitions, however, are based on another crucial assumption, viz. that all people give the same meaning to a specific verbal description in terms of a welfare evaluation, and that people are able to estimate the income level needed to reach the verbally described situation. With the answers they give we obtain, on these assumptions, income levels for different households that are associated with one, interpersonally comparable welfare level.

This method of obtaining information on the relationship between income and welfare may be put to further use by asking people to answer this question for several different verbal descriptions, that denote several different welfare levels, like "good", "bad", "insufficient", et cetera. In this chapter we will describe how these answers may be used to derive a poverty line,[2] to be called the Leyden poverty line (LPL), that has the following properties:
- The poverty line may be differentiated according to a variety of household characteristics, like family size, age, employment, et cetera.
- The relationship between the poverty line and the general standard of living in society is established empirically, not a priori.
- Most other poverty line definitions may be seen as special cases of the Leyden poverty line, when the relationship between welfare and income as hypothesized happens to coincide with a specific a priori notion on welfare, implicit in one of these other definitions.

Throughout this book we will consider the household to be the relevant unit of welfare measurement. Within a household, joint decisions are made with respect to labour supply, household production, investments in human capital; these decisions result in cash income and non-cash income in the form of home production or human wealth. The household members derive welfare from the total of this command over resources. It will therefore be the welfare level of the total household that we are concerned with.[3]

In section 2.1 the poverty line to be used in this monograph is formally derived. This section is a summary of a voluminous body of research, developed in the Leyden Income Evaluation Project. In order to avoid extensive lists of references in the text, the appropriate references are given in the notes to this chapter. In section 2.2 a formalization of other poverty line definitions is given, and in section 2.3 the poverty line to be used is shown to be a generalization of all others. Sections 2.2 and 2.3 are also largely based on earlier work, especially on Van Praag (1984) and Hagenaars and Van Praag (1985).

## 2.1 A welfare definition of poverty

In this section the poverty line definition to be used in this monograph[4] will be formally derived. Remembering that a definition of poverty is implicitly a definition of welfare, the Leyden poverty line is found by first defining and measuring welfare, and then defining poverty as a situation of low welfare. As we have seen in chapter 1, the definition and measurement of welfare has been the subject of a long debate in economic science. Our conclusion in reviewing this discussion was that in poverty research a certain amount of interpersonal comparability is unavoidable. We have to be able to say whether two households have the same level of welfare or not; and if not, which of the two is better off. Van Praag (1971) proposed a method to measure the relationship between welfare and income. The method is based on the assumption that people associate verbal qualifications like "good", "bad", "sufficient", with certain welfare levels. By asking people what income level they need for an evaluation of the situation of their household as "good", we ask them to give us one point on their household welfare function. Hence the information on welfare is obtained by direct questioning; a six-level version of this so-called income evaluation question (IEQ) runs as follows:

> "Please try to indicate what you consider to be an appropriate amount of money for each of the following cases.
>
> Under my (our) conditions I would call an after-tax income per week/month/year (please encircle the appropriate period) of:
>
> | about £....... | very bad |
> | about £....... | bad |
> | about £....... | insufficient |
> | about £....... | sufficient |
> | about £....... | good |
> | about £....... | very good" |

The assumption that each verbal qualification has the same emotional meaning to all respondents now enables us to compare the welfare levels as classified by these verbal qualifications between respondents: if one person has an income level which is between the income levels he states as "good" and "very good", his welfare level is higher than that of another with an income classified between "sufficient" and "good". Hence, for this global comparison of welfare levels no more assumptions are needed; notably, no assumption on the precise form of the underlying dependency between income and welfare is needed. The assumption used sofar is sufficient for comparison of people between different discrete welfare "classes", defined by the verbal qualifications. The number of classes that may be distinguished depends on the number of verbal qualifications that one can reasonably ask. However, if two people both classify their own income as between "just sufficient" and "good" we cannot, following this procedure, compare their welfare levels although we can say that they will not be too different. Sometimes this may be sufficient, for instance, for the purpose of measuring the incidence of poverty, if everybody classifying his own income as less than "sufficient" would be defined as poor. We can also use the income level people think is "sufficient" to derive a poverty line, corresponding to this verbal description.[5] This may be done in two ways: by calculating a point of intersection of the income level, associated with "sufficient" and the actual income level (the "Leyden" method) or by averaging all answers of people who say their actual income is "sufficient" (the "Deleeck" method). Either method will result in a poverty line, corresponding to the welfare level "sufficient".

Hence both the incidence of poverty (within broad welfare classes) and poverty lines may be derived using one assumption only: that the verbal qualifications have the same meaning to different respondents. However, if one wants to summarize the extent of poverty in one index number, some way of comparing people within a certain welfare class is desired. Besides, for analytical purposes we prefer to describe the relationship between income y and welfare U derived from it by a mathematical relationship $U = U(y)$, which we shall call the welfare function of income (WFI), rather than by a step function. We therefore wish to interpolate within the welfare classes between the six points, in other words, to describe the six points by some convenient mathematical function.

If we now consider the six answers to the IEQ - to be denoted by $y_1, \ldots,$

$y_6$ - to be points on the household welfare function of the respondent, we have to know to what numerical welfare levels these six verbal evaluations correspond. If we assume that people try to maximize the information on their WFI by the answers they give, it can be shown under fairly general assumptions that the verbal qualifications will tend to correspond to the means of equal quantiles of the welfare scale, if the range of U is taken to be a finite interval.[6] If we take the interval [0-1] to be the welfare range, the six answers divide this interval into six equal parts, of 1/6 each. The lowest qualification, "very bad", covers the first quantile, and hence the income level $y_1$ will represent on the average a welfare level of 1/12. In general, the i-th answer on a six-level scale is associated with a welfare level of

$$U(y_i) = \tfrac{1}{2} \left[ \frac{i-1}{6} + \frac{i}{6} \right] = \frac{i-\tfrac{1}{2}}{6} \qquad\qquad i = 1,\ldots 6$$

This is called the equal quantile assumption.[7]

The six points of the welfare functions of two hypothetical respondents are depicted in figure 2.1.

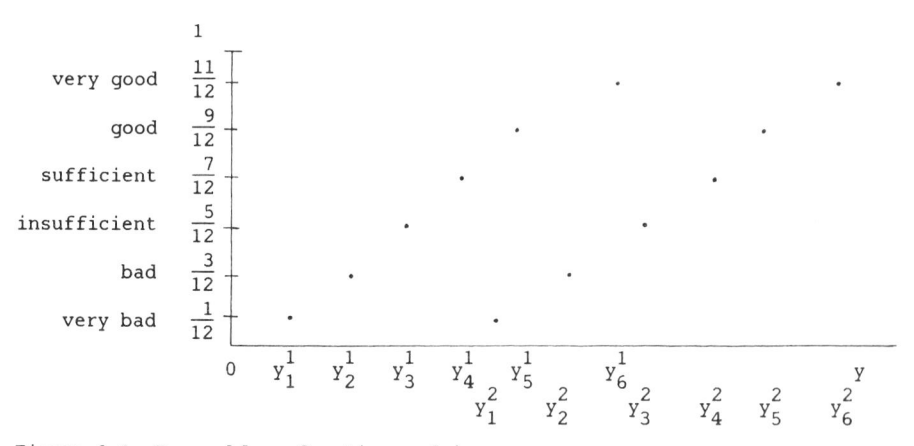

Figure 2.1 Two welfare functions of income

In drawing this figure, we have thus far made the assumptions that
(1) the verbal qualifications represent a certain notion of "welfare", that is the same to all respondents;
(2) people's response behaviour is aimed to maximize information on their welfare function;

(3) the welfare axis is a finite interval, that may be represented by the [0-1] interval.

The six points $[y_i, (i-\tfrac{1}{2})/6]$, $i = 1,\ldots,6$, may now be used to fit for each respondent a function representing the welfare function of income.

Van Praag (1968) introduced a theory of consumer behaviour resulting in the proposition that the welfare function of income may be approximately described as a lognormal distribution function, that is:

(2.1) $\quad U_n(y) = \Lambda(y;\mu_n,\sigma_n) = \Phi(\ln y;\mu_n,\sigma_n),$

where $\Lambda$ and $\Phi$ stand for the lognormal and normal distribution function, respectively.[8]

This theory assumes that the welfare range is a finite interval; the distribution functions are scaled between zero and one, and hence one is able to compare changes in welfare resulting from a certain change in income, at different points of the function.

In Van Herwaarden and Kapteyn (1981) it was shown that the lognormal function fitted the data, obtained by the IEQ, better than a score of other functions. Only the logarithmic function was found to be slightly better; in the range of answers of interest, however, the lognormal function was found to be a very good description of the data. Moreover, economic theory on uncertainty yields arguments in favour of a bounded welfare function [see Von Neumann and Morgenstern (1953)]. The lognormal function is bounded while the logarithmic function is not; moreover, the lognormal distribution function has the Friedman-Savage S-shape, which follows from Friedman's relation between risk preference and income.

If we accept the lognormal distribution function as a good approximation, the information contained in the six points of the welfare function may be summarized in the two parameters of the lognormal distribution function, namely $\mu$, a location parameter, and $\sigma$, a dispersion parameter. From the six answers to the IEQ of an individual n, called $y_{1n}$ to $y_{6n}$, the individual parameters $\mu_n$ and $\sigma_n$ may be estimated, as we have, according to the equal quantile assumption,

(2.2) $\quad U_n(y_{in}) = \Lambda(y_{in}; \mu_n, \sigma_n)$

$\quad\quad\quad\quad\quad\quad = \Phi(\ln y_{in}; \mu_n, \sigma_n)$

$\quad\quad\quad\quad\quad\quad = \Phi(\dfrac{\ln y_{in} - \mu_n}{\sigma_n}; 0,1) = \dfrac{i-\frac{1}{2}}{6} \quad\quad\quad\quad i = 1,\ldots,6$

This may be rewritten as:

(2.3) $\quad \dfrac{\ln y_{in} - \mu_n}{\sigma_n} = \Phi^{-1}[\dfrac{i-\frac{1}{2}}{6};0,1] \quad\quad\quad\quad i = 1,\ldots,6$

or

(2.4) $\quad \ln y_{in} = \mu_n + \sigma_n u_i,$

$\quad\quad$ where $u_i$ is defined as: $u_i = \Phi^{-1}[\dfrac{i-\frac{1}{2}}{6};0,1]$, $\quad\quad\quad i = 1,\ldots,6$

After adding an i.i.d. error term $\varepsilon_{it}$ with $E(\varepsilon_{it}) = 0$ for all i and t to equation (2.4), we can estimate $\mu_n$ and $\sigma_n$ for each individual separately by ordinary least-squares regression.

To illustrate their meaning two figures are drawn for different values of $\mu_n$ and $\sigma_n$. In figure 2.2 three WFIs are drawn for three different values of $\mu$, with the same value of $\sigma$.

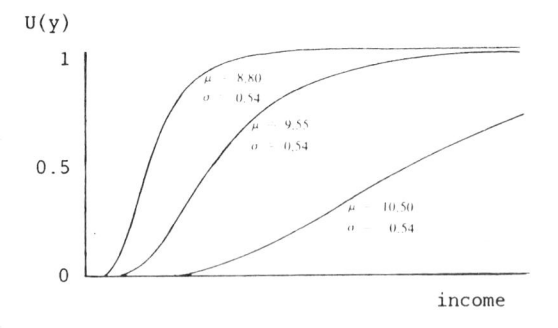

U(y)

```
                μ = 8.80
                σ = 0.54
                        μ = 9.55
                        σ = 0.54
                                μ = 10.50
                                σ = 0.54
                    income
```

Figure 2.2  The welfare function of income for different values of µ

```
                                          U(y)
                                            1
                                          0.5
                                            0
                                                              income
```

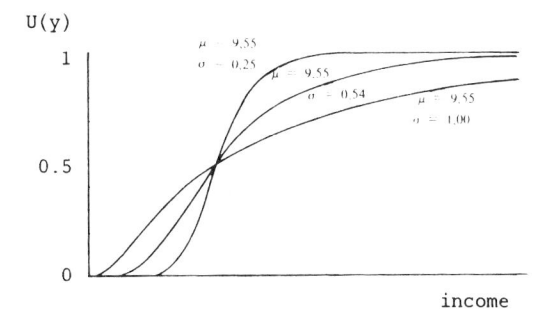

Figure 2.3  The welfare function of income for different values of σ

The quantity $\exp(\mu)$, called the natural unit of income,[9] is the income level evaluated by 0.5, just halfway on the welfare scale. It is seen that the higher μ, the higher the income necessary for an evaluation of 0.5. The quantity $\exp(\mu)$ is a location parameter, representing the needs or wants of a household in terms of monetary income.

In figure 2.3 three welfare functions have been drawn for different values of σ, with the same value of μ. It is seen that the higher σ, the more income levels are evaluated substantially different from zero or one. The quantity σ is called the welfare sensitivity of income.

The two parameters describe the welfare function of income completely. However, the parameters may differ over households, as suggested by our illustration in figure 2.1. The explanation of systematic differences in $\mu_n$ and $\sigma_n$ over households has been the subject of numerous studies in the Leyden Income Evaluation Project.[10]

A first explanation for differences in the location of the welfare function is that households differ in size and composition. A family of four will need a higher monetary income to obtain a certain welfare level than a family of two, other things being equal. The extra income needed is the net result of cost and benefits of the two additional household members. An assessment of the extra income needed to obtain the same welfare level for households of different size may be made by estimating the relationship between μ and family size. Because the net effect of family size is estimated, the possible positive non-monetary effect on welfare of having children is also taken into account.

A second explanation for differences in the location of the welfare function is that households may differ in other respects that influence their command over resources. Farm households may have a considerable amount of non-cash income, and therefore need a lower monetary income for the same welfare level than non-farm households. A student who is investing in human capital may need a lower monetary income than someone of his age who is not studying. Households with large variations in income may need as a risk premium a larger monetary income for a certain welfare level than a household without fluctuations in income. Hence all variables that should be included in the "generalized command over resources" of a household may give rise to differences in the location of the welfare functions of households. By estimating the effect of these variables on μ we may calculate the income differentials needed in order to provide these households with the same welfare level.

Hence, equivalence scales may be calculated for family size, farm/non-farm households, human wealth, fluctuations in income, et cetera. Suppose, however, that households are similar with respect to all these variables. We may then still observe systematic differences in the location of their welfare function.

The explanation of such remaining differences may be found in psychological and sociological theories on human behaviour.[11] In chapter 4 we shall elaborate on these aspects.

In the remainder of this chapter a simplified model will be used in order to derive poverty lines, using the welfare function of income. In this simplified model we exclude all differentiating variables except family size. We furthermore assume $\sigma_n$ to be constant in each country.

An empirically successful equation explaining μ, that will be the starting point of our poverty line definition, is

(2.5)    $\mu_n = \beta_0 + \beta_1 \ln fs_n + \beta_2 \ln y_n + \beta_3 m_n$

where $fs_n$ is the household size, $y_n$ is the household's income, and $m_n$ the mean log income in n's social reference group. Parameter $\beta_1$ is called the "family size elasticity".[12] Coefficient $\beta_2$ is called "preference drift",[13] as it depicts the trend that preferences drift upwards with income, and $\beta_3$ is called "reference drift",[14] as it reflects a similar phenomenon with respect to the incomes of people in the social reference group,[15] i.e. people we refer to in our attitudes.

For each household n the income level that is evaluated by δ is now seen to be

(2.6) $\quad U_n(\ln y_{\delta,n}) = \Phi(\ln y_{\delta,n}; \mu_n, \sigma_n) = \delta$

or

(2.7) $\quad \dfrac{\ln y_{\delta,n} - \mu_n}{\sigma_n} = \Phi^{-1}(\delta; 0, 1)$

yielding

(2.8) $\quad \ln y_{\delta,n} = \mu_n + \sigma_n u_\delta$

where $u_\delta$ is defined as $u_\delta = \Phi^{-1}(\delta; 0, 1)$.
Substituting (2.5) and assuming $\sigma_n$ to be a constant $\bar\sigma$ we get

(2.9) $\quad \ln y_{\delta,n} = \beta_0 + \beta_1 \ln \text{fs} + \beta_2 \ln y_n + \beta_3 m_n + \bar\sigma u_\delta$

We may now assess for each household whether he evaluates his own income as higher or lower than δ:

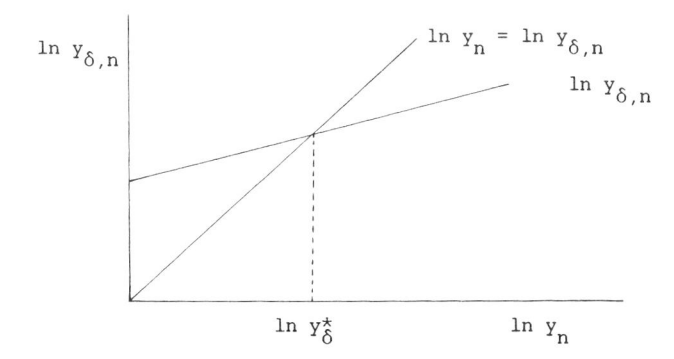

If $y_n > y_{\delta,n}$, we have $U_n(y_n) > U_n(y_{\delta,n}) = \delta$ and

if $y_n < y_{\delta,n}$, we have $U_n(y_n) < U_n(y_{\delta,n}) = \delta$.

Figure 2.4  The definition of the poverty line $y_\delta^*$

For people on the borderline there holds $y_n = y_{\delta,n}$, yielding

(2.10) $\quad \ln y_{\delta,n} = \beta_0 + \beta_1 \ln fs + \beta_2 \ln y_{\delta,n} + \beta_3 m_n + \bar{\sigma} u_\delta$

If we assume for the moment that the social reference group is the same for all households, which we represent by

(2.11) $\quad m_n = \bar{m}$

the national poverty line $y_\delta^*$ is found by solving for $y_{\delta,n}$:

(2.12) $\quad \ln y_\delta^* = \dfrac{1}{1-\beta_2} (\beta_0 + \beta_1 \ln fs + \beta_3 \bar{m} + \bar{\sigma} u_\delta)$

We might also arrive at this expression by calculating for each household its own poverty line, which depends on the income in its social reference group. By then taking the geometric mean income of all poverty lines of all households, the same national poverty line $y_\delta^*$ would be obtained, where $\bar{m}$ represents the mean log income of all social reference groups in society.[16] Hence, the assumption of equal $\bar{m}$ for everybody in society is not as restrictive as it seems; it is an aggregation method to arrive at a national poverty line. Let us now look at the properties of this poverty line.

It is seen that the resulting poverty line is differentiated according to family size. The level of the poverty line obviously depends on the welfare level $\delta$: the higher $\delta$, the higher the poverty line. Hence the poverty line defined in this way is nothing but the income level that is needed for a welfare evaluation of $\delta$; the value of $\delta$ is the welfare level that one chooses as a poverty threshold. The threshold value may be interpreted both in terms of welfare units and of verbal qualifications: a 0.5 poverty line, for instance, is found if the poverty threshold is chosen to be halfway on the welfare scale. Another interpretation of the same line is that the 0.5 line is found if the poverty threshold is the verbal evaluation between "sufficient" and "insufficient".

For each family size, the poverty line defined in (2.12) yields the same welfare level $\delta$. Hence, the poverty line is said to be differentiated according to family size in a welfare neutral way. A similar differentiation may be made for other socio-economic characteristics.

The question whether this poverty line is relative or absolute depends on the value of the parameter $\beta_3$ and on the composition of the social reference group. The assumption that the social reference group is the same for everybody, that was made in (2.11), implies that $\beta_3$ cannot be identified in (2.12): an intercept $\beta_0 + \beta_3 \bar{m}$ is estimated, from which $\beta_0$ and $\beta_3$ cannot be found separately. Hence, $\beta_3$ can only be estimated if respondents with different social reference groups may be identified. This may be done in various ways; the method used in this chapter is to assume that the social reference group is the same for everybody within a certain country, but that it differs over countries. We furthermore assume that the social reference group consists equally of all other people in one's country; the geometric mean income in the social reference group then equals median income in society.

In this case we have $\bar{m} = \mu_y$, where $\mu_y$ denotes the logarithm of median income in society. Similarly, rather than assuming $\bar{\sigma}$ to be the same for all people in all countries, we assume that $\bar{\sigma}$ is the same for everybody within a certain country, and possibly related to the standard deviation of log incomes in a country, $\sigma_y$.

We will denote the relationship between $\bar{\sigma}$ and $\sigma_y$ as a general functional relation $\bar{\sigma} = f(\sigma_y)$.

Equation (2.12) may now be written

$$(2.13) \quad \ln y_\delta^* = \frac{1}{1-\beta_2} [\beta_0 + \beta_1 \ln fs + \beta_3 \mu_y + f(\sigma_y) u_\delta]$$

The elasticity of the poverty line with respect to median income may be used as a measure for the relativity of the poverty line; this elasticity is defined as

$$(2.14) \quad \frac{d \ln y_\delta^*}{d \mu_y} = \frac{\beta_3}{1-\beta_2}.$$

It is seen that the elasticity equals zero if $\beta_3$ equals zero, and equals 1 if $\beta_3 = 1-\beta_2$ ($\beta_2 \neq 1$). Hence the poverty line is absolute if the reference drift equals zero, i.e. if people do not refer to other people when evaluating their welfare. Such an absolute poverty line results irrespective of the value of $\beta_2$ (as long as $\beta_2 \neq 1$). On the other hand the poverty line is completely relative if the preference drift and reference drift add up to one. The interpretation of this situation is found by looking at the effect of a percentage income increase of $\gamma$ for everybody. This would imply $\mu'_y = \mu_y + \ln(1+\gamma)$ and $\ln y'_n = \ln y_n + \ln(1+\gamma)$. Hence equation (2.5) implies:

(2.15) $\quad \mu'_n = \beta_0 + \beta_1 \ln fs_n + \beta_2 \ln y'_n + \beta_3 \mu'_y$

$\quad\quad\quad = \mu_n + \beta_2 \ln(1+\gamma) + \beta_3 \ln(1+\gamma)$

$\quad\quad\quad = \mu_n + \ln(1+\gamma)$

The percentage change in $\mu_n$ would be the same for everybody, and equal to the percentage change in income. Nobody would consider such a change in income to be a change in welfare, as

$$\Phi(\frac{\ln y'_n - \mu'_n}{\sigma'_n}; 0, 1) = \Phi(\frac{\ln y_n - \mu_n}{\sigma_n}; 0, 1) \text{ for all } n$$

($\sigma'_n$ will be equal to $\sigma_n$ as a percentage increase in all incomes does not change the variance of log incomes). Hence, if welfare is completely relative, i.e. $\beta_2$ and $\beta_3$ add up to one, the resulting poverty line will reflect this by an elasticity of 1.

It is furthermore seen that the poverty line depends on $\sigma_y$, except for the line $\delta = 0.5$, for which holds $u_\delta = \Phi^{-1}(0.5; 0, 1) = 0$.

Resuming the results of this section, we have described a measurement method to observe points on a welfare function of households, by asking people to tell us what income levels they evaluate as "good", "bad", "insufficient", et cetera. These points allow us to identify people as being below a certain welfare level, associated with, for instance, "insufficient". By calculating the average income of people with an actual income that they evaluate between "sufficient" and "insufficient", a poverty line is calculated according to the Deleeck method. However, the points on the welfare function may also be used to estimate the welfare function of income completely for each individual; for this procedure another assumption is needed, viz. that the verbal qualifications divide the total welfare space into equal intervals. By a normalization of 0 for the worst situation possible and 1 for the best situation possible the welfare function may be fitted through six points that map income levels to a welfare level between 0 and 1. The mathematical function chosen is the lognormal distribution function.

A number of variables influence the location of this welfare function, like family size, actual household income, and income in the social reference group. The effect of family size allows us to calculate equivalence scales that provide the same welfare level to different households. The relationship with actual income is used to calculate a poverty line as a point of intersection between actual income and income needed for a certain welfare level; in this way a poverty line may be defined as a welfare level between 0 and 1 that is chosen to be the poverty threshold. The effect of income in the social reference group, finally, may be used to estimate the extent to which the poverty line changes when median income in society changes; in other words, it enables us to assess empirically whether the poverty line is absolute, relative, or somewhere in between.

## 2.2 Comparison with other poverty line definitions

We will now compare the poverty line $y_\delta^*$ with some well-known other poverty line definitions, described in the previous chapter [see Hagenaars and Van Praag (1985)].

All poverty line definitions can be placed on a scale between completely absolute and completely relative, in other words, will have an elasticity with respect to median income between 0 and 1. We will calculate this elasticity for all poverty line definitions.

We will furthermore consider the effect of a change in income inequality, to be measured by the standard deviation of log incomes $\sigma_y$. We will assume that the income distribution function may be described by the normal distribution of log incomes $\Phi(\ln y; \mu_y, \sigma_y^2)$. Hence $\exp(\mu_y)$ equals median income in society. We furthermore assume for the moment that all incomes will be incomes per equivalent adult [implying $\beta_1 = 0$ for equation (2.13)]; we will return to the effect of family size on the poverty lines later in this section.

(a) **A basic needs approach; Rowntree's poverty line**

As described in the previous chapter, Rowntree estimates a poverty line by calculating (minimum) "cost of food", $c_0$, and (minimum) "other cost", $oc_0$, separately. The resulting poverty line is

(2.16)  $z_1 = c_0 + oc_0$

This poverty line is obviously absolute; the elasticity of this line with respect to median income is zero.

(b) **A basic needs approach; Orshansky's poverty line**

Orshansky calculated the poverty line by multiplying the cost of food by an average of the ratio of total income to food expenditures in society. Suppose that the relationship between expenditures on food c and family income y may be described by a double logarithmic Engel function:[17]

(2.17)  $\ln c = \alpha_0 + \alpha_1 \ln y$,

If the geometric mean[18] $\bar{r}$ is chosen as the average food-income ratio, used to transform expenditures on food into a poverty line, we have

(2.18)  $\bar{r} = \exp[E(\ln \frac{c}{y})]$

$= \exp[E(\ln c - \ln y)]$

$= \exp[E(\alpha_0 + (\alpha_1 - 1)\ln y)]$

$= \exp[\int_{-\infty}^{+\infty} (\alpha_0 + (\alpha_1 - 1)\ln y) d\Phi(\ln y; \mu_y, \sigma_y^2)]$

$= \exp[(\alpha_0 + (\alpha_1 - 1)\mu_y)]$

where $E(.)$ stands for the mathematical expectation with respect to the distribution of incomes.
The poverty line corresponding to a specific food basket $c_0$ is now found to be

(2.19) $$z_2 = c_0 (\bar{r})^{-1} = c_0 \exp[-\alpha_0+(1-\alpha_1)\mu_y]$$

It appears that the resulting poverty line depends on median income in society, $\exp(\mu_y)$, if the food-income ratio is regularly adapted to changes in society. The elasticity of this poverty line with respect to median income equals $(1-\alpha_1)$. A food elasticity of 0.3, for example, yields an elasticity of the poverty line with respect to median income of 0.7.

(c) A basic needs approach; Friedman's poverty line

A third way of calculating a poverty line from minimum food expenditures $c_0$ is to multiply with the Engel coefficient of the poor, i.e.

$$z_3 = c_0 \left(\frac{y_0}{c_0}\right)$$

In other words, the poverty line is defined as the income level at which the minimum food basket $c_0$ is consumed, where $y_0$ is found from the Engel function. From the loglinear Engel function we have $\ln c_0 = \alpha_0 + \alpha_1 \ln y_0$, from which $y_0$ may be solved as

$$y_0 = \exp\left(\frac{\ln c_0 - \alpha_0}{\alpha_1}\right)$$

Hence

(2.20) $$z_3 = y_0 = c_0^{1/\alpha_1} \exp\left(-\frac{\alpha_0}{\alpha_1}\right)$$

This poverty line is absolute; the elasticity with respect to median income is zero.

(d) Food ratio method

One might alternatively derive a poverty line from the Engel function by setting a maximum value $y_0$ for the ratio of food expenditures to total income; if someone's food-income ratio $c/y$ is higher than $y_0$, he is called poor; if $c/y$ is lower than $y_0$, he is called non-poor.

If once again equation (2.17) describes the relationship between food and income in society, the poverty line corresponding to $y_0$ is the solution for y of

(2.21) $\quad \ln y_0 = \ln \frac{c}{y} = \alpha_0 + (\alpha_1 - 1) \ln y$

yielding:

(2.22) $\quad z_4 = \exp \left( \frac{\alpha_0 - \ln y_0}{1 - \alpha_1} \right)$

If $y_0$ does not change with $\mu_y$ or $\sigma_y$, this method thus results in an absolute poverty line.

(e) Fraction of median income

If the poverty line is chosen as a fraction of median income, this poverty line can be denoted by

(2.23) $\quad z_5 = \tau_0 \exp(\mu_y) \quad\quad\quad (0 \leq \tau_0 \leq 1)$

The welfare proxy used in the derivation of this line is the ratio of actual income to median income in society. This poverty line is obviously relative; the elasticity with respect to median income equals 1.

(f) Fraction of mean income

If instead of median income, mean income is chosen as the indicator of the standard of living in society, and if the income distribution may be approximated by a lognormal distribution function, the resulting poverty line is

(2.24) $\quad z_6 = \tau_{00} \exp(\mu_y + \tfrac{1}{2}\sigma_y^2)$

Again, the poverty line is relative with an elasticity of one; in this definition, however, an increase in income inequality will increase the poverty line as well.

### (g) Percentile of the income distribution

Finally, a poverty line may be defined as a certain percentile $\varepsilon_0$ of the income distribution:

$$(2.25) \qquad \int_{-\infty}^{\ln z_7} d\Phi(\ln y, \mu_y, \sigma_y^2) = \varepsilon_0$$

The poverty line now equals

$$(2.26) \qquad z_7 = \exp[u_{\varepsilon_0} \sigma_y + \mu_y]$$

where $u_{\varepsilon_0}$ is defined as $\Phi(u_{\varepsilon_0}; 0,1) = \varepsilon_0$, and $\Phi$ denotes the normal distribution function.

In this definition the welfare proxy used is someone's relative position in the income distribution. This poverty line depends both on average income and on income inequality; for values of $\varepsilon_0$ smaller than 0.5 (implying that the poverty line is smaller than median income), the poverty line increases if income inequality decreases.
The elasticity with respect to median income is again equal to 1.

### 2.3 Evaluation of different definitions

The poverty lines and poverty percentages corresponding to the various definitions can be summarized in the following table. For the calculation of the poverty percentages it is again assumed that incomes are lognormally distributed.
The poverty lines vary from absolute ($z_1$, $z_3$ and $z_4$) to entirely relative ($z_5$, $z_6$ and $z_7$). The other poverty line definitions ($z_2$ and $z_8$) may be anywhere on this scale, dependent on the values of the coefficients. These coefficients are to be estimated using survey data; the estimates are denoted by a hat. If $\hat{\alpha}_1 = 1$, implying that the elasticity of food consumption with respect to income equals 1, the Orshansky line becomes absolute; if $\hat{\alpha}_1 = 0$, implying that expenditures on food are inelastic with respect to income, the Orshansky method yields a completely relative poverty line.

In other words, if food expenditures increase less than proportionally with increasing income, as is stated by Engel's law, we will find a relative poverty line. If, on the other hand, food expenditures increase at the same rate as income, the fraction of total income spent on food is constant when income rises, and we find an absolute poverty line.[19] Analogously the Leyden definition is an absolute poverty line if $\beta_3 = 0$, and a completely relative line if $\beta_2 = 1 - \beta_3$.
Moreover, the Leyden poverty line definition appears to be a generalization of almost all other poverty line definitions:

Specialization to $z_1$, $z_3$, and $z_4$

If $\beta_3 = 0$, $\beta_1 = 0$, and $\delta = 0.5$, we have a Rowntree definition with

$$\ln (c_0 + oc_0) = \frac{\beta_0}{1 - \beta_2}$$

or a Friedman definition with

$$\frac{\ln c_0 - \hat{\alpha}_0}{\hat{\alpha}_1} = \frac{\beta_0}{1 - \beta_2}$$

or a food-ratio definition where

$$\frac{\hat{\alpha}_0 - \ln y_0}{1 - \hat{\alpha}_1} = \frac{\beta_0}{1 - \beta_2}$$

Specialization to $z_2$

If $\delta = 0.5$ and $\beta_1 = 0$, we have an Orshansky definition with

$$\ln c_0 - \hat{\alpha}_0 = \frac{\beta_0}{1 - \beta_2} \text{ and } (1-\hat{\alpha}_1) = \frac{\beta_3}{1 - \beta_2}$$

Specialization to $z_5$

If $\beta_3 = 1 - \beta_2$, $\beta_1 = 0$, and $\delta = 0.5$, we have a fraction of median income definition, with

$$\ln \tau_0 = \frac{\hat{\beta}_0}{1 - \hat{\beta}_2}$$

Specialization to $z_6$

If $\hat{\beta}_3 = 1 - \hat{\beta}_2$, $\hat{\beta}_1 = 0$, we have a fraction of median income definition, with

$$\ln \tau_{00} = \frac{f(\sigma_y)u_\delta}{(1-\hat{\beta}_2)} - \tfrac{1}{2}\sigma_y^2$$

Specialization to $z_7$

If $\hat{\beta}_3 = 1 - \hat{\beta}_2$, $\hat{\beta}_1 = 0$, $f(\sigma_y) = \sigma_y$, and $\hat{\beta}_0 = 0$, (2.13) specializes to

$$\ln y^*_\delta = \mu_y + \frac{\sigma_y u_\delta}{(1-\hat{\beta}_2)}$$

which is a percentile definition with

$$u_{\varepsilon_0} = \frac{u_\delta}{(1 - \hat{\beta}_2)}$$

Hence all poverty lines described may be found as special instances of the Leyden poverty line depending on the values of the coefficients $\hat{\beta}_0$, $\hat{\beta}_2$ and $\hat{\beta}_3$, and the welfare level $\delta$.

The nature of the poverty line, either relative or absolute, thus arises from the estimation of parameters $\beta_0$, $\beta_2$ and $\beta_3$ from survey data, instead of being implicitly imposed by the researcher by the choice of a specific poverty line definition.

The basic needs and food ratio definitions are both based on survey data from budget surveys. As budget surveys require a strong effort from the respondents, the response is usually low and the resulting data sets are not always representative for the society as a whole. The advantage of the Leyden poverty line in this respect is that it does not require a budget survey, but can be derived from any survey that includes an IEQ and information on household income. Moreover, a second advantage of our subjective poverty line is that it is based on direct measurement of welfare, instead of on a proxy of welfare via the expenditures on food, especially as so many difficulties arise in the definition of the basic food basket. See for a further comparison Van Praag, Spit and Van de Stadt (1982), whose research also provides us with an indication for the values of the coefficients $\alpha_0$, $\alpha_1$ and $\alpha_2$, in the following estimates of the Engel function:

$$\ln c = 4.24 + 0.38 \ln fs + 0.39 \ln y$$
$$(0.21) \quad (0.06) \quad\quad (0.02)$$

(standard errors are given within parentheses). This results in a poverty line elasticity of the Orshansky line of 0.61. The coefficient of the Leyden poverty line has not been estimated in that paper; for estimation of all of these parameters either panel data or data on several countries or separate societies are needed that provide us with varying levels of median income and income inequality needed to identify the parameters $\beta_0$ and $\beta_3$ separately. If no such variation is available, the poverty line may still be calculated; however, as median income is then constant for all observations, all terms pertaining to median income will be included in the intercept. Lack of variation in income inequality leads, moreover, to the assumption of a constant value of the welfare sensitivity parameter $\sigma$ over the population. The resulting expression is of the form

(2.27) $$\ln y_\delta^* = \frac{1}{1 - \beta_2} [\beta_0 + \bar{\sigma} u_\delta],$$

where $\beta_0$ is the intercept, and $\beta_2$ the coefficient of log income in the μ-equation. In this book both the more general form of the poverty line equation given in (2.13) will be estimated, using data from several European countries, and the more simple form (2.27) for each country separately.

We have so far assumed that all income and welfare measurements are independent of family size. As we have seen in chapter 1, the derivation and use of equivalence scales introduces another difference between the various poverty line definitions. The poverty line definitions based on survey data may be easily adapted to yield family size differentiated poverty lines by the inclusion of family size in the Engel function and the welfare function to be estimated. All other methods except these two need some exogenously determined equivalence scale, to be applied both in the calculation of the parameters of the income distribution and in the differentiation of the poverty line itself.

The Leyden poverty line has been differentiated according to family size by the inclusion of family size in equation (2.5). As this equation measures welfare directly, the effects of family size on welfare may be found in a "natural" way [see also Van Praag, Spit and Van de Stadt, (1982)].

These welfare neutral equivalence scales may also be derived for various other characteristics, as we have mentioned above.[20] We will return to these characteristics in chapter 4, where the theory explaining $\mu$ and $\sigma$ is discussed in more detail.

Summarizing, the Leyden poverty line definition described in this chapter has the following properties: it is a definition of an income level that provides a certain minimum welfare level. It may be differentiated according to various socio-economic variables such that it provides the same welfare level to different households. Finally, it is based on the perception of welfare in society, as measured in a representative survey. All other poverty lines are seen to be special cases of the Leyden poverty line.

Table 2.1 Eight poverty lines and poverty percentages

| Definition | Poverty line | Poverty percentage | Elasticity |
|---|---|---|---|
| 1. Basic needs, Rowntree | $\ln z_1 = \ln(c_0 + oc_0)$ | $\pi_1 = \phi\left[\dfrac{\ln(c_0+oc_0)-\mu_y}{\sigma_y}, 0, 1\right]$ | 0 |
| 2. Basic needs, Orshansky | $\ln z_2 = \ln c_0 - \hat{\alpha}_0 + (1-\hat{\alpha}_1)\mu_y$ | $\pi_2 = \phi\left(\dfrac{\ln c_0 - \hat{\alpha}_0 - \hat{\alpha}_1\mu_y}{\sigma_y}; 0, 1\right)$ | $1-\hat{\alpha}_1$ |
| 3. Basic needs, Friedman | $\ln z_3 = \dfrac{\ln c_0 - \hat{\alpha}_0}{\hat{\alpha}_1}$ | $\pi_3 = \phi\left(\dfrac{\ln c_0 - \hat{\alpha}_0 - \hat{\alpha}_1\mu_y}{\hat{\alpha}_1\sigma_y}; 0, 1\right)$ | 0 |
| 4. Food ratio | $\ln z_4 = \dfrac{\hat{\alpha}_0 - \ln y_0}{1-\hat{\alpha}_1}$ | $\pi_4 = \phi\left[\dfrac{\hat{\alpha}_0 - \ln y_0 - (1-\hat{\alpha}_1)\mu_y}{(1-\hat{\alpha}_1)\sigma_y}\right]$ | 0 |
| 5. Percentage median income | $\ln z_5 = \ln \tau_0 + \mu_y$ | $\pi_5 = \phi\left(\dfrac{\ln \tau_0}{\sigma_y}\right)$ | 1 |
| 6. Percentage mean income | $\ln z_6 = \ln \tau_{00} + \mu_y + \tfrac{1}{2}\sigma_y^2$ | $\pi_6 = \phi\left(\dfrac{\ln \tau_{00} + \tfrac{1}{2}\sigma_y^2}{\sigma_y}; 0, 1\right)$ | 1 |
| 7. Percentile | $\ln z_7 = u_{\varepsilon_0}\sigma_y + \mu_y$ | $\pi_7 = \varepsilon_0$ | 1 |
| 8. Leyden poverty line | $\ln z_8 = \dfrac{\hat{\beta}_0 + \hat{\beta}_1\ln fs + \hat{\beta}_3\mu_y + f(\sigma_y)u_\delta}{1-\hat{\beta}_2}$ | $\pi_8 = \phi\left[\dfrac{(\hat{\beta}_3-1)\mu_y + \hat{\beta}_1\ln fs + f(\sigma_y)u_\delta}{(1-\hat{\beta}_2)\sigma_y}; 0, 1\right]$ | $\dfrac{\hat{\beta}_3}{1-\hat{\beta}_2}$ |

(Coefficients that are obtained from estimation of survey data are denoted with a hat)

NOTES TO CHAPTER 2

[1] In this chapter we will write "income" instead of "command over resources"; we will return to the difference between the two in chapter 3.

[2] In fact more than one poverty line may be derived with this information, as will be shown in this chapter.

[3] This does not imply that all household members necessarily benefit equally from their total command over resources, or that they participate equally in the decision making process; for the purpose of this monograph, however, we will abstain from these inequalities. For a discussion of the assumption made here we refer to chapter 3.

[4] The definition was introduced by Goedhart, Halberstadt, Kapteyn and Van Praag (1977) and elaborated upon in Van Praag, Goedhart and Kapteyn (1980), Van Praag, Hagenaars and Van Weeren (1982), Van Praag (1984), and Hagenaars and Van Praag (1985).

[5] Van Praag (1984) proposed this method to calculate so-called "true cost functions" at all welfare levels described by the available verbal descriptions.

[6] See for a formal derivation Van Praag (1971), and for a generalization Kapteyn (1977).

[7] The equal quantile assumption was tested in Buyze (1982).

[8] The theory described here was elaborated upon by Van Praag (1971), Kapteyn (1977), Van Praag (1981), Kapteyn and Wansbeek (1982), and numerous other publications [see for a summary the "Leyden Income Evaluation Project: A Summary of Activities" (1984)].

[9] The natural unit to measure a certain variable X is $\exp[E(\ln X)]$ which in this application equals the geometric mean income. See Van Praag (1968) for a motivation of the terminology.

[10] Van Praag (1971), Van Praag and Kapteyn (1973), Kapteyn (1977), Kapteyn, Van Praag and Van Herwaarden (1978), Kapteyn, Wansbeek and Buyze (1978), Kapteyn and Wansbeek (1982), Van Praag (1981), and Van Praag and Spit (1982), to name but a few. A complete list of publications is given in "The Leyden Income Evaluation Project: A Summary of Activities" (1984).

[11] Kapteyn (1977), Kapteyn, Van Praag and Van Herwaarden (1978), Kapteyn, Wansbeek and Buyze (1978), Van Praag, Kapteyn and Van Herwaarden (1979), Van Praag (1981).
A similar theory has been described by Duesenberry as early as 1949 and more recently by Layard (1980) in his formulation of a status ranking principle.

[12] Van Praag (1971).

[13] Van Praag (1971).

[14] Kapteyn (1977).

[15] Hyman (1942), Kapteyn (1977).

[16] This procedure yields expression (2.12) for all family size only if the value of $m_n$ does not vary over household size.

[17] See Watts (1967), Cramer (1969), and Van Praag, Spit and Van de Stadt (1982).

[18] If another indicator of the average food-income ratio is used, (2.18) will become slightly more complicated. For any specific form of the income distribution, however, the poverty line may again be derived, analytically or numerically.

[19] Again, it should be noted that an absolute poverty line is also found if the food ratio of one specific time period is chosen as a constant multiplier of food expenditures for years to follow, where only the food expenditures are adapted to price inflation.

[20] See Van Praag, Hagenaars and Van Weeren (1982) for an empirical example of this differentiation.

Chapter 3
DETERMINANTS OF INCOME

The poverty concept used in this book is income poverty, implying that a household is considered to be poor if its household income falls below its poverty line. If we want to assess which socio-economic characteristics determine poverty, we have to study the determinants of the poverty lines of different households and the determinants of household income.

We have seen in chapter 2 that a household is considered to be poor if its household income y is smaller than $y_\delta^*$. If $y_\delta^*$ is the same for all households in society, the determinants of poverty are equivalent to the determinants of low household income. If $y_\delta^*$ varies over households, e.g. with family size, a household with family size fs is considered to be poor if $y(fs) < y_\delta^*(fs)$. Hence, if we want to determine whether households with a specific family size are in poverty, we have to compare their income with their specific needs, as reflected by the family size differentiated poverty line. This does not hold for family size only; if we want to know, for instance, whether farm households are more often in poverty than non-farm households, we have to compare farm and non-farm household incomes with their respective poverty lines. As the non-cash income of a farm household will be reflected in a lower monetary poverty line, the answer will depend on the difference between farm and non-farm household incomes compared to the difference between farm and non-farm poverty lines. The same holds for all other variables that influence the household's total command over resources, like human wealth, employment, fluctuations in income, et cetera. Hence, by looking at the effect of these variables both on income and on the poverty line, determinants of poverty are found.

In this chapter we will concentrate on the components of household income. Chapter 4 will discuss the determinants of welfare, and chapter 5 will combine the two preceding chapters in discussing the determinants of poverty.

## 3.1 The income concept used

The income concept to be used is monetary after-tax annual household income. Before describing the components this household income consists of, and explaining the variation in these components, we should motivate the choice of this specific income concept.

The choice of monetary income implies that all non-cash components of command over resources are excluded. Among these are fringe benefits, home produced goods and services, and benefits from government expenditure like food stamps, medical aid, public housing, education, public transport, et cetera. The non-cash benefits from public goods and services may form an important part of total command over resources in some countries. Smeeding (1977) shows that the total market value of non-cash transfers exceeds public assistance in cash in the U.S.A. by an ever increasing margin. Chiswick and O'Neill (1977) present estimates of the effect that exclusion of some of these variables has on estimates of income inequality; a variance of log income of 0.75, rather than 0.52 is found.[1] The difficulties involved in including these non-cash components in studies of income distribution are enormous [see, e.g., Smeeding (1977)]. The main difficulty is that one wishes to assess the amount of money that would make the household indifferent between the non-cash benefit and the monetary cash equivalent. This implies that we have to know the effect of the non-cash benefit on household welfare. As we have mentioned above, we will estimate the effect of various characteristics on welfare directly. The cash value of different non-cash components may hence be derived from the poverty line, that is based on this welfare measurement. Rather than adding the value of non-cash components to monetary household income, and then comparing the corrected incomes to one uniform poverty line, we compare each monetary income to the appropriate poverty line, where the value of non-cash income is implicitly deducted.

The choice of after-tax income is made because it is after-tax, rather than pre-tax income that is perceived as command over resources by most households. Both the poverty line and the actual household income are therefore measured as after-tax concepts.

The choice of current annual income rather than attempting to measure permanent income by estimating economic status, like Garfinkel and Haveman (1977), is motivated by arguments similar to those mentioned in our choice for monetary income: we will measure the effect on welfare directly of variables influencing permanent income. Students, for example, who are investing in human capital and hence have a temporarily low income, will take their human capital into account when answering the questions on welfare; the poverty line for students will as a result also take account of this human wealth.

Finally, we have to motivate our choice of household income. As indicated in the previous chapter, this choice is made because household members usually derive welfare not only from their own income, but from total household cash and non-cash income. The choice of the family as the income unit in research on income distribution and poverty has been discussed by Danziger and Taussig (1979) and Datta and Meerman (1980). Danziger and Taussig showed that measures of both income inequality and poverty are sensitive to the choice of the income unit, as well as to the weight that is given to each income unit in the total population. They do not advocate one specific income unit, but suggest that each income unit should be weighted in the total income distribution with the number of persons in the family. Cowell (1984) analyzes the effect of the choice of income unit and income receiving unit on income inequality. He suggests that one should use as income concept household income per equivalent adult, and as income receiving unit each person in the household. Datta and Meerman (1980) follow Kuznets (1976) in abandoning household income in favour of household _per capita_ income. They show that by using household income, income inequality is usually overestimated. This results from the fact that household income usually reaches a maximum at the period when the family size is largest; young people and old people, who have relatively low incomes, form one or two person households, while middle-aged have highest incomes and highest family size. Hence by dividing household incomes by family size, the differences between households decrease. Estimates of the percentage of people in poverty are also found to be different for the two income concepts. Finally, they show that the effect of using _per capita_ household income instead of household income is to flatten the life-cycle income profile.

In fact, there are two aspects of this problem, as has been clarified by Sen (1983). Firstly, a criterion has to be found to derive poverty lines for different family types, e.g. by the determination of family equivalence scales. Secondly, after having determined equivalent poverty lines for different families, weights have to be given to families of different

size in some aggregate index of poverty to be calculated. With respect to the first problem, we reject the method followed by Datta and Meerman, as it excludes the possibility of economies of scale within a household.
The second problem, that arises when aggregate indices of poverty are to be calculated, will be solved in chapter 6.

Having specified the income concept to be used, we will now look at the components of this monetary after-tax annual household income. We may write:[2]

(3.1) $\quad y = y_m + y_p + cb$

where
$\quad y$ = monetary after-tax annual household income

$\quad y_m$ = monetary after-tax annual income of the main breadwinner, that is per definition the one who contributes most to household income

$\quad y_p$ = monetary after-tax annual income of the partner

$\quad cb$ = child benefits per year

Hence we split up total household income into the incomes of its contributors, where we assume, for convenience, that no more than two breadwinners are found in a household. The income of the main breadwinner is in some households the only component of household income; in all households it is per definition the largest component. The explanation of this income component will therefore be most important in this monograph. The income of the partner may be the second part of household income. Apart from the determinants of this income itself, the determinants of the fact whether or not the partner is working are also of interest to our purpose. The third part, finally, is the monetary income from child benefits. As these are institutionally determined their explanation is not relevant in the present framework; we will return to the child benefits when discussing the effect of family size on welfare, in chapter 5.

Hence, we will continue to discuss the determinants of personal income, of both main breadwinner and partner, and the decision of the partner to participate in the labour market.

## 3.2 Determinants of individual income

In this section we will briefly review the main theories explaining individual income. Our aim in surveying these theories is to derive variables that should be included in the empirical income equations, and to facilitate the interpretation of the results. No test of the various theories is intended (or feasible, given the data available).

A considerable number of more or less competing theories to explain differences in personal income have been developed in economic history. Sahota (1978) distinguishes ten different schools of thought, between some of which a wide divergence is found. In this survey we shall classify these theories into one of the five following categories:
(1) individual choice
(2) inheritance
(3) chance
(4) market imperfections
(5) public income redistribution

Although hardly any theory restricts the causes of income differences to one of these five categories exclusively, they all emphasize one of these causes particularly.

(1) Individual choice

Among the theories hypothesizing that income differences largely result from individual choice are the human capital theory, the life-cycle theory, and theories on compensating differentials. In each of these theories the essential assumption is that people maximize expected life-time welfare. Given their individual tastes and endowments, the maximization procedure results in different income patterns over life-time. In the human capital theory, started off by Mincer (1958) and Becker (1962), income differences are the result of heterogeneity of labour, which in turn is the result of individual choice. Knowledge and experience is seen as a form of capital, that will increase productivity. This knowledge may be acquired by investments in schooling. As a result of increased productivity, people with more human capital will be able to earn higher labour incomes. As these higher incomes will be paid after a period of schooling, individuals will compare these future benefits to the cost of schooling, both in the form of direct cost (e.g. school fees) and in the form of earnings foregone during the schooling period. They will choose to invest in human capital, if the present value of future earnings is greater than or equal to the present value of total cost. This basic model was developed by Mincer (1958) and elaborated upon by numerous scholars.[3] Human capital cannot only be increased by schooling; a variety of post-school investments can also result in increased experience, and hence productivity. Assuming that marginal productivity of this experience decreases after a certain period, this results in the well-known concave age-income profiles. The relationship between age and income has been described in many articles. The life-cycle pattern of income has been studied for various reasons, in actuarial studies [see e.g. Kiker (1966)], studies on saving behaviour [see Somermeyer and Bannink (1966)], and in the human capital studies mentioned above. In all studies it appeared that income increases with age until at some age a maximum is reached, after which income declines. This is the pattern when cross-sectional data are used; Becker showed that the income of an individual over time not necessarily shows the same pattern, due to increases in real income and changes in the income distribution over time. However, given data on these changes the "time-series" age-income profiles may be estimated from cross-sectional data. Becker (1964) estimated these time-series for individuals with varying educational levels. The age-income profile tends to be much steeper for people with a high education than for people with low education.

Of the numerous articles on this topic we mention Mincer (1974) who, besides age-income profiles, studied experience-income profiles, where experience is the number of years worked.

Recent extensions of the human capital framework incorporate a variety of other decisions that people make to maximize lifetime welfare, e.g. with respect to job search [Spence (1973)], home production [Becker (1975)], family and population [Nerlove (1974)].

A similar procedure of balancing cost and benefits from alternative actions is the basis of Friedman's (1953) life-cycle theory. People have different tastes for risk, and choose between occupations with different risks. Risk averters can only be induced to enter a risky occupation by a high risk premium. The higher incomes of self-employed are thus interpreted as a compensation for the uncertainty of their income. This compensatory principle is one of the oldest theories explaining differences in individual incomes. Adam Smith (1776, p.202) states that higher wages will be paid to make up for negative aspects of certain employments, while advantages of other employments will result in comparatively low wages. As examples of circumstances giving rise to wage differences of this sort, Smith mentions the attractiveness of the employment, the cost of acquiring the required skills, the stability of employment, the responsibility of the job, and the probability of success, the latter being the result of both luck and talent. With respect to the pleasantness of the employment Smith states that jobs that are difficult, dirty, or have a low social status, will pay more than jobs that are easy, or honourable; a higher pecuniary gain has to compensate for these disadvantages in order to induce people to enter these employments. Recent empirical evidence is given by Atrostic (1982), who found a negative correlation between positive job characteristics and wages, if the sample is split up into subgroups with an equal amount of human capital.

The stability of employment is Smith's third motive for income inequality. Workers with insecure employments will ceteris paribus have higher wages than people with secure employments; not only in order to maintain them during unemployment, but also to compensate them for the psychic cost of insecurity.

Another factor mentioned by Smith that still appears in theories on income is the responsibility of the job. The more responsibility, the higher are the wages paid. Tinbergen (1975), for instance, has used two variables that may be interpreted as reflecting responsibility; the first is the effort required by the job (expressed in years of schooling), the second is the "tension" of the job (expressed by a possible divergence between required and actual schooling) [see for empirical evidence also Bouma, Van Praag and Tinbergen (1976)]. In Tinbergen's theory this tension may arise both if job requirements are too high and too low, compared to actual schooling. Incomes will differ over individuals in order to compensate for these inconveniences.

Hence human capital theory, life-cycle theory and the theory of compensating differentials all basically state that differences in monetary income may be the result of individual choices in which all cash and non-cash cost and benefits of their actions are balanced such that the life-time welfare of all these different individuals is maximized.

(2) Inheritance

The most comprehensive theory in this category is Meade's inheritance theory (1964). His analysis follows the emphasis of classical economic theories on factors of production and social class.[4] Meade distinguishes cash and non-cash inheritance; among the latter are genetic make-up, parental nurture and training, and social contacts. Both positive and negative feedbacks to a favourable inheritance are distinguished; the positive feedbacks, however, dominate, resulting in a persisting division of society in poor and rich families. Meade hence incorporates earlier theories in which income differences were exclusively explained in terms of inherited mental and physical abilities; he is more general in the sense that abilities resulting from the (inherited) social environment are also taken into account. Whereas the individual choice theories emphasize that abilities are produced by education and are acquired by individual choice, the inheritance theories consider abilities to be gifts from one generation to another.

An inheritance theory which may be generalized to take account of human capital is Hartog's multicapability theory [Hartog (1980)] which states that earnings depend on the supply of capabilities, not on the available levels. By emphasizing the supply, individual tastes and preferences are allowed for.

(3) Chance

A third cause of income inequality is found in random events, luck, chance. Gibrat (1931) formulated the stochastic theory of income inequalities, which implied that a normally distributed random component of log income is responsible for the well-known lognormal distribution of incomes. Fase (1969) studied age-income profiles in the context of a stochastic model, where income at each age is assumed to be a random variable, following a lognormal distribution. Furthermore he assumed log income to increase systematically with a decreasing percentage until a certain maximum is reached, after which log income decreases at an increasing rate. This amounts to a model in which expected yearly log income is a quadratic function of age, corresponding to one of the specifications used by Mincer on the basis of human capital theory [Mincer, 1974)]. Although

Fase's results imply that the age at which the maximum income is reached is higher for people with a university degree than for others, his findings do not confirm the expected difference in steepness of the age-income profiles that human capital theory would imply.
Although in all empirical studies a considerable part of income variance is still unexplained, the present tendency in research is to try and analyse additional systematical causes, rather than to call all unexplained variance the result of luck [see, e.g., Shorrocks (1975)].

(4) Market imperfections

Another cause of income differences is non-competitiveness of labour markets. The labour market may be non-competitive for a variety of reasons. Monopolistic powers may be present in the form of labour unions, causing union members to have higher wages (ceteris paribus) than non-union members. Various social, legal and cultural institutions may be an impediment to complete mobility. In certain occupations only a limited number of people are admitted, resulting in relatively high wages.
Stratification of the labour market may also be the result of discrimination according to e.g. race or sex; a recent study of Brown et al. (1980) shows that only 14 to 17 percent of the wage differential between men and women is attributable to differences in endowments; the remainder reflects both discrimination and occupational segmentation. Lack of mobility of labour causes regional wage differences, as well as differences between rural and urban areas. Though both higher incomes and lower unemployment rates in large cities cause migration from the country to the cities, which partly diminishes these income differences, complete mobility is often inhibited by e.g. lack of housing [Rothenberg Pack (1973)].[5]
One of the theories explaining income differences in terms of non-competitiveness is the segmented labour market theory [see, e.g., Piore and Doeringer (1971), Vietorisz and Harrison (1973)]. The theory states that the labour market is dichotomized into a primary sector and a secondary sector. The primary sector offers high wages, good working conditions, employment stability, and good opportunities for on-the-job training. In the secondary sector low wages, bad working conditions, high turnover rates, and no opportunities for training are found. There is little or no mobility between these two sectors, as workers in both sectors develop

different ways of living and different attitudes. The attitudes of workers in the secondary sector will often prevent them from entering the first sector. The difficulty of moving out of the secondary sector is larger for blacks and for women than for whites and for men, as a result of discrimination by both employers and co-workers.

Some of the predictions based on the compensatory principle are contradicted by the dual labour market theory; the latter implies for instance that stable employments will pay higher wages than the unstable employments.

Non-competitiveness is also the main cause of income inequality in Lydall's (1968) managerial hierarchy theory, Thurow's (1975) job competition theory, and the screening or signalling theory, as described by, e.g., Spence (1973), to the extent that the screens or signals do not reflect true ability, but the taste of employers for discrimination; see Cain (1977) for a critical review of all theories in this category.

(5) Public income redistribution

Although after the Paretian revolution in economics interpersonal welfare comparisons are no longer considered part of positive economics by most economists, in actual government policies interpersonal comparisons are made all the time. The tendency of most public finance programs in European countries has been to redistribute from the rich to the poor sections of society [see, e.g., OECD (1976), Tinbergen (1975)].[6] The effect of these programs on the income distribution is twofold. On the one hand a direct effect of taxes and income transfers is found on the after-tax income distribution; in the form of programs providing social assistance, unemployment and disability benefits, old-age and widow pensions, and in the form of tax expenditures, like allowing for various deductions for family maintenance, work related cost, et cetera. The direct effects, especially of transfers, is of crucial importance in reducing poverty. A second, indirect effect of taxes and transfers is that they may affect the choices that people make with respect to labour supply, savings, and possibly marital status and living arrangements. A survey of literature on both the direct and the indirect effect of transfer programs is given by Danziger, Haveman and Plotnick (1981). They conclude that the results reviewed imply, with due caution, that reduction of benefits will increase income poverty and achieve only small increases in work effort and savings. In a comparison of the welfare state in the U.S. and the Netherlands, however, Haveman (1985) suggests that the losses associated with the welfare state might be reduced by a reorientation of the transfer programs.

Although most theories reviewed tend to concentrate upon one of the five causes mentioned of income differences, recent studies try either to test these theories against each other [Taubman and Wales (1974), Taubman (1975), Leigh (1978)] or to integrate them into a more complete model of income distribution [Ghez and Becker (1975), Griliches (1977), Ritzen (1977), Hartog (1980)]. With respect to the testing of theories, evidence is given by Taubman (1975) that implications of the human capital theory, the life-cycle theory and inheritance theory all stand to test. Leigh (1978) tests some of the implications of the dual labour market theory versus the human capital theory, and concludes that "... while a two-sector view of the labour market is too simple to yield realistic policy prescriptions, the existence of a more complex structure of segmentation cannot be dismissed". This points to the idea that by integrating the various theories into more complete models the determinants of income distributions will be more fully explained.

Not all variables mentioned here will appear in our empirical equations. We have no data on ability, family background, inherited property, on-the-job training, and a number of other characteristics that we would need in order to incorporate all important factors in our analysis. Moreover, we have no panel data, but cross-sectional data only. We list the variables that will be included in the income equation, with the expected effect according to the theories described above. A detailed description of the way these variables are measured in our survey is given in the appendix.

Hypotheses on individual incomes

(a) Degree of urbanization

Due to incomplete mobility, higher incomes are expected for people living in larger cities. The effect of the "flight to the suburbs" may disturb this phenomenon. An extra problem with this variable is in the definition of, e.g., "large city". Suburbs may be included in one country and excluded in the other. This will complicate international comparison.

(b) Fluctuations in income

Following the life-cycle theory it is expected that people with large fluctuations in income will have a higher (average) income than people without fluctuations in income. According to the dual labour market theory, however, people with large fluctuations in income are expected to have lower average earnings. It is not certain which of these hypotheses will prevail. Moreover, as only cross-sectional data are available, the period of measurement may also be important: even if on average people with large fluctuations in income have a higher income than people without fluctuations in income, the reverse might be observed if the survey takes place during a recession.

(c) Occupation

Based on theories of risk aversion it is expected that people who are self-employed will have a higher income on average than people who are employees. Again, this may or may not show up in the data, as we do not measure averages over a period of time but incomes at one specific moment only.

(d) Level of schooling

Based on the theory of human capital, a higher level of education is expected to result in a higher after-tax personal income. The same effect is found according to screening theories.

(e) Age

Using data from cross-sectional surveys, we expect income to rise with age until a certain maximum is reached, after which income will decline. This profile will differ for persons with varying levels of schooling: the higher the educational level, the steeper the age-income profile is expected to be, and the higher the age at which the maximum income is reached.

(f) Sex

Men are expected to have a higher income, ceteris paribus, than women, due to different labour market behaviour and possible discrimination.

(g) Taxes

Two persons with the same pre-tax income may have different after-tax incomes if the tax structure is such that different personal exemptions or different tax rates are imposed for different household types. In the Netherlands, for example, single persons without children have a lower personal exemption than that of one- or two-parent families. These differences are at least partly based on the notion that taxes should be lower if the needs of a certain family are higher. Hence, we will have to allow for additional differences in incomes according to household composition. As most tax systems allow deductions for family maintenance we expect after-tax income for large families to be higher than for small families. In some tax systems total household income is taken into account in the individual tax exemption allowed; this implies that people whose partner is also earning an income may have relatively low after-tax income.

The equation explaining individual income for the main breadwinner in our empirical work may be specified for all observations as

(3.2) $\quad \ln y_m = X_m \gamma_m + e_1$

where $\ln y_m$ is an individual observation on log income, $X_m$ a row vector containing for each observation dummy variables denoting urbanization, occupation, fluctuations in income and continuous variables referring to age and education, and $e_1$ is a normal, independently and identically distributed error term with $E(e_1) = 0$ and $Var(e_1) = \sigma_{11}$ for all observations. As it is likely that the determinants of income have a different effect for working persons than for non-working persons, we will estimate this relation for both groups separately. Moreover, the equation is estimated for male and female main breadwinners separately.

### 3.3 Participation of the partner in the labour force

We have seen that the income of the main breadwinner is expected to be determined by age, education, urbanization, income stability, and occupation. The same variables with different impacts may be expected to be determinants of the income function of the partner. The income equation of the partner hence is specified as

(3.3) $\quad \ln y_p = X_p \gamma_p + \varepsilon_2'$

where $X_p$ consists of the same variables as $X_m$, observed for the partner. There is, however, an additional problem in estimating the effect of all these variables on $y_p$: as we only observe incomes for partners who actually work, a truncated sample is observed. This may result in biased estimates of the coefficients. A method to solve this problem has been described by Heckman (1976): whether an income is observed, depends on the participation decision of the partner - if she (or he) decides to participate an income will be observed, if she decides not to participate no income will be observed. The bias mentioned above is a result of the fact that the sample of incomes observed is conditional upon this participation decision being positive. The solution proposed is to add to the income equation the expected value of this bias, which will depend on the expected participation decision. Hence, apart from the income function, the decision to participate will have to be explained.

We specify the unobservable $\pi^*$, the inclination to participate as

(3.4) $\quad \pi^* = \alpha_0 + \alpha_1 \ln\text{age}_p + \alpha_2 \ln^2\text{age}_p + \alpha_3 \text{educ}_p +$

$\alpha_4 \text{children} + \alpha_5 y_m + \varepsilon_1$

We observe the discrete proxy of $\pi^*$, part, that is equal to 1 iff $\pi^* > 0$
$\qquad\qquad\qquad\qquad\qquad\qquad\qquad\qquad\qquad\qquad\qquad$ 0 iff $\pi^* \leq 0$.

We expect the inclination to participate on the labour market to depend on age of the partner ($\text{age}_p$), number of children younger than 18 (children), education ($\text{educ}_p$), and income of the main breadwinner ($y_m$) [see, e.g., Heckman (1974), Hausman (1980)]. $\alpha_3$ is expected to be positive, and $\alpha_4$ and $\alpha_5$ are expected to be negative. If the error term $\varepsilon_1$ is assumed to follow a normal distribution, the parameters in (3.4) may be estimated by probit maximum likelihood, and the resulting coefficients may be used to define for each partner in the sample a calculated inclination to participate on the labour market, say the variable pârt,

(3.5) $\quad \text{pârt} = \hat{\alpha}_0 + \hat{\alpha}_1 \ln\text{age}_p + \hat{\alpha}_2 \ln^2\text{age}_p + \hat{\alpha}_3 \text{educ}_p + \hat{\alpha}_4 \text{children} + \hat{\alpha}_5 y_m$

This expected value of the inclination to participate, given the characteristics, is used to correct for sample selection bias, yielding:

(3.6)  $\ln y_p = X_p \gamma_p + \kappa \dfrac{\phi(\hat{p}art;0,1)}{1-\Phi(\hat{p}art;0,1)} + \varepsilon_2$

where $\phi(.)$ and $\Phi(.)$ are the density function and the distribution function of the normal distribution respectively. The ratio $\phi/(1-\Phi)$ is Mill's ratio [see e.g. Johnson and Kotz (1972)]. Equation (3.6) can now be estimated using OLS-regression [see for the procedure followed Heckman (1976) and Maddala (1983)].

Equations (3.3) and (3.6) will be used to compare (household) income with household needs. The specification used to estimate household needs will be discussed in the next chapter.

## NOTES TO CHAPTER 3

[1] Figures by the Dutch Social and Cultural Planning Bureau, on the other hand, indicated that inclusion of benefits of government expenditures increases income inequality, because of higher consumption of some public goods and services in higher income classes [Sociaal en Cultureel Planbureau (1977)]. Their result, however, depends also on the selection of public goods and services analysed, and the definition of "household" used.

[2] The income concept used in the empirical part of this study includes both earned and non-earned income in $y_m$ and $y_p$

[3] A survey of the "vintage" human capital theory has been given by Kiker (1968). Mincer (1970) reviews the literature of the first decade of the new human capital theory. A review of recent developments in human capital theory is found in Sahota (1978).

[4] A review of theories based on production factors is given by Pen (1971).

[5] Recent studies in the United States showed that the resulting general pattern of relatively high incomes in large cities is changing due to a "flight to the suburbs". For a variety of reasons, the high income population of the cities tends to choose a suburb as a place of residence [see, e.g., Frey (1980), Bradford and Kelejian (1973)]. As a result, the mean income in large cities decreases, and in suburbs it increases. This may reduce the income differentials according to degree of urbanization, and even invert the relationship. It is to be expected that the extent of this flight to the suburbs varies considerably over countries. It is beyond the scope of the present study to explain these flows into and out of the cities; we will only try to assess the resulting income differences.

[6] Hartog and Veenbergen (1978), however, found a significant positive effect of social security increases on income inequality for Dutch data from 1914-1972; they also found slightly increasing income inequality after the early 1960s, in contrast to a downward trend in the period before.

[7] This was the common assumption in the "ability" school of personal income distribution; see, e.g., Staehle (1943). For our purpose the assumption of normality is merely a convenient way of enabling scaling of the variable; the assumption is not tested in our research.

APPENDIX TO CHAPTER 3

According to the hypotheses derived we expect individual incomes to be determined to a large extent by age, education, degree of urbanization, fluctuations in income, and occupation. In this appendix the specification of this relationship will be discussed for each of these variables.
The individual income concept used in our research is after-tax monetary income, including asset income, holiday allowances, bonuses, and other extra income.

(a) <u>Age</u>

A common specification of the relationship between income and age, resulting from, among others, human capital theory [see e.g. Mincer (1974)] is

$$\ln y_m = \sum_{k=1}^{K} x_k \gamma_k + \gamma_{K+1} \text{AGE} + \gamma_{K+2} \text{AGE}^2 + u$$

where $y_m$ is individual income, AGE is age (in years) and $x_k$, $k = 1,\ldots,K$ denote all other explanatory variables. The coefficients $\gamma_{K+1}$ and $\gamma_{K+2}$ are expected to be positive and negative, respectively. However, this specification implies that the log income profile over age is symmetric around its maximum, which may not always be the case. An alternative specification, which implies that the decline after the maximum is less strong than the increase before reaching the maximum, is the specification

$$\ln y_m = \sum_{k=1}^{K} x_k \gamma_k + \gamma_{K+1} \ln \text{AGE} + \gamma_{K+2} \ln^2 \text{AGE}^2 + u$$

Again, $\gamma_{K+1}$ is expected to be positive and $\gamma_{K+2}$ negative.
In this specification the age at which a maximum income is reached equals $\exp(-\gamma_{K+1}/2\gamma_{K+2})$. The choice for one or the other of the alternative specifications will depend on their empirical performance. Both specifications may be extended to allow for varying age-income profiles for different levels of education, by adding cross-products of the variable denoting education and the terms representing age. We will now turn to the other variables, denoted by $x_k$, $k = 1,\ldots,K$.

(b) <u>Education</u>

Education has been measured as a qualitative variable indicating the highest level of schooling attained.
With the specification of education two problems have to be solved. Firstly, the variable cannot always be classified unambigously on one ordinal scale. Technical and professional education are hard to classify in terms of general education levels. Secondly, the ordinal procedures that may be used with dummy variables are not very satisfactory. We might include all educational levels as dummy variables in the equation. In some countries this would increase the number of explanatory variables considerably (in the Netherlands, for instance, eight different educational levels are distinguished). If, however, those educational levels are grouped to avoid this, we lose information. These difficulties are avoided if the educational dummies are transformed into a continuous variable. In order to attempt this, the ordering problem has to be solved first.
Instead of imposing a more or less arbitrary ordering on the variables, two kinds of educational careers are distinguished, a technical and a general education. Both are different dimensions of the education concept; within each dimension a higher or a lower level may be attained. This implies that for both ordinal categories a transformation into an interval-scaled variable is needed.
The transformation chosen is a "normalization" procedure. Assuming that the phenomenon underlying educational success (that may be called general ability and technical ability for the two categories respectively) follows a normal distribution over the population,[7] the levels of education may be transformed to a score on this variable. If, for instance, L different levels of general education are distinguished, classified in increasing order, the new continuous variable EDUC is found to be

$$EDUC(k) = \Phi_{0,1}^{-1} [\sum_{i=1}^{k-1} (p_i) + \tfrac{1}{2} p_k] \text{ for } k = 1,\ldots,L$$

where $p_k$ is the relative frequency in the population that has attained educational level k [see for the procedure followed e.g. Bross (1958)], and $\Phi(.)$ is the standard normal distribution function. In applying this transformation some assumptions are made, notably about the normality of the distribution of education. When presenting simple tables or figures, we will in general maintain the original classification of education.

(c) Urbanization

Urbanization has been measured in the form of dummy variables denoting rural areas (less than 20,000 inhabitants), small towns (between 20,000 and 100,000 inhabitants) and big cities (more than 100,000 inhabitants).

(d) Fluctuations in income

The fluctuations in income are also measured as a dummy variable, indicating small fluctuations, large fluctuations or no fluctuations at all, as defined by the respondents themselves.

(e) Occupation

The classification of occupation differs across countries. In the design of the questionnaires it has been tried to include at least the following categories: farmers, other self-employed, manual workers, employees, and civil servants. However, in some countries one category had to be omitted, as will be described in chapter 6.
These categories are included not only for people who are presently working, but also for people who are retired, ill or unemployed; in that case it refers to their former occupation. The reason for this is that social security benefits and pensions, and hence income received while not working, may depend heavily on the previous occupation. In order to account for people who do not (yet) have any job experience a category "has never worked" is included.

Chapter 4
DETERMINANTS OF WELFARE PARAMETERS

We have defined poverty as a situation where the actual household income is lower than the income needed by the household for a certain welfare evaluation. Hence, two aspects are important in the identification of the poor: the household income and the income needed for a certain welfare level. The former has been discussed in chapter 3; in this chapter we will analyse the determinants of the income level $y_\delta$ needed for a specific welfare level $\delta$. As we have seen in chapter 2, this income depends on the parameters of the individual welfare function of income, $\mu$ and $\sigma$, and the welfare level $\delta$:

$$\ln y_\delta = \mu + \sigma u_\delta$$

where $u_\delta$ is defined as $\Phi(\delta;0,1) = u_\delta$.
If the minimum welfare level chosen to be the poverty threshold equals $\delta = 0.5$, we have $u_\delta = 0$, and we only have to consider the determinants of $\mu$. However, if the minimum welfare level does not equal 0.5, the determinants of $\sigma$ will also be of interest.

The structure of this chapter is as follows. First a general description of the theory explaining the determinants of the individual welfare function of income is given in section 4.1. This theory will result in two sets of hypotheses on the effects of socio-economic variables on the two parameters of the welfare function of income; the hypotheses on $\mu$ are presented in section 4.2, and the hypotheses on $\sigma$ in section 4.3. In an appendix to this chapter, the implications of the theoretical considerations for elasticity of the poverty line are derived.

## 4.1 Determinants of the individual welfare function of income

As described in chapter 2, two different kinds of variables are expected to be of influence on $\mu$, variables influencing the command over resources and reference variables. The former are variables that reflect cost differences between households. An example is family size: the larger the number of household members, the more money is needed for a welfare evaluation of 0.5. Another example is income in kind: households enjoying a certain amount of income in kind, e.g. farmers, will need less money income, ceteris paribus, for a welfare evaluation of 0.5 than other households. All variables that reflect choices made in households between cash and non-cash income may have an effect on μ, and hence on $y_\delta$. Students will allow for their investment in human wealth, and may have a lower μ as a result; risk averse people with large fluctuations in income will have a risk premium incorporated in their μ; one-earner households who have decided to spend relatively much time on household production will have a lower μ than two-earner households. By calculating the monetary income needed by these differentiated households, we may assess for each household whether they are in poverty by comparing their actual money income with their appropriate $y_\delta$. The effects hypothesized here are ceteris paribus, however; it will appear that some of the variables distinguished here may also have a reference effect on μ which is opposite. These reference effects result from the theory that μ and σ may be partly explained by the fact that the welfare function of income reflects the income distribution of perceived incomes, in which the social reference group plays a vital role [see Kapteyn (1977), Van Praag et al. (1979), Van Praag (1980, 1981)]. The hypothesis is that someone tends to evaluate an income level $\tilde{y}$ by x, 0 < x < 1, if he thinks that 100x % of the population has an income lower than or equal to $\tilde{y}$. This perceived income distribution is not necessarily equal to the actual income distribution. One might say that the income distribution is partly absorbed and distorted by a social filter process, before it is perceived by an individual and is incorporated in his attitudes and behaviour. This social filter process, that determines someone's perception of the income distribution is caused by the fact that people do not know the actual income distribution. Their (vague) estimate of this distribution will be based on the incomes of persons they know. This means that their perception of the present income distribution will be biased by their own income (preference effect), and the incomes of people in their "social reference group" (reference effect). This social reference group may be defined as the group to which an individual relates his attitudes [see e.g. Cartwright and Zander (1968)].

The effect of the actual income distribution and its filtered image, the income distribution in the social reference group, may be summarized in the working hypothesis that the mean $\mu_n$ of the perceived present income distribution is a function of, among others, actual household log income and the mean of log incomes of households in the social reference group of individual n.

A second reason why someone's perception of the present income distribution may differ from the actual distribution is that it also depends on incomes he has perceived in the past, i.e. both his own income in the past and the incomes of the social reference group in the past. Moreover, expected future income may also influence the perception of the present income distribution [see Van Praag and Van Weeren (1983)]. These hypotheses culminate in the following equation:

$$(4.1) \quad \mu_n = \sum_{t=-\infty}^{+\infty} a_n(t) \sum_{k=1}^{N} w_{nk}(t) \ln y_k(t)$$

where $w_{nk}(t)$ is the weight that person n attaches to the log income of individual k at time t, and $a_n(t)$ is the weight that the income distribution at time t gets from individual n at the present, where $\sum_{k=1}^{N} w_{nk} = 1$ and $\sum_{t=-\infty}^{+\infty} a_n(t) = 1$. Future income $y(t)$, $t = 1, \ldots, \infty$, should be interpreted as expected future incomes. We may rewrite (4.1) as

$$(4.2) \quad \mu_n = \sum_{t=-\infty}^{-1} a_n(t) [\sum_{\substack{k=1 \\ k \neq n}}^{N} w_{nk}(t) \ln y_k(t) + w_{nn}(t) \ln y_n(t)]$$

$$+ \quad a_n(0) [\sum_{\substack{k=1 \\ k \neq n}}^{N} w_{nk}(0) \ln y_k(0) + w_{nn}(0) \ln y_n(0)]$$

$$+ \sum_{t=1}^{+\infty} a_n(t) [\sum_{\substack{k=1 \\ k \neq n}}^{N} w_{nk}(t) \ln y_k(t) + w_{nn}(t) \ln y_n(t)]$$

from which equation we see that the welfare parameter μ depends on incomes in past, present and future; both someone's actual income and the weighted income in someone's social reference group in these different periods are of importance.

Analogously, the welfare parameter $\sigma_n^2$ is hypothesized to be a weighted average over time of all perceived variances of log incomes. These perceived variances are the weighted variances of log incomes about the perceived mean income $\mu_n$. We hypothesize:

$$(4.3) \quad \sigma_n^2 = \sum_{t=-\infty}^{+\infty} a_n(t) \sum_{k=1}^{N} w_{nk}(t)[\ln y_k(t)-\mu_n]^2$$

where $\mu_n$ represents the perceived mean income.
The different factors that influence $\sigma_n^2$ are seen from

$$(4.4) \quad \sigma_n^2 = \sum_{t=-\infty}^{-1} a_n(t)\{\sum_{\substack{k=1 \\ k \neq n}}^{N} w_{nk}(t)[\ln y_k(t)-\mu_n]^2 + w_{nn}(t)[\ln y_n(t)-\mu_n]^2\}$$

$$+ \quad a_n(0)\{\sum_{\substack{k=1 \\ k \neq n}}^{N} w_{nk}(0)[\ln y_k(0)-\mu_n]^2 + w_{nn}(0)[\ln y_n(0)-\mu_n]^2\}$$

$$+ \sum_{t=1}^{\infty} a_n(t)\{\sum_{\substack{k=1 \\ k \neq n}}^{N} w_{nk}(t)[\ln y_k(t)-\mu_n]^2 + w_{nn}(t)[\ln y_n(t)-\mu_n]^2\}$$

Hence the variance of the perceived distribution depends on variances of incomes in past, present and future, both of one's own income and of incomes in one's social reference group.

The basic idea, described in these two formulae has been elaborated upon and tested in a number of articles, e.g. Kapteyn (1977), Kapteyn et al. (1978), Van Praag et al. (1979), Kapteyn and Wansbeek (1982), Van Praag (1981, 1982), Van Praag and Van Weeren (1983).
Before formulae (4.1) and (4.2) can be written in a tractable form, suitable for estimation purposes, a number of difficulties have to be solved.
A first problem concerning the estimation of (4.1) and (4.3) is that longitudinal or panel data would be required. In the Netherlands, series of panel data suitable for this use have been collected for the period 1980-1984. Partial tests of these ideas on this dataset have been performed by Van de Stadt, Kapteyn and Van de Geer (1982), Van Praag and Spit (1982), and Van Praag and Van Weeren (1983). For other years and other countries, however, only cross-sectional data are observed. If no panel data are

available, we can only use current income data. This may be represented by putting $a_n(t) = 0$ for all $t \neq 0$. Equations (4.1) and (4.2) then reduce to

$$(4.5) \qquad \mu_n = a_n(0)[\sum_{n \neq k} w_{nk}(0) \ln y_k(0) + w_{nn} \ln y_n(0)]$$

By omitting the other four terms of (4.2), a specification error is introduced. We will try to reduce the effect of this specification error by including, if possible, proxy variables reflecting past own income. The empirical studies using panel data show that a relatively high income in the past has an increasing effect on $\mu$. Similarly, (4.4) reduces to

$$(4.6) \qquad \sigma_n^2 = a_n(0)\{\sum_{n \neq k} w_{nk}(0)[\ln y_k(0)-\mu_n]^2 + w_{nn}[\ln y_n(0)-\mu_n]^2\}$$

The terms omitted from this equation reflect the variance of log incomes in one's social reference group in the past and in the future, and one's own variance of log income in the past and future. They represent two different sources of variance; the first is due to the dispersion of incomes over different persons, and the second is due to instability of individual or household income over time. The variation of observed incomes in one's social reference group may be caused both by permanent and transient inequality of incomes in the reference group.[1] A second problem to be solved is that the social reference group is unobservable. If we call the (also unobservable) mean log income in the social reference group of individual $n$ $m_n$, and the log variance $s_n^2$, equations (4.5) and (4.6) become

$$(4.7) \qquad \mu_n = a_n(0)\{\sum_{\substack{k=1 \\ k \neq n}}^{N} w_{nk} m_n + w_{nn} \ln y_n(0)\}$$

$$(4.8) \qquad \sigma_n^2 = a_n(0)\{s_n^2 \sum_{\substack{k=1 \\ k \neq n}}^{N} w_{nk} + \sum_{\substack{k=1 \\ k \neq n}}^{N} w_{nk}[m_n-\mu_n]^2 + w_{nn}[\ln y_n(0)-\mu_n]^2\}$$

A third problem is that the theory described above in equations (4.1) to (4.8) applies to individuals; before applying it to household incomes, all incomes have to be transformed using some equivalent adult scale. This problem has been considered in Van Praag and Kapteyn (1973), Kapteyn and Van Praag (1976) and Van de Stadt (1979), among others. It appeared that (4.7) and (4.8) still hold, if all income terms are replaced by income per equivalent adult, denoted by $\tilde{y}_n(t) = y_n(t)/f_n(t)$, where $f_n(t)$ stands for the number of equivalent adults in family n at time t. The specification of $f_n(t)$ may involve both family size and family composition; in the remainder we will use the following, simple specification:

(4.9)   $\ln f_n(t) = \gamma_0 + \gamma_1 \ln fs_n(t)$

where $fs_n(t)$ is the number of family members in family n at time t. The coefficients $\gamma_0$ and $\gamma_1$ are not determined <u>a priori</u>, but will be estimated along with other parameters.

If we assume   $\beta_0 = \gamma_0 a_n(0)$
$\beta_1 = \gamma_1 a_n(0) w_{nn}$
$\beta_2 = a_n(0) w_{nn}$
$\beta_3 = a_n(0) \sum_{\substack{k=1 \\ k \neq n}}^{N} w_{nk}$

and omit all indices referring to time periods, we have

(4.10)   $\mu_n = \beta_0 + \beta_1 \ln fs_n + \beta_2 \ln y_n + \beta_3 m_n$

which is the expression used in the derivation of the poverty line in chapter 2. Parameter $\beta_1$ is called the family size elasticity, reflecting cost differences between households of different size, $\beta_2$ is the preference drift and $\beta_3$ is the reference drift. All three parameters are hypothesized to have a positive effect on $\mu$. Coefficient $a_n(0)$ cannot be identified and is, for convenience, considered to be equal to 1. As $a_n(0)$ reflects the relative importance of the present, compared to past and future, this assumption is not restrictive in our static model.
Using the same notation, the expression for $\sigma_n^2$ now becomes

(4.11)   $\sigma_n^2 = \beta_3 s_n^2 + \beta_3 (m_n - \mu_n)^2 + \beta_2 (\ln y_n - \mu_n)^2$

It is seen that (4.10) and (4.11) involve the same parameters $\beta_0$, $\beta_1$, $\beta_2$ and $\beta_3$. When (4.10) is substituted in (4.11) it appears that (4.11) is highly non-linear in the unknown coefficients. In order to estimate these parameters we still need additional hypotheses on $m_n$ and $s_n$. In earlier research the social reference group has been operationalized in various ways. In most of these operationalizations, a proxy of the social reference group is formed by the introduction of social types; i.e. people who are the same with respect to a vector of socio-economic characteristics like education, job type, degree of urbanization, employment, age and region. It is then supposed that people who belong to the same social type assign the same reference weights to people of other social types. A social reference group then consists of all other people in society, weighted with the reference weight of the social type to which they belong. For the specification of the welfare parameters this implies that the weights $w_{nk}$ depend on the social types to which n and k belong. In some applications of the theory these reference weights $w_{nk}$ are estimated [see Kapteyn (1977), Van Praag et al. (1979)]. However, as their estimation is rather complicated and problematic, in later research those complications are circumvented, by assuming that someone's social reference group consists of other people of the same social type only. Within this reference group everybody gets an equal weight, resulting in the same value for $w_{nk}$ for everybody. Following this assumption one can calculate the log income in someone's social reference group by calculation of the mean log income of all people with the same social characteristics, like age, occupation, and education.

The approach to be followed in this research is different. We will operationalize the social reference group in two different ways. The first operationalization is the result of our intention to analyse for each country the determinants that make people poverty prone. This analysis requires the estimation of the effect of various characteristics both on income and on the poverty line, which is defined in terms of parameters of the μ and σ equations. If we want to estimate the effect of, for instance, education on the welfare parameters, two effects may be found; people with higher education may have a higher level of μ because they have to get their returns to previous investment in human capital, and people with higher education may have a social reference group consisting of relatively many other people with higher education; as they will all have a relatively high income, the reference effect will also increase μ. Hence by including education as an explanatory variable in μ, we will estimate the net total effect of education on welfare, without making additional assumptions on the composition of the social reference group. The underlying notions of reference effect and cost effect may help us, however, in deriving hypotheses on the sign of the effect of various characteristics on μ. Hence we estimate for each country the total effect on μ of all characteristics that are hypothesized to have either a cost effect, or a reference effect, or both. The specification of those characteristics is given in the next section.

A second operationalization of the social reference group is prompted by the fact that we wish to establish to what extent poverty lines are relative, i.e. change when the average standard of living changes. As we have data on different countries, we may estimate the degree of relativity of the poverty line by assuming that everyone's social reference group consists of all other people in the same country. Although this assumption obviously abstracts from the more complex social reality of life, it may still be valid in the context of international comparison, where the general standard of living, as reflected by median income in society, will have an effect on incomes in all social reference groups in that country. Our second proxy for the social reference group is hence to assume $m_n = \mu_y$ and $s_n^2 = \sigma_y^2$ for everybody within one country, yielding:

(4.12) $\quad \mu_n = \beta_0 + \beta_1 \ln fs_n + \beta_2 \ln y_n + \beta_3 \mu_y$

(4.13) $\quad \sigma_n^2 = \beta_3 \sigma_y^2 + \beta_3 (\mu_y - \mu_n)^2 + \beta_2 (\ln y_n - \mu_n)^2$

which may be estimated if cross-national data are available.

Although the resulting equation for $\mu_n$ is similar to the one used in chapter 2 in the derivation of the poverty line, the equation for $\sigma_n^2$ is rather more complicated. In chapter 2 it was simply assumed that $\sigma_n = f(\sigma_y)$, which implies that the poverty line is the implicit solution of

(4.14) $\quad \ln y_\delta^* = \beta_0 + \beta_1 \ln fs + \beta_2 \ln y_\delta^* + \beta_3 \mu_y + u_\delta f(\sigma_y)$

which can easily be solved for $\ln y_\delta^*$.

Using the more complicated specification for $\sigma_n^2$, however, we have

(4.15) $\quad \ln y_\delta^* = \beta_0 + \beta_1 \ln fs + \beta_2 \ln y_\delta^* + \beta_3 \mu_y +$

$$u_\delta \sqrt{\beta_3 \sigma_y^2 + \beta_3 [\mu_y - \mu_n (\ln y_\delta^*)]^2 + \beta_2 [\ln y_\delta^* - \mu(\ln y_\delta^*)]^2}$$

which is not so easily solved for $\ln y_\delta^*$.
In the appendix to this chapter the elasticity of this more complicated poverty line definition with respect to median income is derived. The calculations result in the following conclusions:

- The elasticity of the poverty line with respect to median income may be written as

$$\frac{d \ln y_\delta^*}{d \mu_y} = \frac{\beta_3}{1-\beta_2} \cdot k$$

k is a correction factor, which equals 1 if $u_\delta = 0$ or $\beta_2 + \beta_3 = 1$.

- The expression for the poverty line derived from (4.15) does not equal the expression implicit in (4.14) unless:[2]
    (a) $u_\delta = 0$, or
    (b) $\beta_2 = 0$, $\beta_3 = 1$
    The last situation is an extreme empirical finding. The first, however, is the result of a particular choice of the poverty threshold. A third situation to be distinguished is
    (c) $\beta_2 = 1$, $\beta_3 = 0$, in which case the poverty line appears to be undefined.

These results lead us to the conclusion that the operationalization of the social reference group by the assumptions $m_n = \mu_y$ and $s_n^2 = \sigma_y^2$ will provide us with an estimate of the elasticity of the poverty line with respect to median income in society at the 0.5 welfare level. The calculation of the effect of various socio-economic characteristics on the poverty line will be made by using the first approach to the social reference group, i.e. by estimating for each country separately all possible effects of socio-eco-

nomic characteristics on $\mu$ and $\sigma^2$.
We will now derive hypotheses for these effects.

## 4.2 Hypotheses on the effects of socio-economic variables on $\mu$

In this section, we will operationalize the theory outlined above by deriving hypotheses on the effects of various socio-economic characteristics on $\mu$. The characteristics may be categorized as follows:
(1) The characteristics representing certain cost effects; the variable "urbanization" may, for instance, reflect high cost of living in a large city.
(2) The characteristics of an individual representing someone's earnings capacity, or permanent income; they may to some extent be considered as a proxy for omitted variables concerning previous and future income, and various kinds of non-cash income.
(3) The characteristics representing reference effects.

The following hypotheses will be based on these possible effects; as one characteristic may reflect more than one effect we will not, however, be able to distinguish between the three effects; only the net result will be observed.

### (a) Household income

As mentioned above, household income is one of the most important variables determining $\mu$; the higher household income, the higher $\mu$. The coefficient of this variable is the preference drift.

### (b) Degree of urbanization

It is hypothesized that living in a large city will imply higher cost of living for households than living in a small town. The reference effect depends on the income differential in general between large cities and small towns; if incomes are overall higher in larger cities, we expect that people living in these cities themselves will mainly have these high incomes in their social reference group. In this case, both cost effect and reference effect will have the same positive effect on $\mu$. If, however, incomes in general are smaller in large cities, the reference effect and cost effect have opposite signs. The net effect of degree of urbanization on μ is uncertain in that case.

(c) Fluctuations in income

According to Manning and Vatter (1964) fluctuations in income may be important for the determination of a poverty line. People with large fluctuations in income will have to build up savings during prosperous times in order to provide for their needs when the income flow becomes smaller. According to the theory of risk aversion this will in general result in higher than average needs.[3]

We do not expect a positive reference group effect, as it is not likely that fluctuations in income are per se an important determinant for someone's social reference group, except when these fluctuations are the result of occupational differences, e.g. for self-employed. However, in that case the reference group effect will appear in the occupational variables.

(d) Changes in financial situations

As mentioned above, it is assumed that incomes in the past will influence the present value of μ. If the financial situation has recently improved, people will remember their previous lower income, and as a result will have a lower welfare parameter μ. If their situation is recently worsened, people will still have their previous higher income in mind and therefore have a higher welfare parameter μ. As an indicator for these changes, dummy variables are included that reflect whether, according to the respondent, the financial situation has improved, worsened, or remained unchanged during the last two years.[4]

(e) Number of breadwinners

The number of breadwinners in a household is expected to have both a cost and a reference effect on μ.

If both the main breadwinner and partner are working, there may be additional household cost, e.g., for child care or time-saving household equipment. Moreover, the larger household production in one-earner households provides income in kind that is absent in two-earner households. A third cost factor in two-earner households may be the larger burden of work related cost. As the household's social reference group is mainly determined by the social class of husband and spouse, irrespective of the question whether it is a one- or a two-earner household, we expect that one-earner households have a somewhat lower and two-earner households have a somewhat higher income than is normal in their social reference group. As a result, the µ of a household where two members are earning an income will due to the reference effect be lower than the µ of a one-breadwinner household. It is not possible to predict which of the two effects, the cost or the reference effect, will be dominant [see Van Praag and Kapteyn (1973), and Homan, Van Praag and Hagenaars (1984)].

(f) <u>Family size</u>

Family size may have both a positive and a negative effect on the cost of a household. The increased cost are a result of increased household consumption. On the other hand, the presence of children may increase household welfare to the extent that it yields parental joy; in this context children may be seen as a consumption good. Another positive effect is that children may increase household production as well, e.g. older children working on their parents' farm. We assume that in most families the consumption aspect dominates the production aspect, as in most countries family allowances are given in addition to the family income in order to compensate at least partly for the presumed net increase in cost. If no other policy aim is to be served by these compensations, one would wish such an allowance to be "welfare neutral"; i.e., if by the birth of a child a family experiences a reduction of family welfare, due to increased cost of living, the family allowance should be such that the family can continue to live at the same welfare level as before the child's birth.
The existing facilities are not always welfare neutral; in the Netherlands for instance, there is reason to assume that large families used to be overcompensated [see e.g. Kapteyn and Van Praag (1976)]. This is partly due to the fact that children <u>per se</u> also yield welfare to their parents, and that household tastes and preferences may change when a child is born. From the relationship between µ and family size we can derive welfare neutral family allowances. These will be compared to the actual family

allowance systems prevailing in the different countries. We will distinguish between the number of adults and the number of children (younger than 18) in our estimates.

(g) Employment

With respect to employment we expect $\mu$ to be lower for families where the head of the household is not working than for families where the head of the household is working. Non-working people usually have a smaller income than their socially equivalent working counterparts. It follows that both their own income and the income of their social reference group are lower than for working households.
A cost effect will arise as well; people who are not working may provide their household with an income in kind, for instance in the form of do-it-yourself activities, or by performing household activities which they otherwise would have to pay for. Finally, the absence of work related cost may result in a lower $\mu$ for not working households.

(h) Occupation

It is expected that occupation will be an important determinant of someone's reference group. Due to this reference group effect it is supposed that people with an occupation with an on average high income will have a higher $\mu$ than people with an occupation with low average income. For the occupational category "farmers" it is expected that cost effects will also be important due to the possible presence of income in kind. This circumstance probably renders the $\mu$ of a farmer's family to be lower than the $\mu$ of other occupations, other things being equal. For self-employed we expect a relatively high $\mu$, in order to compensate for the uncertainty in income that goes with the occupation.

(i) Sex

It is not supposed a priori that reference effects will arise due to the sex of the main breadwinner, as there is no reason to assume that sex is an important determinant of one's social reference group with respect to incomes. Whether cost of female breadwinners will be significantly lower than cost of male breadwinners will be assessed empirically.

(j) Education

Education is, like occupation, probably one of the main variables determining a social reference group. As higher education will result in higher incomes, it is supposed that the reference effect of higher education on μ is positive.
There is also a cost effect as the investment in education is made in view of expected higher incomes after the end of the study. These expected returns to education will also increase μ.
Both effects will cause μ to be higher for people with higher education.

(k) Age

The age of the main breadwinner gives another opportunity for including a proxy for the income history of a person. As people who are still in the increasing part of their age-income profile have experienced previous incomes that are mainly lower than their present income, we expect their μ to be lower, ceteris paribus, than that of people who have already passed the age at which their maximum income was earned. We may also find a positive effect of age on μ if age is seen as experience, produced by on-the-job training, for which one expects higher incomes in later years.

Summarizing, the relationship describing μ may be written for all respondents as

$$\mu = X\beta + e_2$$

where X is a row vector containing for each household log household income, urbanization, fluctuations in income, changes in financial situations, number of breadwinners, family size, employment, occupation, sex, education, and age. Error term $e_2$ is assumed to be normally identically and independently distributed with $E(e_2) = 0$ and $Var(e_2) = \sigma_{22}$.

4.3 Hypotheses on the effects of socio-economic variables on $\sigma$

Analogously to the previous section, we may operationalize the general theory described above in the following hypotheses on $\sigma$ [see Kapteyn (1977), pp.119-125]:

(a) Fluctuations in income

The more fluctuations in household income someone experiences, the higher the dispersion of transitory income, and hence the higher $\sigma$.

(b) Changes in financial situation

If someone's financial situation has improved or worsened the dispersion of incomes he has experienced is higher than for someone whose income has not changed; hence we expect a higher $\sigma$.

(c) Education

People with higher education will usually experience a larger increase in income than people with lower education, according to the human capital theory; hence they will have a higher $\sigma$.

(d) Occupation

People who are self-employed will probably have less stable incomes, and hence a higher dispersion of transitory income than people who are employed or not working; this will result in a higher value of $\sigma$.

(e) Number of breadwinners

If more than one person in a household is working, probably a larger variation in household income is experienced, implying a higher $\sigma$. This is due to the fact that partners often work intermittently, with interruptions for child-bearing and -raising. However, as the household with one earner in the survey period may also have been a two-earner household some time earlier, the relationship is not expected to be very strong.

The relationship between σ and these characteristics will be described as

$$\ln \sigma = X\alpha + e_3$$

where row vector X contains the same variables included in the μ equation, α is a vector of coefficients which are put equal to zero for all variables not listed in our hypotheses, and $e_3$ is again a normally identically and independently distributed error term with $E(e_3) = 0$ and $Var(e_3) = \sigma_{33}$. Having described the parameters of the welfare function, we may combine them with the information on income to derive poverty determinants. This is the subject of the next chapter.

## NOTES TO CHAPTER 4

[1] In the terms pertaining to the social reference group both sources of variance may be present.
These different sources of variance may be illustrated by assuming that log income $\ln y_k(t)$ of individual k consists of a structural part $\ln \eta_k$, which is constant over time, and a transitory part $\varepsilon_k(t)$ which is a random variable with $E[\varepsilon_k(t)] = 0$ and $\text{Var}[\varepsilon_k(t)] = \sigma^2_{\varepsilon_k}$.

The observed variance of incomes $y_k(t)$ over time is now written as

$$E\{\ln y_k(t) - E[\ln y_k(t)]\}^2 = E[\ln \eta_k + \varepsilon_k(t) - \ln \eta_k]^2 = \sigma^2_{\varepsilon_k}$$

Hence a large value of $\sigma^2_{\varepsilon_k}$, reflecting a large instability of income, will result in a large variation of incomes over time of individual k. On the other hand, a large variance of incomes in one's social reference group is observed, at any point in time t, if

$$E\{\ln y_k(t) - E[\ln y_k(t)]^2\}^2 =$$

$$E\{\ln \eta_k(t) + \varepsilon_k(t) - \overline{\ln \eta_k(t)}\}^2 = \sigma^2_\eta + \bar{\sigma}^2_\varepsilon$$

is large.
This may be due to a large value of $\sigma^2_\eta$, reflecting a large inequality of structural incomes in one's social reference group, or to a large value of the average $\bar{\sigma}^2_\varepsilon$, which is the average income instability.

[2] Of course, the extent to which the solution at other welfare levels differs from the simpler solution in chapter 2 depends on the quality of the explanation of $\sigma^2_n$: if no systematic variation in $\sigma^2_n$ is found, apart from the effect of income inequality, we may maintain the simple assumption $\sigma_n = f(\sigma_y)$. This is an empirical question, that will be dealt with in chapter 11.

[3] Another aspect of income stability is that for people with stable incomes their present income will be highly correlated with their incomes in former periods. The specification error introduced by the omission of these terms will result in higher values of $\beta_2$ for people with stable incomes. However, this differentiation is not made in our empirical work.

[4] Van Praag and Van Weeren (1983) described and estimated the time-discounting mechanism by which previous income influences µ; they conclude that the effect of the past is large for old people and young people, and moderate for the middle-aged.

## APPENDIX TO CHAPTER 4

In this appendix we will solve for the elasticity of $\ln y_\delta^*$ with respect to $\mu_y$ in the following system:

(A.1)  $\ln y_n = \ln y_{\delta,n} = \ln y_\delta^*$

(A.2)  $\mu_n = \beta_0 + \beta_2 \ln y_n + \beta_3 \mu_y$

(A.3)  $\sigma_n^2 = \beta_3 \sigma_y^2 + \beta_3(\mu_y - \mu_n)^2 + \beta_2(\ln y_n - \mu_n)^2$

(A.4)  $\ln y_{\delta,n} = \mu_n + \sigma_n u_\delta$

where $u_\delta = \Phi^{-1}(\delta; 0, 1)$.

For the general solution of $\ln y_\delta^*$ the elasticity may be solved by taking the total differential of the system (A.1) - (A.4), after having substituted (A.1):

(A.5)  $\mu_n = \beta_0 + \beta_2 \ln y_\delta^* + \beta_3 \mu_y$

(A.6)  $\sigma_n^2 = \beta_3 \sigma_y^2 + \beta_3(\mu_y - \mu_n)^2 + \beta_2(\ln y_\delta^* - \mu_n)^2$

(A.7)  $\ln y_\delta^* = \mu_n + \sigma_n u_\delta$

Taking the total differential of all equations, we have (assuming $\sigma_y^2$ to be constant)

(A.8)  $d\mu_n = \beta_2 d\ln y_\delta^* + \beta_3 d\mu_y$

(A.9)  $2\sigma_n d\sigma_n = 2\beta_3(\mu_y - \mu_n)(d\mu_y - d\mu_n) + 2\beta_2(\ln y_\delta^* - \mu_n)(d\ln y_\delta^* - d\mu_n)$

(A.10)  $d\ln y_\delta^* = d\mu_n + u_\delta d\sigma_n$

Substituting (A.8) and (A.9) into (A.10) yields

(A.11) $\quad d\ln y_\delta^* = \beta_2 d \ln y_\delta^* + \beta_3 d\mu_y + u_\delta[\beta_3(\mu_y - \mu_n)(d\mu_y - d\mu_n) +$

$\beta_2(\ln y_\delta^* - \mu_n)(d\ln y_\delta^* - d\mu_n)]/\sigma_n$

Again substituting (A.8) and (A.5) gives

(A.12) $\quad d\ln y_\delta^* = \beta_2 d\ln y_\delta^* + \beta_3 d\mu_y + u_\delta[\beta_3\{(1-\beta_3)\mu_y - \beta_0 - \beta_2 \ln y_\delta^*\}$

$\times \{(1-\beta_3)d\mu_y - \beta_2 d \ln y_\delta^*\} +$

$\beta_2\{(1-\beta_2)\ln y_\delta^* - \beta_0 - \beta_3\mu_y\}\{(1-\beta_2)d\ln y_\delta^* - \beta_3 d\mu_y\}]/\sigma_n$

(A.13) $\quad (1-\beta_3)\mu_y - \beta_0 - \beta_2 \ln y_\delta^* = \mu_y - \ln y_\delta^* + \sigma_n u_\delta \quad$ (from A.5 and A.7)

(A.14) $\quad (1-\beta_2)\ln y_\delta^* - \beta_0 - \beta_3 \mu_y = \sigma_n u_\delta$

Substituting these expressions in (A.12) and regrouping yields

$d \ln y_\delta^*\{1 - \beta_2 + \beta_2\beta_3[(\mu_y - \ln y_\delta^*) + \sigma_n u_\delta]u_\delta - (1-\beta_2)\beta_2 u_\delta\}$

$= d \mu_y \{\beta_3 + (1-\beta_3)\beta_3[(\mu_y - \ln y_\delta^*) + \sigma_n u_\delta]y_\delta - \beta_3\beta_2 u_\delta\}$

Hence

$$\frac{d\ln y_\delta^*}{d\mu_y} = \frac{\beta_3[1 + (1-\beta_3)\{(\mu_y - \ln y_\delta^*)u_\delta + \sigma_n u_\delta^2\} - \beta_2 u_\delta]}{(1-\beta_2)[1 + \frac{\beta_2\beta_3}{1-\beta_2}\{(\mu_y - \ln y_\delta^*)u_\delta + \sigma_n u_\delta^2\} - \beta_2 u_\delta]} \quad (\beta_2 \neq 1)$$

From this expression we see that:

(a) $\quad \dfrac{d \ln y_\delta^*}{d\mu_y} = \dfrac{\beta_3}{1-\beta_2} \quad$ if $u_\delta = 0$, i.e. if $\delta = 0.5$

(b) $\quad\quad\quad\quad\quad = 0 \quad\quad\quad$ if $\beta_3 = 0$, irrespective the value of $\delta$

(c) $\quad\quad\quad\quad\quad = 1 \quad\quad\quad$ if $\beta_3 = 1-\beta_2$, irrespective the value of $\delta$.

## Chapter 5
## DETERMINANTS OF POVERTY

Poverty has been defined as a situation in which the welfare, derived from income, is less than a certain minimum welfare level. In the previous chapters we have derived hypotheses on the effect of socio-economic variables on income and the two parameters that determine the welfare function, i.e. $\mu$ and $\sigma$. Whether certain socio-economic characteristics make people poverty prone, depends on the net effect of these two relationships. If income is a decreasing function of a certain variable, and $\mu$ is an increasing function of this variable, and $\sigma$ is not affected by it, the variable may be said to be a determinant of low welfare, and hence of poverty, as $(\ln y - \mu)$ decreases in this variable. If both income and $\mu$ are increasing functions of a certain variable, the net effect of this variable on welfare will be positive if the effect on income is larger than the effect on $\mu$, and vice versa.

In this chapter we will describe how we can make use of the equations explaining welfare parameters and income for the derivation of poverty lines and poverty determinants. We have described in chapter 3 the equation explaining income of the main breadwinner as

(5.1)  $\ln y_m = X_m \gamma_m + e_1$

where $X_m$ contains age, education, occupation, urbanization and fluctuations in income of the main breadwinner.

In chapter 4 the equation explaining $\mu$ was described as

(5.2)  $\mu = X\beta + e_2$

where X may be partitioned as

$$X = [X_m, X_0, \ln y]$$

where $X_m$ is identical to the row vector of explanatory variables of $y_m$, $X_0$ are all other variables explaining $\mu$, apart from $\ln y$, log household income, that is included as a separate variable. If $\beta$ is partitioned accordingly as $\beta' = [\beta_m, \beta_0, \beta_y]$, we may rewrite (5.2) as

(5.3) $\quad \mu = X_m \beta_m + X_0 \beta_0 + \beta_y \ln y + e_2$

However, household income consists, as we have seen in chapter 3, of

$$\ln y = \ln (y_m + y_p + cb)$$

where $y_p$ and cb are income of the partner and child benefits respectively. In order to make the exposition of the method to be used as simple as possible, we will assume for the moment $y_p = 0$ and cb = 0, yielding ln y = ln $y_m$. This assumption will be relaxed later in this chapter.

The chapter is organized as follows. In section 5.1 the derivation of poverty lines is given. Section 5.2 describes some methods of estimating the probability of being poor. In section 5.3 the effects of income of the partner and child benefits are discussed. Section 5.4 hypothesizes the effects of various socio-economic characteristics on the probability of being poor.

## 5.1 Derivation of the poverty line

(i) Poverty line, differentiated according to socio-economic characteristics

In chapter 2, we derived for the income level evaluated by $\delta$

$$\ln y_\delta = \mu + \sigma u_\delta$$

Substituting the estimated equation (5.3) yields

(5.4) $\quad \ln y_\delta = X_m \beta_m + X_0 \beta_0 + \beta_y \ln y + \sigma u_\delta$

The poverty line is the point of intersection between (5.4) and the line ln y = ln $y_\delta$, which yields:

(5.5) $\quad \ln y_\delta^*(X_m) = \dfrac{X_m \beta_m + X_0 \beta_0 + \sigma u_\delta}{1 - \beta_y}$

One may substitute for $\sigma$ the equation

(5.6)  $\ln \sigma = X_m \hat{\alpha}$

or choose σ to be constant, dependent on the explanatory value of (5.6). We assume σ to be constant in the remainder.

Given the specification of $X_m$, and the choice of a household type without children or additional income of the partner, (5.5) defines a poverty line for this household type which is differentiated according to age, education, occupation, urbanization, and fluctuations in income. Given the number of differentiating variables, (5.5) approaches the concept of an individual poverty line; it may differentiate according to a large number of socio-economic characteristics. However, one may wonder whether all these differences in characteristics should be allowed for in the poverty line. The choice of characteristics to be differentiated is a political choice: one may, e.g., decide to differentiate according to age only. If that is the political consensus, we need a method to aggregate or average over all other characteristics. It should be noted, however, that even if it is politically agreed that these other characteristics "do not count", they still affect the individual perception of poverty.

(ii) Average poverty lines

If one, for instance, does not want to differentiate with respect to the characteristics $X_m$, a geometric mean poverty line can be found by substituting in (5.5) the average value of $X_m$, say $\bar{x}_m$, yielding

(5.6) $\quad \overline{\ln y_\delta^*} = \dfrac{\bar{x}_m \beta_m + X_0 \beta_0 + \sigma u_\delta}{1 - \hat{\beta}_y}$

(5.6) defines a poverty line for the household type $(\bar{x}_m, X_0)$ aggregated over all other variables. If one does not want to differentiate according to variables $X_0$ either, one averages over $X_0$ as well:

(5.7) $\quad \overline{\overline{\ln y_\delta^*}} = \dfrac{\bar{x}_m \beta_m + \bar{x}_0 \beta_0 + \sigma u_\delta}{1 - \hat{\beta}_y}$

where $\bar{x}_0$ denotes the row vector containing the average values of all other characteristics included in μ. (5.7) might be seen as a national average poverty line, without any differentiation according to household type, age, occupation, et cetera.

Which poverty line should be used depends on the political choice of differentiating characteristics that a society makes. As was seen in chapter 2, one will make an error of a certain type, when averaging over certain characteristics: people who feel poor according to the poverty line differentiated for their type may be defined as non-poor according to the average poverty line (type II error), and people who were not poor according to their type specific poverty line may be defined as poor (type I error). The first situation will arise for people with

$$\frac{x_m \beta_m + x_0 \beta_0 + \sigma u_\delta}{1-\beta_y} > \ln y > \frac{\bar{x}_m \beta_m + \bar{x}_0 \beta_0 + \sigma u_\delta}{1-\beta_y}$$

i.e. for those who score higher than average on some characteristics that increase the poverty line.

The second situation occurs when

$$\frac{x_m \beta_m + x_0 \beta_0 + \sigma u_\delta}{1-\beta_y} < \ln y < \frac{\bar{x}_m \beta_m + \bar{x}_0 \beta_0 + \sigma u_\delta}{1-\beta_y}$$

i.e. for those who score lower than average on some characteristics that increase the poverty line.

If, for example, family size increases the poverty line, but an average national poverty line is used which does not differentiate according to family size, single persons may be considered poor while they do not consider themselves poor, while large families may be considered non-poor while they consider themselves poor. Of course, the larger the effect of the differentiating factor, the larger the error made. If, in a democratic process, the majority of the population has characteristics $[\bar{x}_m, \bar{x}_0]$, they may decide to average over all characteristics. Minorities that have characteristics different from $[\bar{x}_m, \bar{x}_0]$ may as a result either benefit from a resulting type II error, or suffer from a type I error. Hence, it is useful, before making decisions on the differentiating variables, to analyse the extent and effect of the error that will be made in the aggregation process. The empirical results, described in chapter 10, will enable such analysis.

## 5.2 Poverty determinants

We have seen that the poverty line may depend on a number of characteristics, denoted by $X_m$ and $X_0$. We also know that household income depends on characteristics $X_m$. By comparing the effect of these characteristics on income with the effect on the poverty line, we may conclude whether the characteristic is liable to make people poverty prone.

Comparing household income with the poverty line, we have

$$\text{if } \ln y(X_m) - \ln y_\delta^*(X_m) < 0 \rightarrow \text{people with characteristics } (X_m) \text{ are poor}$$
$$> 0 \rightarrow \text{people with characteristics } (X_m) \text{ are non-poor.}$$

As $\ln y(X_m) - \ln y_\delta^*(X_m) = X_m \gamma_m + e_1 - \dfrac{X_m \beta_m + X_0 \beta_0 + \sigma u_\delta + e_2}{1-\beta_y}$, each increase in a socio-economic characteristic may be seen either to increase the gap between income and needs, or to decrease the gap. In the former case we say that this characteristic makes people poverty prone, in the latter case the characteristic is poverty reducing. For characteristics $X_0$ it is easily seen whether they increase the poverty line, and hence make people poverty prone.

For the other characteristics the comparison of $\gamma_m$ and $\dfrac{1}{1-\beta_y}\beta_m$ will give us the required information.

The effect of these characteristics on poverty may be expressed in a poverty probability PPOV which gives the probability that someone with characteristics $X_m$ is in poverty.

The derivation of such a poverty probability follows from (5.3) and (5.5):

(5.8)    $\text{PPOV} = P[\ln y_\delta^*(X_m) > \ln y(X_m)]$

$= P[\dfrac{1}{1-\beta_y}(X_m \beta_m + X_0 \beta_0 + \sigma u_\delta + e_2) > X_m \gamma_m + e_1]$

$= P[e_1 - \dfrac{1}{1-\beta_y} e_2 < \dfrac{1}{1-\beta_y}(X_m \beta_m + X_0 \beta_0 + \sigma u_\delta) - X_m \gamma_m]$

$= \Phi(z;0,1)$

where

(5.9) $$z = \frac{\frac{1}{1-\beta_y}(X_m\beta_m + X_0\beta_0 + \sigma u_\delta) - X_m\gamma_m}{\sqrt{\sigma_{11} + (\frac{1}{1-\beta_y})^2 \sigma_{22} - \frac{2}{1-\beta_y}\sigma_{12}}}$$

$\Phi$ is the standard normal distribution function, and $\sigma_{12}$ is the covariance between $e_1$ and $e_2$ (if this covariance is assumed or found to be zero, the last term under the square root vanishes).

Hence for each socio-economic type $X_m$ a probability of being in poverty may be derived by calculating from (5.9) the value of z for this specific type and the value of the standard normal distribution function in this point.

A similar model was used by Garfinkel and Haveman (1977), who estimated the effect of various socio-economic characteristics on the probability of being poor by a regression of the (0-1) dummy variable denoting the poverty status (according to different definitions).

The resulting poverty probability equals 0.5 for socio-economic types with $\ln y^*_\delta(X_m) = \ln y(X_m)$, i.e. socio-economic types that are exactly on the brink of poverty. For families with socio-economic characteristics that make people poverty prone, we have PPOV (the probability of being in poverty) larger than 0.5; for households with characteristics that do not make people poverty prone, we have PPOV smaller than 0.5.

In the derivation of PPOV we have allowed all characteristics $X_m$ to vary. If we do not want to differentiate according to all characteristics, but restrict ourselves, e.g., to differentiation according to variables $X_0$ only, we have:

$$\overline{\ln y^*_\delta} = \frac{\bar{x}_m\beta_m + X_0\beta_0 + \sigma u_\delta + e_2}{1-\beta_y}$$

and

$$\overline{\ln y} = \bar{x}_m\gamma_m + e_1$$

Hence:

$$P[(\overline{\ln y}) < \overline{\ln y_\delta^*}] =$$

$$P[\bar{x}_m\gamma_m + e_1 < \frac{\bar{x}_m\beta_m + X_0\beta_0 + \sigma u_\delta + e_2}{1-\beta_y}] =$$

$$P[e_1 - \frac{e_2}{1-\beta_y} < \frac{\bar{x}_m\beta_m + X_0\beta_0 + \sigma u_\delta - (1-\beta_y)\bar{x}_m\gamma_m}{1-\beta_y}] =$$

$$\Phi(z;0,1)$$

where

$$(5.10) \quad z = \frac{\frac{1}{1-\beta_y}(\bar{x}_m\beta_m + X_0\beta_0 + \sigma u_\delta) - (1-\beta_y)\bar{x}_m\gamma_m}{\sqrt{\sigma_{11} + (\frac{1}{1-\beta_y})^2\sigma_{22} - \frac{2}{1-\beta_y}\sigma_{12}}}$$

That expression denotes the probability that an average household of this type is under the poverty line.

Finally, we may wish to analyse whether the society as a whole has an average welfare level lower than the poverty line. We may calculate the average welfare level in a society as

$$\overline{U(y)} = \int_0^\infty U(\ln y) \, dF(\ln y; \mu_y, \sigma_y^2)$$

where F denotes the distribution of log incomes in society. If F is chosen to be the lognormal distribution function, we have

$$\overline{U(y)} = \int_0^\infty \Lambda(y;\mu,\sigma^2) d\Lambda(y;\mu_y,\sigma_y^2)$$

$$= \int_0^\infty \Lambda(y;\beta_y \ln y + \bar{x}_m\beta_m + \bar{x}_0\beta_0, \sigma^2) d\Lambda(y,\mu_y,\sigma_y^2)$$

$$= \int_0^\infty \Lambda(y^{1-\beta_y};\bar{x}_m\beta_m + \bar{x}_0\beta_0, \sigma^2) d\Lambda(y,\mu_y,\sigma_y^2)$$

If we apply the convolution theorem of lognormal distributions [see e.g. Aitchison and Brown (1957)], this results in

$$\overline{U(y)} = \Lambda[1; \bar{x}_m \beta_m + \bar{x}_0 \beta_0 - (1-\beta_y)\mu_y, \sigma^2 + (1-\beta_y)^2 \sigma_y^2]$$

$$= \Phi\left(\frac{(1-\beta_y)\mu_y - \bar{x}_m \beta_m - \bar{x}_0 \beta_0}{\sqrt{\sigma^2 + (1-\beta_y)^2 \sigma_y^2}}; 0,1\right)$$

We will have $\overline{U(y)} < \delta$ if

$$\frac{(1-\beta_y)\mu_y - \bar{x}_m \beta_m - \bar{x}_0 \beta_0}{\sqrt{\sigma^2 + (1-\beta_y)^2 \sigma_y^2}} < u_\delta$$

or  $$\mu_y < \frac{1}{1-\beta_y}[\bar{x}_m \beta_m + \bar{x}_0 \beta_0 + u_\delta \sqrt{\sigma^2 + (1-\beta_y)^2 \sigma_y^2}]$$

At welfare level 0.5 this implies that average welfare is lower than 0.5, if median income is lower than the poverty line. At other welfare levels the probability $\overline{U(y)} < \delta$ increases if income inequality in a society increases.

## 5.3 Poverty determinants for other household types

In the derivation of the poverty line, we have thus far restricted ourselves to one household type, viz. households without income of the partner or child benefits. The reason for this restriction was that we would like to avoid the complication of additions to household income by $y_p$ or cb.

In this section we will outline the procedure of determining poverty characteristics for other household types. We will first discuss the effect of an income of the partner (5.3.1), and then the effect of child benefits (5.3.2)

### 5.3.1 Two-earner households

If we want to determine the probability that a two-earner household is below the poverty line, we have:

$$P[\ln y_m + \ln(1 + \frac{y_p}{y_m}] < \ln y_\delta^* (X_m, X_0)]$$

The poverty line $y_\delta^*$ for this household type is seen to be

$$\ln y_\delta^* = \frac{1}{1-\beta_y} [X_m \beta_m + X_0 \beta_0 + \sigma u_\delta]$$

where $X_0$ includes variables that denote the effect of the household type on the poverty line.

We may write log household income as

$$\ln y_m + \ln(1 + \frac{y_p}{y_m}) =$$

$$= X_m \gamma_m + \ln\{1 + \exp[X_p \gamma_p + \varepsilon_2 - X_m \gamma_m - e_1]\} + e_1$$

where $X_p$ is defined as in (3.6).

If we look at the terms that have been added to household income and the poverty line, we may wonder whether the increase in the poverty line, as denoted by $\frac{X_0 \beta_0}{1-\beta_y}$, is compensated by the increase in household income, as denoted by $(1 + \frac{y_p}{y_m})$. If so, two-earner families have a smaller probability of being poor than their one-earner equivalents (ceteris paribus). We may calculate the extra income due to the partner's income for each combination $(X_m, X_p)$. In fact, we will also allow for the possibility that taxes are higher for the main breadwinner, if additional income is coming into the household, by adding dummy variables for taxes per household type to $X_m$. The total effect of the partner's working on income and poverty line is calculated numerically for some combinations of $(X_m, X_p)$.

## 5.3.2 Child benefits

If, in addition to the main breadwinner's income, child benefits are received, log household income equals

$$\ln y = X_m \gamma_m + \ln(1 + \frac{cb}{y_m}) + e_1$$

Again, we may assume that the presence of children influences $y_m$ as well through taxes by differentiating $X_m$ according to household type. We then wonder whether the total increase in income compensates for the increase in needs, reflected by a poverty line which is expected to be higher for families with children:

$$\ln y_\delta^* = \frac{1}{1-\beta_y} [X_m \beta_m + \tilde{x}_0 \beta_0 + \sigma u_\delta]$$

where the number of children is included in $\tilde{x}_0$. We will calculate numerically for different family sizes whether child benefits actually overcompensate, undercompensate or just compensate the cost of children at the poverty line.

## 5.4 Hypotheses on determinants of poverty

In table 5.1 we summarize the hypothesized effects described in chapters 3 and 4 of socio-economic variables on y, μ and σ. Firstly, the determinants of individual income are given (rows a through h). Secondly, the effects of an additional adult person in the household are explored (i and j). Thirdly, the effect of children in a household is described (k).
In addition to the hypothesized effects on y, μ and σ, the effect of each variable on the probability of being poor is predicted. The poverty line is for this use defined at the 0.5 level because at that level the determinants of σ may be disregarded.

In the first part of the table we find the characteristics that are assumed to influence individual income. It appears that only three characteristics have an unambiguous effect on the probability of being poor. Firstly, people who are experiencing an increase in income have a lower probability of being poor than people who, although at the same income level, experience a decrease in income or no change at all. Secondly, old people will usually fall back in income, while their needs are still relatively high; the net effect is to increase their probability of being poor. Thirdly, the probability of a woman being poor is larger than this

Table 5.1 Hypothesized effects of socio-economic variables on income, welfare parameters, and the probability of being poor, defined at the 0.5 level

|  | Effect on y | Effect on μ | Effect on σ | Effect on $P(y<y^*_{0.5})$ |
|---|---|---|---|---|
| **I. Single person households** |  |  |  |  |
| a. large degree of urbanization | ± | + | 0 | ± (+) |
| b. large fluctuations in income | ± | + | + | ± (0) |
| c. improvement in financial situation | + | − | + | − |
| d. not working | − | − | 0 | ± (+) |
| e. occupation: self-employed | + | ± | + | ± (0) |
|                farmers | − | − | + | ± (+) |
| f. high education | + | + | + | ± (−) |
| g. age: young | − | − | 0 | ± (+) |
|        old | − | + | 0 | + |
| h. sex: female | − | 0 | 0 | + |
| **II. Additional adult person** |  |  |  |  |
| i. not working | + | + | 0 | ± |
| j. working | ++ | ± | + | ± (−) |
| **III. Additional children** |  |  |  |  |
| k. large number of children | + | + | 0 | ± |

probability for a man, because her income is hypothesized to be lower than his. Hence old-aged and female heads of household are expected to be poverty prone.

For the other characteristics the net effect depends on the relative magnitudes of the effects on μ and y. If we make further assumptions on these relative magnitudes, the net effect of some of these characteristics on the probability of being poor may be predicted as well. These hypothesized effects are given in parentheses in the last column.

The degree of urbanization has a positive effect on cost of living whereas the effect on income is not determined; it results in a positive effect on the probability of being poor. For fluctuations in income no specific effect is predicted; it depends on the question whether the resulting increase in needs is sufficiently compensated by extra income. If this is the case, we should have a net effect of zero on the probability of being poor.

The effect of not working is negative, both on income and on μ; it is supposed that the negative effect on income is larger than the effect on µ. Hence we hypothesize that people who are not working have a higher probability of being poor. For self-employed we have, following the line of thought set out for fluctuations in income, hypothesized no specific effect on the probability of being poor. For farmers, however, we expect that the decrease in µ due to their income in kind is not sufficient to compensate for the low income they usually appear to have in empirical studies; hence we hypothesize that farmers are poverty prone. Education has positive effects both on y and on µ; the effect on y is supposed to be larger, resulting in a lower poverty probability for people with a high level of education. For young people, finally, we expect their income to be lower than the relatively low µ due to reference effects; hence they are hypothesized to be poverty prone.

Turning now to the additional effects that may be found if we look at couples rather than single persons, we see that the presence of an additional person who is not working expected to have a positive effect, both on y and on µ. The reason that y increases is that taxes are usually lower for couples than for single persons. Whether the net effect will be positive or negative depends on the extent to which tax facilities are welfare neutral between couples and single persons. If they are, the net effect should be zero. If taxes overcompensate the higher cost of living of a couple, the net effect on the poverty probability is negative, and if they undercompensate, the effect on the poverty probability is positive. As this may vary considerably over countries, no general hypothesis is to be made. If the additional adult person is working, more income is earned in the household. The effect on µ is two-sided: extra cost of living result for working couples because of their loss in household production and their higher work related cost, which increase µ; on the other hand, lower income in their social reference groups may decrease µ. The net effect is not unambiguous; we may hypothesize, however, that the additional income earned will in general be sufficient to cover these extra cost. If so, the net effect on the probability of being poor is negative.

Finally, the effect of children in the household is given; we have assumed that income increases with children, both because of family allowances and because of tax facilities. Moreover, hours of work of the main breadwinner may increase with children. The total effect on the main breadwinner's income is positive. The increase in income is intended to compensate for the higher cost of living, due to children, which is reflected by a positive effect on μ. If this compensation is welfare neutral, the probability of being poor should not be influenced by the presence of children. If cost of children are not fully accounted for, large families will be poverty prone; if cost of children are overcompensated, large families will have a lower probability of being in poverty than couples.

As we have seen, the household income may be split up into different components. The most important is the income of the main (or single) breadwinner. Additions to the household income may be the income of the partner (if any), family allowances and tax facilities. All hypothesized effects on income of additional adults and children in a family are additional effects on this basic income. We shall develop our empirical research along these lines and we shall analyse the determinants of the income of the main breadwinner, both when he is working and when he is not working, and the extent to which the household composition influences this income via taxes. We then look at the other components of household income, viz., the income of the partner and family allowances. By including these household components as possible determinants of μ, we will be able to differentiate in our analysis between the following household types:

( 1) Single person, working
( 2) Single person, not working
( 3) One-parent family, working
( 4) One-parent family, not working
( 5) Couples, both adults working, no children
( 6) Couples, one adult working, no children
( 7) Couples, no adult working, no children
( 8) Families, both adults working, children
( 9) Families, one adult working, children
(10) Families, no adults working, children
(11) Extended families, two or more adults working
(12) Extended families, one or no adult working.

Within more-person household types we will give special attention to the effects of the number of children and the number of breadwinners in a family. The category "one-parent family" has been included, as in these families the earnings capacity of the one breadwinner will be restricted by the necessity to perform household activities as well, yielding a lower income; this may, moreover, increase cost, yielding a higher µ. In addition, both a memory and a reference effect may enforce these higher needs: if these families have been used to a two-parent family situation (divorced, widowed) their former income probably used to be higher, and they will probably still have other two-parent families in their social reference group. All categories are differentiated according to working or not working of the adults in the household. The category "extended family" is defined as a household where more than two adults are living (with or without children). This category has been split up into families where more than one person is working, and families where one or no person is working.

The effect of all other characteristics, like education, occupation, sex, etc., will be examined for each of these categories separately.

It will further be analysed whether some of these household types are more poverty prone than others. Following the hypotheses in table 5.1, it is in general to be expected that the more adults are working in the household, the lower the probability of being poor. There is no unambiguous statement to be given, however, about the differences in the probability of being poor between household types. This depends upon the values that the effects on µ and y will get in our empirical research.

Chapter 6
THE EXTENT OF POVERTY

6.1  Introduction

Once a certain poverty line definition is agreed upon, and an empirical level of the poverty line is assessed, one can attempt to measure the extent of poverty in a certain population by a poverty index. In a famous article in <u>Econometrica</u> (1976) Sen describes the problems involved in the definition of a poverty index, that is meant to summarize the available information on the poor. Basically, Sen distinguishes three elements that ought to be included in a poverty index; the (relative) number of poor, indicating the incidence of poverty, the average income shortfall of the poor, indicating the average deprivation of the poor, and the distribution of income amongst the poor, indicating the relative deprivation of the poor.
The first two elements are usually measured in respectively the head-count ratio H, defined as the number of poor q divided by the total number of people in the population n and the income gap ratio I, defined as the average income gap of the poor, divided by the poverty line, $I = (z-\bar{y}_p)/z$, where $\bar{y}_p$ is the average income of the poor, and z is the poverty line.
Sen introduces a poverty index that combines these two familiar indices with the third element, income inequality amongst the poor. His index is defined as the weighted average of the individual income shortfalls, where the weights depend on the rank order of the individual in the welfare ordering of the poor.
Sen's pioneering article has been followed by numerous others. Takayama (1979) suggests using a censored income distribution, where the incomes of all the non-poor are put equal to the poverty line. His poverty index is defined as the Gini inequality measure of this censored distribution. Kakwani (1980) generalizes Sen's index by weighting each income gap by the rank order to the power k, where k is some positive number, that may be chosen according to the importance one attaches to the lowest incomes. Blackorby and Donaldson (1980) show that Sen's index is a specialization of a general framework in which a poverty index is equal to the head-count ratio times the relative income gap of an equally distributed equivalent income of the incomes of the poor, according to some social welfare func-

tion defined over the population of poor. Sen's index is found if in this framework the Gini welfare function is chosen. Clark, Hemming and Ulph (CHU) (1981) combine Takayama's censored distribution and Blackorby and Donaldson's framework of equally distributed equivalent incomes, using an Atkinson (1970) social evaluation function, to get a poverty index. Thon (1983) shows that a number of existing poverty indices violate the essential transfer axiom, if the number of poor decreases as a result of a transfer from a rich to a poor person. His alternative weights the income gaps of the poor with their rank order in the total income distribution. Foster, Greer and Thorbecke (FGT) (1984) propose a class of decomposable poverty indices that vary with a "poverty aversion" parameter.

Reviewing a number of these indices, however, Kundu and Smith (1984) in a recent contribution to the International Economic Review argue that no existing poverty index can possibly meet three specific axiomatic requirements, that are widely used, simultaneously. If these axioms are accepted, none of this wide variety of indices is acceptable as a general poverty index. No ready solution to circumvent this impossibility theorem is available; Kundu and Smith even doubt whether any general index of poverty can be meaningful. They conclude that one should measure the three different elements of poverty (incidence, absolute deprivation, income inequality) separately, depending on the poverty aspect one is interested in, rather than combine them into one single index. The state of affairs may, however, not be as bad as they suggest.

We set out to show firstly that some indices are better than others, even if Kundu and Smith's axioms are accepted, and hence none can meet all requirements. Moreover, we develop a social welfare framework which yields a class of poverty measures that do meet an alternative set of axioms. If these alternative axiomatic requirements are accepted, Kundu and Smith's impossibility theorem no longer holds, and two of the indices mentioned above, namely Clark, Hemming and Ulph's index and Foster, Greer and Thorbecke's index are performing best, both being members of the general class to be derived.

Finally, we show that all other indices may be seen to be special cases of the social welfare framework, although they violate one or more of the axiomatic requirements.

This chapter is structured as follows. Section 6.2 discusses the axiomatic requirements that a poverty index should meet. Section 6.3 reviews the indices mentioned, and shows that two indices meet a set of axioms that are desirable in a social welfare framework. In section 6.4 this framework is formulated and used to develop a class of poverty indices that meet these axioms. In section 6.5 it is shown that all other indices are implicitly part of this social welfare structure without, however, meeting all requirements. Section 6.6 gives some extensions of the concept, while in section 6.7 the relation between the poverty index and the individual welfare function of income is discussed. In chapter 12, the empirical results of the various indices, discussed in this chapter, will be presented with respect to the eight countries considered.

## 6.2 Axiomatic requirements

In order to evaluate different indices an axiomatic framework is needed that lists the desirable properties of a poverty index. Though some of these properties are chosen by all researchers as a matter of course, others may be less easy to agree upon, as they reflect either value judgments or emphasis of the researcher on a certain aspect of poverty. This problem usually arises if a choice has to be made between two conflicting axiomatic requirements, that are both per se believed to be desirable.

A list of desirable properties that most researchers (including me) will accept is:

(1) Monotonicity

A decrease in the income of a poor person should increase the poverty index, and vice versa.

(2) Transfer

A transfer from a poor person to a richer person should increase the poverty index, and vice versa.

(3) Population symmetry

If two or more identical populations are pooled, the poverty index should not change.

(4) Proportion of poor

An increase in the relative number of poor should increase the poverty index.

The monotonicity and transfer requirements have been used in one form or another in the derivation of all poverty indices. In addition a stronger axiom, the ranked relative deprivation axiom has been used by Sen, Thon and Takayama, which assumes that relative deprivation depends on the rank order of welfare.[1] The axiom is applied to poverty indices of a certain structure, i.e. weighted poverty gaps, where the weight of each person depends on his rank order in the welfare distribution. A weaker version of the ranked relative deprivation axiom would merely require that the impact of a poor person on the poverty index should be stronger, the poorer a person is, without specifying this impact by the rank order in the welfare distribution. This weaker axiom is implied by the transfer axiom.

The population symmetry axiom, although well-known in income inequality literature, has not yet been given much attention in poverty research. The theoretical desirability of the axiom *per se* will probably be generally acknowledged. The property holds for the head-count ratio, the relative income gap and all well-defined income inequality measures; hence if one combines these three elements into one poverty index, one would wish this index to have the same property. The only reason one may have for dismissing this axiom is that one may be interested in the absolute number of poor, rather than the relative number of poor. No existing poverty index, however, has claimed such intention. The population symmetry property is also desirable for empirical applications, when a dataset has to be re-weighted in order to be representative for the population.

The fourth axiom has caused most problems in the derivation of poverty indices. It will be useful to distinguish various ways in which the relative number of poor may increase, dependent on the question whether the increase takes place in a population of constant size, or in a situation where the size of the population varies. We will discuss these two situations separately.

(i) <u>The size of the total population, n, does not change</u>

In this situation an increase in the relative number of poor may be due to one of the following reasons:

(4.a) A rich man's income $y_r$ decreases with an amount a such that $y_r - a < z < y_r$ (MON).

(4.b) A rich person r transfers an amount a to another person such that $y_r - a < z < y_r$, and the receiver either remains poor or rich, i.e. the receiver does not cross the poverty line as a result of the transfer (TRAN).

(4.c) The poverty line z increases with an amount $\varepsilon$ such that at least one additional person p falls below the poverty line: $z < y_p < z+\varepsilon$ (Z).

It is obvious that increases in the relative number of poor due to MON and TRAN are closely related to the axioms of monotonicity and transfer, respectively. The first relation does not cause any problem. The monotonicity axiom states that a decrease in income of a poor person should increase the poverty index, and we may now add that a decrease in a rich man's income should also increase the poverty index if as a result of this decrease the man crosses the poverty line.

The second possible cause of an increase in the relative number of poor is the transfer from one person r to another person q, such that r falls below the poverty line. If person q is a rich person, no problem arises; however, if q is a poor person we may have conflicting axioms. The increase in the relative number of poor should increase the poverty index, but the transfer axiom implies that the "equalizing" transfer from a rich to a poor person should decrease the poverty index. This conflict has been described by Thon (1979). He proposes to give priority to the transfer axiom, and to use poverty indices that do not explicitly take the number of poor into account.

In fact, the problem we face is one of interpersonal comparison of welfare: does the increase in income of a poor person lead to an increase in welfare that is larger than the loss of welfare experienced by the rich person when the latter crosses the poverty line? It seems unavoidable to make such a comparison to solve the conflict. The choice Thon makes is in fact a Rawlsian choice: the increase in welfare of the poorer person is considered to be more important than the loss of welfare of a richer person.

However, if such a choice is to be made, one may as well start in choosing a social welfare function, and hence make the choice explicit. We will return to this later in this section.

The third possible increase in the relative number of poor is the result of an increase in the poverty line. Again, this may give rise to conflicting axioms. As long as the poverty line is at a level which is, at least in theory, obtainable for all people in society, i.e. as long as $z < \bar{y}$, no problem arises. However, if z increases above average income in society ($z > \bar{y}$), it is hard to reconcile "income inequality among the poor" with the monotonicity axiom. A decrease in income of someone between average income and the poverty line decreases income inequality in society, and hence increases social welfare, if income equality is associated with optimal social welfare. However, such a decrease is an obvious violation of the monotonicity axiom. Hence, a change in income that would increase an overall index of social welfare would simultaneously increase the poverty index.

Again it seems that, as such a choice is unavoidable, we may prefer to use a social welfare function that makes such a choice explicit.

It is seen that in the situation of constant population size, a number of choices have to be made between conflicting axioms. Let us now see what happens if we also allow the size of the population to change.

(ii) The size of the population varies

In addition to the increases in the relative number of the poor as a result of the changes we discussed before, the relative number of poor may now increase as a result of two more reasons:
- a poor person is added to the population,
- a rich person leaves the population.

We may think either of birth and death, respectively, or of immigration and emigration. It is for this situation that Kundu and Smith derived their impossibility theorem. The transfer axiom, population symmetry theorem and proportion of poor theorem cannot hold simultaneously in a situation of varying population size. Their theorem implies that all attempts to combine income inequality, the relative number of poor and the average poverty gap lead to conflicting requirements. Hence, Thon's conclusion in a situation of constant population size holds a fortiori in a situation of varying population size: one has to choose between various axioms. However, rather than dismissing the notion of a general poverty index altogether, we may try to base a poverty index on a framework which makes these choices explicit and which is general enough to enable all possible choices to be made.

A social welfare function is such a framework that enables us to derive different poverty indices, depending on our views on welfare in society. Before developing such a framework we will review the performance of various poverty indices on the criteria mentioned.

## 6.3 Performance of various poverty indices

We start our review with the situation of constant population size. In this situation the relative number of poor may increase as a result of a monotonic decrease in income of the rich (MON), a transfer from a rich person to a poor person (TRANS) and as a result of an increase in the poverty line z (Z). In table 6.1 a review of the indices and their performance on these criteria is given.[2] For a more detailed description of the indices we refer to the publications in which they have been introduced.

As mentioned in section 6.2, two possible conflicts may arise between different axioms in this situation. First the transfer axiom will always be in conflict with the proportion of poor axiom when the relative number of poor changes as a result of a transfer. Second, several axioms may be in conflict with general notions of social welfare if the poverty line is higher than average income. This latter problem will be discussed in section 6.4; let us for the moment assume that $z < \bar{y}$. We are now left with the choice between the transfer axiom and the relative number of poor. Even before making this choice, however, it is seen that two indices, CHU's $P_5$ and FGT's $P_7$, are performing better than all others, in the sense that they meet all requirements, apart from this unavoidable choice.

The choice itself should, we think, depend on both the nature of the poverty line and the nature of welfare. If the poverty line is an absolute borderline between survival and starvation [see, e.g., the "hungerline" described by Sharma (1983)], the proportion of poor axiom should get priority over all others. However, in that case neither average deprivation nor income inequality among the poor are relevant; the only measure of importance is in fact the simple head-count.

However, as poverty lines in Western countries are usually not of such nature, the only choice consistent with the notion of decreasing marginal

Table 6.1 Review of poverty indices

| | (The size of the population does not change) | | Monotonicity | Transfer | Symmetry | Proportion of poor MON | TRANS | Z |
|---|---|---|---|---|---|---|---|---|
| H | Head-count ratio | $\dfrac{q}{n}$ | no | no | yes | yes | yes | yes |
| I | Income gap ratio | $\dfrac{z-\bar{y}_p}{z}$ | yes | no | yes | no | no | no |
| $P_1$ | Sen | $\dfrac{2}{(q+1)nz} \sum_{i=1}^{q} (q+1-i)(z-y_i)$ | yes | no | no[1] | yes | yes | yes |
| $P_2$ | Takayama | $1 + \dfrac{1}{n} - \dfrac{z}{\mu^* n^2} \sum_{i=1}^{n} (n+1-i) y_i^*$ | no | no | yes | no | no | no |
| $P_3$ | Kakwani | $\dfrac{2}{(q+1)nz} \sum_{i=1}^{q} (q+1-i)^k (z-y_i)$ | yes | no | no[1] | yes | yes | yes |
| $P_4$ | Blackorby and Donaldson | $\dfrac{q}{n} \cdot \dfrac{z - Y_{EDE\,P}}{z}$ | yes | no | yes | yes | yes | yes |
| $P_5$ | Clark, Hemming and Ulph | $1 - \left\{ \dfrac{q}{n}\left(\dfrac{Y^A_{EDE\,P}}{z}\right)^\beta + \left(1-\dfrac{q}{n}\right) \right\}^{1/\beta}$ | yes | yes | yes | yes | no | yes |
| $P_6$ | Thon | $\dfrac{2}{n(n+1)z} \sum_{i=1}^{q} (n+1-i)(z-y_i)$ | yes | yes | no[2] | yes | no | yes |
| $P_7$ | Foster, Greer and Thorbecke | $\dfrac{1}{n} \sum_{i=1}^{q} \left(\dfrac{z-y_i}{z}\right)^\alpha$ | yes | yes | yes | yes | no | yes |

Notes: [1] It does asymptotically fulfil this requirement, assuming $q = q + 1$.
[2] It does asymptotically fulfil this requirement, assuming $n = n + 1$.

Notation: $q$ = number of poor
$n$ = number of persons in the population
$z$ = poverty line
$\bar{y}_p$ = average income of the poor

$y^*$ = truncated income vector; $y_i^* = z$ if $y_i \geqq z$ and $y_i^* = y_i$ if $y_i < z$.
$\mu^*$ = average income of the truncated distribution.
$Y_{EDE\,P}$ = equally distributed equivalent income of the poor, according to a general social evaluation function, defined over the poor only.
$Y^A_{EDE\,P}$ = equally distributed equivalent income of the poor, according to an Atkinson social evaluation function, defined over the poor only.

welfare is to give priority to the transfer axiom over the proportion of poor axiom. That is, to follow Thon (1979) in his choice for an index that does not explicitly depend on the relative number of poor. This is precisely the choice made in CHU's and FGT's index. Thon (1983) has remarked upon the good performance of CHU's $P_5$. His own index asymptotically meets all requirements as well. We conclude that in the situation of constant population size, CHU's $P_5$ and FGT's $P_7$ are performing better than all others, if the poverty line is not a threshold between life and death, and if the notion of decreasing marginal welfare is accepted.

Let us now see to what extent these two indices survive the introduction of varying population size.
According to Kundu and Smith (1983) the four axioms cannot hold simultaneously in this situation. A change in the relative number of poor may result from the addition of a poor person to society. Such an addition should, according to Kundu and Smith, always increase a poverty index. However, in fact the same dilemma is posed as the one discussed above: if the poverty line is of a truly absolute nature, the addition of a person below this line should indeed increase our measure of poverty. If, however, the poverty line is not as absolute as that, it may be that the addition of a poor person who is richer than most other poor increases the average income of the poor, and hence average social welfare of the poor. Again, if one introduces income inequality and average deprivation into a poverty index, we should accept that in some situations the addition of a poor person may decrease the poverty index. We would wish these situations, however, to be described by some social welfare function, which describes whether average social welfare is increased or decreased by such an addition. This is exactly what is done in the derivation of CHU's index: it is based on a social welfare function, defined over the truncated population, such that the addition of a poor person to the population increases the poverty index if the income of the additional poor person is lower than the equally distributed equivalent of the censored income distribution $y^*_{EDE}$, defined as $U^{-1}(SW(y^*))$. If the additional poor has an income higher than $y^*_{EDE}$, the poverty index decreases. The choice of a social welfare function enables us to make explicit the social trade-off between changes in the number of poor and the distribution of incomes; if one wants to maintain the proportion of poor axiom, no matter what income

the additional poor has got, one may choose a social welfare function such that $y^*_{EDE} = z$. Hence a social welfare function includes choices between conflicting axioms; its advantage is that these choices are made explicit. Given the choices that we made above, CHU's index still meets all our requirements; it is performing best (with FGT) if the population size is not allowed to vary, and it increases when average social welfare of the truncated population decreases. We now proceed to generalize CHU's derivation to describe a general class of poverty measures, that meet the same requirements. FGT's index will be shown to be a member of this class, as well as (asymptotically) Thon's index. It will furthermore be shown that all other indices may be rewritten to fit in this social welfare function.

## 6.4 Generalization of CHU's index

A general class of poverty indices is found by applying the well-known income inequality measures of Dalton (1920) and Atkinson (1970) to poverty measurement.[3]

Dalton's inequality index may be written as

$$D = 1 - \frac{SW(y)}{SW(\tilde{y})}$$

where SW is a social welfare function, y is a vector representing the actual income distribution, and $\tilde{y}$ is a vector representing the optimal income distribution, i.e. the income distribution that maximizes social welfare, given the available total national income.

Let the social welfare function be defined in the utilitarian tradition as

$$SW(y) = \frac{1}{n} \sum_{k=1}^{n} U(y_k)$$

If all (utility) functions U are equal, and U is concave, the optimal income distribution is found when incomes are equally distributed, yielding

$$D = 1 - \frac{SW(y)}{U(\bar{y})} \ .$$

Atkinson (1970) transformed Dalton's measure back to income space by a transformation $\phi(SW) = U^{-1}(SW)$, yielding

$$A = 1 - \frac{Y_{EDE}}{\bar{y}}$$

where $Y_{EDE} = U^{-1}(SW(y))$.

This expression has the advantage of being invariant to linear transformations of the U-function. A necessary condition for this transformation is, of course, that U is a monotonous function. The specification Atkinson chose was $U = \frac{1}{\beta} y^{\beta}$.

The social welfare function is a useful starting point for the derivation of a poverty index. Our interest is in the poor; this may be formalized by defining the social welfare function as

$$SW(y^*) = \frac{1}{n} \sum_{k=1}^{n} \min\{U(y_k), U(z)\}$$

This is equivalent to the social welfare function given above applied to the censored income distribution $y^*$, where

$$y_k^* = y_k \quad \text{if} \quad y_k < z$$
$$= z \quad \text{if} \quad y_k \geq z$$

Let us first assume that $z < \bar{y}$. In that case the constraint of total available income is not binding for the calculation of optimal social welfare of the censored income distribution; the optimal distribution of censored incomes is found when all incomes equal the poverty line: max $SW(y^*) = U(z)$.

The Dalton measure, applied to poverty measurement, is

$$D_p = 1 - \frac{SW(y^*)}{U(z)}.$$

If, following Atkinson, a transformation $U^{-1}$ is applied, we have

$$A_p = 1 - \frac{Y_{EDE}^*}{z},$$

where $Y_{EDE}^* = U^{-1}[SW(y^*)] = U^{-1}\{\frac{1}{n}[\sum_{i=1}^{q} U(y_i) + (n-q)U(z)]\}$.

These expressions represent a class of poverty indices, depending on the functional specification of U. However, the class may be limited to those indices that meet the axioms mentioned above by deriving from these axioms necessary and sufficient conditions for U.

(1) Monotonicity axiom
   If $U(y)$ is a continuous, increasing function, $D_p$ and $A_p$ satisfy the monotonicity axiom.

(2) Transfer axiom
   If $U(y)$ is a continuous, increasing strictly concave function, $D_p$ and $A_p$ satisfy the transfer axiom.

(3) Population symmetry axiom
   By the specification of the social welfare function the population symmetry axiom is warranted, as replication of the income distribution changes neither the relative frequencies of incomes, nor U.

(4) Proportion of poor
   (a) $D_p$ and $A_p$ increase with an increase in the relative number of poor as a result of a monotonic decrease in the income of a rich person, causing him to fall below the poverty line, for all continuous increasing functions U (MON).
   (c) $D_p$ and $A_p$ increase with an increase in the relative number of poor as a result of an increase in the poverty line z for all continuous increasing functions U (Z).

Hence the necessary and sufficient requirements to be made with respect to U, in order that $D_p$ and $A_p$ meet all desirable axioms in the situation (i), is that U is a strictly concave, continuous, increasing function. A proof of these statements is given in appendix A.

For all members of this class holds that, if the size of the population is allowed to vary, the poverty indices increase if the income of an additional poor person is lower than $y^*_{EDE}$, and decrease if the income of an additional poor person is higher than $y^*_{EDE}$.

An illustration of the Atkinson type class of poverty measures is given in figures 6.1 and 6.2. Suppose that in a two-person world P represents the actual income distribution $(y_{1a}, y_{2a})$. Given the requirements for the U-function and the specification of the social welfare function, this society will be inequality averse, which is represented by convex social

indifference curves, like the one through P.
If everybody would have the same income, the same social welfare would be found at point B, given by $(y_{EDE}, y_{EDE})$.
Hence the society would be willing to sacrifice at most $\bar{y}-y_{EDE}$, in order to arrive at an equal income distribution. BD represents the loss in social welfare, due to inequality. The corresponding Atkinson inequality measure is $\frac{BD}{OD}$.
If we now look at figure 6.2, the social welfare function is truncated at the poverty line; a higher income than the poverty line for one of the two persons will not result in a higher level of social welfare. Optimal social welfare is hence reached at point C, and the difference between C and A represents the loss in social welfare, due to poverty. The corresponding Atkinson poverty index is $\frac{AC}{OC}$.

Figure 6.1 Atkinson inequality measure

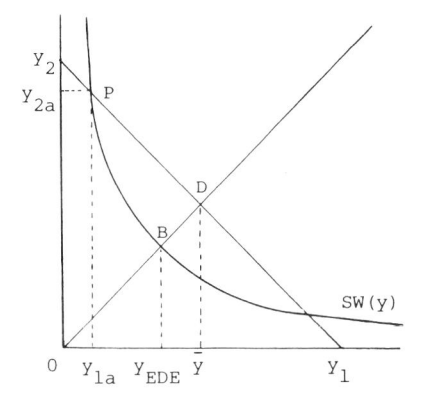

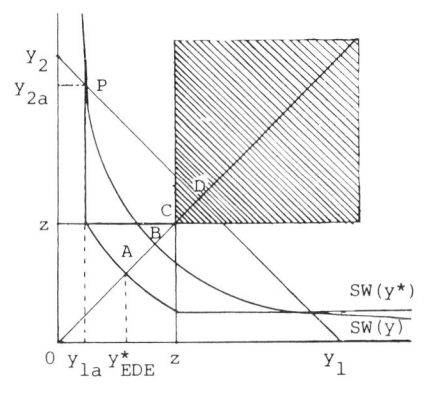

Figure 6.2 Atkinson poverty measure
In the shaded area no ordering is defined

Before turning to some special members of the class, we will consider the situation that $z > \bar{y}$. In this situation we will have to make the choice described in section 6.2, between desirable properties of the poverty index and desirable properties of a general index of social welfare. As we have seen in the description of the Dalton and Atkinson inequality indices, maximum social welfare of the total population is found for equally distributed incomes, $y_i = \bar{y}$, $i = 1,\ldots,n$. Hence if everybody is on the poverty line, maximum social welfare of the truncated distribution is larger than maximum social welfare of the total distribution. Hence we have to choose whether we measure the situation of the poor compared to $SW(z)$ or $SW(\bar{y})$. If we maintain $SW(z)$ to be the measuring rod, we measure the (im)possibility of society to alleviate the poverty burden. If, on the other hand, we choose $SW(\bar{y})$ to be the measuring rod, we are measuring the condition of the poor compared to others in society. In the latter case we have

$$\lim_{z \to \infty} D_p = \lim_{z \to \infty} \{1 - \frac{SW(y^*)}{SW(\bar{y})}\} = 1 - \frac{SW(y)}{SW(\bar{y})} = D$$

and

$$\lim_{z \to \infty} A_p = \lim_{z \to \infty} \{1 - \frac{U^{-1}(SW(y^*))}{\bar{y}}\} = 1 - \frac{U^{-1}(SW(y))}{\bar{y}} = A$$

Hence, the Dalton and Atkinson poverty measures tend to be Dalton and Atkinson income inequality measures asymptotically, when the poverty line tends to infinity. An objection to the choice of $SW(\bar{y})$ rather than of $SW(z)$ is that the resulting poverty indices do no longer satisfy the monotonicity axiom. If someone's income is decreased, $\bar{y}$ decreases as well, and the effect on the poverty index is not always positive. However, this is the implication of a social welfare function which stresses equality. Again, whether this is acceptable in this poverty context depends on the purpose of the measurement: within a certain society it may be useful to measure to what extent obtainable social welfare is reached; when comparing between countries, however, one may wish to measure to what extent the final aim of a society, even though not obtainable at present, is met.
The social welfare framework enables us to measure both aspects of poverty.

## 6.5 Special cases of the general class of poverty indices

We have shown that the generalization of CHU's index leads to a class of poverty indices that is better than all others if the population size is constant, and that provides an appealing solution to Kundu and Smith's impossibility theorem if the size of the population varies. We will now discuss some proper members of the general class, as well as some degenerate members.

First we have, of course, CHU's index; it is a member of the Atkinson type with

$$U(y) = \frac{1}{\beta} y^\beta$$

U satisfies all requirements for $\beta < 1$.

Secondly, we see that FGT's index is a member of the Dalton type, with

$$U(y) = z^\alpha - (z-y)^\alpha,$$

as

$$D_p^{FGT} = 1 - \frac{\sum_{i=1}^{n} z^\alpha - (z-y_i^*)^\alpha}{nz^\alpha} = \frac{nz^\alpha - nz^\alpha + \sum_{i=1}^{q}(z-y_i)^\alpha}{nz^\alpha} = \frac{1}{n} \sum_{i=1}^{q} (\frac{z-y_i}{z})^\alpha$$

U satisfies all requirements for $\alpha > 1$.

Thirdly, we propose another member of the class which is easily calculated and interpreted. It follows by the choice of

$$U(y) = \ln y \qquad (y > 0)$$

yielding

$$D_p = 1 - \frac{\sum_{i=1}^{n} \ln y_i^*}{\sum_{i=1}^{n} \ln z} = \frac{n \ln z - \sum_{i=1}^{q} \ln y_i - (n-q) \ln z}{n \ln z} = \frac{q}{n} [\frac{\ln z - \ln \bar{\bar{y}}_p}{\ln z}]$$

where $\bar{\bar{y}}_p$ is the geometric mean income of the poor,

and

$$P_8 = A_p = 1 - \frac{\exp[\frac{1}{n} \sum_{i=1}^{n} \ln y_i^*]}{z} = 1 - (\frac{\bar{\bar{y}}_p}{z})^{q/n}$$

Both expressions are simple functions of the geometric mean income of the poor, the poverty line, and the relative number of poor. $U(y)$ satisfies all requirements for $y > 0$.

If we extent our social welfare concept to include functions of the Gini type, e.g.

$$SW(y) = \sum_{i=1}^{n} w_i y_i,$$

where all incomes $y_i$ are ordered such that $y_i < y_{i+1}$ for all i, various other poverty indices are seen to be special cases of the Dalton type where this social welfare function is again defined over the truncated distribution:

$$D_p^w = 1 - \frac{\sum_{i=1}^{n} w_i y_i^*}{z \sum_{i=1}^{n} w_i},$$

where $D_p^w$ stands for Dalton indices based on social welfare functions of the weighted income type. We may derive[4] sufficient properties that the weights $w_i$ should have in order to meet the axioms (with the same qualifications as before):

(1) $D_p^w$ satisfies the monotonicity axiom if all weights are positive.

(2) $D_p^w$ satisfies the transfer axiom if the weights are decreasing, $w_{i+1} < w_i$, for all i, and if maximum social welfare, defined as $z \sum_{i=1}^{n} w_i$, does not depend on q.

(3) $D_p^w$ satisfies the population symmetry axiom if the weights $w_i$ change proportionally when the income distribution is replicated, i.e. $\tilde{w}_i = Tw_i$ if the income distribution is replicated T times.

(4) a. $D_p^w$ increases with the relative number of poor as a result of a decrease in a rich man's income, causing him to fall below the poverty line, if all weights are positive (MON).

c. $D_p^w$ increases when the poverty line shifts upward if all weights are positive and do not depend on q, the number of poor (Z).

Thon's index is obviously a member of the class $D_p^w$, with $w_i = (n+1-i)$. It is easily seen that Thon's index satisfies all requirements except the third, which it satisfies only asymptotically. In fact, various other indices are seen to be a member of the $D_p^w$ class, as is shown in table 6.2,

Table 6.2 Members of the $D_p^w$ class

| index | $w_i$ | $SW_{max}$ |
|---|---|---|
| H (Head-count) | $w_i = 0 \quad y_i < z$ | $z$ |
|  | $w_i = \frac{1}{n} \quad y_i \geq z$ |  |
| I (Income gap) | $w_i = \frac{1}{n} \quad y_i \leq z$ | $\frac{q}{n} z$ |
|  | $w_i = 0 \quad y_i > z$ |  |
| $P_1$ (Sen) | $w_i = \frac{1}{n}(q+1-i) \quad y_i < z$ | $\frac{1}{2} z(q+1)$ |
|  | $w_i = \frac{1}{n}\frac{1}{q}\sum_{i=1}^{q}(q+1-i) \quad y_i \geq z$ |  |
| $P_2^5$ (Takayama) | $w_i = \frac{1}{n}(2n-2i+1) \quad \forall i$ | $n\mu^*$ |
| $P_3^6$ (Kakwani) | $w_i = \frac{1}{n}(q+1-i)^k \quad y_i < z$ | $\frac{1}{2} z(q+1)$ |
|  | $w_i = \frac{1}{n}\frac{1}{q}\sum_{i=1}^{q}(q+1-i)^k \quad y_i \geq z$ |  |
| $P_6$ (Thon) | $w_i = \frac{1}{n}(n+1-i) \quad \forall i$ | $\frac{1}{2} z(n+1)$ |

where $\quad D_p^w = 1 - \dfrac{\sum_{i=1}^{n} w_i y_i^*}{SW_{max}}$, $\quad SW_{max} = z \sum_{i=1}^{n} w_i$

It is easily checked that no index satisfies all the sufficient conditions on $w_i$.

Finally, we note that Blackorby and Donaldson's index, which is also based on social welfare functions but defined over the population of poor only, equals our Dalton measure $D_p$ if

$$U^{-1}[\sum_{i=1}^{q} U(y_i) + (n-q) U(z)] = qU^{-1}[\frac{1}{q}\sum_{i=1}^{q} U(y_i)] + (n-q)z$$

which holds for the linear function $U(y) = y$ only. In that case we have

$$D_p = 1 - \frac{\sum_{i=1}^{n} y_i^*}{nz} = \frac{q}{n}[\frac{z-\bar{y}_p}{z}]$$

which is the product of head-count and poverty gap ratio, which was used by Sen as a normalization index. However, as $U(y)$ is not concave, the index does not meet the transfer axiom.

## 6.6 Extensions

The general framework described above may be extended in various ways. A first useful extension is to allow for different functions U for people with different characteristics $\vartheta$; $\vartheta$ may for instance indicate family size. The Dalton measure for the poor might be written as

$$D_p = 1 - \frac{\frac{1}{n}\sum_{\ell=1}^{L}\sum_{k=1}^{n(\ell)} U(y_k^*|\vartheta_\ell)}{\max_y \frac{1}{n}\sum_{\ell=1}^{L}\sum_{k=1}^{n(\ell)} U(y_k^*|\vartheta_\ell)},$$

where $n(\ell)$ is the number of people with characteristics $\theta_\ell$, L is the total number of characteristics and $n = \sum_{\ell=1}^{L} n(\ell)$. It is likely that in this case poverty lines may vary according to $\vartheta$ as well. Let us denote $z(\theta_\ell)$ for a poverty line for a family with characteristics $\theta_\ell$. If welfare neutral poverty lines are aimed at, that is, poverty lines that yield the same welfare for each family, it should hold that

$$U(z(\vartheta_\ell)|\vartheta_\ell) = \bar{U} \quad \text{for all } \ell = 1,\ldots,L.$$

Hence if an equivalence scale can be derived that transforms all incomes into some $\vartheta_0$-equivalent income:[7]

$$U(ye|\vartheta_0) = U(y|\vartheta_\ell)$$

where $\quad ye = \dfrac{z(\vartheta_0)}{z(\vartheta_\ell)} y$,

$D_p$ may be rewritten as

$$D_p = 1 - \frac{\frac{1}{n} \sum_{k=1}^{n} U(ye_k^* | \vartheta_0)}{U(z(\vartheta_0) | \vartheta_0)}$$

which gives $U^{-1}(. | \vartheta_0)$ as the obvious transformation to income space, such that

$$A_p = 1 - \frac{U^{-1}\{\frac{1}{n} \sum_{k=1}^{n} U(ye_k^* | \vartheta_0)\}}{z(\vartheta_0)}$$

has all the properties of the Atkinson measure derived above.

A second possible extension is to allow for a two-dimensional poverty border, e.g., in income and leisure t, rather than to concentrate on income alone. In that case we have

$$D_p(y,t) = 1 - \frac{\sum_{\ell=1}^{L} \sum_{k=1}^{n} U(y_k^*, t_\ell)}{\max_{y,t} \sum_{\ell=1}^{L} \sum_{k=1}^{n} U(y_k^*, t_\ell)}$$

The optimalization of the denominator should be under the constraint of available national income, available total time per person, and a possible income-time constraint. In extensions of this kind, however, no obvious transformation to income-leisure space is available.

Thirdly, the Dalton type index may be decomposed into subgroup indices, as was shown by Foster, Greer and Thorbecke (1984) for their index. Suppose the income vector y is decomposed into (m) vectors $y^{(1)}, \ldots, y^{(m)}$ with $n_j$, $j=1,\ldots,m$ persons in each subgroup j. It is easily derived that

$$D_p(y,z) = \sum_{j=1}^{m} \frac{n_j}{n} D_p(y^{(j)}, z)$$

Hence the Dalton class also satisfies the "subgroup monotonicity axiom" proposed by Foster, Greer and Thorbecke.

Fourthly, the index may be used to describe dynamic processes if the poverty line is allowed to vary. If the poverty line depends on the income distribution in society, like in our study, changes in the income distribution affect the extent of poverty both by a direct and an indirect effect. First the number of people under the "old" poverty line change, and then the poverty line itself will change. This may be incorporated in a dynamic model from which poverty developments may be analysed.

## 6.7 Poverty measurement and the individual welfare function of income

The various poverty indices proposed essentially differ, as we have seen, with respect to the question whether poverty is such a different state from other situations on the welfare scale, that one is justified in foregoing the general notion of decreasing marginal welfare below and above the poverty line. Sen and others have in their index given priority to the relative number of poor over the transfer axiom. In doing so, it is implied that welfare is substantially different below the poverty line and above the poverty line. Some kink in the welfare function of income may be the reason. Basically, this is the line of reasoning that Townsend (1979) pursued, who defined the poverty line as the income level below which a more than proportional decrease in welfare is perceived. If one could find evidence for this hypothesis, the index Sen proposes might again be applied. Unfortunately, the evidence presented by Townsend is not very convincing. Without such evidence, and an accurate estimate of the location of the income level where this kink in the welfare function is found, it seems rather arbitrary to assume that below a certain income level the welfare function is suddenly quite different.

If we would know what the individual welfare function looks like, the general Dalton and Atkinson indices for poverty measurement may be even further argued to be the proper indices to use: they simply aggregate individual welfare of the poor, and compare it to the welfare threshold at which the poverty line is set. If the welfare function is empirically found to have a concave shape, the index $D_p$ will behave as CHU's $D_5$. If the welfare function has a kink at the poverty line, the index will behave like Sen's.

In this book we have estimated the location and variance of the welfare function of income. This instrument, which has proved valuable in the derivation of poverty lines and poverty determinants, may also prove useful for this final problem of poverty measurement. By calculating $U(y_k)$ for each family in the sample, as

$$U(y_k) = \Lambda(\ln y_k, \mu_k, \sigma_k^2)$$

and truncating the welfare function at the poverty threshold:

$$U(y_k^*) = U(y_k) \quad \text{if } U(y_k) < \delta$$
$$U(y_k^*) = \delta \quad \text{if } U(y_k) \geq \delta,$$

we may apply the Dalton index straightforwardly as

$$D_p^{WFI} = 1 - \frac{\frac{1}{n}\sum_{k=1}^{n} U(y_k^*)}{\delta}$$

The advantage of this index is, apart from the fact that we do not have to assume *a priori* whether a kink is found in the welfare function of income at the poverty line, that it enables us to incorporate all other determinants of poverty as well. We may allow for all possible individual circumstances, without having to specify them in the poverty line. The only choice to be made is the welfare level $\delta$. Once $\delta$ is chosen, the Dalton index may be calculated both for countries as a whole and for subgroups within a country. The decomposition property of $D_p$ implies that the weighted average of all subgroup poverty indices add up to the total poverty index.

Summarizing the main conclusions of this chapter, we have developed a general class of poverty indices that is based on a social welfare framework. Most other poverty indices are seen to be a member of this class.

The properties of these indices depend on the implicit assumptions on welfare that are made. The direct measurement of welfare by means of the income evaluation question enables us to calculate an aggregate index of poverty in each country, without further assumptions on welfare. The general class may be decomposed into poverty indices of social subgroups. The empirical results of this poverty measurement are given in chapter 12.

## NOTES TO CHAPTER 6

[1] Although the axiom is based on welfare orderings, the practice is to operationalize welfare by income.

[2] The statements may be verified using the general framework developed later in this chapter, for which proofs are given in the appendices.

[3] See also Van Praag (1977) for a reappraisal of the Dalton measure.

[4] The sufficient conditions are derived in appendix B.

[5] $SW_{max}$ is defined as $\mu^* \sum_{i=1}^{n} w_i$, where $\mu^*$ is the mean income of the truncated distribution.

[6] The weights are normalized such that $\sum_{i=1}^{q} (q+1-i)^k = \frac{q(q+1)}{z}$

[7] This requires homotheticity of the utility function.

## APPENDIX A TO CHAPTER 6

In this appendix we will derive the properties that U should have, in order that $D_p$ meets the axioms in the situation that the size of the total population does not change. We will denote $D_p^a$ for the poverty index after the change, relevant to a certain axiom, and $D_p^b$ for the poverty index before this change. The derivations will be given for $D_p$; the proofs for $A_p$ may be derived analogously.

### (1) Monotonicity

Suppose the income of a poor person j is decreased with an amount a. This results in an increase of the poverty index if

$$1 - \frac{1}{nz} \left[ \sum_{k=1}^{n} U(y_k^*) - U(y_j) + U(y_j - a) \right]$$

$$> 1 - \frac{1}{nz} \left[ \sum_{k=1}^{n} U(y_k^*) \right]$$

Hence

$$D_p^a > D_p^b \quad \text{if} \quad \frac{1}{n} \left[ \sum_{k=1}^{n} U(y_k^*) - U(y_j) + U(y_j - a) \right]$$

$$< \frac{1}{n} \left[ \sum_{k=1}^{n} U(y_k^*) \right]$$

$$\rightarrow -U(y_j) + U(y_j - a) < 0$$

$$U(y_j - a) < U(y_j)$$

which holds for all $y_j < z$, if U is a monotonous increasing function. Hence the monotonicity axiom requires that U is an increasing function.

### (2) Transfer

Suppose an amount a is transferred from a poor person j to a (richer) person $\ell$.

$$D_p^a = 1 - \frac{1}{nz} [\sum_{k=1}^{n} U(y_k^*) - U(y_j) + U(y_j-a) - U(y_\ell^*) + U(y_\ell+\overset{*}{a})]$$

$$D_p^b = 1 - \frac{1}{nz} [\sum_{k=1}^{n} U(y_k^*)]$$

Hence $D_p^a > D_p^b$ if

$$\frac{1}{n}[\sum_{k=1}^{n} U(y_k^*) - U(y_j) + U(y_j-a) - U(y_\ell^*) + U(y_\ell+\overset{*}{a})] < \frac{1}{n}[\sum_{k=1}^{n} U(y_k^*)]$$

or $U(y_j-a) - U(y_j) + U(y_\ell+\overset{*}{a}) - U(y_\ell^*) < 0$.

If $y_\ell > z$ this implies $U(y_j-a) < U(y_j)$, which implies that U should be an increasing function of y.

If $y_\ell+a < z$ this implies $U(y_\ell+a) - U(y_\ell+a-a) < U(y_j) - U(y_j-a)$ which implies that U should be a strictly concave function.

If $y_\ell+a > z$ ($\ell$ crosses the poverty line as a result of the transfer) we have $U(z) - U(y_\ell) < U(y_j) - U(y_j-a)$.

Now $U(y_\ell) > U(z-a) \rightarrow$

$U(z) - U(y_\ell) < U(z) - U(z-a)$

and $U(z) - U(z-a) < U(y_j) - U(y_j-a)$ if U is strictly concave.

Hence the transfer axiom leads to the requirement that U should be strictly concave.

(3) <u>Population symmetry</u>

Let the income distribution be replicated T times.

$$D_p^a = 1 - \frac{1}{zTn} \sum_{k=1}^{n} U(y_k^*)T$$

$$= 1 - \frac{1}{nz} \sum_{k=1}^{n} U(y_k^*) = D_p^b$$

(4) Relative number of poor

(a) As a result of a monotonic decrease in income $y_\ell$ of a rich person, causing him to cross the poverty line.

$$D_p^a = 1 - \frac{1}{nz} [\sum_{k=1}^{n} U(y_k^*) + U(y_\ell - a) - U(z)], \text{ where } z < y_\ell < z+a.$$

$$D_p^b = 1 - \frac{1}{nz} \sum_{k=1}^{n} U(y_k^*)$$

$$D_p^a > D_p^b \text{ if } U(y_\ell - a) < U(z)$$

which holds for all monotonous increasing functions U.

c.  As a result of an increase $\varepsilon$ in poverty line $z$, such that one additional person $q+1$ with $z < y_{q+1} < z+\varepsilon$ falls below the poverty line.

$$D_p^a = 1 - \frac{\frac{1}{n}[\sum_{i=1}^{q+1} U(y_i) + (n-q-1)U(z+\varepsilon)]}{U(z+\varepsilon)}$$

$$D_p^a > D_p^b \text{ if } \frac{\frac{1}{n}[\sum_{i=1}^{q+1} U(y_i) + (n-q-1)U(z+\varepsilon)]}{U(z+\varepsilon)} < \frac{\frac{1}{n}[\sum_{i=1}^{q} U(y_i) + (n-q)U(z)]}{U(z)}$$

$$\rightarrow U(z) [\sum_{i=1}^{q+1} U(y_i) + (n-q-1)U(z+\varepsilon)] < U(z+\varepsilon) [\sum_{i=1}^{q} U(y_i) + (n-q)U(z)]$$

$$\rightarrow U(z) [\sum_{i=1}^{q} U(y_i) + U(y_{q+1}) - U(z+\varepsilon)] < U(z+\varepsilon) [\sum_{i=1}^{q} U(y_i)]$$

which holds for all $\varepsilon$, as $U(y_{q+1}) < U(z+\varepsilon)$ for increasing functions U.

## APPENDIX B TO CHAPTER 6

In this appendix we will derive the properties that $w_i$ should have, in order that $D_p$ satisfies the set of axioms described in the text (that is, axiom (1) to (3), (4a) and (4c)). For a general social welfare function

$$SW = \sum_{i=1}^{n} w_i y_i$$

where $y_i$ are the ordered incomes $y_i < y_{i+1}$ $\forall i$, applied to the truncated distribution:

$$D_p = 1 - \frac{\sum_{i=1}^{n} w_i y_i^*}{z \sum_{i=1}^{n} w_i}$$

Again $D_p^a$ is the index after the relevant changes and $D_p^b$ is the index before the change.

### (1) Monotonicity

Suppose the income $y_m$ of a poor person is decreased with an amount a, such that $y_{k-1} < y_m - a < y_k$.

$$D_p^a = 1 - \frac{[\sum_{i=1}^{k-1} w_i y_i + w_k(y_m - a) + \sum_{i=k}^{m-1} w_{i+1} y_i + \sum_{i=m+1}^{n} w_i y_i^*]}{z \sum_{i=1}^{n} w_i}$$

$$D_p^a > D_p^b \text{ if } \sum_{i=1}^{k-1} w_i y_i + w_k(y_m - a) + \sum_{i=k}^{m-1} w_{i+1} y_i + \sum_{i=m+1}^{n} w_i y_i^* < \sum_{i=1}^{n} w_i y_i^*$$

$$\rightarrow w_k(y_m - a) + \sum_{i=k}^{m-1} w_{i+1} y_i < w_k y_k + \sum_{i=k}^{m-1} w_{i+1} y_{i+1}$$

which holds for all positive $w_i$, as $y_i < y_{i+1}$ $\forall i$ and $y_m - a < y_k$.

(2) **Transfer**

Suppose a poor person $\ell$ transfers an amount a to a richer person m, such that $y_{k-1} < y_\ell - a < y_k$ and $y_p < y_m + a < y_{p+1}$.

(i) Suppose $SW_{max} = z \sum_{i=1}^{n} w_i$ does not change as a result of this transfer. We have

$$D_p^a = 1 - \frac{1}{SW_{max}} [\sum_{i=1}^{k-1} w_i y_i + w_k(y_\ell - a) + \sum_{i=k}^{\ell-1} w_{i+1} y_i + \sum_{i=\ell+1}^{m-1} w_i y_i^* +$$

$$\sum_{i=1}^{p-1} w_i y_{i+1}^* + w_p(y_m + a)^* + \sum_{i=p+1}^{n} w_i y_i^*]$$

$D_p^a > D_p^b$ if $w_k(y_\ell - a) + \sum_{i=k}^{\ell-1} w_{i+1} y_i + \sum_{i=m}^{p-1} w_i y_{i+1}^* + w_p(y_m + a)^*$

$$< w_k y_k + \sum_{i=k}^{\ell-1} w_{i+1} y_{i+1} + \sum_{i=m}^{p-1} w_i y_i^* + w_p y_p^*$$

$\rightarrow \sum_{i=m}^{p-1} w_i(y_{i+1}^* - y_i^*) + w_k(y_\ell - a) + w_p(y_m + a)^*$

$< \sum_{i=k}^{\ell-1} w_{i+1}(y_{i+1} - y_i) + w_k y_k + w_p y_p^*$

Now $\sum_{i=m}^{p-1} w_i(y_{i+1}^* - y_i^*) < a \max_{[m,p-1]} w_i$

and $\sum_{i=k}^{\ell-1} w_{i+1}(y_{i+1} - y_i) > a \max_{[k-1,\ell]} w_i$

Hence $D_p^a > D_p^b$ if $a \max_{[m,p-1]} w_i + w_k(y_\ell - a) + w_p(y_m + a)^*$

$< a \max_{[k-1,\ell]} w_i + w_k y_k + w_p y_p^*$

$\rightarrow a \max_{[m,p-1]} w_i + aw_p < a \max_{[k-1,\ell]} w_i + aw_k$

which holds for all $w_i$ with $w_{i+1} < w_i$ $\forall i$.
Hence $w_i$ should be monotonously decreasing in $i$.

(ii) Suppose $SW_{max} = z \sum_{i=1}^{n} w_i$ is a function of $q$, the number of poor.

If $SW_{max}$ would be an increasing function of $q$ ("positively concerned with the number of poor") we may follow Thon's argument (1979) that a transfer $\varepsilon$ from a poor person with $y_\ell$ to someone on the poverty line with income $y_m$ (=z) would give ($\varepsilon$ is so small that $y_{\ell-1} < y_\ell - \varepsilon < y_\ell$)

$$D_p^a = 1 - \frac{\sum_{i=1}^{n} w_i y_i^* - w_\ell \varepsilon}{SW(q-1)} \text{ and } D_p^b = 1 - \frac{\sum_{i=1}^{n} w_i y_i}{SW(q)}$$

Now $D_p^a > D_p^b$ if $SW(q) (\sum_{i=1}^{n} w_i y_i^* - w_\ell \varepsilon) < SW(q-1) \Sigma(w_i y_i^*)$

as $SW(q) > SW(q-1)$ there may be such transfers that decrease the poverty index, violating the transfer axiom.

If, on the other hand, $SW_{max}$ is a decreasing function of $q$ ("negatively concerned with the number of poor"), we may consider a monotonic decrease of a rich man's income $y_m$ to $y_m - \varepsilon$.

Such a decrease ought to increase the poverty index, according to the monotonicity axiom; however, if $SW_{max}$ decreases as a result, the net effect may be the opposite.

Hence, the only index satisfying both transfer and monotonicity axiom is an index defined such that the sum of the weights $w_i$ does not depend on $q$.

(3) Population symmetry

Suppose the income distribution $y$ is replicated $T$ times. We have

$$D_p^a = 1 - \frac{\sum_{j=1}^{Tn} w_j y_j^*}{z \sum_{j=1}^{Tn} w_j} = 1 - \frac{\sum_{i=1}^{n} y_i^* \sum_{k=T(i-1)+1}^{Ti} w_k}{z \sum_{i=1}^{n} \sum_{k=T(i-1)+1}^{Ti} w_k}$$

$D_p^a = D_p^b$ if $\sum_{k=T(i-1)+1}^{Ti} w_k = Tw_i$, which holds for constant functions $w_i = a$ only.

(4) <u>Relative number of poor</u>

(a) <u>Monotonicity</u>

Suppose a rich person's income $y_m$ is decreased such that $y_{k-1} < y_m - a < y_k < z$. Given the argument in (2), we assume that maximum social welfare does not depend on q. We have

$$D_p^a = 1 - \frac{\sum_{i=1}^{k-1} w_i y_i + w_k(y_m - a) + \sum_{i=k}^{m-1} w_{i+1} y_i + \sum_{i=m+1}^{n} w_i y_i^*}{SW_{max}}$$

$D_p^a > D_p^b$ if, analogously to (1), the weights $w_i$ are positive.

(c) <u>Increase in z</u>

Suppose the poverty line z is increased with $\varepsilon$ such that one additional poor person falls below this line: $z < y_{q+1} < z+\varepsilon$. Assume that, following the argument in (2), $SW_{max}$ does not change with q. We have:

$$D_p^a = 1 - \frac{\sum_{i=1}^{q+1} w_i y_i + (z+\varepsilon) \sum_{i=q+2}^{n} w_i}{(z+\varepsilon) \sum_{i=1}^{n} w_i}$$

$D_p^a > D_p^b$ if $z \sum_{i=1}^{n} w_i [\sum_{i=1}^{q+1} w_i y_i + (z+\varepsilon) \sum_{i=q+2}^{n} w_i] < (z+\varepsilon) \sum_{i=1}^{n} w_i [\sum_{i=1}^{n} w_i y_i^*]$

$\rightarrow z[w_{q+1} y_{q+1} + (z+\varepsilon) \sum_{i=q+2}^{n} w_i] < (z+\varepsilon)[\sum_{i=q+1}^{n} z w_i]$

$zw_{q+1} y_{q+1} < zw_{q+1}(z+\varepsilon)$

which holds for all positive weights $w_i$.

Chapter 7

DESCRIPTION OF THE DATA

In this chapter the dataset used for the empirical part of this book is described. The chapter is organized as follows. First some general information on the organization of the survey is given (section 7.1), and on the sampling method used (section 7.2). In sections 7.3 and 7.4 the interview and questionnaire are described. Section 7.5 informs on the actual interview. In section 7.6 the response rates are discussed. Section 7.7 describes the representativeness of the sample, and section 7.8 discusses the use of weights in regression analysis to correct for non-representativeness. Section 7.9 describes the way we have dealt with missing observations, and section 7.10 discusses possible measurement errors.

7.1 Organization

The data used in this project have been collected especially for poverty research in a "conditions-of-living survey" (COL) by the Center for Research in Public Economics (CERPEC) in Leyden, supported financially by the "Struggle Against Poverty" program of the European Communities.
The survey was designed and analyzed by Van Praag and the present author at the CERPEC in Leyden. For the actual data collection the collaboration of statistical institutes and opinion agencies in the member countries was sought. In the Netherlands and in Ireland a cooperation was started with the national statistical institutes. For the other countries, the Gesellschaft für Konsum-, Markt- und Absatzforschung (GFK) at Nuremberg, Germany, was willing to coordinate the data collection in cooperation with their associates in those countries.
The basic questionnaire has been discussed by the researchers with experts of these institutes, and some modifications have been made to adapt the questionnaire to specific national situations, especially with respect to income sources and the definition of net income. In all countries, this questionnaire has been pretested on a small sample of about 200 respondents. These surveys have also resulted in some improvements in the questionnaires. We will give a brief account of the resulting differences in the questionnaires in section 7.4.

## 7.2 Sampling methods

In general, two sampling designs can be used, random sampling and sampling based on a quota system. In the latter method, the sample is structured to consist of a certain percentage of different social categories, that may or may not correspond to the national percentages of these strata, depending on the objectives of the data collection. Categories to be used are, e.g., region, age, family size, occupation, education, urbanization, social class, sex of head of household, employment, et cetera. In practice, a combination of one to three of these categories is used.

In a system of random sampling, addresses or persons are chosen at random from some register (e.g., an electoral register). The two systems can be combined by first calculating the number of addresses to be drawn from each stratum, according to the quota system, and then drawing this number of addresses at random from each stratum. In most of the countries this combined method has been used.

## 7.3 Written questionnaires versus oral interviews

In principle it was intended to collect the data by a written questionnaire linked to a consumer survey, a survey that is periodically carried out in EC member countries or to some other omnibus survey (hereafter to be referred to as 'main survey'). The main reason for wanting a written questionnaire was to minimize the influence of the interviewer on the answers of the respondents (interview bias). Moreover, by linking a written questionnaire to another survey, the cost of the research could be relatively low. It was impossible, however, to have a written questionnaire in all countries. In Ireland and Italy the risk of a low response rate from certain groups was considered too high. Therefore it was decided to have oral interviews in Italy and Ireland, where we had to put up with the risk of interview bias. In all other countries a written questionnaire has been left with the respondent, explained by the interviewer after finishing the oral interview for the omnibus or consumer survey. This questionnaire had to be sent back in a pre-stamped envelope.

## 7.4 Differences in questionnaires

Due to the procedure mentioned above, various differences arose between questionnaires. First of all, there are differences caused by the way of interviewing: the oral questionnaires could be more compact than the written questionnaires, as the written questionnaires needed a longer introduction to certain questions. Secondly, adaptations for different national situations had to be made. A third source of variation in the questionnaires resulted from translation of the questionnaire in the national language(s). The fourth source of variation was due to the fact that in some countries our questionnaire was linked to the consumer survey, where a specific occupational classification was used that was not identical to the classification used in other countries.

The differences in questionnaires that are caused by one of the reasons mentioned above are minor, and will probably not greatly diminish the international comparability of the data. They do cause, however, differences in occupational categories included in various countries, as well as differences in educational categories. The main differences between countries are:

- In Belgium and the UK, farmers have not been included as a separate category; they are included in the category "self-employed".
- In Ireland, civil servants have been joined with "employees".
- In the Netherlands, no category "has never worked" was included; housewives are asked to give their (former) husband's occupation, and students their future occupation.
- In France, Belgium and the Netherlands, technical or vocational education has been included as a separate category; in the Netherlands three different levels of technical/vocational training have been distinguished.

## 7.5 The interview

In all countries the questionnaire could eventually be linked to another, oral survey. In principle all interviews were completed in the months October and November of 1979. In France, however, the survey was carried out in three stages. The first stage was conducted in October 1979, the second in November and the last one in February 1980. In all countries

reminders have been sent to respondents who did not send back their questionnaires. If necessary, this was repeated after a few more weeks.
In some countries, additional oral interviews have been conducted in order to get a more representative sample (in the other countries a sample of about 3000 respondents was reached without additional interviews). In the Netherlands oral interviews were conducted when the interviewer thought it highly unlikely that the respondent would fill out the questionnaire himself (this happened in about 450 cases). In Denmark 1000 oral interviews have been conducted in order to assure a proper response rate.
After coding and putting the data on tape, these tapes were sent to Leyden where the data have been screened and analysed.

## 7.6 Analysis of response

As has been pointed out, the questionnaire (written or oral) was linked to the main oral survey. For this reason two possible sources of non-response arise. Firstly, respondents may refuse to answer the questions of the main survey. Secondly, they may be willing to participate in the main survey but may refuse afterwards to fill out the mail-back questionnaire. The first filter is therefore the non-response to the main survey. This non-response may vary a lot over the countries because of the different types of surveys employed. The second source of non-response is expected to be of the same quantitative order in all countries except in Ireland and Italy, where our questionnaire has been answered in an oral interview, directly following the main survey. Unfortunately it was impossible to trace the non-response for the main survey in all countries. Therefore the specific non-response of our COL survey cannot be distinguished from the non-response to the main survey.

Table 7.1 gives the total number of the gross sample, the number of respondents to the COL survey, and the overall response rates.

Table 7.1 Response rates

|  | BEL | DEN[1] | FRA | GER | IRE[2] | ITA | NET | UK |
|---|---|---|---|---|---|---|---|---|
| Gross sample | 5010 |  | 4000 | 6000 |  | 3200 | 5230 | 5122 |
| COL survey | 2994 | 2972 | 3014 | 3126 | 3106 | 2987 | 2590 | 2943 |
| Response | 60 % | 70 % | 75 % | 52 % | 79 % | 93 % | 50 % | 57 % |

Obviously, the rather high response rates for Ireland and Italy are caused by the fact that interviews were oral.

When looking at the response rates we also have to bear in mind that there have been differences in the reminding of interviewees in the different countries. All statistical institutes have been asked to provide us with a representative sample of about 3000 completed questionnaires. In Germany this number has been reached before any reminding took place. In this case, only selected reminders have been sent out in order to assure the representativeness of the sample. If in this country reminders would have been sent to all non-respondents, the response rate might have improved even further. In Denmark the sampling institute has carried out about 1000 oral interviews, besides the usual mail-back procedure. We now turn to the more important point of representativeness.

## 7.7 Representativeness of the sample

The gross sample is structured according to the quota sampling method mentioned in section 7.4 to reflect the composition of the total population. If, however, certain groups of this gross sample have a lower response rate than other groups, the net sample of returned questionnaires may not be representative. The net sample was therefore compared in all countries to some national statistics with respect to occupation, family size, urbanization, region, etc. Partly to account for the specific national situation, and partly because of the availability of recent statistics on some of these characteristics a selection of these characteristics was made for each country. The appendix to this chapter gives a survey of the characteristics selected, the national population percentages for each of these characteristics, and the percentage found in the samples.

For each characteristic a chi-square statistic is calculated, which is a measure for the representativeness of the sample. Its formula is

$$\chi^2 = \sum_{k=1}^{K} \frac{(\text{number in the sample} - \text{number in the population})^2}{\text{number in the population}}$$

where the summation is taken over all classes of the characteristic used. For each characteristic the 95 % critical value is given as well. We see that for almost all characteristics in all countries the hypothesis that the ideal frequency equals the observed frequency has to be rejected with a probability of 95 %. In Italy the hypothesis cannot be rejected for region, in Belgium for region and city size, and in the Netherlands for employment. For all countries a reweighting procedure has been applied according to the characteristics given in the appendix. We will outline this reweighting procedure for the case where there are three characteristics (generalization to more characteristics is straightforward). This procedure is known as the RAS technique,[3] which has been developed by Deming and Stephan (1940).

Suppose the three characteristics are classified in respectively $n_1$, $n_2$ and $n_3$ classes. The observed joint frequency for each combination of characteristics in our sample is denoted by $f_{ijk}$, where $i = 1,\ldots,n_1$, $j = 1,\ldots,n_2$ and $k = 1,\ldots,n_3$.

We are now looking for correction factors in order to get "corrected" joint frequencies $f^*_{ijk}$, $i = 1,\ldots,n_1$, $j = 1,\ldots,n_2$, $k = 1,\ldots,n_3$. We assume that these correction factors can be split up into three parts, one for each characteristic. We obtain

(7.1) $\qquad f^*_{ijk} = C_1(i)C_2(j)C_3(k)f_{ijk} \qquad\qquad i = 1,\ldots,n_1$
$\qquad\qquad\qquad\qquad\qquad\qquad\qquad\qquad\qquad\qquad j = 1,\ldots,n_2$
$\qquad\qquad\qquad\qquad\qquad\qquad\qquad\qquad\qquad\qquad k = 1,\ldots,n_3$

where $C_n(m)$ is the correction factor if characteristic n has the value m. Notice that $C_1(i) = 1$ if persons belonging to class i with respect to the first characteristic have "average" response behaviour, that $C_1(i) > 1$ means that these persons are less responsive than average while $C_1(i) < 1$ implies that they are over-responsive.

We do not have at our disposal the joint population frequencies $f^*_{ijk}$, but only the marginal population frequencies $f^*_{i..}$, $f^*_{.j.}$ and $f^*_{..k}$, which are taken from national statistics. For instance, let characteristic 1 be age and characteristic 2 be region: the national age distribution may be known, but an age distribution per region is frequently unknown. There holds

$$f^*_{i..} = \sum_{j=1}^{n_2} \sum_{k=1}^{n_3} f^*_{ijk} \qquad i = 1,\ldots,n_1$$

(7.2) $$f^*_{.j.} = \sum_{i=1}^{n_1} \sum_{k=1}^{n_3} f^*_{ijk} \qquad j = 1,\ldots,n_2$$

$$f^*_{..k} = \sum_{i=1}^{n_1} \sum_{j=1}^{n_2} f^*_{ijk} \qquad k = 1,\ldots,n_3$$

Combining (7.1) and (7.2) we have the $n_1 + n_2 + n_3$ equations:

$$f^*_{i..} = \sum_{j=1}^{n_2} \sum_{k=1}^{n_3} c_1(i)c_2(j)c_3(k)f_{ijk} \qquad i = 1,\ldots,n_1$$

(7.3) $$f^*_{.j.} = \sum_{i=1}^{n_1} \sum_{k=1}^{n_3} c_1(i)c_2(j)c_3(k)f_{ijk} \qquad j = 1,\ldots,n_2$$

$$f^*_{..k} = \sum_{i=1}^{n_1} \sum_{j=1}^{n_2} c_1(i)c_2(j)c_3(k)f_{ijk} \qquad k = 1,\ldots,n_3$$

from which the $n_1 + n_2 + n_3$ unknown $c_1(i)$, $c_2(j)$ and $c_3(k)$ can be solved by a simple iteration procedure.

The reweighting procedure provides us with a corrected dataset for all countries, according to the marginal population frequencies given in formulae 7.2.

However, in case of non-representation reweighting is impossible. Almost certainly three groups will not be represented in the survey, viz.

(1) the illiterates in countries with written questionnaires,

(2) people without permanent address,

(3) foreigners who do not speak the national language

(these groups may overlap to a certain extent). The third point implies that foreign migrants are severely underrepresented or not represented at all. The illiteracy is presumably a smaller problem; where most illiteracy was expected, in Ireland and Italy, the survey has been carried out on an oral basis. As the three groups that are under-represented can be expected to have relatively low incomes, the estimates of poverty percentages in our survey are probably under-estimates of the actual poverty percentages in society.

## 7.8 The use of weights in regression analysis

The weights, calculated according to the method described in the last section, are seen to be indicators of the extent to which people with certain characteristics have responded in the survey. In this section we will describe when and why these weights should be used in regression analysis. Suppose we have a sample of T persons out of a population of N persons. The total population N may be classified in K different strata of "inclination to cooperate when asked for an interview"; in each stratum k $N_k$ persons are found, and $\sum_{k=1}^{K} N_k = N$. Suppose furthermore that in each stratum the relationship we are interested in is given as

(7.4) $\quad y_k = X_k \beta_k + \varepsilon_k \qquad\qquad k = 1,\ldots,N$

where $X_k$ is a $[N_k \times p]$ matrix of explanatory variables, $\beta_k$ is a $[p \times 1]$ vector of coefficients, $y_k$ is the $[N_k \times 1]$ vector of observations of the variable to be explained, and $\varepsilon_k$ is a $[N_k \times 1]$ vector of i.i.d. error terms with $E(\varepsilon_k) = 0$. When enough observations on each stratum are available, we may estimate $\beta_k$ for each stratum separately. If, however, we are merely interested in a national average for the relationship, and we do not have ample data on each stratum, we may also estimate the coefficient for the total population instead of (7.4),

(7.5) $\quad y = X\beta + \varepsilon$

where $y$ and $\varepsilon$ are $[N \times 1]$ vectors and X is a $[N \times p]$ matrix. The OLS estimator for $\beta$ based on the total population equals

(7.6) $\quad \beta_{OLS}^P = (X'X)^{-1}X'y = [\sum_{k=1}^{K} \frac{N_k}{N} \frac{(X_k'X_k)}{N_k}]^{-1} [\sum_{k=1}^{K} \frac{N_k}{N} \frac{(X_k'y_k)}{N_k}]$

$\qquad\qquad = [\sum_{k=1}^{K} (X_k'X_k)]^{-1} [\sum_{k=1}^{K} X_k'X_k \beta_k]$

If we wish to follow this procedure using a sample, rather than the total population, the representativeness of the sample becomes important. Suppose the sample is drawn using a sample design matrix S. S is a $[T \times N]$ matrix with elements

$S_{ij} = 1$    if the j-th person in the population is the i-th person in the sample;

$S_{ij} = 0$    otherwise.

Hence, S transforms the N persons in the population to the T sample observations by deleting from the $[N \times N]$ unit matrix the T-N rows corresponding to observations that are not in the sample. The sample is said to be representative if all different strata in the population are proportionally present in the sample, i.e. in frequencies $T_k$, k=1,....K, with

$$\frac{N_k}{N} = \frac{T_k}{T} \text{ for all } k.$$

It is not always possible to design the sample in such a way that representativeness is guaranteed. If it is known that certain strata in the sample are under-represented, and others are over-represented, we may calculate weights that correct for this non-representativeness; the weights are defined as $w_k = \frac{N_k T}{NT_k}$ for all persons in the sample stratum k. The weighted sample is now said to be representative for the population. If we estimate (7.5) by the sample observations, without using these weights, we have:

(7.7)    $Sy = SX\beta + S\varepsilon$          with $E(S\varepsilon) = 0$ and $Var(S\varepsilon) = \sigma_\varepsilon^2 I_T$

Hence, ordinary least squares would give:

(7.8)    $\hat{\beta}_{OLS}^S = (X'S'SX)^{-1} X'S'Sy$

$$= [\sum_{k=1}^{K} X'S_k'S_k X]^{-1} \sum_{k=1}^{K} X'S_k'S_k y,$$

where $S_k X$ and $S_k y$ denote the matrices and vectors found in sample stratum k, respectively.

If we assume that within each stratum, the second order moments of the sample are approximately equal to the population moments:

$$\frac{X'S_k'S_k X}{T_k} \cong \frac{X_k'X_k}{N_k} \text{ and } \frac{X'S_k'S_k y}{T_k} \cong \frac{X_k'y_k}{N_k}$$

the estimate $\hat{\beta}^S_{OLS}$ in (7.8) will not in general equal the estimate in (7.6). We have

$$(7.9) \quad \hat{\beta}^S \cong [\sum_{k=1}^{K} \frac{T_k}{T} (\frac{X'_k X_k}{N_k})]^{-1} [\sum_{k=1}^{K} \frac{T_k}{T} (\frac{X'_k y_k}{N_k})]$$

$$= [\sum_{k=1}^{K} \frac{T_k}{T} (\frac{X'_k X_k}{N_k})]^{-1} [\sum_{k=1}^{K} \frac{T_k}{T} (\frac{X'_k X_k}{N_k}) \hat{\beta}_k]$$

which does not equal $\hat{\beta}^P_{OLS}$ from (7.6), unless $\frac{N_k}{N} = \frac{T_k}{T}$, i.e. if the sample is representative.

The weights $w_k$ satisfy $\frac{w_k T_k}{T} = \frac{N_k}{N}$. We will use this property to correct for non-representativeness.

If we write W for a [T×T] diagonal matrix with element
$W_{jj} = w_k$ if the j-th person in the sample belongs to stratum k
$W_{ij} = 0$ for all $i \neq j$,
we may write the weighted sample estimator as

$$(7.10) \quad \hat{\beta}^S_{WOLS} = (X'S'WSX)^{-1} X'S'WSy$$

$$\cong [\sum_{k=1}^{K} \frac{w_k T_k}{T} (\frac{X'_k X_k}{N_k})]^{-1} [\sum_{k=1}^{K} \frac{w_k T_k}{T} (\frac{X'_k y_k}{N_k})]$$

$$= [\sum_{k=1}^{K} \frac{N_k}{N} (\frac{X'_k X_k}{N_k})]^{-1} [\sum_{k=1}^{K} \frac{N_k}{N} (\frac{X'_k y_k}{N_k})] = \hat{\beta}^P_{OLS}$$

which approximately equals the estimator from (7.6) that we would have got if the sample would have been representative.

## 7.9 Missing observations

As is to be expected, not all respondents have filled out their questionnaire completely. For instance, sometimes information on income is missing, or the income evaluation question has not been answered, while other questions have been answered correctly.

Although a number of ingenious methods to account for these missing observations is available,[4] we have preferred to drop the whole questionnaire when one of the relevant items was missing. The reason for doing this was that the sample size was large enough to start with, so there was no need to economize on the number of questionnaires. However, missing observations may be found more often in some strata of our sample than in others; the correction procedure outlayed in the former section hence has been applied to the remaining net dataset, rather than to the sample before deletion of missing observations.

## 7.10 Measurement errors

Finally, some remarks are in order on the extent to which measurement errors may distort our results. Research on observation errors in income data show that substantial measurement errors may be found; systematical under-reporting of incomes was found by Smeeding (1977) and modelled by, e.g., Hartley and Revankar (1974); Van Praag, Hagenaars and Van Eck (1983) found that measurement errors may account for 17 % of the observed variance of log income. In our research, however, both income information and the answers to the income evaluation question are important. We think it likely that someone who under-reports actual income will also underestimate his IEQ answers. Hence these measurement errors would not impair the identification of the poor. The resulting poverty lines may, however, be underestimates.

NOTES TO CHAPTER 7

[1] As in Denmark the response rate with respect to the additional oral interviews is unknown only the response rate with respect to the mail-back questionnaires is given here.

[2] In Ireland the interviewees were taken from a random subsample of the respondents to the consumer survey. It appeared that almost everybody who was willing to answer questions for the consumer survey was willing to respond to the COL survey as well. This is probably because the COL survey is oral in Ireland, as well as the main survey. We have therefore taken the response rate of the consumer survey as the response rate for the COL survey.

[3] The derivation RAS stems from the three matrices used in the introduction of the method by Deming and Stephan (1940).

[4] See e.g. Afifi and Elashof (1966) for a review of the early literature on the subject. More recent contributions are made by e.g. Beale and Little (1975), Dagenais (1973), Kmenta (1978), Van Praag and Wesselman (1984), Van Praag, Dijkstra and Van Velzen (1985).

APPENDIX TO CHAPTER 7

SAMPLE VS. POPULATION FREQUENCIES FOR ALL COUNTRIES

BELGIUM

Regions

| classification: | frequencies: | |
|---|---|---|
| | sample | pop. |
| Antwerp | 16.7 | 15.7 |
| Flemish Brabant | 8.6 | 8.5 |
| Brussels | 12.8 | 13.9 |
| Walloon Brabant | 2.5 | 2.3 |
| West Flanders | 10.8 | 10.1 |
| East Flanders | 13.4 | 13.1 |
| Hainault | 13.0 | 14.1 |
| Liege | 10.2 | 11.2 |
| Limburg | 5.3 | 5.3 |
| Luxemburg | 2.6 | 2.1 |
| Namur | 4.2 | 3.8 |
| Total | 100 | 100 |

Value of $\chi^2$ statistic: 16.02
95 % critical value: 18.3

Age of head of household

| classification: | frequencies: | |
|---|---|---|
| | sample | pop. |
| 14 - 24 | 2.4 | 4.4 |
| 25 - 29 | 10.4 | 7.3 |
| 30 - 44 | 36.9 | 27.6 |
| 45 - 59 | 31.0 | 27.1 |
| 60 - 64 | 5.7 | 9.2 |
| 65 - 69 | 6.8 | 8.8 |
| 70 - 74 | 4.0 | 7.8 |
| 75 and over | 2.9 | 7.8 |
| Total | 100 | 100 |

Value of $\chi^2$ statistic: 357.24
95 % critical value: 14.1

Size of the household

| classification: | frequencies: | |
|---|---|---|
| | sample | pop. |
| 1 person | 10.8 | 18.8 |
| 2 persons | 22.1 | 30.2 |
| 3 persons | 21.6 | 20.1 |
| 4 persons | 24.9 | 14.8 |
| 5 persons or more | 20.6 | 16.1 |
| Total | 100 | 100 |

Value of $\chi^2$ statistic: 387.72
95 % critical value: 9.49

Size of the city

| classification: | frequencies: | |
|---|---|---|
| | sample | pop. |
| up to 5000 inh. | 27.9 | 28.0 |
| 500-100.000 | 42.4 | 42.0 |
| 100.000 and over | 29.6 | 30.0 |
| Total | 100 | 100 |

Value of $\chi^2$ statistic: 0.26
95 % critical value: 5.99

DENMARK

Regions

| classification: | frequencies: | |
|---|---|---|
| | sample | pop. |
| Capital | 28.8 | 31.0 |
| Frederiksberg | 4.2 | 4.0 |
| Roskilde | 3.3 | 3.0 |
| Westseeland | 4.7 | 5.0 |
| Storstroms | 4.9 | 5.0 |
| Bornholm | 0.2 | 1.0 |
| Fünen | 9.0 | 9.0 |
| Süd Jütland | 5.3 | 6.0 |
| Ribe | 4.7 | 4.0 |
| Vejle | 5.3 | 4.0 |
| Ringkobing | 4.7 | 4.0 |
| Aarhus | 10.1 | 11.0 |
| Viborg | 4.5 | 4.0 |
| Nordjütland | 10.3 | 9.0 |
| Total | 100 | 100 |

Value of $\chi^2$ statistic: 56.51
95 % critical value: 22.4

Occupation of main wage earner

| classification: | frequencies: | |
|---|---|---|
| | sample | pop. |
| farmers | 6.8 | 6.0 |
| self-employed | 9.3 | 10.0 |
| civil-servants/ employees | 29.5 | 26.0 |
| workers | 28.0 | 31.0 |
| non-working | 26.0 | 27.0 |
| Total | 100 | 100 |

Value of $\chi^2$ statistic: 26.65
95 % critical value: 9.49

Size of household

| classification: | frequencies: | |
|---|---|---|
| | sample | pop. |
| 1 person | 20.9 | 24.0 |
| 2 persons | 33.4 | 29.0 |
| 3 persons | 16.5 | 19.0 |
| 5 persons | 19.7 | 17.0 |
| 5 persons and more | 9.5 | 11.0 |
| Total | 100 | 100 |

Value of $\chi^2$ statistic: 60.49
95 % critical value: 9.49

FRANCE

Regions

| classification: | frequencies: | |
|---|---|---|
| | sample | pop. |
| North | 10.7 | 7.0 |
| East | 9.6 | 9.0 |
| East Paris Basin | 8.3 | 8.5 |
| West Paris Basin | 8.5 | 9.0 |
| West | 11.2 | 12.5 |
| South West | 13.7 | 10.0 |
| Rhone Alps | 11.5 | 12.0 |
| South East | 10.5 | 11.0 |
| Greater Paris | 16.1 | 21.0 |
| Total | 100 | 100 |

Value of $\chi^2$ statistic: 139.64
95 % critical value: 15.5

Age of head of household

| classification: | frequencies: | |
|---|---|---|
| | sample | pop. |
| 15 - 24 | 10.8 | 5.8 |
| 25 - 34 | 29.0 | 19.0 |
| 35 - 44 | 17.2 | 17.0 |
| 45 - 54 | 19.4 | 19.0 |
| 55 - 64 | 10.9 | 14.0 |
| 65 and over | 12.6 | 26.0 |
| Total | 100 | 100 |

Value of $\chi^2$ statistic: 579.40
95 % critical value: 11.1

Size of the city

| classification: | frequencies: | |
|---|---|---|
| | sample | pop. |
| up to 20.000 inh. | 11.9 | 14.0 |
| 20.000-100.000 | 19.5 | 15.0 |
| 100.000 and over | 29.1 | 26.0 |
| Greater Paris | 14.5 | 18.0 |
| rurals | 25.0 | 27.0 |
| Total | 100 | 100 |

Value of $\chi^2$ statistic: 84.33
95 % critical value: 9.49

Size of the household

| classification: | frequencies: | |
|---|---|---|
| | sample | pop. |
| 1 person | 20.0 | 22.2 |
| 2 persons | 27.7 | 28.2 |
| 3 persons | 19.4 | 19.2 |
| 4 persons | 18.6 | 15.2 |
| 5 persons | 8.7 | 8.2 |
| 6 persons and over | 5.6 | 7.2 |
| Total | 100 | 100 |

Value of $\chi^2$ statistic: 40.58
95 % critical value: 11.1

GERMANY

Region

| classification: | frequencies: | |
|---|---|---|
| | sample | pop. |
| Schleswig-Holstein | 4.1 | 4.1 |
| Hamburg | 3.3 | 2.8 |
| Niedersachsen | 16.4 | 11.7 |
| Bremen | 1.5 | 1.2 |
| Nordrheinwestfalen | 22.4 | 27.8 |
| Hessen | 11.7 | 9.1 |
| Rheinland-Pfalz | 5.3 | 6.0 |
| Baden-Württemberg | 13.2 | 14.9 |
| Bayern | 17.5 | 17.5 |
| Saarland | 2.5 | 1.6 |
| Berlin | 2.2 | 3.3 |
| Total | 100 | 100 |

Value of $\chi^2$ statistic: 129.81
95 % critical value: 18.3

Occupation head of household

| classification: | frequencies: | |
|---|---|---|
| | sample | pop. |
| worker | 32.2 | 23.4 |
| employee | 24.8 | 25.0 |
| civil servant | 11.2 | 11.5 |
| free profession and self-employed | 5.8 | 3.3 |
| farmers | 2.9 | 1.2 |
| non-working | 23.7 | 35.6 |
| Total | 100 | 100 |

Value of $\chi^2$ statistic: 345.08
95 % critical value: 11.1

Size of the city

| classification: | frequencies: | |
|---|---|---|
| | sample | pop. |
| less than 5000 inh. | 28.7 | 21.9 |
| 5000-9999 | 9.7 | 10.6 |
| 10.000-19.999 | 11.9 | 12.3 |
| 20.000-99.999 | 22.8 | 22.5 |
| 100.000 and over | 26.9 | 32.7 |
| Total | 100 | 100 |

Value of $\chi^2$ statistic: 92.24
95 % critical value: 9.49

Size of household

| classification: | frequencies: | |
|---|---|---|
| | sample | pop. |
| 1 person | 16.0 | 25.5 |
| 2 persons | 27.4 | 27.4 |
| 3 persons | 22.1 | 19.5 |
| 4 persons and more | 34.5 | 27.5 |
| Total | 100 | 100 |

Value of $\chi^2$ statistic: 162.85
95 % critical value: 7.81

IRELAND

Age of head of household

| classification: | frequencies: | |
|---|---|---|
| | sample | pop. |
| 20 - 29 | 10.9 | 22.3 |
| 30 - 39 | 22.6 | 17.1 |
| 40 - 49 | 18.3 | 17.7 |
| 50 - 59 | 22.3 | 17.9 |
| 60 - 64 | 10.0 | 7.7 |
| 65 and over | 15.9 | 17.4 |
| Total | 100 | 100 |

Value of $\chi^2$ statistic: 295.29
95 % critical value: 11.1

Education

| classification: | frequencies: | |
|---|---|---|
| | sample | pop. |
| primary | 59.7 | 66.2 |
| secondary | 8.6 | 15.8 |
| vocational | 21.7 | 8.8 |
| secondary and vocational | 2.5 | 3.9 |
| university | 7.5 | 5.3 |
| Total | 100 | 100 |

Value of $\chi^2$ statistic: 784.98
95 % critical value: 9.49

ITALY

Size of the household

| classification: | frequencies: | |
|---|---|---|
| | sample | pop. |
| 1 person | 10.1 | 7.3 |
| 2 persons | 23.9 | 23.2 |
| 3 persons | 24.9 | 26.1 |
| 4 persons | 25.6 | 25.6 |
| 5 persons | 10.0 | 11.1 |
| 6 persons and more | 5.7 | 6.7 |
| Total | 100 | 100 |

Value of $\chi^2$ statistic: 40.20
95 % critical value: 11.1

Regions

| classification: | frequencies: | |
|---|---|---|
| | sample | pop. |
| North West | 31.9 | 30.7 |
| North East | 19.1 | 18.6 |
| Central | 18.7 | 19.0 |
| South | 20.1 | 21.0 |
| Islands | 10.2 | 10.7 |
| Total | 100 | 100 |

Value of $\chi^2$ statistic: 3.50
95 % critical value: 9.49

## THE NETHERLANDS

### Employment

| classification: | frequencies: | |
|---|---|---|
| | sample | pop. |
| manual worker | 21.8 | 22.4 |
| employer | 37.4 | 35.0 |
| independent farmer | 3.1 | 2.8 |
| self-employed | 6.8 | 5.8 |
| unemployed | 1.0 | 2.0 |
| military service | 0.1 | 0.01 |
| full-time training | 1.4 | 2.1 |
| home duties | 5.6 | 8.6 |
| retired | 15.8 | 16.4 |
| sick/disabled | 7.2 | 5.0 |
| Total | 100 | 100 |

Value of $\chi^2$ statistic: 81.17
95 % critical value: 16.9

### Age and sex of head of household

| classification: | frequencies: | |
|---|---|---|
| | sample | pop. |
| head of household, <65 | 72.4 | 69.6 |
| head of household, >64 | 10.8 | 11.5 |
| single, man, <65 | 4.2 | 4.9 |
| single, man, >64 | 1.7 | 1.5 |
| single, woman, <65 | 5.0 | 6.1 |
| single, woman, >64 | 6.0 | 6.4 |
| Total | 100 | 100 |

Value of $\chi^2$ statistic: 13.37
95 % critical value: 11.1

## UNITED KINGDOM

### Size of the household

| classification: | frequencies: | |
|---|---|---|
| | sample | pop. |
| 1 person | 5.7 | 18.1 |
| 2 persons | 27.2 | 31.3 |
| 3 persons | 21.5 | 18.8 |
| 4 persons | 10.7 | 8.3 |
| 6 persons and more | 5.5 | 6.3 |

Value of $\chi^2$ statistic: 485.41
95 % critical value: 9.49

### Age of head of the household

| classification: | frequencies: | |
|---|---|---|
| | sample | pop. |
| less than 25 years | 4.8 | 4.2 |
| 25 - 29 | 12.7 | 8.2 |
| 30 - 44 | 41.4 | 25.2 |
| 60 - 64 | 6.0 | 9.2 |
| 65 and over | 10.9 | 27.2 |

Value of $\chi^2$ statistic: 624.27
95 % critical value: 9.49

Source: The information on Belgium, Denmark, France, Germany, Great Britain and Italy has been provided by the G.F.K. at Nuremberg, Germany. The Dutch figures are provided by the Central Bureau of Statistics. For the Irish figures we have used the results of the Census of Population 1971, published in the Irish Statistical Abstract, 1976, by the Central Statistics Office in Dublin.

Chapter 8
EMPIRICAL RESULTS: DIFFERENCES IN WELFARE

After the theoretical exposition of the first six chapters and the description of our dataset of the previous chapter we may now look at some empirical results. In this chapter we give some general information on average welfare, as measured in our survey, both in different countries and in different household types per country. In later chapters we present the determinants of welfare parameters and income separately; the present chapter describes the net effect of these two aspects, in terms of an actual welfare score between zero and one. For all categories distinguished the average welfare score of all households belonging to the category is calculated. This will give us information on the welfare distribution over categories and over countries. We may also use the average welfare score as an indicator of the fact whether a country or category is on average poor, i.e. has a welfare level lower than the welfare level at which the poverty threshold is set. The choice of this poverty threshold in this research is the welfare level 0.5, just halfway the welfare scale. Our reason for choosing this level is that it corresponds to a verbal qualification between "sufficient" and "insufficient", which appears to be an appealing definition of a poverty border. This choice has furthermore the advantage that the determinants of the welfare parameter µ are sufficient to derive the poverty line, as the parameter σ does not have an effect on the poverty line at the 0.5 level.

The choice of 0.5 as a poverty threshold implies that a category with an average welfare level lower than 0.5 is on average poor. Individual welfare levels may be higher or lower than this average; these additional differences in welfare will be explained in chapter 11.

A first impression of welfare differences between these household types is given in table 8.1, in which the average welfare levels in each of the twelve different household types are given for all countries.

Table 8.1 shows large differences in welfare both between categories and between countries. The differences between categories are the same for almost all countries: in all countries highest welfare is found in households (with or without children) where both main breadwinner and partner are working. In all countries lowest welfare is found in non-working single-parent and single-person households. Furthermore, we find in almost

Table 8.1 Average welfare levels for different household types in eight European countries

|  | BEL | DEN | FRA | GER | IRE | ITA | NET | UK |
|---|---|---|---|---|---|---|---|---|
| Single person, working | 0.60 | 0.53 | 0.44 | 0.68 | 0.56 | 0.61 | 0.67 | 0.63 |
| Single person, not working | 0.53 | 0.47 | 0.34 | 0.60 | 0.38 | 0.47 | 0.59 | 0.41 |
| One-parent family, working | 0.69 | 0.51 | 0.52 | 0.68 | 0.54 | 0.66 | 0.60 | 0.66 |
| One-parent family, not working | 0.62 | 0.34 | 0.47 | 0.54 | 0.39 | 0.52 | 0.45 | 0.35 |
| Couple, both working | 0.79 | 0.62 | 0.66 | 0.82 | 0.71 | 0.78 | 0.81 | 0.74 |
| Couple, one working | 0.71 | 0.60 | 0.48 | 0.76 | 0.59 | 0.61 | 0.69 | 0.63 |
| Couple, not working | 0.69 | 0.53 | 0.51 | 0.69 | 0.38 | 0.54 | 0.61 | 0.57 |
| Families, two working adults | 0.82 | 0.62 | 0.65 | 0.82 | 0.70 | 0.77 | 0.75 | 0.72 |
| Families, one working adult | 0.77 | 0.59 | 0.55 | 0.75 | 0.60 | 0.63 | 0.67 | 0.62 |
| Families, no working adults | 0.59 | 0.41 | 0.44 | 0.58 | 0.38 | 0.66 | 0.57 | 0.55 |
| Extended families, two or more working | 0.79* | 0.56* | 0.58 | 0.74 | 0.62 | 0.79 | 0.79* | 0.73 |
| Extended families, one or none working | 0.73 | 0.71 | 0.51 | 0.77 | 0.55 | 0.68 | 0.70 | 0.67 |

Note: Average welfare levels marked with an * are calculated on a subgroup consisting of less than 10 households.

all countries a systematically lower welfare level for non-working households, compared to their working equivalents. The differences between countries are also striking: in some countries (Belgium, Germany) not one category is poor on average ($U(y) < 0.50$)); in others (Italy, the Netherlands, the United Kingdom) poverty is on average concentrated in single-person households or one-parent families. In Denmark, France and Ireland poverty is also found on average in non-working families with children. In France couples with one breadwinner, and in Ireland non-working couples are also found to be in poverty. In Ireland the welfare level of all these poor household types is on average even lower than 0.40; besides Ireland, figures as low as this are only found in France and Denmark. Whereas Germany has no household category with average welfare lower than 0.54, France has no category with average welfare level higher than 0.66. This is lowest of all countries; even Ireland has a maximum welfare level of 0.70 (for families with two working adults).

As mentioned above, these welfare levels are averages per household type. Within these household types, differences in welfare may exist due to differences in, e.g., education, age, and sex.
In order to restrict the number of tables within this text, the full tables with welfare levels differentiated according to education, age and, if relevant, occupation and age of the main breadwinner are given in the appendix to this chapter. No differentiation is given for extended families, as their number was too small in some countries.
The main conclusions these tables yield are:

(1) Single person, working

As we have seen in table 8.1 this category was poor on average in France; from table 8.4 in the appendix it appears that this holds for all ages, all educational levels, all occupations and both sexes. Differentiated with respect to age, poverty amongst working single persons is found in Ireland in age class 50-60 and in Denmark in age class 60-67. In Ireland manual workers in this category are found to be poor on average.

(2) Single person, not working

In the three countries where this category was found to be poor on average (France, Italy, Ireland), it appears that poverty is found in all age groups, for all levels of education, for all occupations and for both sexes. With respect to age, people younger than about 50 in this category are found to be poor in Denmark, Belgium and Germany. The lowest level of education gives an additional group of poor in Italy, the UK and Denmark. With respect to sex we find in two countries males within this category are above the poverty threshold, while females are below (Belgium and UK).

(3) One-parent family, working

Although this category is not poor on average in any country, in all countries certain subgroups are found to be poor. No single characteristic prevails in all countries.

(4) One-parent family, not working

This household type, which is poor on average in almost all countries, does not yield main differences for subcategories according to age and education. With respect to sex it should be noted that in most countries the main breadwinners in this category are almost always women.

(5) Couples, both working

This category is relatively well off in all countries, in all subcategories: one exception is France, where farmers within this category are found to be in poverty.

(6) Couples, one working

The poor in this category in France are found in various occupational classes, among which manual workers and farmers/self-employed. Farmers in the Netherlands and Ireland are also found to be poor.

(7) Couples, not working

Non-working couples are poor in Ireland in all age, educational and occupational classes. Vulnerable groups in other countries are farmers, manual workers and lower educational groups.

(8) Families, both adults working

Families with both adults working are overall well off, except in Denmark for the subgroup 60-67 years.

(9) Families, one working

Families where one person is working are in general above the poverty threshold, except for old-aged families, and farmers in France, Belgium and UK.

(10) Families, not working

Non-working families are overall found to be in poverty in Ireland,

France and Denmark. In addition various subgroups according to age, education and former occupation are found to be poor in all countries.

For all categories it is furthermore striking that
- Poverty is concentrated on average in the categories non-working. If the age categories between household types are compared, it appears that non-working old-aged do not have systematical lower welfare than other age categories that are not working. If, however, one compares the welfare of non-working pensioners with the welfare level of working families, couples or single persons, it appears that there is a decrease in welfare when one stops working. That holds, however, for all ages, and the difference in welfare between working and non-working families is in some countries much larger for younger people (unemployed or disabled).
- A higher education does not in general yield a higher welfare level. Especially in households where both adults are working, the increase in welfare needs appears to be of the same order of magnitude as the increase in income due to education.[2]

This finding may be interpreted in different ways. It may indicate that the human capital theory with respect to education holds, in a situation of perfect competition and equal access to education for everybody. Everybody maximizes life-time welfare, given different tastes and preferences, and chooses a certain amount of investment in human capital. Everybody ends up at the same welfare level, because in the situation of perfect competition they are paid exactly the amount of money that makes them indifferent between their actual education and another level of education. The result may also be explained in terms of Tinbergen's theory of compensating differentials for effort and tension; everybody is exactly compensated for the investment in education and responsibility that goes with the job, resulting in equal welfare levels. The fact that people do have different levels of education is the result of individual tastes and abilities. A third explanation, however, is in terms of preference and reference effects: people with higher education will have higher incomes and a social reference group with higher incomes; they tend to adapt their welfare function of income accordingly. If the reference and preference effects add up to one, no increase in welfare is perceived, as a result of the increase in income. This last interpretation implies that there may very well be separate labour markets with restricted access, but that the monopoly rents of certain professions do not in the end lead to higher welfare.

We will not be able to conclude from our data which of these interpretations reflects reality best, as reference effects and cost effects cannot be separated in our study. A future extension of research along these lines seems, however, interesting.

Finally, it should be noted that we have compared welfare levels, not income levels. Two different household types may derive a similar welfare level from quite different incomes. As an illustration, in table 8.2 the income levels in Denmark are given for two different categories, which both on average have a welfare level of 0.62.

Table 8.2 Household types within one country (Denmark) with different incomes but equal welfare levels

|  | both working couples | both working families |
|---|---|---|
| $\overline{y}$ [a] | 30,879 | 34,170 |
| $\overline{\exp(\mu)}$ [a] | 27,013 | 30,082 |
| $\overline{\sigma}$ | 0.34 | 0.32 |
| $\overline{U(y)}$ | 0.62 | 0.62 |

[a] In Dutch guilders per year.[3]

We see there are both differences in income levels, probably reflecting child benefits and tax structures, and differences in needs as reflected by $\exp(\mu)$, reflecting the cost of children. If the differences in income are only the result of child benefits, the family allowance system in Denmark can according to this comparison be said to be welfare neutral.

A similar comparison may be made between countries; a welfare level for a certain household type may be the same in two countries, although it may be the result of different income levels.

We see, e.g., that for "both working" families in Belgium and Germany the average welfare level equals 0.82 while their income levels differ considerably as shown in table 8.3.

Table 8.3  Working families in different countries with different incomes but similar welfare levels

|  | Belgium | Germany |
|---|---|---|
| $\bar{y}$ [a] | 49.174 | 42.948 |
| exp ($\mu$) | 31.059 | 27.638 |
| $\bar{\sigma}$ | 0.44 | 0.44 |
| $\overline{U(y)}$ | 0.82 | 0.82 |

[a] In Dutch guilders per year.[3]

The higher average income in Belgium results in higher needs than in Germany, while the same welfare level is derived from a different income. These differences may also be the result of non-cash transfers and government expenditures.

This first impression of the data gives some insight in the characteristics that make people poverty prone. In all countries non-working families have a welfare level which is considerably lower than working families. Moreover, single persons and one-parent families appear to have low welfare on average. As mentioned, this is due to the net effect of these characteristics on the income and welfare parameters. In order to examine these two effects separately, we will now discuss the determinants of income and needs separately. We will return to a multivariate analysis of poverty determinants in chapter 11.

## NOTES TO CHAPTER 8

[1] This is the result of our definition
$\ln y_\delta^* = \mu + \sigma u_\delta$, and $u_{0.5} = \Phi^{-1}(0.5;0,1) = 0$.

[2] In the Netherlands, the United Kingdom and, to some extent, in Belgium we even find decreasing welfare levels with education for both working families.

[3] In these and following tables all income levels all converted to Dutch guilders per year using the exchange rate at the survey period, and a correction factor for differences in purchasing power. The exchange rates for October 1, 1979 are (1 Dutch guilder = ... "national currency"):

| | |
|---|---|
| Belgium | 14.49 BFr. |
| Denmark | 2.63 DKr. |
| France | 2.12 FFr. |
| Germany | 0.90 DM |
| Great Britain | 0.24 £ |
| Ireland | 0.24 £ |
| Italy | 414 Liras |

The purchasing power parities used give the equivalent amount of 1 Dutch guilder for each country (in Dutch guilders):

| | |
|---|---|
| Belgium | Dfl. 1.05 |
| Denmark | Dfl. 1.30 |
| France | Dfl. 1.00 |
| Germany | Dfl. 1.03 |
| Great Britain | Dfl. 0.94 |
| Ireland | Dfl. 0.89 |
| Italy | Dfl. 0.74 |

Source: Central Bureau of Statistics, Monthly Price Bulletin, March, 1980.

APPENDIX TO CHAPTER 8

Table 8.4  Average welfare levels; single person, working
(welfare levels marked by an asterisk are based on subgroups smaller than 10)

|  |  | BEL | DEN | FRA | GER | IRE | ITA | NET | UK |
|---|---|---|---|---|---|---|---|---|---|
| age | < 30 | 0.59 | 0.53 | 0.44 | 0.68 | 0.65 | 0.57 | 0.69 | 0.61 |
|  | 30 - 40 | 0.63 | 0.55 | 0.44 | 0.68 | 0.61* | 0.63 | 0.65 | 0.76 |
|  | 40 - 50 | 0.59* | 0.50 | 0.42 | 0.68 | 0.64* | 0.52 | 0.69 | 0.47* |
|  | 50 - 60 | 0.57* | 0.51 | 0.45 | 0.68 | 0.38 | 0.66 | 0.71 | 0.58 |
|  | 60 - 67 | - | 0.49 | 0.47* | 0.71* | 0.64 | 0.60 | 0.56* | - |
|  | > 67 | 0.67* | 0.63* | 0.39* | 0.72* | 0.79* | 0.63* | 0.10* | - |
| education | 1 | 0.71* | 0.52 | 0.39 | 0.67 | 0.53 | 0.51 | 0.53 | 0.56 |
|  | 2 | 0.51 | 0.54 | 0.44 | 0.69 | 0.79* | 0.57 | 0.63 | 0.67* |
|  | 3 | 0.52* | 0.53 | 0.42 | 0.68 | 0.58 | 0.61 | 0.65 | 1.00* |
|  | 4 | 0.63* | 0.51 | 0.48 | 0.61* | 0.54* | 0.61 | 0.77 | 0.67* |
|  | 5 | 0.61 | 0.52 | 0.44 | 0.72 | - | 0.67 | 0.64* | 0.83* |
| occupation | manual | 0.61* | 0.50 | 0.40 | 0.71 | 0.49 | 0.54 | 0.56 | 0.66 |
|  | employee | 0.67 | 0.52 | 0.43 | 0.66 | 0.56 | 0.65 | 0.69 | 0.60 |
|  | civil servant | 0.71 | 0.62 | 0.47 | 0.72 | - | 0.59 | 0.72 | 0.66* |
|  | self-employed | 0.38 | 0.54 | 0.48 | 0.59 | 0.74 | 0.66 | 0.54 | 0.53* |
|  | farmer | - | 0.39* | 0.29* | 0.61* | 0.58 | 0.47* | 0.78* | - |
| sex | male | 0.60 | 0.51 | 0.46 | 0.68 | 0.56 | 0.63 | 0.66 | 0.63 |
|  | female | 0.60 | 0.54 | 0.41 | 0.69 | 0.56 | 0.56 | 0.68 | 0.60 |

Table 8.5  Average welfare levels; single person, not working

|  |  | BEL | DEN | FRA | GER | IRE | ITA | NET | UK |
|---|---|---|---|---|---|---|---|---|---|
| age | < 30 | - | 0.32 | 0.26 | 0.39 | - | 0.81* | 0.54 | - |
|  | 30 - 40 | 0.29* | 0.33 | 0.35 | 0.48* | - | - | 0.49 | - |
|  | 40 - 50 | 0.25* | 0.45 | 0.17 | 0.10* | 0.17* | 0.11 | 0.52* | - |
|  | 50 - 60 | 0.51 | 0.46 | 0.41 | 0.64 | 0.37 | 0.34 | 0.50 | 0.23* |
|  | 60 - 67 | 0.62 | 0.45 | 0.38 | 0.66 | 0.34 | 0.44 | 0.57 | 0.46* |
|  | > 67 | 0.51 | 0.53 | 0.35 | 0.62 | 0.39 | 0.50 | 0.62 | 0.38* |
| education | 1 | 0.50 | 0.47 | 0.37 | 0.61 | 0.37 | 0.44 | 0.58 | 0.30 |
|  | 2 | 0.58 | 0.53 | 0.17 | 0.57 | 0.35* | 0.41 | 0.64 | 0.60* |
|  | 3 | 0.60* | 0.30 | 0.30 | 0.61 | 0.41 | 0.54 | 0.54 | 0.68* |
|  | 4 | 0.41* | 0.31 | 0.35 | 0.66 | 0.17* | 0.74 | 0.60 | - |
|  | 5 | 0.73 | 0.54 | 0.31 | 0.60 | 0.49 | 0.62* | 0.83* | - |
| sex | male | 0.59 | 0.47 | 0.35 | 0.68 | 0.34 | 0.47 | 0.64 | 0.58* |
|  | female | 0.49 | 0.47 | 0.34 | 0.58 | 0.39 | 0.47 | 0.57 | 0.32 |

Table 8.6    Average welfare levels; one-parent family, working

|  |  | BEL | DEN | FRA | GER | IRE | ITA | NET | UK |
|---|---|---|---|---|---|---|---|---|---|
| age | < 30 | 0.68* | 0.51 | 0.47 | 0.66 | 0.56 | 0.67 | 0.72* | 0.71 |
|  | 30 - 40 | 0.67 | 0.54 | 0.48 | 0.70 | 0.51 | 0.73 | 0.60 | 0.58 |
|  | 40 - 50 | 0.62 | 0.51 | 0.59 | 0.68 | 0.55 | 0.64 | 0.48 | 0.68 |
|  | 50 - 60 | 0.81 | 0.49 | 0.57 | 0.64 | 0.58 | 0.61 | 0.66 | 0.66* |
|  | 60 - 67 | - | 0.38* | 0.48 | 0.79* | 0.45 | 0.48* | 0.68* | 0.80* |
|  | > 67 | - | 0.22* | 0.56* | - | 0.47 | 0.69* | 0.88* | - |
| education | 1 | 0.54* | 0.55 | 0.49 | 0.66 | 0.51 | 0.67 | 0.60 | 0.62 |
|  | 2 | 0.69 | 0.48 | 0.59 | 0.69 | 0.63 | 0.63 | 0.55 | 0.90* |
|  | 3 | 0.73 | 0.50 | 0.41 | 0.67 | 0.50 | 0.71 | 0.71* | 0.71* |
|  | 4 | 0.67* | 0.44* | 0.52 | - | 0.57* | 0.60 | 0.67* | 0.77* |
|  | 5 | 0.73 | 0.44* | 0.56 | 0.82* | 0.75 | 0.72 | 0.90* | 0.69* |
| occupation | manual | 0.54 | 0.48 | 0.44 | 0.70 | 0.55 | 0.74 | 0.54 | 0.65 |
|  | employee | 0.72 | 0.53 | 0.53 | 0.70 | 0.57 | 0.61 | 0.67 | 0.63 |
|  | civil servant | 0.71 | 0.52 | 0.60 | 0.82* | - | 0.68 | 0.75 | 0.70* |
|  | self-employed | 0.98* | 0.31* | 0.49 | 0.72* | 0.50 | 0.61 | 0.68* | 0.97* |
|  | farmer | - | 0.60 | 0.51 | 0.51 | 0.51 | 0.70 | 0.47* | - |
| sex | male | 0.80 | 0.49 | 0.61 | 0.67 | 0.54 | 0.71 | 0.63 | 0.73 |
|  | female | 0.67 | 0.51 | 0.49 | 0.69 | 0.54 | 0.60 | 0.58 | 0.55 |

Table 8.7    Average welfare levels; one-parent family, not working

|  |  | BEL | DEN | FRA | GER | IRE | ITA | NET | UK |
|---|---|---|---|---|---|---|---|---|---|
| age | < 30 | 0.42* | 0.31 | 0.48 | - | 0.30* | - | 0.41 | 0.29* |
|  | 30 - 40 | 0.54 | 0.25* | 0.35 | 0.61* | 0.43* | 0.54* | 0.30 | 0.72* |
|  | 40 - 50 | 0.60 | 0.34* | 0.63 | 0.57 | 0.34 | 0.61* | 0.53 | 0.34* |
|  | 50 - 60 | 0.71 | 0.36 | 0.48 | 0.44 | 0.32 | 0.51 | 0.48 | 0.17* |
|  | 60 - 67 | 0.74* | 0.57* | 0.52* | 0.56* | 0.41 | 0.63* | 0.47 | 0.31* |
|  | > 67 | 0.37* | 0.43* | 0.38 | 0.60 | 0.43 | 0.45 | 0.55 | 0.39* |
| education | 1 | 0.76 | 0.36 | 0.46 | 0.46 | 0.37 | 0.41 | 0.49 | 0.41 |
|  | 2 | 0.51 | 0.56* | - | 0.65 | 0.30* | 0.37 | 0.38 | 0.10* |
|  | 3 | 0.52* | 0.31 | 0.38 | - | 0.49 | 0.65 | 0.53 | 0.17* |
|  | 4 | 0.64 | 0.24* | 0.36* | - | 0.36* | 0.60 | 0.45 | - |
|  | 5 | 0.37* | 0.30* | 0.76* | 0.35* | 0.51* | 0.18* | - | 0.40* |
| sex | male | 0.57 | 0.48 | 0.68* | 0.66 | 0.48 | 0.53 | 0.36* | 0.29 |
|  | female | 0.63 | 0.30 | 0.45 | 0.52 | 0.33 | 0.52 | 0.46 | 0.44* |

Table 8.8   Average welfare levels; couple, both working

|  |  | BEL | DEN | FRA | GER | IRE | ITA | NET | UK |
|---|---|---|---|---|---|---|---|---|---|
| age | < 30 | 0.81 | 0.60 | 0.65 | 0.82 | 0.69 | 0.80 | 0.82 | 0.75 |
|  | 30 - 40 | 0.79 | 0.61 | 0.70 | 0.85 | 0.78 | 0.80 | 0.82 | 0.77 |
|  | 40 - 50 | 0.64 | 0.60 | 0.64 | 0.82 | 0.82* | 0.82 | 0.81 | 0.68 |
|  | 50 - 60 | 0.83* | 0.68 | 0.64 | 0.77 | 0.68* | 0.69 | 0.75 | 0.68 |
|  | 60 - 67 | - | 0.56 | 0.71* | 0.73* | - | 0.75 | 0.87* | 0.79 |
|  | > 67 | - | 0.65 | 0.65* | 0.98* | - | 0.78* | - | - |
| education | 1 | 0.80 | 0.58 | 0.54 | 0.75 | 0.71 | 0.58* | 0.72 | 0.75 |
|  | 2 | 0.75 | 0.64 | 0.67 | 0.83 | 0.68 | 0.72 | 0.81 | 0.77 |
|  | 3 | 0.82 | 0.68 | 0.71 | 0.81 | 0.73 | 0.84 | 0.81 | 0.70 |
|  | 4 | 0.80 | 0.54 | 0.70 | 0.85 | 0.73* | 0.79 | 0.83 | 0.61* |
|  | 5 | 0.75 | 0.64 | 0.68 | 0.84 | 0.74 | 0.79 | 0.90 | 0.74 |
| occupation | manual | 0.84 | 0.62 | 0.67 | 0.78 | 0.72 | 0.84 | 0.77 | 0.73 |
|  | employee | 0.79 | 0.63 | 0.68 | 0.83 | 0.68 | 0.80 | 0.82 | 0.76 |
|  | civil servant | 0.77 | 0.61 | 0.65 | 0.85 | - | 0.74 | 0.84 | 0.71 |
|  | self-employed | 0.69 | 0.64 | 0.60 | 0.85 | 0.70* | 0.79 | 0.83 | 0.70 |
|  | farmer | 0.72* | 0.55 | 0.47 | 0.74* | 0.89* | 0.63 | - | - |

Table 8.9   Average welfare levels; couple, one working

|  |  | BEL | DEN | FRA | GER | IRE | ITA | NET | UK |
|---|---|---|---|---|---|---|---|---|---|
| age | < 30 | 0.79 | 0.61 | 0.49 | 0.68 | 0.69* | 0.61 | 0.70 | 0.65 |
|  | 30 - 40 | 0.84 | 0.45* | 0.44 | 0.75 | 0.60 | 0.69 | 0.70 | 0.52 |
|  | 40 - 50 | 0.66 | 0.54 | 0.53 | 0.76 | 0.56* | 0.52 | 0.70 | 0.68 |
|  | 50 - 60 | 0.67 | 0.59 | 0.48 | 0.77 | 0.65 | 0.62 | 0.68 | 0.62 |
|  | 60 - 67 | 0.74 | 0.65 | 0.53 | 0.78 | 0.57 | 0.56 | 0.69 | 0.60 |
|  | > 67 | 0.58* | 0.55 | 0.28* | 0.89* | 0.48 | 0.72 | 0.71 | 0.72* |
| education | 1 | 0.69 | 0.59 | 0.41 | 0.75 | 0.51 | 0.58 | 0.72 | 0.63 |
|  | 2 | 0.67 | 0.67 | 0.51 | 0.76 | 0.74 | 0.57 | 0.67 | 0.66 |
|  | 3 | 0.71 | 0.61 | 0.44 | 0.75 | 0.74 | 0.65 | 0.66 | 0.70 |
|  | 4 | 0.75 | 0.54 | 0.49 | 0.77* | 0.65* | 0.61 | 0.73 | 0.68* |
|  | 5 | 0.73 | 0.63 | 0.62 | 0.71* | 0.86* | 0.77 | 0.72 | 0.48* |
| occupation | manual | 0.71 | 0.64 | 0.43 | 0.77 | 0.60 | 0.64 | 0.67 | 0.64 |
|  | employee | 0.72 | 0.58 | 0.63 | 0.75 | 0.67 | 0.64 | 0.74 | 0.61 |
|  | civil servant | 0.75 | 0.64 | 0.48 | 0.68 | - | 0.61 | 0.69 | 0.66 |
|  | self-employed | 0.59 | 0.61 | 0.58 | 0.80 | 0.60 | 0.59 | 0.65 | 0.67* |
|  | farmer | - | 0.52 | 0.19 | 0.81* | 0.47 | 0.59 | 0.45* | - |
| sex | male | 0.73 | 0.61 | 0.50 | 0.76 | 0.59 | 0.62 | 0.70 | 0.63 |
|  | female | 0.56 | 0.55 | 0.39 | 0.73 | 0.69* | 0.57 | 0.64 | 0.63 |

Table 8.10  Average welfare levels; couples, not working

|  |  | BEL | DEN | FRA | GER | IRE | ITA | NET | UK |
|---|---|---|---|---|---|---|---|---|---|
| age | < 30 | - | 0.29 | 0.36 | 0.43* | - | - | 0.57* | - |
|  | 30 - 40 | - | 0.36* | 0.25* | 0.62* | 0.10* | 0.70* | 0.47* | - |
|  | 40 - 50 | - | 0.36* | 0.67* | - | 0.18* | - | 0.63* | - |
|  | 50 - 60 | 0.76 | 0.59 | 0.49 | - | 0.34* | 0.53 | 0.49 | 0.55* |
|  | 60 - 67 | 0.67 | 0.55 | 0.54 | 0.72 | 0.46 | 0.55 | 0.61 | 0.52 |
|  | > 67 | 0.68 | 0.53 | 0.51 | 0.67 | 0.35 | 0.54 | 0.63 | 0.62 |
| education | 1 | 0.67 | 0.53 | 0.47 | 0.69 | 0.38 | 0.45 | 0.59 | 0.59 |
|  | 2 | 0.63 | 0.57 | 0.53 | 0.67 | 0.16* | 0.55 | 0.58 | 0.52 |
|  | 3 | 0.80 | 0.43* | 0.55 | 0.81 | 0.20 | 0.57 | 0.66 | 0.51* |
|  | 4 | 0.70 | 0.24* | 0.58 | 0.65* | 0.43* | 0.74 | 0.68 | 0.48* |
|  | 5 | 0.67* | 0.62* | 0.58 | 0.55* | 0.52* | 0.63* | 0.90* | - |

Table 8.11  Average welfare levels; families, both working

|  |  | BEL | DEN | FRA | GER | IRE | ITA | NET | UK |
|---|---|---|---|---|---|---|---|---|---|
| age | < 30 | 0.81 | 0.62 | 0.67 | 0.82 | 0.48* | 0.78 | 0.75 | 0.75 |
|  | 30 - 40 | 0.81 | 0.63 | 0.66 | 0.84 | 0.68 | 0.76 | 0.78 | 0.71 |
|  | 40 - 50 | 0.86 | 0.64 | 0.65 | 0.80 | 0.71 | 0.76 | 0.72 | 0.73 |
|  | 50 - 60 | 0.75 | 0.56 | 0.57 | 0.82 | 0.75 | 0.80 | 0.73 | 0.69 |
|  | 60 - 67 | 0.48* | 0.45 | 0.60* | 0.74* | 0.73 | 0.82 | 0.74* | 0.91* |
|  | > 67 | 0.97* | - | - | - | - | 0.89* | - | - |
| education | 1 | 0.84 | 0.62 | 0.59 | 0.74 | 0.73 | 0.74 | 0.78 | 0.73 |
|  | 2 | 0.84 | 0.62 | 0.65 | 0.83 | 0.66 | 0.74 | 0.74 | 0.71 |
|  | 3 | 0.78 | 0.61 | 0.65 | 0.81 | 0.62 | 0.78 | 0.76 | 0.72 |
|  | 4 | 0.82 | 0.64 | 0.68 | 0.85* | 0.71 | 0.79 | 0.76 | 0.67 |
|  | 5 | 0.81 | 0.60 | 0.71 | 0.83 | 0.75 | 0.80 | 0.72 | 0.63 |
| occupation | manual | 0.86 | 0.63 | 0.59 | 0.80 | 0.69 | 0.78 | 0.77 | 0.74 |
|  | employee | 0.83 | 0.65 | 0.70 | 0.84 | 0.72 | 0.80 | 0.76 | 0.70 |
|  | civil servant | 0.79 | 0.58 | 0.68 | 0.80 | - | 0.76 | 0.76 | 0.70 |
|  | self-employed | 0.77 | 0.60 | 0.69 | 0.86 | 0.66 | 0.78 | 0.72 | 0.65 |
|  | farmer | 0.81 | 0.58 | 0.54 | 0.79 | 0.64 | 0.63 | 0.69 | - |

Table 8.12  Average welfare levels; families, one working

|  |  | BEL | DEN | FRA | GER | IRE | ITA | NET | UK |
|---|---|---|---|---|---|---|---|---|---|
| age | < 30 | 0.77 | 0.57 | 0.53 | 0.72 | 0.58 | 0.65 | 0.64 | 0.59 |
|  | 30 - 40 | 0.77 | 0.61 | 0.58 | 0.76 | 0.58 | 0.61 | 0.68 | 0.62 |
|  | 40 - 50 | 0.77 | 0.59 | 0.54 | 0.74 | 0.62 | 0.61 | 0.67 | 0.65 |
|  | 50 - 60 | 0.76 | 0.58 | 0.51 | 0.73 | 0.62 | 0.64 | 0.64 | 0.59 |
|  | 60 - 67 | 0.79 | 0.55 | 0.56 | 0.83 | 0.61 | 0.70 | 0.71 | 0.63 |
|  | > 67 | 0.16* | 0.60* | 0.47* | - | 0.53 | 0.74 | 0.78* | - |
| education | 1 | 0.74 | 0.56 | 0.48 | 0.72 | 0.57 | 0.60 | 0.66 | 0.61 |
|  | 2 | 0.75 | 0.63 | 0.56 | 0.74 | 0.59 | 0.58 | 0.65 | 0.59 |
|  | 3 | 0.79 | 0.63 | 0.65 | 0.77 | 0.65 | 0.63 | 0.68 | 0.66 |
|  | 4 | 0.77 | 0.61 | 0.59 | 0.76 | 0.54 | 0.66 | 0.70 | 0.54 |
|  | 5 | 0.77 | 0.58 | 0.58 | 0.76 | 0.66 | 0.75 | 0.70 | 0.61 |
| occupation | manual | 0.77 | 0.58 | 0.51 | 0.73 | 0.58 | 0.59 | 0.63 | 0.60 |
|  | employee | 0.79 | 0.63 | 0.62 | 0.77 | 0.64 | 0.69 | 0.67 | 0.64 |
|  | civil servant | 0.74 | 0.57 | 0.57 | 0.76 | - | 0.58 | 0.71 | 0.60 |
|  | self-employed | 0.73 | 0.58 | 0.52 | 0.71 | 0.65 | 0.62 | 0.70 | 0.67 |
|  | farmer | - | 0.53 | 0.48 | 0.75 | 0.55 | 0.68 | 0.74 | 0.15* |
| sex | male | 0.77 | 0.59 | 0.55 | 0.74 | 0.60 | 0.63 | 0.67 | 0.62 |
|  | female | 0.70* | 0.50 | 0.41 | 0.91* | 0.54 | 0.61 | 0.71* | 0.24* |

Table 8.13  Average welfare levels; families, not working

|  |  | BEL | DEN | FRA | GER | IRE | ITA | NET | UK |
|---|---|---|---|---|---|---|---|---|---|
| age | < 30 | 0.61* | 0.43* | 0.62* | 0.24* | 0.19 | - | 0.32* | 0.16 |
|  | 30 - 40 | 0.57* | 0.51 | 0.19 | 0.51* | 0.34 | 0.91* | 0.48* | 0.67* |
|  | 40 - 50 | 0.41* | - | 0.37 | 0.67 | 0.35 | 0.73* | 0.42 | 0.53* |
|  | 50 - 60 | 0.60 | 0.30* | 0.35 | 0.49 | 0.34 | 0.58 | 0.58 | 0.52 |
|  | 60 - 67 | 0.63 | 0.40* | 0.54 | 0.69 | 0.40 | 0.57 | 0.62 | 0.61 |
|  | > 67 | 0.67 | 0.12* | 0.69 | 0.67 | 0.47 | 0.64 | 0.66 | 0.39 |
| education | 1 | 0.56 | 0.39 | 0.38 | 0.51 | 0.38 | 0.51 | 0.49 | 0.50 |
|  | 2 | 0.49* | 0.36* | 0.58 | 0.64 | 0.90* | 0.60 | 0.60 | 0.73* |
|  | 3 | - | 0.71* | 0.38 | 0.40* | 0.39 | 0.59 | 0.56 | 0.76* |
|  | 4 | 0.63* | - | 0.63* | 0.86* | 0.35* | 0.65 | 0.78 | - |
|  | 5 | 0.73* | 0.37* | 0.64* | 0.58* | 0.44* | 0.62 | - | 0.61* |

## Chapter 9
## EMPIRICAL RESULTS: DETERMINANTS OF INCOME

In this chapter we will discuss the results of the estimation of income functions for all countries. As mentioned in chapter 3, we have estimated individual income functions for men and women who are working, and for households where the main breadwinner is not working. With respect to the functional specification of the income functions, both the specifications in age and in log age have been estimated (see the appendix to chapter 3); it appeared that in all countries except Italy the specification with log age fitted significantly better to our data. For the Italian data the difference in fit was negligible. Therefore we used the specification with log age for all countries.

For the definition of the variables used we refer to the appendix to chapter 3. The results for male incomes are given in section 1, for female incomes in section 2, and the non-earned incomes in section 3. Section 4 compares the three different income functions, and draws some conclusions on household income. Within each section, the results are discussed per country; in the presentation of the results of Belgium, the first country, the interpretation of the coefficients is discussed extensively as an example. In all tables, standard errors are given in parentheses.

### 9.1 Individual income functions for working men

The income functions are presented in three different specifications: firstly, a general specification where the age-income profile is supposed to be the same for everybody; secondly, a specification where the age-income profile varies with education, and thirdly, a specification where the age-income profile varies with occupation. Hence, the intercepts for different occupations and for education in the first version will indicate their average effect on income. The specific effects of education and occupation on the age-income profile will be illustrated graphically for each country in the appendix to this chapter.

All age-income profiles presented are based on cross-sectional data and may not be interpreted as life-time income profiles. They do reflect differences in income structure for different age cohorts in the year of the survey rather than individual changes over time.

### 9.1.1 Belgium

In table 9.1 the OLS results of the estimation of the income equation are given for the Belgian data. If we first look at the estimates in column 1, it is seen[1] that the degree of urbanization does not have a significant influence on income.[2] The coefficients of the variable "fluctuations in income" are positive, in line with the risk aversion hypothesis; they are not, however, significantly different from zero. There appears to be a significant occupational effect on income for employees, who have a higher income than men in other occupations.

Two educational variables are distinguished in Belgium; general education and technical education. General education has been normalized following the procedure described in the appendix to chapter 3. In interpreting the coefficients of this variable, it should be reminded that a standard person, with a value for general education of zero, is in the fifth decile of the education distribution. This implies that someone in the ninth decile has an income which is $\exp[0.166 \times \phi^{-1}(0.90;0,1)] = 1.25$ times the income of a standard person. Someone in the first decile, on the other hand, has an income which is $\exp[0.166 \times \phi^{-1}(0.10;0,1)] = 0.80$ times the income of a standard person. Technical education has been included as a dummy variable; its coefficient reflects that the income of someone with technical education is $\exp[-0.020] = 0.98$ times the income of a person with standard general education. The coefficients of ln age and ln²age appear to be significantly different from zero, and have the expected signs. The age at which the maximum income in our cross-section is reached is equal to $\exp[\frac{4.328}{2(0.546)}]$, which is 53 years.

The $\bar{R}^2$ of this equation is 0.31; the number of observations was 952.

Let us now turn to column 2, where cross-products of age and education have been added.

With respect to general education, significant differences in age-income profiles arise for different educational levels. The coefficients can be interpreted as follows. If there holds

$$\ln y = \alpha_0 - \alpha_1 \ln^2 \text{age} + \alpha_2 \ln \text{age} - \alpha_3 \text{educ} \ln^2 \text{age} + \alpha_4 \text{educ} \ln \text{age}$$

where "educ" is a score on the increasing educational scale, the age at

Table 9.1  Income function for working men in BELGIUM

| | | | |
|---|---|---|---|
| intercept | 1.483 (1.937) | 2.517 (2.406) | 4.722 (3.329) |
| small town | -0.046 (0.025) | -0.047 (0.025) | -0.033 (0.025) |
| large town | -0.041 (0.024) | -0.047 (0.023) | -0.042 (0.023) |
| small fluctuations | 0.023 (0.024) | 0.020 (0.024) | 0.030 (0.024) |
| large fluctuations | 0.093 (0.052) | 0.096 (0.051) | 0.071 (0.051) |
| employee | 0.110 (0.028) | 0.119 (0.027) | -7.220 (4.453) |
| civil servant | 0.017 (0.029) | 0.018 (0.028) | 1.019 (4.991) |
| self-employed/farmer | 0.008 (0.042) | 0.017 (0.042) | -11.559 (6.025) |
| general education | 0.166 (0.015) | -7.254 (2.494) | 0.156 (0.015) |
| tech. educ. (dummy) | -0.020 (0.023) | 0.624 (4.301) | -0.039 (0.022) |
| ln age | 4.328 (1.072) | 3.852 (1.323) | 2.837 (1.845) |
| ln²age | -0.546 (0.147) | -0.489 (0.181) | -0.378 (0.255) |
| gen. educ. × ln age | | 3.808 (1.358) | |
| gen. educ. × ln²age | | -0.484 (0.184) | |
| tech. dummy × ln age | | -0.264 (2.387) | |
| tech. dummy × ln²age | | 0.022 (0.330) | |
| employee × ln age | | | 3.597 (2.461) |
| employee × ln²age | | | -0.432 (0.339) |
| civil servant × ln age | | | -1.040 (2.751) |
| civil servant × ln²age | | | 0.210 (0.378) |
| self-empl./farmer × ln age | | | 6.511 (3.325) |
| self-empl./farmer × ln²age | | | -0.908 (0.456) |
| one-parent family | 0.126 (0.146) | 0.052 (0.144) | 0.037 (0.143) |
| couple, both working | 0.184 (0.090) | 0.127 (0.089) | 0.126 (0.089) |
| couple, one working | 0.172 (0.090) | 0.143 (0.089) | 0.104 (0.089) |
| family, both working | 0.212 (0.084) | 0.165 (0.083) | 0.169 (0.083) |
| family, one working | 0.323 (0.083) | 0.270 (0.082) | 0.266 (0.082) |
| extended family, working | 0.264 (0.096) | 0.227 (0.095) | 0.208 (0.095) |
| number of observations | 952 | 952 | 952 |
| $\bar{R}^2$ | 0.307 | 0.335 | 0.346 |

Note: a) Farmers are not included as a separate category; they are included in the category self-employed.
b) Technical education has been included as a dummy variable, which equals 1 if the respondent has a technical education, and 0 otherwise.
c) Standard errors in parentheses.

which the maximum income is earned is

$$\text{age}_{max} = \exp\left[\frac{\alpha_2 + \alpha_4 \text{educ}}{2(\alpha_1 + \alpha_3 \text{educ})}\right]$$

Hence the maximum age is larger with increasing education if

$$\frac{d \ln age_{max}}{d\, educ} = \{\frac{2[\alpha_4(\alpha_1 + \alpha_3 educ) - \alpha_3(\alpha_2 + \alpha_4 educ)]}{2^2(\alpha_1 + \alpha_3 educ)^2}\} > 0,$$

or $\alpha_1\alpha_4 - \alpha_2\alpha_3 > 0$.

For Belgium we have $\alpha_1\alpha_4 - \alpha_2\alpha_3 = 0.501 \times 3.426 - 3.945 \times 0.432 > 0$, implying that people with a higher level of general education reach their maximum income at a later age.

These results are illustrated in figure 9.1.a in the appendix, where age-income profiles are given for different educational levels in Belgium. The intercept is found by substituting the marginal frequency found in the population of all other variables for each educational subgroup:

$$\ln y(educ) = a_0(educ) + (a_1 + a_3 educ) \ln^2 age + (a_2 + a_4 educ) \ln age$$

where $a_0(educ) = \sum_{k=1}^{K} fx_k(educ)\hat{y}_k$, which is the average value of all other characteristics found in the sample for education level "educ". The age-income profiles, presented for five educational groups show that at the lowest educational level hardly any differences are found over age, while for the highest education a rather steep increasing profile is found until about 50 years of age, after which income decreases considerably. Below the age of 25, however, we see that lower educational groups have relatively high incomes.

The results in the third column show that the age-occupation terms do not have coefficients significantly different from zero. This should be borne in mind when looking at the occupationally differentiated age-income profiles in figure 9.1.b in the appendix. Manual workers have relatively high incomes when very young, while between 25 and 30 the self-employed earn most. Between about 30 and 50 this holds for employees, and for older cohorts the civil servants are found to be best off.

Finally we note that a single person in Belgium has lowest after-tax income, and a single breadwinner in a family with children has highest after-tax income. This reflects different tax structures for different household types and possibly longer working weeks for main breadwinners in a family.

## 9.1.2 Denmark

Table 9.2 shows the estimation results of the income function for the Danish men. It is seen that men living in a large city (more than 100.000 inhabitants) have a significantly lower log income; this indicates that the effect of the "flight to the suburbs" is stronger than migration to the towns in Denmark. The coefficients of fluctuations in income do not confirm the risk aversion hypothesis; no positive risk premium is found in Denmark. The occupational dummies show that employees have the highest log income, and civil servants come next. The income of farmers is significantly lower than all occupational categories. It should be remembered, though, that only monetary income is included in ln y; there may be a substantial income in kind. The table shows that income increases significantly with level of education. In Denmark all educational levels could be ordered unambiguously on one scale, so there are no separate variables for technical and general education. In Denmark somebody in the ninth educational decile has an income that is 1.11 times the income of a standard person while someone in the first decile has an income of 90 % of the standard person.

The coefficients of ln age and ln²age are also significantly different from zero; the age at which the maximum income is reached equals 40. The $\bar{R}^2$ for this equation is 0.276. $\bar{R}^2$ increases to respectively 0.288 and 0.300 if cross-product terms for education and occupation are added to the equation. This is shown in the second and third column of table 9.2. It is seen that the higher the education, the higher the age at which a maximum income is earned. The age at which higher education starts to pay off is about 30. Employees reach their maximum income at 42 years of age, manual workers at 40 and self-employed at 42; farmers reach their (low) top income at 31 years of age. Civil servants have highest incomes in young and old age cohorts; employees have highest incomes for cohorts between 25 and 55. Farmers have, after the age of 25, considerably lower incomes than all others. The results are illustrated in figures 9.2.a and 9.2.b in the appendix. With respect to household composition the same pattern is found as in Belgium: single persons have lowest after-tax income, while single breadwinners of a family with children have highest after-tax income.

Table 9.2  Income function for working men in DENMARK

| | | | |
|---|---|---|---|
| intercept | -5.707 (1.659) | -1.542 (1.812) | -5.128 (2.302) |
| small town | -0.018 (0.028) | -0.022 (0.027) | -0.020 (0.028) |
| large town | -0.079 (0.028) | -0.072 (0.028) | -0.082 (0.028) |
| small fluctuations | -0.025 (0.030) | -0.014 (0.030) | -0.023 (0.030) |
| large fluctuations | -0.066 (0.043) | -0.047 (0.043) | -0.063 (0.043) |
| employee | 0.131 (0.030) | 0.140 (0.029) | -2.825 (3.856) |
| civil servant | 0.080 (0.038) | 0.079 (0.037) | 11.168 (5.177) |
| self-employed | 0.032 (0.038) | 0.018 (0.038) | 0.344 (5.421) |
| farmer | -0.403 (0.047) | -0.367 (0.046) | 2.809 (8.407) |
| general education | 0.079 (0.015) | -1.626 (1.852) | 0.082 (0.015) |
| ln age | 8.382 (0.922) | 6.220 (0.995) | 8.097 (1.293) |
| ln$^2$age | -1.133 (0.127) | -0.850 (0.136) | -1.099 (0.180) |
| gen. educ. × ln age | | 0.592 (1.012) | |
| gen. educ. × ln$^2$age | | -0.034 (0.138) | |
| employee × ln age | | | 1.468 (2.145) |
| employee × ln$^2$age | | | -0.179 (0.297) |
| civil servant × ln age | | | -6.255 (2.853) |
| civil servant × ln$^2$age | | | 0.876 (0.391) |
| self-employed × ln age | | | -0.251 (2.919) |
| self-employed × ln$^2$age | | | 0.045 (0.392) |
| farmer × ln age | | | -1.098 (4.372) |
| farmer × ln$^2$age | | | 0.073 (0.568) |
| one-parent family | 0.181 (0.108) | 0.137 (0.107) | 0.170 (0.108) |
| couple, both working | 0.146 (0.050) | 0.113 (0.050) | 0.154 (0.050) |
| couple, one working | 0.283 (0.059) | 0.255 (0.058) | 0.295 (0.059) |
| family, both working | 0.214 (0.049) | 0.178 (0.049) | 0.222 (0.049) |
| family, one working | 0.359 (0.053) | 0.311 (0.053) | 0.364 (0.053) |
| extended family, working | 0.117 (0.106) | 0.066 (0.104) | 0.089 (0.106) |
| number of observations | 1369 | 1369 | 1369 |
| $\bar{R}^2$ | 0.276 | 0.301 | 0.288 |

### 9.1.3 France

In table 9.3 the French estimation results of the income equation are given. It is seen that men living in a large town have a significantly higher income than those living in rural areas. Men with large fluctuations in income have an income which is significantly lower than the income of people with a steady income. We furthermore see that highest incomes are found for self-employed, while farmers have an income which is much, and significantly, lower than that of manual workers. In France two variables for education have been distinguished, general and technical education. It is seen that the higher the general education, the higher the income level. Someone in the ninth educational decile earns

Table 9.3  Income function for working men in FRANCE

| | | | |
|---|---|---|---|
| intercept | 0.939 (1.422) | 0.740 (1.677) | 5.942 (2.086) |
| small town | 0.048 (0.027) | 0.045 (0.027) | 0.045 (0.026) |
| large town | 0.072 (0.023) | 0.073 (0.022) | 0.068 (0.022) |
| small fluctuations | 0.014 (0.023) | 0.013 (0.023) | 0.021 (0.023) |
| large fluctuations | -0.079 (0.034) | -0.077 (0.033) | -0.084 (0.033) |
| employee | 0.181 (0.027) | 0.188 (0.026) | -5.592 (3.426) |
| civil servant | 0.143 (0.029) | 0.153 (0.028) | -3.186 (3.944) |
| self-employed | 0.248 (0.033) | 0.245 (0.033) | -5.454 (4.360) |
| farmer | -0.239 (0.052) | -0.220 (0.052) | -17.223 (6.517) |
| general education | 0.194 (0.016) | -2.198 (2.019) | 0.195 (0.015) |
| tech. educ. (dummy) | 0.030 (0.022) | 5.243 (2.984) | 0.016 (0.022) |
| ln age | 4.535 (0.801) | 4.661 (0.937) | 1.818 (1.182) |
| ln²age | -0.579 (0.112) | -0.595 (0.130) | -0.213 (0.166) |
| gen. educ. × ln age | | 1.026 (1.119) | |
| gen. educ. × ln²age | | -0.100 (0.154) | |
| tech. dummy × ln age | | -2.842 (1.685) | |
| tech. dummy × ln²age | | 0.382 (0.237) | |
| employee × ln age | | | 2.891 (1.933) |
| employee × ln²age | | | -0.354 (0.271) |
| civil servant × ln age | | | 1.543 (2.244) |
| civil servant × ln²age | | | -0.169 (0.314) |
| self-employed × ln age | | | 3.189 (2.419) |
| self-employed × ln²age | | | -0.442 (0.334) |
| farmer × ln age | | | 9.984 (3.530) |
| farmer × ln²age | | | -1.441 (0.476) |
| one-parent family | 0.231 (0.073) | 0.208 (0.072) | 0.217 (0.073) |
| couple, both working | 0.049 (0.040) | 0.058 (0.039) | 0.074 (0.039) |
| couple, one working | 0.119 (0.041) | 0.105 (0.041) | 0.122 (0.041) |
| family, both working | 0.167 (0.035) | 0.152 (0.035) | 0.171 (0.035) |
| family, one working | 0.232 (0.034) | 0.217 (0.034) | 0.239 (0.034) |
| extended family, working | 0.144 (0.067) | 0.139 (0.066) | 0.162 (0.066) |
| number of observations | 1545 | 1545 | 1545 |
| $\bar{R}^2$ | 0.341 | 0.362 | 0.371 |

$\exp[0.197 \times \Phi^{-1}(0.9;0,1)] = 1.29$ times the income of someone halfway on the educational range, while someone in the first educational decile earns $\exp[0.197 \times \Phi^{-1}(0.1;0,1)] = 0.77$ times the standard income. People with a technical education have a slightly higher income than a standard person in the fifth decile of the general educational distribution. The coefficients for ln age and ln²age are significantly different form zero; the age at which a maximum income is reached equals 50. The $\bar{R}^2$ value of the estimated equation is 0.341. $\bar{R}^2$ increases slightly by adding age-education and age-occupation interaction terms. The age at which the maximum income is reached increases with increasing level of general education, from 36 for the first decile to 62 for men in the last decile. For men with technical education increasing incomes over life-time are found. These results are illustrated in figures 9.3.a and 9.3.b in the appendix. The age-income profiles differentiated according to occupation show that manual workers, employees and civil servants have increasing incomes during working life, while self-employed and farmers reach their maximum at 46 and 36 respectively. Again farmers have lowest incomes at almost all ages, except 25-40 years, when manual workers have lowest incomes.

Finally we note that, although again single persons have lowest and male breadwinners in a one-earner family have highest after-tax income, one-parent families in France have a <u>ceteris paribus</u> after-tax income almost as high.

### 9.1.4 Germany

The German results are shown in table 9.4. In Germany income increases with increasing degree of urbanization; both urbanization dummmies are significantly different from zero. The dummy variables for fluctuations in income are somewhat surprising: people who have small fluctuations in income appear to have significantly higher incomes than those who have either no fluctuations at all or large fluctuations. Self-employed in Germany have the highest incomes; manual workers the lowest. It is seen that income increases with increasing educational level. The age coefficients are both significantly different from zero, and have the expected signs. The age at which the maximum income is reached is 44. The $\bar{R}^2$ for this equation is 0.327. $\bar{R}^2$ increases to 0.350 and 0.349 in columns 2 and 3 after addition of the age-education and age-occupation interaction terms.

The age-income profiles for different educational levels show the expected pattern. The age at which a maximum is reached is higher for higher educational levels, ranging from 31 years for the first decile to 47 years for the highest decile. These results are illustrated in figure 9.4.a in the appendix. In figure 9.4.b age-income profiles are presented for different occupations. It is seen that manual workers have their maximum income at 39, while self- employed have their maximum income at 47. The income of farmers is decreasing with age, but is always higher than the income of manual workers.

Finally, it is seen that men living in an extended family have highest after-tax income, and single persons lowest.

Table 9.4  Income function for working men in GERMANY

| | | | |
|---|---|---|---|
| intercept              | -1.803 (1.524) | -0.154 (1.604) | -1.743 (2.248) |
| small town             |  0.047 (0.022) |  0.044 (0.022) |  0.042 (0.022) |
| large town             |  0.080 (0.022) |  0.078 (0.022) |  0.075 (0.022) |
| small fluctuations     |  0.041 (0.020) |  0.034 (0.020) |  0.038 (0.020) |
| large fluctuations     | -0.005 (0.038) | -0.012 (0.038) |  0.016 (0.038) |
| employee               |  0.141 (0.024) |  0.148 (0.024) | -2.571 (3.438) |
| civil servant          |  0.139 (0.029) |  0.143 (0.029) |  5.021 (4.597) |
| self-employed          |  0.252 (0.037) |  0.258 (0.037) | -4.189 (5.794) |
| farmer                 |  0.091 (0.048) |  0.123 (0.047) | 10.975 (9.240) |
| general education      |  0.121 (0.013) | -4.899 (1.788) |  0.117 (0.013) |
| ln age                 |  6.250 (0.847) |  5.417 (0.890) |  6.406 (1.253) |
| ln$^2$age              | -0.827 (0.117) | -0.723 (0.123) | -0.874 (0.174) |
| gen. educ. × ln age    |                |  2.525 (0.983) |                |
| gen. educ. × ln$^2$age |                | -0.314 (0.135) |                |
| employee × ln age      |                |                |  1.134 (1.909) |
| employee × ln$^2$age   |                |                | -0.106 (0.264) |
| civil servant × ln age |                |                | -3.096 (2.565) |
| civil servant × ln$^2$age |             |                |  0.480 (0.356) |
| self-employed × ln age |                |                |  2.070 (3.113) |
| self-employed × ln$^2$age |             |                | -0.233 (0.417) |
| farmer × ln age        |                |                | -5.782 (4.957) |
| farmer × ln$^2$age     |                |                |  0.767 (0.663) |
| one-parent family      |  0.099 (0.075) |  0.089 (0.074) |  0.085 (0.077) |
| couple, both working   |  0.008 (0.045) |  0.023 (0.044) |  0.005 (0.044) |
| couple, one working    |  0.052 (0.049) |  0.053 (0.049) |  0.032 (0.049) |
| family, both working   |  0.131 (0.043) |  0.132 (0.043) |  0.127 (0.043) |
| family, one working    |  0.144 (0.041) |  0.140 (0.041) |  0.138 (0.041) |
| extended family, working | 0.197 (0.061) | 0.211 (0.060) |  0.208 (0.061) |
| number of observations | 1078           | 1078           | 1078           |
| $\bar{R}^2$            | 0.327          | 0.350          | 0.349          |

## 9.1.5 Ireland

The Irish estimation results are given in table 9.5. The degree of urbanization is quite important for the income level in Ireland: the larger the city, the higher the household income. Men living in a large town have a household income which is 24 % higher than that of men living in the country. This difference is largest of all countries. The dummy variables on income stability are in line with the risk premium hypothesis: the larger the fluctuations in income, the higher the household income is. It is seen that employed (including civil servants) and self-employed have a higher

Table 9.5  Income function for working men in IRELAND

| | | | |
|---|---|---|---|
| intercept | 7.516 (1.680) | 7.610 (1.732) | 10.819 (2.455) |
| small town | 0.061 (0.045) | 0.060 (0.045) | 0.066 (0.045) |
| large town | 0.213 (0.028) | 0.213 (0.028) | 0.210 (0.028) |
| small fluctuations | 0.042 (0.028) | 0.042 (0.028) | 0.042 (0.028) |
| large fluctuations | 0.180 (0.038) | 0.180 (0.038) | 0.181 (0.038) |
| employee/civil servant | 0.061 (0.034) | 0.065 (0.034) | -2.900 (4.348) |
| self-employed | 0.078 (0.042) | 0.078 (0.042) | 1.474 (5.786) |
| farmer | -0.139 (0.038) | -0.131 (0.038) | -3.623 (4.303) |
| general education | 0.176 (0.018) | 2.715 (2.189) | 0.174 (0.018) |
| ln age | 0.895 (0.920) | 0.838 (0.945) | -1.058 (1.356) |
| ln$^2$age | -0.112 (0.125) | -0.103* (0.128) | 0.173 (0.186) |
| gen. educ. × ln age | | -1.436 (1.192) | |
| gen. educ. × ln$^2$age | | 0.201 (0.162) | |
| empl./civil servant × ln age | | | 1.601 (2.382) |
| empl./civil servant × ln$^2$age | | | -0.215 (0.325) |
| self-employed × ln age | | | -0.348 (3.145) |
| self-employed × ln$^2$age | | | -0.006 (0.426) |
| farmer × ln age | | | 2.395 (2.328) |
| farmer × ln$^2$age | | | -0.385 (0.313) |
| one-parent family | 0.273 (0.101) | 0.268 (0.101) | 0.246 (0.101) |
| couple, both working | 0.282 (0.126) | 0.277 (0.126) | 0.304 (0.125) |
| couple, one working | 0.238 (0.106) | 0.238 (0.106) | 0.216 (0.105) |
| family, both working | 0.298 (0.105) | 0.297 (0.105) | 0.294 (0.104) |
| family, one working | 0.488 (0.095) | 0.486 (0.095) | 0.487 (0.094) |
| extended family, working | 0.469 (0.099) | 0.466 (0.099) | 0.452 (0.098) |
| number of observations | 1230 | 1230 | 1230 |
| $\bar{R}^2$ | 0.300 | 0.301 | 0.316 |

Note: Civil servants are not included as a separate category, but included in the category "employees".

income than manual workers. Farmers have the lowest income of all occupations. Income is increasing with education. With respect to age, none of the coefficients is significantly different from zero. The age-income profile is very flat; a maximum is reached at the age of 57. The $\bar{R}^2$ of this equation is 0.298.

The fit does not improve if cross-product terms are added to account for different age-income profiles for different educational levels. None of the cross-product terms is significantly different from zero. Moreover, the sign of the cross-products imply that the age-income profiles tend to be flatter with increasing education. These results point at a system where people are "screened" by employers according to their education, and where age is not an important factor in determining income. The age-income profiles are illustrated in figure 9.5.a in the appendix. The cross-product terms of age and occupation do not have coefficients significantly different from zero either. The resulting occupation-income profiles are presented in figure 9.5.b. Finally we see that large differences in after-tax income exist between family types: a man, earning the family income, has an income that is 64 % higher than the income of a single person.

## 9.1.6 Italy

The estimation results for Italy are given in table 9.6. Living in a large city results in a higher income than living in the country or in a small town; the coefficient, however, is not significantly different from zero. This may be because of the large differences between the north and south of Italy. The more income fluctuations, the higher income appears to be, which is in line with the risk premium hypothesis. Employees have highest incomes, while farmers have lowest of all occupations. It is seen that income increases with the level of education attained. The income level of a family where the main breadwinner has attained the ninth educational decile is $\exp(0.182 \times \Phi^{-1}(0.9;0,1)] = 1.27$ times the income of a family where the main breadwinner has the standard educational level. The overall age-income profile does not have a maximum during working age, which appears to be because of large differences in age profiles for different education levels and different occupations. However, the coefficients of ln age en ln²age are not significantly different from zero. The $\bar{R}^2$ of the equation is 0.196. The fit increases slightly if interaction terms are added. The coefficients of the cross-product terms with education are significantly different from zero. The age at which a maximum is reached does not increase with education: someone in the first educational decile has decreasing income during working life, while someone in the ninth educational decile reaches his maximum income at 47 years. This is illustrated in figure 9.6.a in the appendix. It is seen that the lowest two educational levels have a rather unusual age-income profile, which is decreasing over age. The cross-product terms with occupation do not have coefficients significantly different from zero, except for employees: whereas for manual workers income is (slowly) increasing with age, employees have a maximum at 46 years of age. For farmers a decreasing age-income profile is found, similar to that of the lowest educational groups.
With respect to family type, we see that one-parent families in Italy have

highest ceteris paribus after-tax income, and single persons lowest.

Table 9.6  Income function for working men in ITALY

| | | | | | | |
|---|---|---|---|---|---|---|
| intercept | 6.015 | (2.103) | 9.391 | (2.211) | 11.423 | (4.086) |
| small town | 0.022 | (0.027) | 0.025 | (0.027) | 0.017 | (0.027) |
| large town | 0.037 | (0.027) | 0.040 | (0.027) | 0.034 | (0.027) |
| small fluctuations | 0.021 | (0.025) | 0.021 | (0.025) | 0.026 | (0.025) |
| large fluctuations | 0.067 | (0.035) | 0.072 | (0.035) | 0.076 | (0.035) |
| employee | 0.088 | (0.035) | 0.096 | (0.035) | -16.676 | (6.284) |
| civil servant | -0.046 | (0.038) | -0.044 | (0.038) | -7.739 | (7.128) |
| self-employed | 0.071 | (0.032) | 0.073 | (0.032) | -1.737 | (5.362) |
| farmer | -0.105 | (0.052) | -0.099 | (0.052) | 9.190 | (11.761) |
| general education | 0.182 | (0.015) | -11.208 | (2.851) | 0.181 | (0.015) |
| ln age | 1.782 | (1.131) | 0.072 | (1.182) | 1.186 | (2.222) |
| ln²age | -0.210 | (0.152) | 0.005 | (0.157) | 0.195 | (0.301) |
| gen. educ. × ln age | | | 5.916 | (1.515) | | |
| gen. educ. × ln²age | | | -0.765 | (0.201) | | |
| employee × ln age | | | | | 9.103 | (3.413) |
| employee × ln²age | | | | | -1.230 | (0.462) |
| civil servant × ln age | | | | | 4.112 | (3.859) |
| civil servant × ln²age | | | | | -0.547 | (0.521) |
| self-employed × ln age | | | | | 1.124 | (2.890) |
| self-employed × ln²age | | | | | -0.170 | (0.388) |
| farmer × ln age | | | | | -4.587 | (6.117) |
| farmer × ln²age | | | | | 0.562 | (0.794) |
| one-parent family | 0.375 | (0.078) | 0.380 | (0.078) | 0.349 | (0.078) |
| couple, both working | 0.107 | (0.072) | 0.127 | (0.072) | 0.113 | (0.072) |
| couple, one working | 0.057 | (0.069) | 0.065 | (0.069) | 0.051 | (0.069) |
| family, both working | 0.091 | (0.062) | 0.092 | (0.062) | 0.088 | (0.063) |
| family, one working | 0.213 | (0.060) | 0.211 | (0.060) | 0.208 | (0.060) |
| extended family, working | 0.255 | (0.069) | 0.257 | (0.069) | 0.256 | (0.069) |
| number of observations | 1402 | | 1402 | | 1402 | |
| $\bar{R}^2$ | 0.196 | | 0.209 | | 0.203 | |

### 9.1.7  The Netherlands

The Dutch results are given in table 9.7. People living in a large town in the Netherlands have a lower income than people living in small cities or in the country-side. People with small fluctuations in income have a higher income than people with a stable income, or people with large fluctuations in income. It is seen that civil servants have highest incomes of all occupations and farmers have lowest. With respect to education, the Dutch specification is slightly different from that in other countries. In the Netherlands the differentiation of educational classes was such that

Table 9.7  Income function for working men in THE NETHERLANDS

| | | | | | | |
|---|---|---|---|---|---|---|
| intercept | 3.567 | (1.414) | 3.563 | (2.465) | 8.702 | (2.235) |
| small town | -0.008 | (0.017) | -0.013 | (0.017) | -0.012 | (0.017) |
| large town | -0.054 | (0.021) | -0.048 | (0.021) | -0.056 | (0.021) |
| small fluctuations | 0.051 | (0.020) | 0.043 | (0.020) | 0.048 | (0.020) |
| large fluctuations | 0.015 | (0.038) | 0.016 | (0.037) | 0.007 | (0.037) |
| employee | 0.108 | (0.022) | 0.118 | (0.021) | -7.808 | (2.999) |
| civil servant | 0.141 | (0.026) | 0.162 | (0.025) | -8.307 | (3.450) |
| self-employed | 0.041 | (0.034) | 0.063 | (0.034) | -7.856 | (5.087) |
| farmer | -0.029 | (0.054) | -0.011 | (0.053) | 4.492 | (10.838) |
| general education | 0.201 | (0.016) | -7.426 | (2.512) | 0.193 | (0.015) |
| technical education | 0.118 | (0.014) | -9.902 | (2.010) | 0.124 | (0.014) |
| tech. educ. (dummy) | 0.004 | (0.017) | 2.856 | (2.913) | -0.006 | (0.017) |
| ln age | 3.272 | (0.776) | 3.328 | (1.344) | 0.627 | (1.237) |
| ln$^2$age | -0.414 | (0.106) | -0.426 | (0.182) | -0.074 | (0.171) |
| gen. educ. × ln age | | | 3.950 | (1.359) | | |
| gen. educ. × ln$^2$age | | | -0.508 | (0.183) | | |
| tech. educ. × ln age | | | 5.391 | (1.107) | | |
| tech. educ. × ln$^2$age | | | -0.721 | (0.152) | | |
| tech. dummy × ln age | | | -1.557 | (1.594) | | |
| tech. dummy × ln$^2$age | | | 0.216 | (0.217) | | |
| employee × ln age | | | | | 4.067 | (1.656) |
| employee × ln$^2$age | | | | | -0.516 | (0.228) |
| civil servant × ln age | | | | | 4.227 | (1.906) |
| civil servant × ln$^2$age | | | | | -0.533 | (0.262) |
| self-employed × ln age | | | | | 4.396 | (2.761) |
| self-employed × ln$^2$age | | | | | -0.606 | (0.373) |
| farmer × ln age | | | | | -2.065 | (5.768) |
| farmer × ln$^2$age | | | | | 0.232 | (0.765) |
| one-parent family | 0.069 | (0.075) | 0.056 | (0.074) | 0.072 | (0.074) |
| couple, both working | 0.053 | (0.045) | 0.036 | (0.044) | 0.041 | (0.044) |
| couple, one working | 0.148 | (0.048) | 0.124 | (0.048) | 0.121 | (0.048) |
| family, both working | 0.143 | (0.044) | 0.120 | (0.043) | 0.119 | (0.043) |
| family, one working | 0.179 | (0.041) | 0.156 | (0.041) | 0.158 | (0.041) |
| extended family, working | 0.045 | (0.073) | 0.046 | (0.072) | 0.049 | (0.072) |
| number of observations | | 1267 | | 1267 | | 1267 |
| $\bar{R}^2$ | | 0.359 | | 0.389 | | 0.385 |

not only general education could be normalized, like in other countries, but also technical/vocational education. The coefficients of these variables are given in the table. Besides these two normalized variables a dummy variable is added to allow for a possible income difference between someone with median general education and someone with median technical education. We now see that both for general and for vocational education the coefficient is positive: more education leads to higher income, though the coefficient of general education is much higher than that correspond-

ing to technical education, indicating that larger income differences are found for people with different general education, than for those with different technical education. The dummy variable is virtually equal to zero, indicating that someone with median technical education has an income equal to someone with median general education. The overall age-income profile has a maximum when age is 54. The $\bar{R}^2$ of this equation is 0.359; it increases to 0.389 if cross-products between age and education are added. For both educational types we find that people with higher education reach their maximum income at a later age; for people with median general education this age is 52 and for people with median technical education (level 3) income is overall increasing during working life, and in between the first and second level of general education. These profiles are illustrated in figure 9.7.a in the appendix. With respect to occupational differences it is seen that manual workers have a very flat, increasing income profile. Civil servants, who have highest incomes of all occupations, reach a maximum at the age of 57.
Finally, we see that one-earner families have highest after-tax income.

## 9.1.8 The United Kingdom

The results for the U.K. are given in table 9.8. The larger the town a family is living in, the higher the household income is (although the coefficients are not significantly different from zero at the 5 percent level). The more income fluctuations, the higher the income is. Employees have highest incomes of all occupations, and manual workers have lowest (farmers are included in the group of self-employed, and cannot be distinguished separately). With respect to education it is found that income increases monotonically with level of education reached, although the effect is not very pronounced. The age-income profile attains its maximum at the age of 44. The fit of the regression in the UK is not very satisfactory; the $\bar{R}^2$ is 0.140.
The improvement in fit if interaction terms with education and occupation are added is only minor; $\bar{R}^2$ becomes 0.151 and 0.158 respectively. The age at which a maximum income is reached increases from 30 for the lowest educational decile to 58 for the highest decile. Manual workers have a very flat income profile, with a maximum at 43 years of age; employees reach their maximum at 41 years, when they have already experienced a much

Table 9.8  Income function for working men in the UNITED KINGDOM

| | | | |
|---|---|---|---|
| intercept | 3.193 (1.807) | 4.002 (1.826) | 6.797 (2.186) |
| small town | 0.038 (0.026) | 0.036 (0.026) | 0.034 (0.026) |
| large town | 0.041 (0.027) | 0.044 (0.027) | 0.038 (0.027) |
| small fluctuations | 0.030 (0.022) | 0.030 (0.022) | 0.027 (0.022) |
| large fluctuations | 0.119 (0.039) | 0.113 (0.039) | 0.117 (0.039) |
| employee | 0.157 (0.026) | 0.159 (0.026) | -12.527 (4.054) |
| civil servant | 0.128 (0.040) | 0.116 (0.040) | -17.284 (6.005) |
| self-employed/farmer | 0.086 (0.041) | 0.082 (0.041) | 0.419 (6.840) |
| general education | 0.081 (0.015) | -0.991 (2.194) | 0.077 (0.015) |
| ln age | 3.462 (1.003) | 3.053 (1.012) | 1.539 (1.217) |
| ln$^2$age | -0.460 (0.138) | -0.407 (0.139) | 0.206 (0.168) |
| gen. educ. × ln age | | 0.392 (1.216) | |
| gen. educ. × ln$^2$age | | -0.026 (0.168) | |
| employee × ln age | | | 6.911 (2.238) |
| employee × ln$^2$age | | | -0.936 (0.308) |
| civil servant × ln age | | | 9.212 (3.306) |
| civil servant × ln$^2$age | | | -1.209 (0.453) |
| self-empl./farmer × ln age | | | -0.355 (3.728) |
| self-empl./farmer × ln$^2$age | | | 0.073 (0.506) |
| one-parent family | -0.029 (0.112) | -0.029 (0.111) | 0.020 (0.112) |
| couple, both working | -0.058 (0.084) | -0.062 (0.084) | -0.032 (0.084) |
| couple, one working | -0.021 (0.090) | -0.022 (0.090) | -0.002 (0.090) |
| family, both working | 0.019 (0.082) | -0.000 (0.082) | 0.033 (0.082) |
| family, one working | 0.069 (0.082) | 0.051 (0.081) | 0.076 (0.081) |
| extended family, working | 0.116 (0.105) | 0.105 (0.104) | 0.132 (0.105) |
| number of observations | 1186 | 1186 | 1186 |
| $\bar{R}^2$ | 0.140 | 0.152 | 0.158 |

Note: In the United Kingdom farmers are included in the category "self-employed".

greater increase in income. Self-employed keep increasing in income with age, but the rate at which it increases is very small. The age-income profiles are presented in figures 9.8.a and 9.8.b.

Finally we see that in the United Kingdom after-tax income is highest for men living in an extended family, while it is lowest for couples who are both working. The coefficients for family type are not, however, significantly different from zero.

### 9.1.9 International comparison

In order to compare the income functions over countries, we have compiled a table where the effect of some important variables is presented. A positive effect on income is represented by +, a negative effect by -.

Table 9.9 Effects of socio-economic characteristics on the income of working men in different countries

|  | BEL | DEN | FRA | GER | IRE | ITA | NET | UK |
|---|---|---|---|---|---|---|---|---|
| urbanization | - | - | + | + | + | + | - | + |
| fluctuations in income | + | - | - |  | + | + |  | + |
| self-employed |  |  | + | + | + |  |  |  |
| farmers | * | - | - |  | - | - | - | * |
| high education | + | + | + | + | + | + | + | + |
| age: young | - | - | - | - | - | - | - | - |
| old | - | - | - | - | - |  | - | - |
| $age_{max}$ | 53 | 40 | 50 | 44 | 57 | 65 | 54 | 44 |

* In these countries farmers are included in the category self-employed.

If we compare the results presented in this table, we see that:

(i) Men living in a large city have higher incomes than men living in small towns or in rural areas for all countries, except Belgium, Denmark and the Netherlands. These three countries are all small, with many small towns within travelling distance of the bigger cities. Presumably many people living in these small towns still work in the bigger cities, implying that we can conclude that overall, higher incomes are earned in big cities.

(ii) The results of the estimation of the effect of fluctuations in income are inconclusive; people with high fluctuations in income have higher income in Belgium, Ireland, Italy and the United Kingdom, while the reverse holds for Denmark and France. In Germany and the Netherlands people with small fluctuations in income have highest income. This may be the result of the economic structure of these countries. The more "laissez-faire" a country is, the higher the risk premium will be. In countries like the Netherlands and Germany, however, the relatively large influence of governmental policies on income distribution may have decreased the amplitude of these fluctuations.

(iii) The effect of education on income varies also widely: it is smallest in Denmark and the United Kingdom, and largest in the Netherlands. The small effect of education in Denmark and the U.K. may be because a general comprehensive school exists in these countries. Another possible explanation is that the educational level is of less importance for one's career than the school at which one has been; in the U.K. private and public schools may both result in the same educa-

tional level, but give other credentials on the labour market.
(iv) Occupational differences are similar in all countries: farmers have lowest incomes, and manual workers come next. Civil servants and employees usually earn most, although in France self-employed have highest incomes.

Finally, we note that the tax systems in the eight countries are such that in general single persons pay highest taxes, resulting in a low after-tax income, while male heads of households pay relatively low taxes, resulting in a relatively high after-tax income. In some countries (Germany and the United Kingdom) males in an extended family have highest after-tax income; this may be the result of special tax facilities if one takes care of parents, or other adult family members.

## 9.2 Individual income function for working women

In this section we present income functions for working women, either living alone or with others in a household. As the determinants of income for a woman who is the single breadwinner may be different from the determinants of an income that is earned in addition to the main breadwinner's income, we estimate income functions separately for female main breadwinners and partners.

In section 9.2.1 the income functions for female breadwinners are given, and in section 9.2.2 those for the partners.

### 9.2.1 Income functions for female breadwinners

The women whose income is explained in this section may be either single persons, or head of a one-parent family, or main breadwinner of a couple or family.

Although we expect that in general the hypotheses derived for male breadwinners to hold for this group as well, it is likely that the extent of certain effects will be different. Age, for instance, may have a smaller impact on earnings for women, because of possible discontinuities in working life. For the same reason the returns to schooling may be expected to be smaller for women. As the group we are concerned with may be rather heterogenous, including divorced or widowed women who have reentered the labour market after a certain period at home, as well as young women who

Table 9.10 Income functions of female breadwinners

| | BEL | DEN | FRA | GER | IRE | ITA | NET | UK |
|---|---|---|---|---|---|---|---|---|
| intercept | 4.491 (9.411) | -3.578 (3.435) | 0.378 (2.842) | -1.799 (3.065) | 5.152 (8.665) | 9.780 (7.699) | 1.901 (4.408) | 5.062 (12.282) |
| small town | -0.140 (0.165) | -0.081 (0.075) | 0.173 (0.069) | -0.068 (0.062) | -0.022 (0.242) | -0.014 (0.121) | 0.076 (0.105) | -0.123 (0.215) |
| large town | -0.049 (0.125) | -0.128 (0.070) | 0.181 (0.057) | 0.020 (0.058) | 0.204 (0.133) | -0.020 (0.117) | 0.031 (0.104) | -0.292 (0.243) |
| small fluctuations | -0.119 (0.129) | -0.041 (0.092) | -0.032 (0.057) | 0.094 (0.063) | 0.431 (0.157) | 0.057 (0.116) | -0.132 (0.118) | -0.146 (0.179) |
| large fluctuations | -0.326 (0.238) | -0.158 (0.138) | -0.050 (0.084) | 0.413 (0.132) | -0.123 (0.220) | -0.263 (0.161) | -0.344 (0.151) | -- |
| employee | 0.443 (0.176) | 0.012 (0.068) | 0.138 (0.069) | 0.241 (0.075) | } 0.056 (0.195) | -0.047 (0.175) | 0.254 (0.131) | 0.003 (0.215) |
| civil servant | 0.547 (0.198) | 0.158 (0.105) | 0.235 (0.078) | 0.149 (0.129) | | 0.037 (0.173) | 0.338 (0.142) | 0.358 (0.387) |
| self-employed | 0.298 (0.253) | -0.230 (0.154) | 0.295 (0.098) | 0.323 (0.144) | 0.464 (0.172) | 0.126 (0.144) | 0.248 (0.181) | -0.101 (0.334) |
| farmer | -- | -0.456 (0.273) | 0.032 (0.220) | -0.557 (0.185) | -- | 0.011 (0.302) | -0.302 (0.331) | -- |
| general education | 0.223 (0.075) | 0.083 (0.045) | 0.140 (0.041) | 0.209 (0.038) | 0.148 (0.082) | 0.170 (0.074) | 0.134 (0.110) | 0.268 (0.115) |
| technical education (dummy) | 0.157 (0.144) | -- | 0.056 (0.063) | -- | -- | -- | 0.051 (0.088) | -- |
| ln age | 2.354 (5.272) | 7.399 (1.967) | 4.852 (1.613) | 6.133 (1.746) | 2.350 (4.745) | -0.068 (4.183) | 3.882 (2.460) | 2.084 (6.967) |
| ln²age | -0.260 (0.732) | -1.023 (0.277) | -0.645 (0.227) | -0.809 (0.246) | -0.343 (0.645) | 0.004 (0.565) | -0.486 (0.341) | -0.235 (0.977) |
| one-parent family | 0.077 (0.138) | -0.020 (0.073) | -0.025 (0.050) | -0.028 (0.063) | 0.046 (0.151) | 0.072 (0.110) | 0.163 (0.109) | -0.224 (0.247) |
| couple without children | 0.061 (0.174) | 0.065 (0.086) | -0.044 (0.102) | 0.023 (0.079) | 0.098 (0.291) | 0.160 (0.252) | -0.209 (0.155) | -0.074 (0.223) |
| family with children | -0.111 (0.229) | 0.036 (0.106) | -0.025 (0.117) | 0.155 (0.168) | -0.275 (0.207) | 0.182 (0.151) | 0.156 (0.223) | -0.601 (0.487) |
| age$_{max}$ | -- | 37 | 43 | 44 | 31 | -- | 54 | -- |
| N | 54 | 187 | 249 | 101 | 71 | 106 | 81 | 30 |
| $\bar{R}^2$ | 0.379 | 0.176 | 0.228 | 0.606 | 0.193 | 0.049 | 0.385 | 0.237 |

have just finished school, we expect the fit of the equation to be considerably worse than the fit for the (large) group of working men. The estimation results are given in table 9.10.

It is seen that again the effect of urbanization varies considerably over countries; in Belgium, Denmark, France and Ireland the same effect is found as for working men. The coefficients are not significantly different from zero in any country except France. In all countries except Germany large fluctuations in income result in a lower income level. This does not coincide with the effects found for working men. Again, however, most coefficients do not differ significantly from zero.

The pattern for occupation is quite similar to the one found for working men; farmers have lowest income, civil servants highest, except in France, Germany and Ireland where self-employed women have highest incomes.

Education has a positive effect on earnings, which is sometimes even larger than the effect found for men (Belgium, Denmark, Germany, Ireland, and the United Kingdom).

However, the coefficients may not be compared in absolute terms, as they reflect the effect of the normalized education level. As the distribution of education is different for men and women, we can only conclude that in the countries mentioned, the differences in earnings over this educational scale are larger for women than for men; as the distribution of education of women has a smaller variance and a lower median, this does not imply that education has a larger return in earnings for women than for men.

The effect of technical or vocational education is to slightly increase the women's income, compared to standard general education.

The age-income profiles have the expected concave shape in all countries except Italy. In Belgium and the United Kingdom, income is increasing with age over life-time; these coefficients are not, however, significantly different from zero. In all other countries the age at which a maximum income is earned is given as "$age_{max}$" in the table. It appears that in all countries the maximum income for women is found at a younger age than for men, except in Germany and the Netherlands, where they are exactly equal (at 44 and 54 respectively).

The effect of household type is rather haphazard, and in no country significantly different from zero; this may be because household type may influence income negatively through hours of work, for example in a one-parent family, and positively through tax benefits. These effects have not been analysed separately in our model. It is seen that the variation explained varies considerably over countries: in Germany $\bar{R}^2$ it is about 0.61, and in Italy it is 0.05.

When we compare the resulting incomes with the incomes found for working men, we see that women overall have lower incomes, <u>ceteris paribus</u>.

As an example, the expected incomes are presented for men and women with the same characteristics, viz. living in the country, no fluctuations in income, manual workers, standard education level, single person, at the age of 40.

|        | BEL    | DEN    | FRA    | GER    | IRE    | ITA    | NET    | UK     |
|--------|--------|--------|--------|--------|--------|--------|--------|--------|
| male   | 22,450 | 17,968 | 17,847 | 22,014 | 10,868 | 16,833 | 22,108 | 16,393 |
| female | 15,319 | 17,960 | 13,358 | 18,339 | 9,251  | 14,524 | 14,886 | 14,073 |

It appears that in all countries men with the same characteristics[3] have higher incomes than women. The difference is almost zero in Denmark, and minor in Ireland, Italy and the United Kingdom, but very large in Belgium and the Netherlands. As mentioned earlier in this section, this difference may result from different working hours, different levels of schooling, different labour market experience and on-the-job training, and discrimination in wages. As this study does not concentrate on the specific issue of labour market behaviour of women, we will confine ourselves to the conclusion that in all countries but Denmark female single breadwinners have an income (considerably) lower than male breadwinners.

### 9.2.2 Income functions for partners

This section is devoted to the estimation of income functions for women in households where the main income is earned by the spouse. As discussed in chapter 3, in these households partners may decide either to participate on the labour market or to spend her time on home production. If the income function is estimated for women who have decided to participate, the resulting estimates may be biased, because the expected value of the error term is conditional upon the partner's participating, and hence not in general equal to zero. The solution to this problem is to estimate the participation decision as well, and to correct for the bias in the income function following a Heckman type correction method.

We expect the participation decision to depend on the presence of children, age, education, and the income of the main breadwinner (see equation (3.4) in chapter 3). Education has been included in the form of dummy variables, denoting increasing levels of education for dummy 1, 2, 4 and 5, and denoting technical education for dummy 3. The income of the man is included as the systematical part of the income equation for the main breadwinner.

This equation has been estimated for all countries using a non-linear least-squares probit procedure from the Statistical Analysis System (SAS) library. The results are presented in table 9.11.

We notice both similarities and differences between countries. The participation is in most countries increasing until about 30 years of age, after which participation decreases. The age at which the highest degree of participation is found is given as "$age_{max}$" per country. Of course, this age may reflect a general cohort effect, as a consequence of emancipation, as well as an individual's preference for homework versus work on the labour market over time. Exceptions to this general age profile are Germany and the Netherlands, where participation is overall decreasing with age. However, the coefficients in both countries do not differ significantly from zero.

As regards education, we see as a rule increasing participation with higher education. Exceptions are found in Denmark, where the fourth educational level does not have a significantly higher participation degree than the lowest educational level, and the United Kingdom, where a sudden decline in participation degree is found at the highest educational level. The effect of children on the participation degree is negative, and significantly different from zero in all countries.

The effect of the husband's income is negative in all countries, although it is not significantly different from zero in Belgium, France, Germany, the Netherlands and the United Kingdom.

We now turn to the explanation of the income of the partner. In addition to the same explanatory variables that have been used for main breadwinners, the correction term to avoid bias is included as $C = \dfrac{\phi(\hat{\pi};0,1)}{1-\Phi(\hat{\pi};0,1)}$,

Table 9.11 The participation decision of the partner

|   | BEL | DEN | FRA | GER | IRE | ITA | NET | UK |
|---|---|---|---|---|---|---|---|---|
| intercept | -29.656 (8.630) | -36.658 (4.262) | -22.325 (4.310) | -0.803 (6.035) | -24.883 (7.093) | -4.199 (6.277) | -0.086 (5.116) | -24.508 (6.231) |
| ln age p | 18.886 (4.942) | 25.615 (3.158) | 13.874 (2.501) | 2.383 (3.688) | 16.760 (4.005) | 11.524 (3.251) | 1.260 (2.829) | 20.012 (3.494) |
| ln²age p | -2.895 (0.707) | -3.693 (0.438) | -2.058 (0.351) | -0.527 (0.506) | -2.395 (0.557) | -1.693 (0.446) | -0.432 (0.392) | -2.948 (0.483) |
| education 2 p | 0.074 (0.156) | 0.319 (0.104) | 0.197 (0.102) | 0.275 (0.102) | 0.279 (0.193) | 0.489 (0.160) | 0.193 (0.099) | 0.241 (0.135) |
| education 3 p | 0.323 (0.160) | -0.019 (0.113) | 0.296 (0.104) | 0.625 (0.135) | 0.325 (0.135) | 0.878 (0.183) | 0.452 (0.123) | 0.151 (0.151) |
| education 4 p | 0.203 (0.193) | -0.001 (0.175) | 0.333 (0.119) | 0.617 (0.345) | 1.243 (0.164) | 1.525 (0.212) | 1.084 (0.270) | 0.440 (0.196) |
| education 5 p | 0.460 (0.148) | 0.344 (0.190) | 0.428 (0.132) | 5.762 (488.9) | 2.073 (0.176) | 2.357 (0.290) | | -0.311 (0.279) |
| children | -0.226 (0.057) | -0.246 (0.059) | -0.347 (0.055) | -0.992 (0.122) | -0.213 (0.038) | -0.197 (0.067) | -1.166 (0.104) | -1.330 (0.105) |
| $\hat{y}_m$ | -0.109 (0.267) | -0.647 (0.313) | -0.092 (0.238) | -0.103 (0.313) | -0.491 (0.237) | -1.572 (0.375) | 0.072 (0.264) | -0.832 (0.583) |
| age_max | 26 | 32 | 29 | -- | 33 | 30 | -- | 30 |
| N | 926 | 1360 | 1497 | 989 | 1327 | 1419 | 1460 | 1109 |
| $\hat{\sigma}^2$ | 0.189 | 0.191 | 0.215 | 0.194 | 0.062 | 0.173 | 0.156 | 0.189 |

Asymptotic standard errors are given in parentheses.

where $\hat{\pi}$ is the predicted probability of participation, obtained by calculating the systematic part of (9.1) with the estimated parameter values of table 9.11 for each partner who participates.

The resulting equations are presented in table 9.12. It is seen that the degree of urbanization does not have a significant effect on income, except in Denmark, where the effect is large and positive. Fluctuations in income tend to have a negative effect on income in most countries; this may refer to irregular jobs which the partner may take up every now and then, in contrast to steady jobs with a constant and higher income. The effect of occupation is comparable to the effect found for female and male breadwinners: civil servants have in general highest incomes, and farmers lowest. It is furthermore striking that self-employed women tend to have small incomes in all countries but Germany; this may be because they are working with their husbands in a firm or shop, and the main income resulting from this work is already included in the main breadwinner's income.

Education in general increases income, with a notable exception in Germany. The only explanation we can offer for this exception is that maybe partners with higher education tend to work less hours a week, from which a lower income may result.

The age-income patterns vary considerably; in France, for example, a proper concave function is found, with a maximum at 40, in other countries the income profile is overall decreasing with age or increasing with age. The coefficients of age are not significantly different from zero in any country.

In all countries the partner's income is highest if she does not have children or other adults living in the family; this is probably the result of a decrease in hours worked if children or others have to be taken care of.

The coefficient of the correction term, finally, is not significantly different from zero, except in the U.K., implying that the coefficients do not differ significantly from OLS estimates without correction for selectivity.

Summarizing we may say that incomes of partners are much less systematical functions of education, occupation and age than the income functions found for male and female breadwinners. This is probably the result of the

Table 9.12 Income functions for working partners

| | BEL | DEN | FRA | GER | IRE | ITA | NET | UK |
|---|---|---|---|---|---|---|---|---|
| intercept | -27.517 (26.623) | 20.271 (16.618) | -1.230 (15.251) | 13.617 (11.968) | -13.890 (43.549) | 6.088 (21.665) | 11.023 (12.362) | 9.346 (5.197) |
| small town | 0.062 ( 0.223) | 0.184 ( 0.161) | -0.081 ( 0.209) | 0.195 ( 0.192) | 0.289 ( 0.852) | -0.424 ( 0.281) | -0.379 ( 0.180) | 0.033 ( 0.073) |
| large town | 0.249 ( 0.246) | 0.351 ( 0.163) | 0.174 ( 0.180) | 0.228 ( 0.191) | -0.517 ( 0.494) | -0.336 ( 0.271) | -0.090 ( 0.210) | 0.008 ( 0.075) |
| small fluctuations | -0.515 ( 0.224) | -0.163 ( 0.171) | 0.197 ( 0.183) | -0.089 ( 0.171) | 0.041 ( 0.586) | 0.160 ( 0.248) | -0.134 ( 0.197) | -0.036 ( 0.063) |
| large fluctuations | -0.330 ( 0.427) | -0.153 ( 0.259) | -0.376 ( 0.265) | -1.091 ( 0.368) | -0.199 ( 0.743) | -1.006 ( 0.360) | -1.039 ( 0.319) | 0.112 ( 0.110) |
| employee | 0.336 ( 0.321) | -0.020 ( 0.157) | -0.222 ( 0.217) | 0.677 ( 0.210) | -0.163 ( 0.617) | 0.113 ( 0.383) | 0.102 ( 0.206) | 0.252 ( 0.070) |
| civil servant | 0.721 ( 0.346) | 0.234 ( 0.248) | -0.140 ( 0.251) | 1.562 ( 0.452) | -- | 0.275 ( 0.414) | 0.522 ( 0.265) | 0.457 ( 0.117) |
| self-employed | -1.095 ( 0.370) | -2.341 ( 0.264) | -3.430 ( 0.317) | 0.699 ( 0.325) | -3.163 ( 1.155) | -1.997 ( 0.382) | 0.310 ( 0.442) | 0.339 ( 0.148) |
| farmer | -- | -5.822 ( 0.289) | -6.872 ( 0.434) | -2.076 ( 0.443) | -- | -3.289 ( 0.565) | 1.775 ( 1.727) | -- |
| general education | 0.140 ( 0.161) | 0.030 ( 0.092) | 0.467 ( 0.146) | -0.249 ( 0.136) | 0.463 ( 0.691) | 0.185 ( 0.345) | -0.053 ( 0.141) | 0.073 ( 0.048) |
| technical education (dummy) | -0.058 ( 0.232) | -- | 0.035 ( 0.198) | -- | -- | -- | -0.228 ( 0.158) | -- |
| ln age | 21.273 (15.386) | -6.117 ( 9.434) | 6.211 ( 8.676) | -2.841 ( 6.804) | 12.856 (24.261) | 2.003 (12.125) | -0.139 ( 6.995) | -0.170 ( 2.927) |
| ln²age | -3.060 ( 2.249) | 0.855 ( 1.343) | -0.841 ( 1.243) | 0.420 ( 0.962) | -1.860 ( 3.390) | -0.325 ( 1.713) | -0.085 ( 0.982) | 0.022 ( 0.409) |
| family, both working | -0.300 ( 0.287) | -0.010 ( 0.181) | -0.334 ( 0.203) | -0.162 ( 0.190) | -0.189 ( 0.689) | 0.579 ( 0.283) | -0.637 ( 0.215) | -0.386 ( 0.082) |
| extended family | -1.986 ( 0.548) | -0.258 ( 0.535) | 0.015 ( 0.489) | -0.434 ( 0.447) | -0.553 ( 0.854) | 0.789 ( 0.399) | -1.446 ( 0.661) | -0.624 ( 0.200) |
| correction term | 0.219 ( 0.764) | -0.567 ( 0.575) | -0.329 ( 0.595) | -0.131 ( 0.256) | 0.463 ( 0.954) | -0.107 ( 0.864) | 0.009 ( 0.187) | -0.152 ( 0.067) |
| N | 315 | 868 | 595 | 371 | 109 | 435 | 424 | 539 |
| $\bar{R}^2$ | 0.161 | 0.448 | 0.483 | 0.154 | -0.010 | 0.239 | 0.118 | 0.156 |

larger variability of hours worked for partners.
However, a thorough study of these two effects requires a more comprehensive analysis of female labour supply, which is beyond the scope of this book. The relatively bad explanation of partners' incomes, especially in Ireland, does not worry us too much, as the partner's income is per definition a smaller contribution to the household income than the main breadwinner's income. Moreover, as we have seen in chapter 8, the average welfare level of families and couples where two persons are working is higher than the poverty threshold in all countries.
We will return to the effect of the partners' income on poverty in chapter 11.

9.3   Incomes of non-working households

In table 9.13 the income functions for households where no one is working are presented. The results will first be discussed per country (in sections 9.3.1 to 9.3.8) and then compared over countries (in section 9.3.9).

9.3.1   Belgium

In large towns people who are not working have significantly higher incomes than in the countryside. This effect is opposite to the results for working men in Belgium who have a higher income in the countryside than in the city. It seems that the effect of the flight to the suburbs is higher for working families and the migration to towns is higher amongst non-working families. Fluctuations in income do not have a significant effect on income. Between the former occupations, however, vast differences are found: non- working civil servants have an income that is 42 % higher than manual workers. Self-employed, on the other hand, have lowest income; amounting to 83 % of the manual workers' income. The effect of general education on income is increasing, but not as strong as for working men. People with technical education have, surprisingly, a significantly higher income than people with standard general education. This effect was not found for working men. The coefficients for ln age and ln$^2$age are slightly higher than those found for working men; they imply that the age at which the maximum income is reached is later, viz. at 61 years, and that the age-income profile is steeper. The differences between household type

Table 9.13 Income function for non-working households

| | DEN | BEL | FRA | GER | IRE | ITA | NET | UK |
|---|---|---|---|---|---|---|---|---|
| intercept | -1.627 (4.724) | -2.209 (1.717) | 1.878 (2.629) | -5.519 (2.816) | -3.688 (3.345) | 34.641 (9.245) | 4.243 (2.049) | 6.489 (5.964) |
| small towns | 0.050 (0.082) | 0.034 (0.040) | -0.005 (0.072) | 0.217 (0.054) | 0.239 (0.069) | -0.066 (0.061) | 0.013 (0.036) | 0.004 (0.091) |
| large towns | 0.159 (0.074) | -0.011 (0.042) | 0.048 (0.056) | 0.226 (0.053) | 0.168 (0.040) | 0.034 (0.058) | -0.013 (0.037) | 0.062 (0.094) |
| small fluctuations | 0.018 (0.070) | 0.064 (0.065) | 0.026 (0.061) | 0.098 (0.073) | 0.094 (0.057) | 0.229 (0.076) | 0.036 (0.046) | 0.109 (0.080) |
| large fluctuations | 0.012 (0.285) | 0.076 (0.088) | -0.043 (0.094) | 0.300 (0.218) | 0.535 (0.182) | -0.005 (0.253) | 0.070 (0.103) | 0.174 (0.259) |
| employees | 0.106 (0.092) | 0.019 (0.046) | 0.196 (0.077) | 0.149 (0.066) | } 0.032 (0.057) | 0.199 (0.091) | 0.136 (0.037) | 0.216 (0.092) |
| civil servants | 0.350 (0.101) | 0.398 (0.068) | 0.366 (0.074) | 0.277 (0.082) | | 0.030 (0.077) | -- | 0.434 (0.144) |
| self-employed | -0.192 (0.102) | 0.021 (0.058) | -0.083 (0.088) | -0.046 (0.088) | -0.100 (0.092) | 0.007 (0.075) | -0.008 (0.051) | } 0.461 (0.178) |
| farmers | | -0.063 (0.064) | -0.063 (0.103) | -0.221 (0.098) | -0.065 (0.074) | 0.133 (0.103) | -0.048 (0.059) | |
| never worked | -0.030 (0.164) | -0.048 (0.056) | 0.133 (0.081) | 0.030 (0.073) | -0.002 (0.087) | -0.112 (0.077) | | -0.057 (0.267) |
| general education | 0.084 (0.048) | 0.059 (0.029) | 0.145 (0.039) | 0.181 (0.034) | 0.155 (0.033) | 0.204 (0.033) | 0.230 (0.029) | 0.151 (0.061) |
| technical education | | | | | | | -0.066 (0.041) | |
| technical education (dummy) | 0.230 (0.098) | | 0.194 (0.079) | | | | 0.151 (0.032) | |
| ln age | 5.472 (2.431) | 5.982 (0.915) | 3.514 (1.440) | 7.454 (1.523) | 6.329 (1.793) | -12.416 (4.529) | 2.478 (1.083) | 1.056 (3.223) |
| ln²age | -0.665 (0.312) | -0.779 (0.121) | -0.423 (0.195) | -0.914 (0.203) | -0.810 (0.238) | 1.503 (0.553) | -0.284 (0.142) | -0.124 (0.431) |
| one-parent family | 0.253 (0.113) | 0.105 (0.062) | 0.461 (0.089) | 0.200 (0.081) | 0.531 (0.058) | 0.319 (0.092) | 0.191 (0.052) | 0.434 (0.172) |
| couple | 0.279 (0.089) | 0.342 (0.045) | 0.389 (0.072) | 0.058 (0.078) | 0.491 (0.068) | 0.484 (0.080) | 0.241 (0.051) | 0.564 (0.149) |
| family | 0.402 (0.115) | 0.474 (0.086) | 0.572 (0.088) | 0.199 (0.093) | 0.893 (0.071) | 0.708 (0.093) | 0.301 (0.059) | 0.719 (0.172) |
| old-age pensioner | -0.121 (0.093) | 0.059 (0.049) | 0.098 (0.081) | 0.046 (0.056) | -0.061 (0.092) | 0.093 (0.098) | -0.044 (0.038) | -0.009 (0.108) |
| unemployed | -0.308 (0.126) | 0.273 (0.074) | 0.044 (0.087) | -0.158 (0.150) | -0.248 (0.104) | 0.322 (0.333) | -0.113 (0.083) | -0.134 (0.163) |
| female breadwinner | -0.092 (0.093) | -0.105 (0.042) | -0.112 (0.069) | -0.285 (0.077) | -0.049 (0.063) | 0.021 (0.087) | -0.110 (0.053) | -0.030 (0.148) |
| number of observations | 186 | 376 | 451 | 294 | 383 | 351 | 451 | 130 |
| $\bar{R}^2$ | 0.440 | 0.469 | 0.385 | 0.500 | 0.531 | 0.458 | 0.487 | 0.421 |

follow the pattern found for working men, though the difference between single persons and others are much higher in non-working families. Unemployed have lower incomes than old-age pensioners.[4] It should be remembered that the latter may have additional pensions or other income sources besides the state pension. They both have lower incomes than the reference group, which consists of all other non-working men (e.g., disabled, students, etc.). Finally, it is seen that female breadwinners have a lower income than men, although the coefficient is not significantly different from zero.

### 9.3.2 Denmark

Neither the coefficients for urbanization nor the coefficients for fluctuations in income are significantly different from zero. With respect to occupation we see that civil servants have again a much higher income, whilst farmers have lowest income. Education has a somewhat smaller effect on income for non-working households than for working men. The age-income profiles in Denmark are less steep for non-working than for working households; the age at which a maximum income is earned is 47 years, 7 years later than for working men. The difference between a single person and a one-parent family is smaller, but the difference between these two subgroups and others, viz. couples and households, has increased. In Denmark unemployed have higher incomes than old age pensioners; the other non-working households have lowest incomes of all. For women we see again a lower, this time significantly lower, income than for men.

### 9.3.3 France

Coefficients for urbanization and fluctuations in income are not significantly different from zero in France. Civil servants maintain their position at the top of the income scale; self-employed and farmers are again lowest. This result for the self-employed is striking if we compare it with their high income position if they are working. The effect of general education on income is rather high, although it is still smaller than the effect for working men. As in Belgium, we see that someone with technical education has a higher non-earned income than someone with a standard general education. The coefficients for age are significantly different from zero; the age at which the maximum income is reached is 64. This is in line with the fact that old-age pensioners have a higher income than unemployed; the high income at 64 does not decrease much after retiring. The difference between single persons and other household types is very high; a family has an income which is 1.77 times as high as a single person. This difference is highest of all countries.

### 9.3.4 Germany

Both in small and in large towns in Germany, the income of non-working households is significantly higher than in the countryside. The effect is much stronger than the effect for working men in this country, especially for small towns. The coefficient for fluctuations in income is large, but not significantly different from zero. As in other countries, civil servants have highest non-earned incomes, while farmers have lowest. The effect of education on income is, surprisingly, larger than the effect found for working men. The steepness of the age-income profile is also stronger than the one found for working men. It appears that one- and two-parent families have highest non-earned income, and single persons have lowest. Unemployed have a lower income than old-age pensioners and other non-working families. Finally, female heads of households have a significantly lower non-earned income than male heads of households; the difference is largest of all countries.

### 9.3.5 Ireland

In Ireland, small and large towns have a significant, positive effect on non-earned income. People with large fluctuations in income have a significantly higher income than others; this may be the result of irregular jobs, that produce a higher income than permanent unemployment. Employees (including civil servants) have highest non-earned income, and self-employed lowest (though not significantly different from manual workers). Education has a positive effect on non-earned income, that is slightly smaller than the effect found for working men. The age-income profile, that was found to be very flat for working men, is much steeper for non-earned incomes; the coefficients for this group are significantly different from zero. The difference between single persons and other families is

huge in Ireland; a family has an income of 2.442 times the income of a single person.
Unemployed have lower non-earned incomes than pensioners and other non-working persons. In Ireland, however, no significant difference is found between the incomes of male and female heads of households.

9.3.6  Italy

In Italy, a deviant age-income profile is found, reflected by a large intercept: incomes are decreasing until about 62 years of age. Urbanization does not have a significant effect on income. People with small fluctuations in income have significantly higher non-earned income. In Italy employees, rather than civil servants have highest non-earned incomes; self-employed and manual workers have low incomes, that are only surpassed by people who have never worked. The effect of education is largest of all countries; it is also larger than the effect found for working men. As in Ireland, differences between single persons and families are very large. Unemployed have higher incomes than old-age pensioners; all other non-working households have lowest. No significant difference, finally, is found between male and female breadwinners.

9.3.7  The Netherlands

In the Netherlands, no significant coefficients are found for urbanization. Families with large fluctuations in income tend to have higher incomes; the differences are not, however, significantly different from zero. Employees have highest non-earned incomes (civil servants could not be distinguished as a separate category among non-working households). Farmers have lowest incomes. General education has an increasing effect on income; the coefficient is even larger than it was for working males. The coefficients for technical education do not follow the expected pattern: someone with standard technical education has a higher income than someone with standard general education; but the higher technical education one has, the lower income is. However, this negative coefficient is not significantly different from zero. The coefficients of $\ln$ age and $\ln^2$ age are slightly smaller than the coefficients found for working males. With respect to different household types, we see that single persons have lowest incomes, and families have highest. Unemployed have lower incomes than old-age pensioners. As regards the sex of the main breadwinner, it is found that women have a significantly lower non-earned income.

### 9.3.8 United Kingdom

Neither degree of urbanization, nor fluctuations in income have a significant effect on income. Self-employed have highest income, followed directly by civil servants, while manual workers and those who have never worked have lowest incomes. The effect of education on income is positive, and slightly smaller than the effect found for working men. The age-income profile is rather flat; no significant coefficients are found. Again, we find large differences between single persons and families, like in Ireland and Italy. Unemployed have lowest incomes, although the coefficient is not significantly different from the coefficients of old-age pensioners and others. Finally, sex of the main breadwinner does not have a significant effect on non-earned income.

### 9.3.9 International comparison

The income functions for non-working households, that may be said to reflect social security regulations and pension schemes in the different countries, may be summarized as follows:
(i)   Living in a large town seems to have a positive effect on non-earned income (with the exception of Denmark).
(ii)  People with fluctuations in income tend to have higher non-earned incomes on average (exceptions in Italy and France). A very large effect is found in Ireland.
(iii) Civil servants have of all occupational categories the most generous social security and pension schemes in all countries except Italy. (In the United Kingdom this favourable position is shared by, surprisingly, the self-employed.) Farmers and self-employed have lowest incomes in all countries, with the exception of the United Kingdom and Italy, where manual workers are worst off.
(iv)  The effect of education on non-earned income is in all countries positive, and in most countries slightly smaller than the effect of education on earnings for working men.

(v) Age-income profiles are in most countries slightly less steep than those found for working men.

(vi) In all countries significant differences between household types are found; single persons have lowest, families have highest non-earned incomes. One parent families and couples are somewhere in between. The differences are especially striking in Ireland, Italy and the United Kingdom.

(vii) In most countries female breadwinners have a lower income than male breadwinners; the difference is very large in Germany.

The effect of the most important characteristics are summarized in table 9.14.

Table 9.14 Effect of socio-economic characteristics on the incomes of non-working families

|  | BEL | DEN | FRA | GER | IRE | ITA | NET | UK |
|---|---|---|---|---|---|---|---|---|
| urbanization | + | - | + | + | + | + |  | + |
| fluctuations in income | + | + | - | + | + |  | + | + |
| self-employed | - |  | - | - | - |  |  | + |
| farmers | - | - | - | - | - | + | - | + |
| high education | + | + | + | + | + | + | + | + |
| age: young | - | - | - | - | - |  | - | - |
| old | - | - | - | - | - |  | - | - |
| sex: female | - | - | - | - | - | + | - | - |

In chapter 11, we will compare the incomes for working and non-working households with their needs, as reflected by the welfare function of income. We will first describe in chapter 10 the estimation results of the equations explaining the welfare parameters μ and σ.

NOTES TO CHAPTER 9

[1] In discussing the results, in this and the following chapters, we will consider the coefficients ceteris paribus.

[2] In this and the subsequent tables all dummy variables are equal to zero for someone living in the country, without fluctuations in income, who is a manual worker with general education, and is a single person.

[3] With respect to education the characteristics may be different, as the standard education of men differs from the standard education of women.

[4] In all tables for non-working households, the dummy variables for unemployed and old-age pensioners are zero for all other households, i.e. disabled, students, housewives, etc.

APPENDIX TO CHAPTER 9

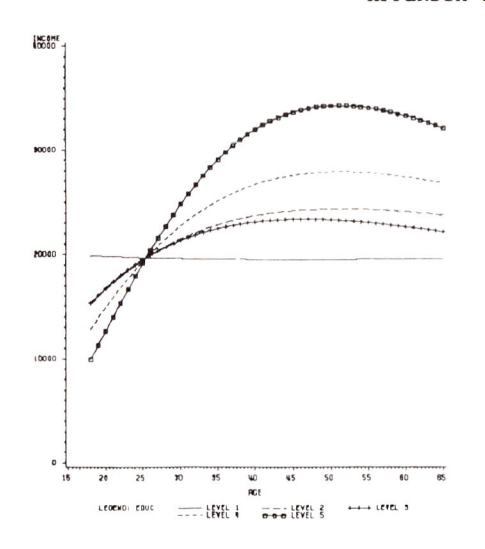

Figure 9.1.a

Age-income profiles
working, education, Belgium

Figure 9.1.b

Age-income profiles
working, job, Belgium

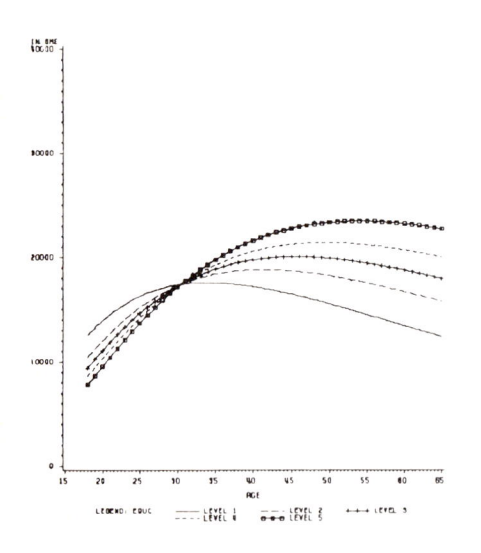

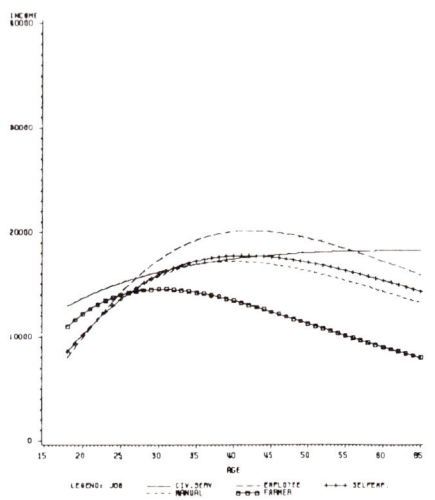

Figure 9.2.a

Age-income profiles
working, education, Denmark

Figure 9.2.b

Age-income profiles
working, job, Denmark

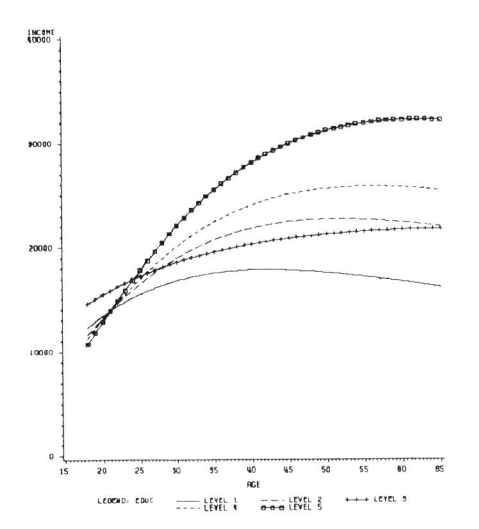

Figure 9.3.a

Age-income profiles
working, education, France

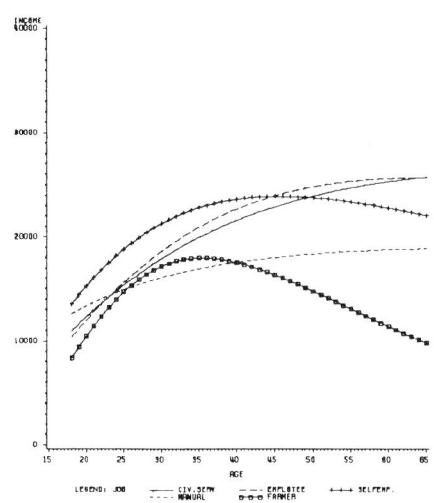

Figure 9.3.b

Age-income profiles
working, job, France

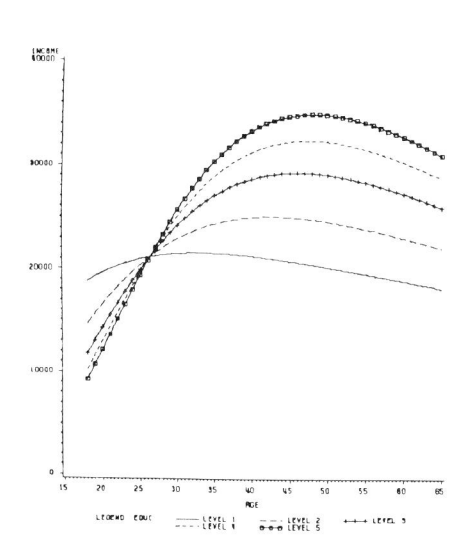

Figure 9.4.a

Age-income profiles
working, education, Germany

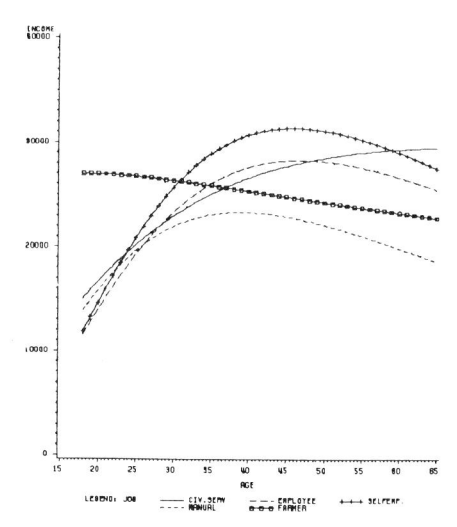

Figure 9.4.b

Age-income profiles
working, job, Germany

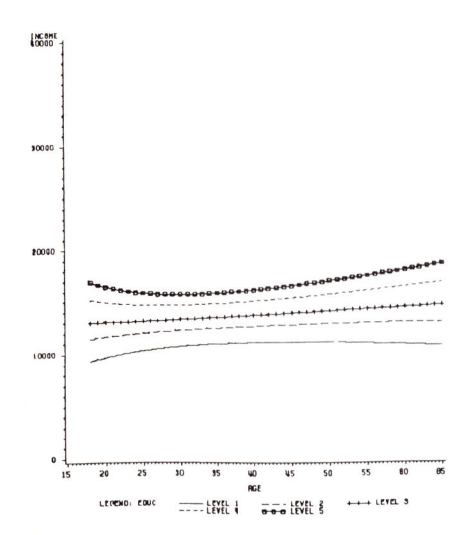

Figure 9.5.a

Age-income profiles
working, education, Ireland

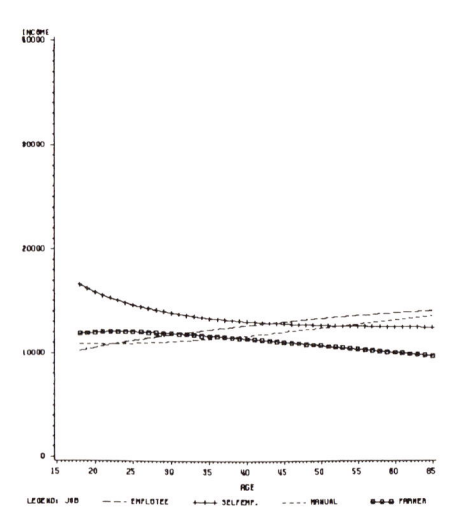

Figure 9.5.b

Age-income profiles
working, job, Ireland

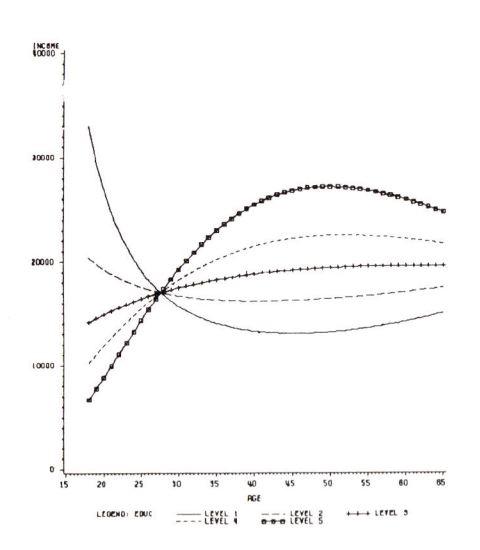

Figure 9.6.a

Age-income profiles
working, education, Italy

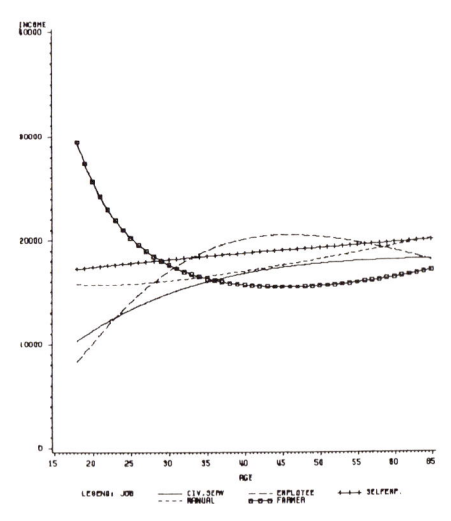

Figure 9.6.b

Age-income profiles
working, job, Italy

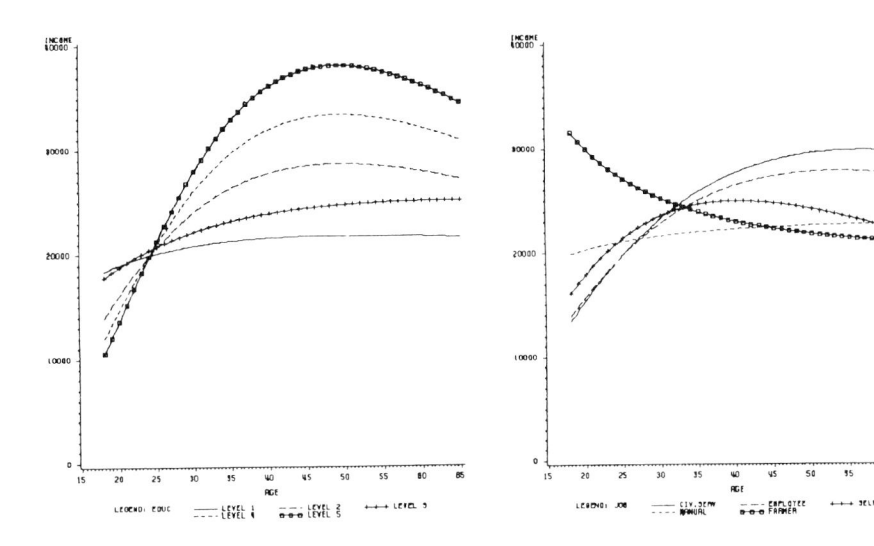

Figure 9.7.a
Age-income profiles,
working, education, the Netherlands

Figure 9.7.b
Age-income profiles
working, job, the Netherlands

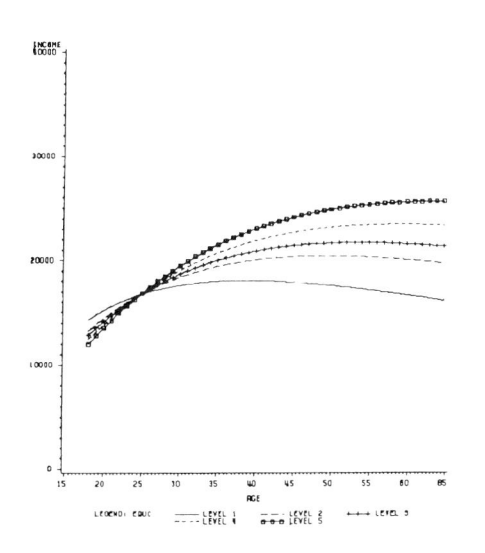

Figure 9.8.a
Age-income profiles
working, education, United Kingdom

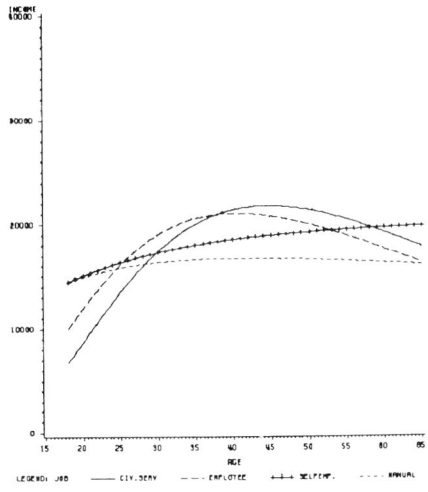

Figure 9.8.b
Age-income profiles
working, job, United Kingdom

Chapter 10

EMPIRICAL RESULTS: DETERMINANTS OF WELFARE

In this chapter the empirical results of the estimation of the welfare parameters μ and σ are presented and discussed. In order to restrict the number of tables, no results including cross-product terms of age and education, respectively occupation are presented. The effect of these cross-product terms is, however, illustrated in age-μ profiles, differentiated according to education and occupation in the appendix. For the calculation of poverty lines, and comparison of income and poverty lines we refer to chapter 11. Section 10.1 presents the results for μ, and section 10.2 concentrates on σ. It may be remembered that μ is a location parameter; exp(μ) is the income level that is evaluated by 0.5, just halfway on the welfare scale. Parameter σ is a dispersion parameter; it indicates the range of incomes that is evaluated significantly different from zero or one. Again, results are first discussed per country and then compared over countries.

## 10.1 Determinants of μ

### 10.1.1 Belgium

The results of the μ equation for Belgium are presented in the first column of table 10.1. It is seen that people living in a large city have a higher μ than people living in the country or in small towns, although the coefficient is not significantly different from zero. Large fluctuations in income also increase μ; someone with large fluctuations needs exp(0.118) = 1.12 times the amount of someone with a constant income for the same welfare evaluation of 0.5. Changes in financial situation over the last two years have the expected effect on μ: in families where household income has increased over the last two years μ is significantly lower than in households without changes in financial situation, whereas for households that have experienced a decrease in income, μ is significantly higher. This reflects the effect of past income, due to habit formation. The dummies for occupation indicate for presently non-working people their former occupation; for people who are working their present occupation. It is seen that employees and civil servants have a significantly higher μ

Table 10.1 The explanation of welfare parameter μ

| | BEL | DEN | FRA | GER | IRE | ITA | NET | UK |
|---|---|---|---|---|---|---|---|---|
| intercept | 1.580 (1.139) | 0.393 (0.606) | 1.706 (0.664) | 2.071 (0.857) | 4.260 (1.024) | 4.072 (1.090) | 1.429 (0.703) | -2.535 (1.086) |
| small town | 0.001 (0.018) | -0.000 (0.012) | -0.016 (0.016) | 0.068 (0.015) | 0.070 (0.027) | -0.032 (0.016) | 0.004 (0.011) | 0.014 (0.016) |
| large town | 0.028 (0.017) | 0.003 (0.012) | 0.040 (0.013) | 0.042 (0.015) | 0.082 (0.016) | 0.037 (0.015) | 0.037 (0.013) | 0.033 (0.017) |
| small fluctuations | 0.002 (0.017) | 0.004 (0.014) | -0.009 (0.013) | 0.023 (0.015) | 0.042 (0.017) | -0.006 (0.015) | 0.003 (0.013) | 0.002 (0.014) |
| large fluctuations | 0.118 (0.037) | 0.011 (0.020) | 0.029 (0.019) | 0.114 (0.029) | 0.073 (0.025) | -0.003 (0.021) | 0.020 (0.023) | -0.027 (0.026) |
| income increased | -0.031 (0.016) | -0.015 (0.012) | 0.004 (0.013) | -0.003 (0.014) | -0.018 (0.016) | -0.034 (0.015) | -0.043 (0.012) | -0.034 (0.016) |
| income decreased | 0.067 (0.021) | 0.070 (0.012) | 0.080 (0.014) | 0.086 (0.020) | 0.058 (0.018) | 0.067 (0.015) | 0.101 (0.015) | 0.027 (0.018) |
| employee | 0.056 (0.020) | 0.026 (0.013) | 0.003 (0.016) | 0.038 (0.017) | } 0.010 (0.020) | 0.073 (0.021) | 0.017 (0.014) | 0.043 (0.017) |
| civil servant | 0.052 (0.021) | 0.020 (0.017) | 0.009 (0.017) | 0.047 (0.021) | | 0.086 (0.021) | 0.021 (0.017) | 0.059 (0.025) |
| self-employed | } 0.006 (0.029) | -0.018 (0.017) | 0.022 (0.019) | -0.013 (0.027) | -0.000 (0.026) | 0.060 (0.018) | -0.035 (0.020) | } 0.022 (0.026) |
| farmer | | -0.103 (0.021) | -0.107 (0.028) | -0.054 (0.032) | -0.024 (0.023) | -0.055 (0.029) | -0.081 (0.026) | |
| never worked | 0.097 (0.096) | 0.007 (0.032) | -0.061 (0.032) | -0.047 (0.040) | -0.028 (0.063) | 0.031 (0.037) | 0.066 (0.011) | 0.107 (0.146) |
| general education | 0.045 (0.011) | 0.017 (0.007) | 0.043 (0.009) | 0.033 (0.009) | 0.032 (0.011) | 0.015 (0.009) | 0.035 (0.010) | 0.060 (0.010) |
| technical education (dummy) | -0.022 (0.017) | | -0.005 (0.014) | | | | 0.008 (0.010) | |
| ln age | 1.911 (0.642) | 1.689 (0.350) | 1.850 (0.377) | 1.052 (0.487) | 0.387 (0.556) | 0.856 (0.583) | 1.948 (0.387) | 4.297 (0.609) |
| ln²age | -0.256 (0.087) | -0.238 (0.048) | -0.253 (0.052) | -0.142 (0.067) | -0.062 (0.075) | -0.124 (0.078) | -0.258 (0.052) | -0.582 (0.083) |
| two adults | 0.055 (0.026) | 0.092 (0.015) | 0.055 (0.015) | 0.019 (0.019) | 0.079 (0.021) | 0.104 (0.019) | 0.118 (0.015) | 0.142 (0.029) |
| three or more adults | 0.100 (0.048) | 0.019 (0.061) | 0.082 (0.042) | 0.026 (0.043) | 0.031 (0.039) | 0.005 (0.033) | 0.173 (0.053) | 0.112 (0.055) |
| one working | 0.064 (0.031) | 0.011 (0.019) | 0.042 (0.020) | 0.012 (0.024) | -0.003 (0.024) | 0.018 (0.024) | 0.007 (0.017) | 0.026 (0.030) |
| two working | 0.075 (0.037) | 0.074 (0.022) | 0.058 (0.024) | -0.009 (0.029) | 0.010 (0.037) | -0.009 (0.029) | -0.007 (0.021) | 0.017 (0.032) |
| one child | 0.006 (0.022) | 0.028 (0.014) | 0.021 (0.016) | 0.048 (0.017) | 0.083 (0.024) | 0.043 (0.017) | 0.039 (0.015) | 0.046 (0.020) |
| two children | 0.027 (0.023) | 0.034 (0.015) | 0.035 (0.017) | 0.068 (0.019) | 0.109 (0.024) | 0.084 (0.018) | 0.036 (0.014) | 0.020 (0.020) |
| three children | 0.031 (0.027) | 0.026 (0.020) | 0.013 (0.021) | 0.107 (0.026) | 0.134 (0.025) | 0.093 (0.025) | 0.065 (0.019) | 0.076 (0.027) |
| four children | 0.086 (0.035) | 0.039 (0.039) | 0.032 (0.033) | 0.143 (0.042) | 0.159 (0.028) | 0.195 (0.039) | 0.017 (0.029) | 0.042 (0.041) |
| five children | 0.142 (0.053) | 0.145 (0.087) | 0.240 (0.051) | 0.231 (0.086) | 0.158 (0.034) | 0.148 (0.069) | 0.083 (0.045) | 0.005 (0.057) |
| six children | 0.363 (0.074) | 0.068 (0.150) | 0.227 (0.061) | 0.129 (0.074) | 0.240 (0.031) | 0.253 (0.109) | 0.291 (0.079) | 0.026 (0.102) |
| income | 0.460 (0.024) | 0.643 (0.014) | 0.481 (0.013) | 0.568 (0.020) | 0.474 (0.018) | 0.408 (0.015) | 0.468 (0.016) | 0.422 (0.021) |
| number of observations | 1269 | 1981 | 2334 | 1572 | 1734 | 1924 | 1890 | 1383 |
| R̄² | 0.593 | 0.824 | 0.642 | 0.653 | 0.631 | 0.526 | 0.636 | 0.511 |

than manual workers and self-employed. People who have never worked have, surprisingly, highest μ of all; the coefficient is, however, not significantly different from zero. General education has a significantly increasing effect on μ, whilst people with technical education have a lower μ than people with standard general education. Age has a significant effect on μ, apart from the effect via income; the effect is illustrated in age-income profiles in the appendix.

The number of adults in a family has a positive effect on μ; the coefficients are not, however, very large (a two-person family has an exp(μ) which is 1.05 times the exp(μ) of a one-person family). This coefficient reflects the net effect of cost of an additional person and the income in kind in the form of, e.g., household production. The number of adults with an income of their own also has a positive effect on μ. The difference between one- and two-earner households is, however, very small, compared to the difference with non-working households: a two-earner household needs exp(0.075) = 1.08 more than a non-working household for the same welfare evaluation of 0.5, while a one-earner household needs exp(0.064) = 1.07 times as much as a non-working household. The number of children has an increasing effect on μ; surprisingly the marginal cost of children increase in Belgium. We will return to the cost of children at the poverty line level in chapter 11.

The dummies denoting the number of adults, the number of income earners and the number of children enable us to compare the welfare needs of households of different types, that were introduced in chapter 5: a family with two children, for instance, where only one adult is working, has an exp(μ) which is exp(0.055 + 0.064 + 0.027) = 1.16 times as high as a single person who is not working. A family with six children, where no adult is working, "needs" 1.53 as much as a non-working single person. Finally, the coefficient of log-household income, the "preference drift", is 0.46; this coefficient differs significantly from zero. The $\bar{R}^2$ of this equation is 0.593.

The coefficients of the cross-product terms with education and occupation are not significantly different from zero. If we replace the variable "log income" in the μ equation by the systematical part of the equation explaining log income as described in the previous chapters, we may write μ in a reduced form as follows:

$$\hat{\mu} = X_m\beta_m + X_0\beta_0 + \beta_y \ln y = X_m(\beta_m + \beta_y\hat{\gamma}_m) + X_0\beta_0$$

where $\hat{\gamma}_m$ represents the estimated coefficients of the income equation.[1] As ln age and ln²age are two of the explanatory variables in $X_m$, this enables us to calculate the reduced form age-µ profiles.

As we have estimated the income equation for working and non-working families separately, these age-µ profiles have to be differentiated accordingly. Hence Belgian age-µ profiles, differentiated according to education and occupation, are presented for both working and non-working families in figures 10.1.a to 10.1.d in the appendix. The deviating profile for people who have never worked in 10.1.d, is the result of a small number of observations; the corresponding coefficients are not significantly different from those of manual workers.

### 10.1.2 Denmark

The results of the µ-equation are presented in the second column of table 10.1. The dummies for urbanization and fluctuations in income do not have coefficients significantly different from zero. The coefficients denoting changes in financial situations have the expected signs; when one's financial situation has decreased, exp(µ) is significantly higher than for someone whose situation has not changed at all. With respect to employment, it is seen that employees and civil servants have a higher µ than manual workers; self-employed and particularly farmers have a lower µ than manual workers. Education has a small positive effect on µ. The coefficients of age are also significantly different from zero; they are illustrated in figures 10.2.a to 10.2.d in the appendix.

The number of adults in a family follows a peculiar pattern; two adults need 10 % more than one adult, but three adults (forming, in our definition, an extended family) have needs that are not significantly different from those of a one-person family. This may indicate dominance of the value of the production in kind in such extended families. The number of people working has a positive effect on µ; in Denmark, the difference between one and two working persons is much higher than that between zero and one working person, indicating large work related cost and cost for child care in two-earner families. The number of children has a small, generally increasing effect on µ (with an exception for six children).

Combined, these dummy coefficients show that in Denmark the largest welfare needs are found in a household with two working adults and with five children; they need 1.36 as much as a non-working single person.
Finally, it is seen that the preference drift in Denmark is rather high, viz. 0.643. The fit of this equation is very good; $\bar{R}^2$ is 0.824. In Denmark the cross-product terms of age and education are significantly different from zero; they are illustrated in figures 10.2.a to 10.2.d in the appendix.

10.1.3 France

The French results of the µ-equation are presented in the third column of table 10.1. Living in a large city has a significant positive effect on µ. Fluctuations in income do not have a significant effect. Households that have experienced a decrease in income have a significantly higher µ than households where no change has taken place; the expected negative coefficient for households who have experienced an increase in income is, however, positive, although not significantly different from zero. Self-employed in France have highest welfare needs, while farmers have the lowest (significantly lower than manual workers). People who have never worked are in between farmers and manual workers. General education has an increasing effect on µ. The coefficients for age (both significantly different from zero) are illustrated in figures 10.3.a to 10.3.d in the appendix.
The number of adults in a household increases µ, with some economies of scale. The number of people working in the household also increases µ. The effect of children is in general to increase µ; µ does not, however, increase monotonously with the number of children. Largest differences between household types are found between extended families with two working adults and five children, and non-working single persons; the former household needs 1.462 times as much as the latter for a welfare evaluation of 0.5.
The preference drift in France is found to be 0.481. The $\bar{R}^2$ of the equation is 0.642. Extension to a model with cross-products of age with education and occupation does not yield significant coefficients; they are illustrated in figures 10.3.a to 10.3.d in the appendix.

## 10.1.4 Germany

The German results are presented in the fourth column of table 10.1. Living in a small town results in a higher µ than living in a large city, which in turn yields a higher µ than living in the country. In Germany, large fluctuations in income have a considerable positive effect on µ. The coefficients for changes in financial situation are as expected. With respect to occupation, we see that civil servants and employees have highest needs, while farmers have lowest. Education has a significant increasing effect on welfare needs. The coefficients for age are significantly different from zero.

The number of adults does not have a significant effect on µ, nor has the number of people working. The number of children does, however, have an increasing, positive effect on µ (with an exception for six children). As a result, the household with highest needs is an extended family with five children, where one person is working. Lowest needs are found again for non-working single persons.

Finally, the preference drift in Germany is found to be 0.568. The $\bar{R}^2$ of the equation is 0.653. Adding cross-products of age and education or occupation does not yield significant coefficients; they are illustrated, however, in figures 10.4.a to 10.4.d in the appendix.

## 10.1.5 Ireland

The Irish results are presented in the fifth column of table 10.1. Degree of urbanization has a significant positive effect on µ, as well as fluctuations in income. Changes in financial situation have the expected signs, although the coefficient of "decrease in financial situation" is rather small, compared to the other countries. Employees and civil servants have highest welfare needs, while farmers and people who have never worked have lowest. Education has a small but significantly positive effect on µ. The coefficients of age are not significantly different from zero.

In Ireland, as in Denmark, extended families have lower welfare needs than a household with two adults. Again this may indicate a dominance of the home production factor in extended families. The coefficients for the number of people who are working are not significantly different from zero. The number of children has, however, a large increasing effect on µ.

The family with highest welfare needs is a family with two working adults and six children.
The preference drift, finally, is found to be 0.474. The $\bar{R}^2$ of this equation was 0.631. Addition of cross-product terms of age and occupation yields significant coefficients for farmers; these effects are illustrated in figures 10.5.a to 10.5.d in the appendix.

### 10.1.6 Italy

The results for Italy are presented in the sixth column of table 10.1. Living in a large city is seen to have a significantly positive effect on µ, whilst living in a small town results in a µ that is significantly lower than for people living in the country. The coefficients for fluctuations in income do not have a significant effect on µ. Changes in financial situation have the expected signs. Civil servants and employees have the highest value of µ, and farmers have lowest. Education does not have a significant effect on µ, nor does age.
A couple needs some 10 % more than a single person; extended families, however, do not need significantly more than a single person. The effect of the number of people working is not significantly different from zero. The larger the number of children, the larger µ (with an exception for five children).
The preference drift, finally, is equal to 0.408. The $\bar{R}^2$ is 0.526. Extension with cross-products of age, education and occupation does not yield significant coefficients; the resulting age-µ profiles are presented in figures 10.6.a to 10.6.d in the appendix. The decreasing age-µ profiles for non-working households in 10.6.b and 10.6.d are the result of the deviant age-income profile for non-working households in Italy; see table 9.13.

### 10.1.7 The Netherlands

The Dutch results are given in the seventh column of table 10.1. Living in a large city significantly increases needs. Fluctuations in income do not have a significant effect on µ. The coefficients of changes in financial situation are highly significant, and very large: someone whose financial situation has become worse has an exp(µ) which is 10 % as high as the

exp(μ) of someone whose financial situation has not changed. Employees have highest μ, and farmers have lowest. The effect of both general and technical education on μ is positive, and significantly different from zero.
The number of adults in a household has a large positive, significant effect on μ. With respect to the number of people working, however, it is seen that one breadwinner has a higher μ than non-working households or two-breadwinner families (although these effects are not significantly different from zero). The higher the number of children, the higher μ (with a non-significant exception for four children).
The preference drift, finally, is found to be 0.468. $\bar{R}^2$ is 0.636. The age-μ profiles are significantly different for different education levels, and for different occupations; they are presented in figures 10.7.a to 10.7.d in the appendix.

## 10.1.8 The United Kingdom

The British results are given in the eighth column of table 10.1. The larger the degree of urbanization, the larger μ. Fluctuations in income do not have significant coefficients. The coefficients of changes in financial situation do have the expected signs. With respect to occupation it is seen that people who have never worked have highest μ, but the coefficient is not significantly different from zero. Education has a significant positive effect on μ. The coefficients of age are significantly different from zero. A couple needs more than extended families and single persons. The effect of the number of people working is not significant. The coefficients for the number of children are not significantly different from zero, except for three children; μ is not increasing with increasing family size.
The preference drift is found to be 0.422. The $\bar{R}^2$ of this equation is 0.511.
Extension with cross-products of age with education and occupation does not yield significant coefficients; they are illustrated in figures 10.8.a to 10.8.d in the appendix.

## 10.1.9 International comparison

The value of the welfare parameter μ is in all countries explained quite well by the explanatory variables; $\bar{R}^2$ varies between 0.511 and 0.824. We may summarize the results as follows:

(i) In all countries except Denmark, living in a large city results in a higher μ; the coefficient varies between 0.028 for Belgium and 0.082 in Ireland. This reflects higher cost of living in large cities than in small cities or in the countryside.

(ii) Fluctuations in income have a significant positive effect on μ in Belgium, Germany and Ireland. This effect indicates the risk-premium that these households need in order to compensate for the uncertainty in income.

(iii) In almost all countries people who have experienced an increase in income have a lower μ, ceteris paribus, than people without changes in income, and people who have experienced a decrease in income have a higher μ, ceteris paribus, than people without changes in income. The extent of this "habit formation" varies over countries; in all countries except the United Kingdom the effect of a decrease in income is larger than the effect of an increase, implying that it is more difficult to get used to a lower income than to a higher income.

(iv) The effect of occupation varies slightly over countries; in most countries employees and civil servants have highest and farmers lowest μ. This latter effect reflects the income in kind of farmers, that results in a lower need in terms of cash income.

(v) Education has a positive effect on μ in all countries. This may be the compensating differential that households need as a return to their investments in human capital. It may also reflect a strong reference effect of education.

(vi) Age has in most countries a significant effect on μ as well; the total effect of age, both per se and via income on μ is that the age at which the maximum μ is found is a few years earlier than the age at which the maximum income is earned. This may be explained by the fact that the period in which a family usually has highest cost is the child-raising period, while maximum income is usually earned later in life.

(vii) With respect to different household types, it is seen that in all countries two adults in a household have higher needs than one adult; the effect of extended families on µ, however, varies across countries. The number of people working in a household has an increasing effect on µ in Belgium, Denmark and France which implies that the loss of home production and higher work related cost dominate the reference effect; in the other countries the difference between families with one, two or no working persons is not significantly different from zero.

The effect of the number of children on µ is in most countries positive; in the United Kingdom, however, no significant effects are found, and in some countries increasing instead of decreasing marginal cost are found.

(viii) The preference drift varies between 0.408 (Italy) and 0.643 (Denmark).

These findings are (partly) summarized in table 10.2.

Table 10.2 The effect of socio-economic variables on welfare parameter µ; synopsis

|  | BEL | DEN | FRA | GER | IRE | ITA | NET | UK |
|---|---|---|---|---|---|---|---|---|
| urbanization | + |  | + | + | + | + | + | + |
| fluctuations in income | + |  | + | + |  |  |  | - |
| self-employed |  |  |  |  |  | + | - |  |
| farmers |  | - | - | - |  | - | - |  |
| high education | + | + | + | + | + | + | + | + |
| age: young | - | - | - | - |  | + | - | - |
| old | - | - | - | - |  | - | - | - |
| family size | + | + | + | + | + | + | + | + |
| number of breadwinners | + | + | + | + |  |  |  |  |
| $age_{max}$ | 47 | 39 | 44 | 43 |  |  | 52 | 43 |

After having estimated the coefficients of the equation explaining µ for each country separately, we may now use the fact that data on several countries are available to estimate the effect of median income on µ. Median income represents some average standard of living; its possible influence on µ will eventually be an indication of the relativity of the poverty line with respect to median income.

To this end the regression equation (4.12), derived in chapter 4, is estimated for all countries jointly, where µ is explained by family size, actual income, and by the national median income and standard deviation of log incomes in the relevant country. The resulting equation writes:[2]

(10.1) $\quad \mu = 1.410 + 0.574 \ln y + 0.224 \mu_y + 0.712 \sigma_y + 0.085 \ln fs$
$\quad\quad\quad\quad (0.175)\ (0.005) \quad\quad (0.017) \quad\ (0.046) \quad\quad (0.005)$

$\bar{R}^2 = 0.616 \quad\quad N = 13,132$

It appears that the preference drift of all countries combined is estimated at 0.574, which implies that almost 60 % of an increase in income will be absorbed by an adjustment of needs. The coefficient of median income is significantly different from zero, and equals 0.224. An increase in median income of 10 % will increase needs with 2.24 %. The preference drift and this reference drift together imply that if a general increase in income of a fraction $\alpha$ occurs the welfare parameter $\mu$ shifts with
$(0.574 + 0.224)\alpha$, which implies that almost 80 % of this economic growth is not perceived as an increase in welfare. Although this is a high percentage, it suggests there is still some welfare gain to be found in economic growth. However, it should be noted that the absence of information on previous incomes may cause a specification error that probably results in underestimation of both preference drift and reference drift. The coefficient of $\sigma_y$, which is also highly significantly different from zero, implies that income inequality per se also tends to increase needs. Perhaps in countries with a high income inequality people have more house holds with relatively high incomes in their social reference group than in countries with a small income inequality, where households in the highest decile of the income distribution may be less conspicious, and therefore not included in the social reference group. The last explanatory variable is family size: the family size coefficient of 0.085 implies that an increase in household size of 100 % results in an increase in household needs of 8.5 %. This figure is an average of the effects of family size in the different countries.

These results will enable us to assess the elasticity of the poverty line with respect to median income, as defined in chapter 2; the empirical value of this elasticity will be discussed in chapter 11.

## 10.2 Determinants of σ

The second welfare parameter is σ, the welfare sensitivity. The estimation results for σ are presented in table 10.3 for all countries. As explanatory variables we have chosen, as argued in chapter 4, fluctuations in income, changes in financial situation, education, occupation and household type (including number of breadwinners). We have furthermore included income, as a possible relationship between σ and income may complicate the definition of poverty lines at welfare levels different from 0.5.

It appears that the explanation of σ by these variables is rather poor; $\bar{R}^2$ varies between 0.024 (Italy) and 0.123 (the Netherlands). Fluctuations in income do have a significant positive effect on σ in Denmark, France, and the Netherlands; in the other countries, however, no significant effects are found. An improvement of the financial situation has a positive effect on σ in Denmark and the United Kingdom. A deterioration of the financial situation has a negative effect in most countries. An exception is the United Kingdom where any change in financial situation increases σ. With respect to occupation, we see that self-employed and farmers systematically have a higher σ than manual workers; the effect is significantly different from zero in all countries. Another effect that is generally found is an increasing influence of education on σ. Looking at the coefficients for household type, we see that in some countries (Denmark, Ireland, the Netherlands, the United Kingdom) σ tends to increase with the number of breadwinners in a household. Other differences between household types exist, but these effects are not the same in all countries. In Denmark, Germany, Ireland, the Netherlands and the United Kingdom single persons have a relatively high σ, while in France and Belgium it is relatively low. Finally, income appears to have a significantly positive effect on σ in Belgium, the Netherlands and the U.K., but a significantly negative effect in Denmark and Ireland.

If we interpret σ as the dispersion parameter of the perceived income distribution, these signs may be interpreted as follows: if the coefficient of income is positive, the perceived income inequality is higher for people with higher incomes; if the coefficient of income is negative, perceived income inequality is lower for people with higher incomes. In the former case, which holds in Belgium, the Netherlands and the U.K., people in high income classes have a social reference group with a large

Table 10.3 Determinants of log σ

|  | BEL | DEN | FRA | GER | IRE | ITA | NET | UK |
|---|---|---|---|---|---|---|---|---|
| intercept | -2.180 (0.260) | -0.397 (0.347) | -1.100 (0.161) | -0.590 (0.321) | -0.233 (0.186) | -0.869 (0.213) | -3.174 (0.313) | -2.058 (0.254) |
| small fluctuations | -0.001 (0.024) | 0.049 (0.034) | 0.019 (0.020) | 0.005 (0.026) | -0.044 (0.022) | 0.004 (0.019) | 0.064 (0.025) | -0.011 (0.021) |
| large fluctuations | -0.025 (0.052) | 0.130 (0.048) | 0.095 (0.029) | -0.070 (0.050) | 0.010 (0.033) | -0.006 (0.027) | 0.124 (0.046) | 0.040 (0.038) |
| increase financial situation | -0.006 (0.022) | 0.067 (0.029) | 0.020 (0.019) | -0.045 (0.023) | -0.037 (0.021) | -0.003 (0.019) | -0.004 (0.022) | 0.048 (0.024) |
| decrease financial situation | -0.013 (0.029) | -0.003 (0.028) | -0.042 (0.020) | -0.053 (0.033) | -0.044 (0.023) | -0.030 (0.019) | -0.028 (0.028) | 0.041 (0.026) |
| employee | 0.008 (0.028) | 0.039 (0.030) | 0.056 (0.023) | 0.014 (0.029) | -0.001 (0.026) | 0.029 (0.026) | 0.074 (0.026) | 0.045 (0.025) |
| civil servant | 0.050 (0.029) | 0.040 (0.041) | 0.054 (0.025) | 0.021 (0.036) | -- | -0.000 (0.023) | 0.077 (0.033) | 0.082 (0.037) |
| self-employed | 0.142 (0.040) | 0.153 (0.040) | 0.171 (0.029) | 0.098 (0.045) | 0.116 (0.033) | 0.114 (0.023) | 0.189 (0.038) | 0.190 (0.038) |
| farmer | -- | 0.102 (0.048) | 0.166 (0.041) | 0.230 (0.055) | 0.106 (0.027) | 0.090 (0.035) | 0.218 (0.052) | -- |
| never worked | 0.192 (0.131) | 0.102 (0.077) | 0.030 (0.051) | 0.064 (0.070) | -0.169 (0.083) | 0.012 (0.048) | -- | 0.091 (0.225) |
| general education | 0.061 (0.015) | 0.061 (0.015) | 0.090 (0.012) | 0.053 (0.015) | 0.041 (0.014) | 0.018 (0.011) | 0.041 (0.020) | 0.002 (0.014) |
| technical education | -- | -- | -- | -- | -- | -- | 0.065 (0.018) | -- |
| technical education (dummy) | 0.007 (0.023) | -- | -0.039 (0.020) | -- | -- | -- | 0.001 (0.020) | -- |
| single person, non-working | 0.068 (0.077) | -0.182 (0.056) | 0.150 (0.041) | -0.013 (0.057) | -0.148 (0.079) | 0.080 (0.055) | 0.011 (0.053) | 0.146 (0.117) |
| one-parent family, working | -0.008 (0.084) | -0.105 (0.071) | 0.028 (0.041) | -0.055 (0.067) | -0.064 (0.072) | 0.090 (0.049) | 0.068 (0.077) | -0.035 (0.091) |
| one-parent family, non-working | 0.123 (0.086) | -0.112 (0.098) | 0.064 (0.066) | -0.012 (0.084) | -0.139 (0.078) | 0.124 (0.070) | 0.070 (0.067) | -0.160 (0.122) |
| couple, two working | 0.071 (0.078) | -0.089 (0.053) | 0.008 (0.038) | 0.012 (0.054) | -0.000 (0.101) | -0.022 (0.052) | -0.108 (0.052) | -0.131 (0.072) |
| couple, one working | 0.003 (0.073) | -0.077 (0.057) | 0.023 (0.036) | -0.027 (0.053) | -0.080 (0.079) | -0.002 (0.048) | -0.052 (0.054) | -0.085 (0.077) |
| couple, non-working | 0.108 (0.075) | -0.138 (0.061) | 0.038 (0.039) | -0.034 (0.057) | -0.147 (0.076) | 0.023 (0.047) | -0.128 (0.051) | -0.211 (0.079) |
| family, two working | -0.013 (0.069) | -0.095 (0.051) | 0.022 (0.033) | 0.014 (0.050) | -0.032 (0.080) | -0.012 (0.044) | -0.058 (0.049) | -0.173 (0.069) |
| family, one working | -0.018 (0.065) | -0.076 (0.053) | 0.000 (0.029) | -0.088 (0.044) | -0.094 (0.068) | -0.017 (0.040) | -0.101 (0.042) | -0.251 (0.068) |
| family, non-working | 0.116 (0.092) | -0.117 (0.137) | 0.062 (0.052) | -0.028 (0.077) | -0.147 (0.075) | 0.036 (0.054) | -0.175 (0.059) | -0.152 (0.093) |
| extended family | 0.016 (0.083) | 0.018 (0.124) | -0.054 (0.059) | -0.017 (0.073) | -0.074 (0.072) | 0.041 (0.049) | -0.233 (0.091) | -0.150 (0.091) |
| log income | 0.140 (0.032) | -0.073 (0.032) | 0.016 (0.020) | -0.036 (0.033) | -0.075 (0.022) | 0.015 (0.019) | 0.200 (0.032) | 0.148 (0.031) |
| R̄² | 0.072 | 0.036 | 0.076 | 0.025 | 0.034 | 0.024 | 0.123 | 0.075 |
| N | 1207 | 1969 | 2302 | 1521 | 1712 | 1891 | 1831 | 1395 |

variance in income; in the latter case (Denmark and Ireland) they have a social reference group with a small variance of income. It may not be a coincidence that the latter two countries have relatively high actual income inequality, and the former three have relatively low income inequality. Possibly people with high incomes in countries with high income inequality tend to close their eyes to these differences, by only taking into account their own income class, while in countries with low income inequality people with high incomes realize that income inequality does exist, as it may have been the subject of economic policy for years.

We have sofar discussed the explanatory variables of $\sigma$ within each country. Let us now turn to the explanation of $\sigma$ by variables that are country specific, like the extent of income inequality within each country. In chapter 4, on theoretical grounds the following specification for $\sigma$ was hypothesized (equation (4.13)):

$$(10.2) \quad \sigma^2 = \alpha_1 \sigma_y^2 + \alpha_2 (\mu_y - \mu)^2 + \alpha_3 (\ln y - \mu)^2$$

where the coefficients $\alpha_1$ and $\alpha_2$ were restricted to be equal to the reference drift, and $\alpha_3$ was assumed to be equal to the preference drift.
We have estimated (10.2) without any restrictions and with the inclusion of an intercept, in order to see to what extent these assumptions are justified. The result reads as

$$(10.3) \quad \sigma^2 = 0.116 + 0.191\sigma_y^2 + 0.053(m_y - \mu)^2 + 0.210(\ln y - \mu)^2$$
$$\phantom{(10.3) \quad \sigma^2 = } (0.009) \ (0.033) \quad\ \ (0.006) \quad\quad\quad (0.007)$$

$$\bar{R}^2 = 0.078 \quad\quad N = 11{,}834$$

When the model is estimated without intercept, we have

$$(10.4) \quad \sigma^2 = 0.607\sigma_y^2 + 0.060(m_y - \mu)^2 + 0.225(\ln y - \mu)^2$$
$$\phantom{(10.4) \quad \sigma^2 = } (0.009) \quad\ \ (0.006) \quad\quad\quad (0.007)$$

It appears that the restriction $\alpha_1 = \alpha_2$ is not justified in either model, nor are the restrictions with respect to the preference and reference drift.

Moreover, the explanation of $\sigma^2$ is rather bad, with an $\bar{R}^2$ of 0.078. In chapter 4, where the implications of specification (10.2) for the derivation of the poverty line were discussed, it was mentioned that the quality of this explanation is of vital importance in the decision whether one is allowed to maintain the simple hypothesis, e.g., $\sigma = f(\sigma_y)$, in the poverty line definition. We think that the empirical result presented in (10.4) shows that, in spite of the relatively low explanatory power of (10.4), this maintained hypothesis is not acceptable, as both additional terms are significantly different from zero. Moreover, as we have seen in table 10.10, even within a country $\sigma$ is sometimes found to be significantly affected by income, which would also complicate the poverty line definition. These results imply that the simple poverty line definition only holds at the 0.5 level, where these complications do not arise. As we have chosen the 0.5 level as a poverty threshold in chapter 8, this additional computational argument strengthens our decision to concentrate on the 0.5 welfare level in the remainder.

## NOTES TO CHAPTER 10

[1] This implies that we have substituted the estimated equation (3.2) for $\ln y_m$, which is the explanatory equation for income in a household without children allowances or partner's income. Hence all age-$\mu$ profiles apply to this specific household type. For working households the coefficients from tables 9.1 to 9.8 are substituted; for non-working households the coefficients from tables 9.13 to 9.20 are used.

[2] These results have also been described in Hagenaars and Van Praag (1985). Although in the theoretical derivation of equation (4.10) the standard deviation of log incomes was not included, it appeared to be significantly different from zero, and is therefore included in the empirical equation.

APPENDIX TO CHAPTER 10

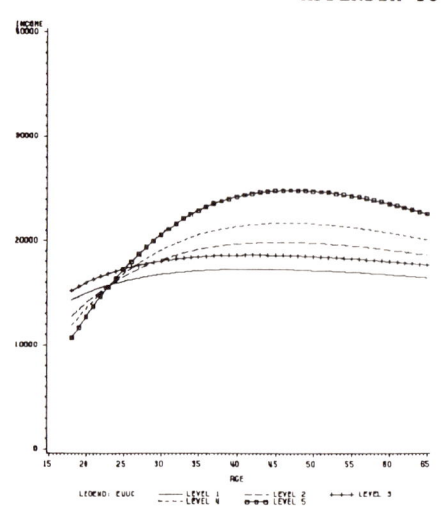

Figure 10.1.a
Age-μ profiles, Belgium
working, education

Figure 10.1.b
Age-μ profiles, Belgium
non-working, education

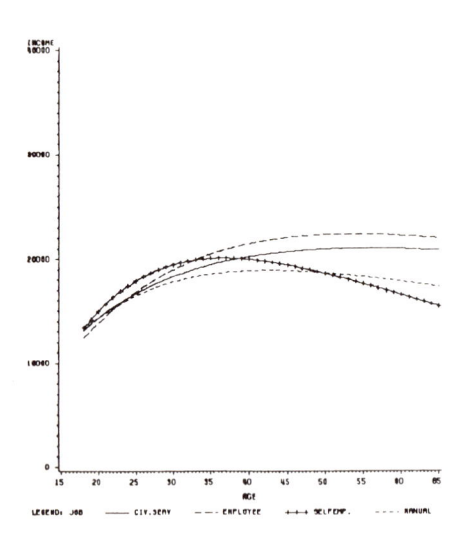

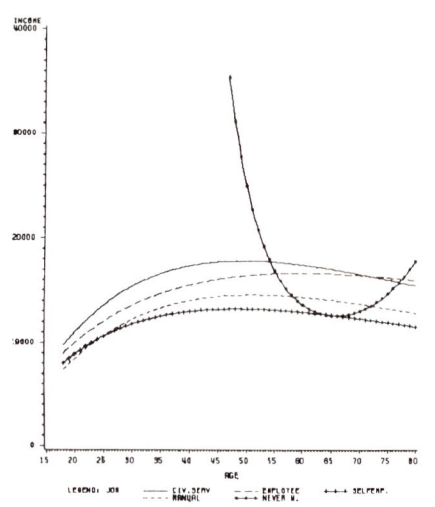

Figure 10.1.c
Age-μ profiles, Belgium
working, job

Figure 10.1.d
Age-μ profiles, Belgium
non-working, job

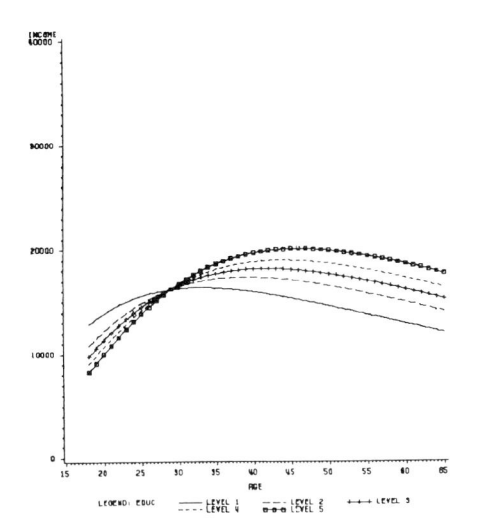

233

Figure 10.2.a
Age-µ profiles, Denmark
working, education

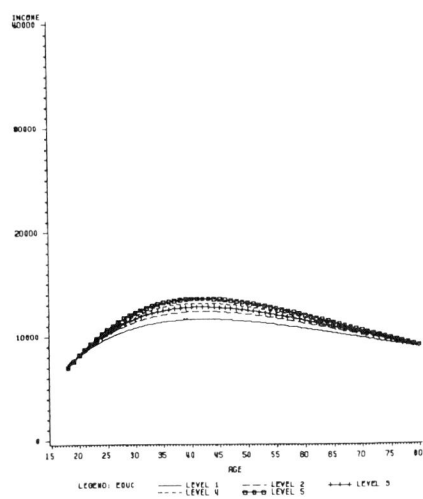

Figure 10.2.b
Age-µ profiles, Denmark
non-working, education

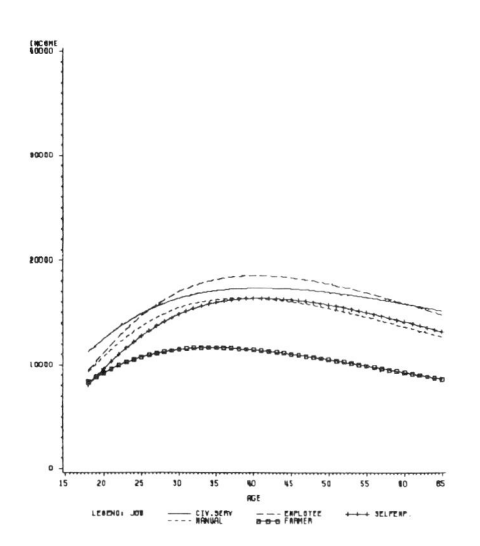

Figure 10.2.c
Age-µ profiles, Denmark
working, job

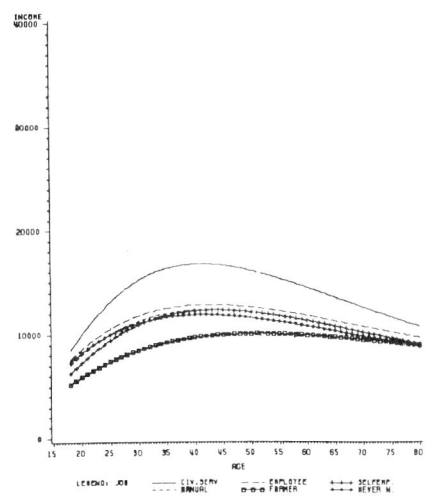

Figure 10.2.d
Age-µ profiles, Denmark
non-working, job

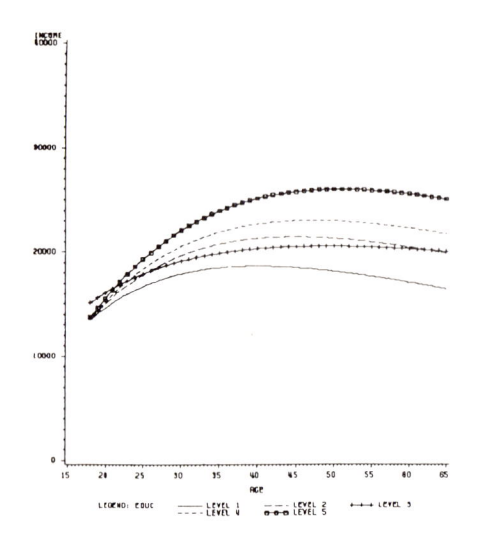

Figure 10.3.a
Age-μ profiles, France
working, education

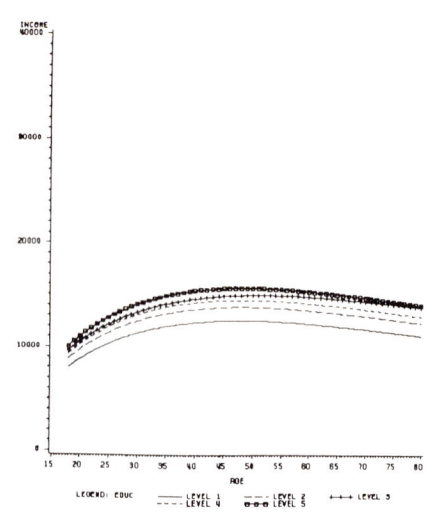

Figure 10.3.b
Age-μ profiles, France
non-working, education

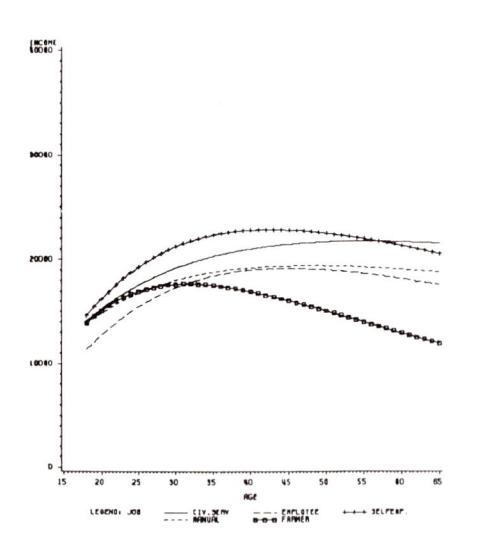

Figure 10.3.c
Age-μ profiles, France
working, job

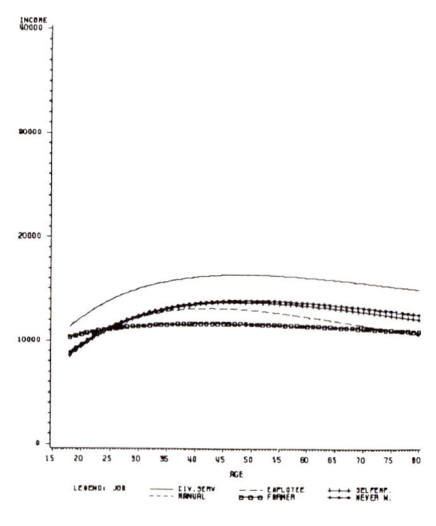

Figure 10.3.d
Age-μ profiles, France
non-working, job

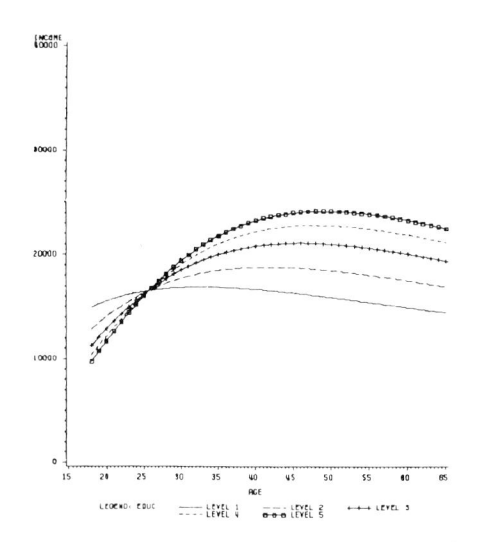

Figure 10.4.a
Age-μ profiles, Germany
working, education

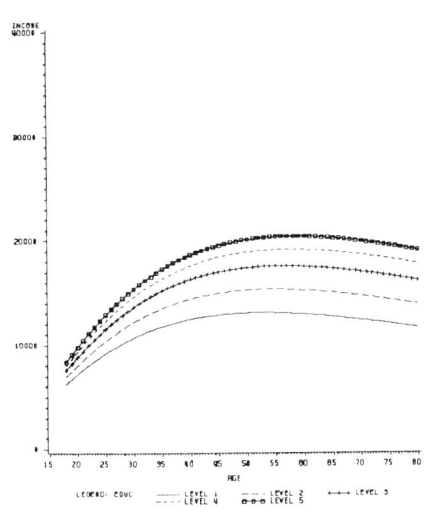

Figure 10.4.b
Age-μ profiles, Germany
non-working, education

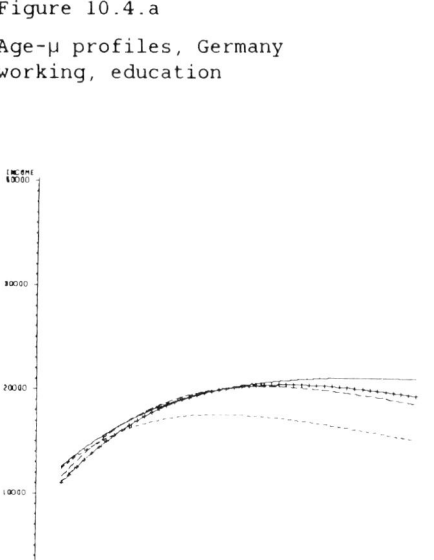

Figure 10.4.c
Age-μ profiles, Germany
working, job

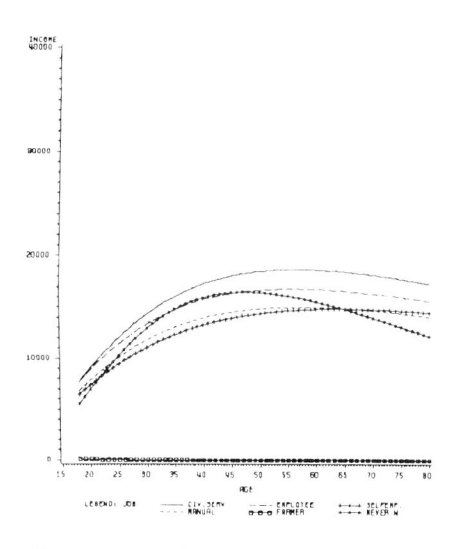

Figure 10.4.d
Age-μ profiles, Germany
non-working, job

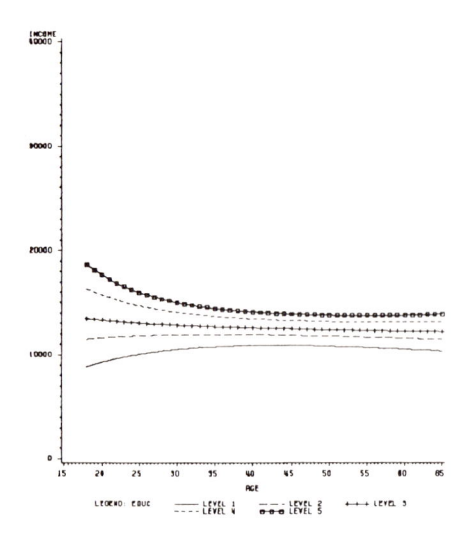

Figure 10.5.a
Age-µ profiles, Ireland
working, education

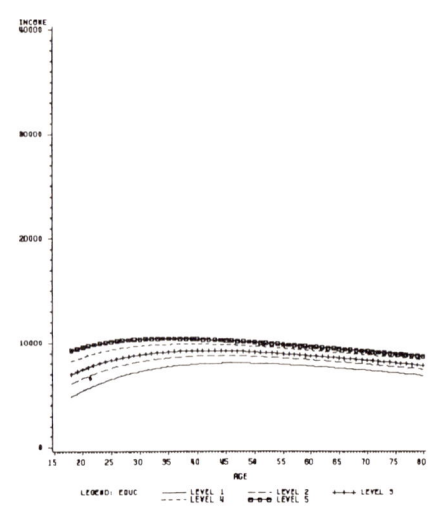

Figure 10.5.b
Age-µ profiles, Ireland
non-working, education

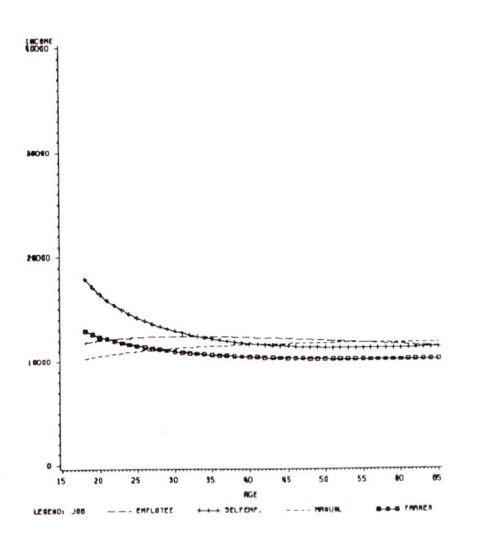

Figure 10.5.c
Age-µ profiles, Ireland
working, job

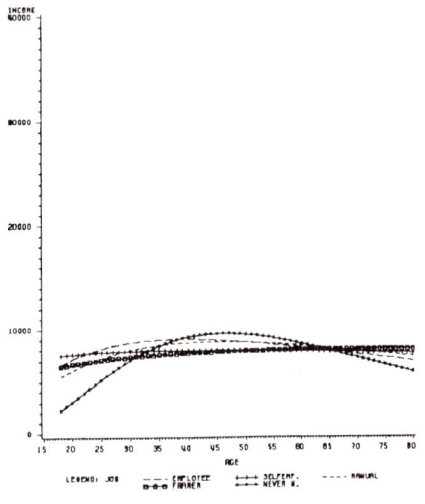

Figure 10.5.d
Age-µ profiles, Ireland
non-working, job

237

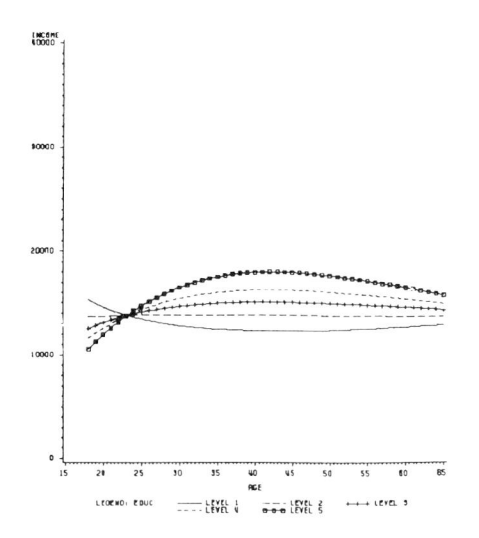

Figure 10.6.a
Age-μ profiles, Italy
working, education

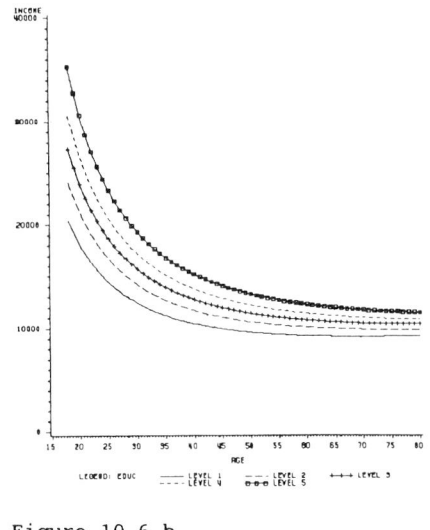

Figure 10.6.b
Age-μ profiles, Italy
non-working, education

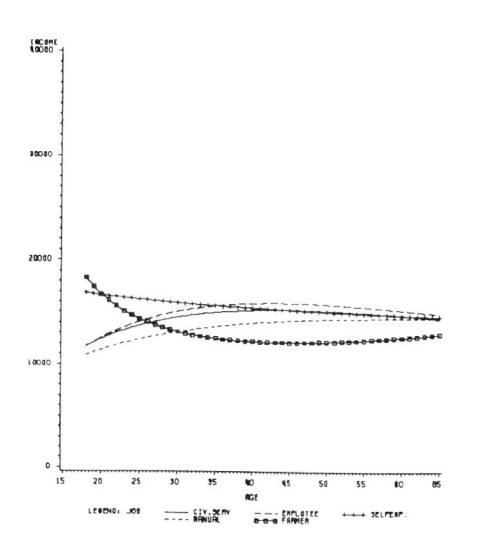

Figure 10.6.c
Age-μ profiles, Italy
working, job

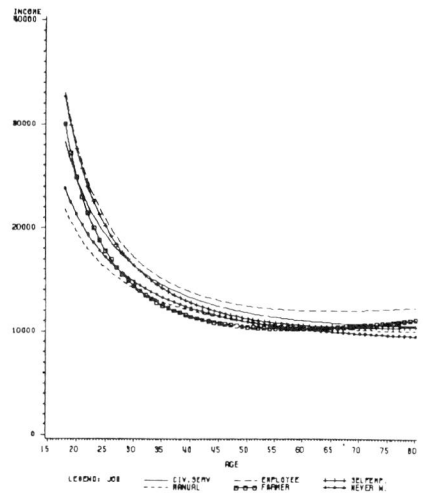

Figure 10.6.d
Age-μ profiles, Italy
non-working, job

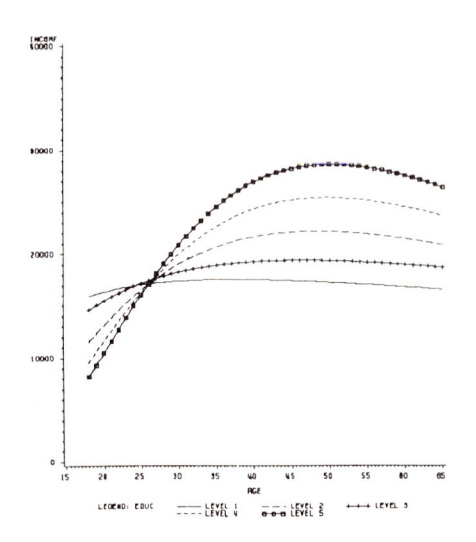

Figure 10.7.a

Age-µ profiles, the Netherlands
working, education

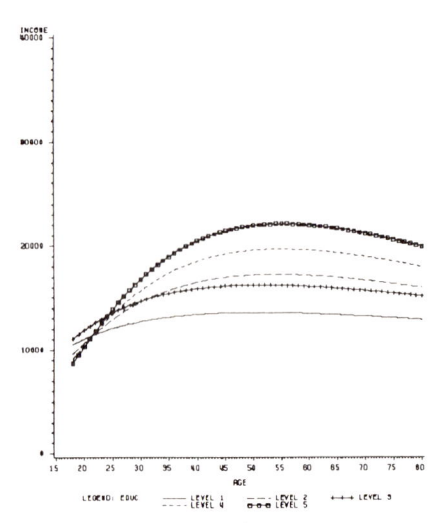

Figure 10.7.b

Age-µ profiles, the Netherlands
non-working, education

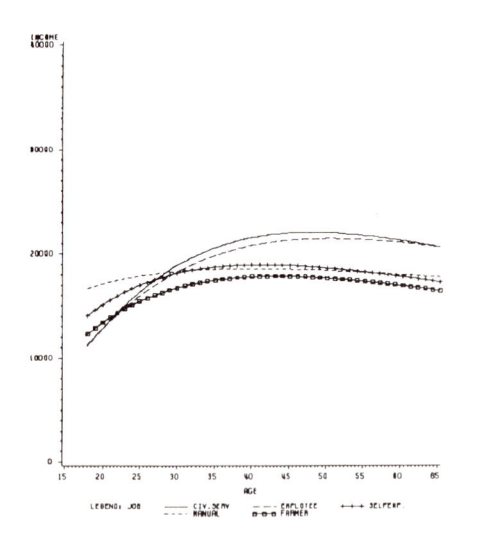

Figure 10.7.c

Age-µ profiles, the Netherlands
working, job

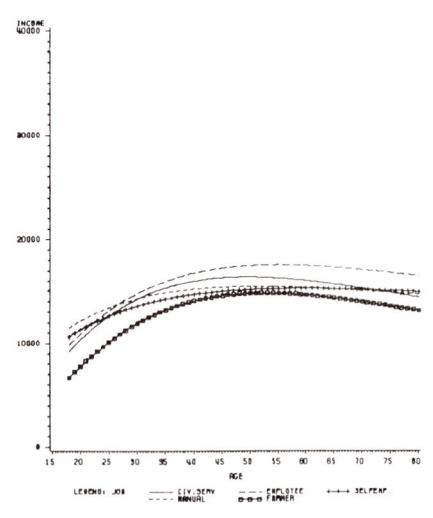

Figure 10.7.d

Age-µ profiles, the Netherlands
non-working, job

239

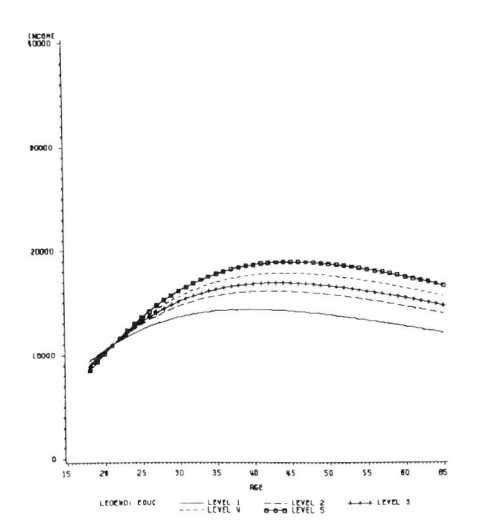

Figure 10.8.a

Age-μ profiles, United Kingdom
working, education

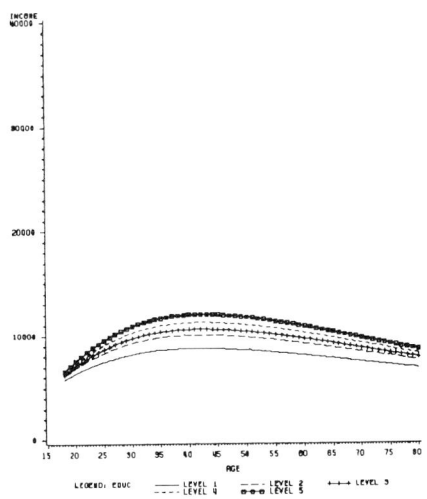

Figure 10.8.b

Age-μ profiles, United Kingdom
non-working, education

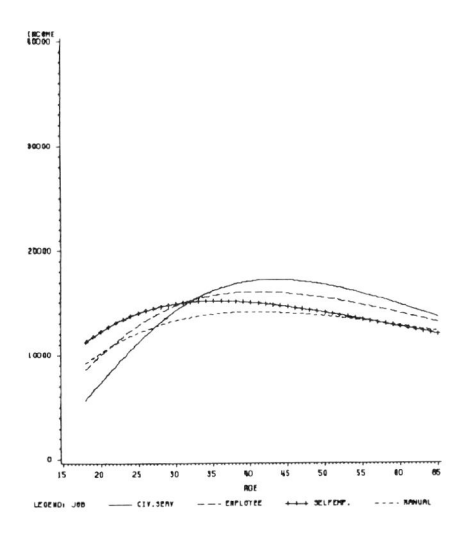

Figure 10.8.c

Age-μ profiles, United Kingdom
working, job

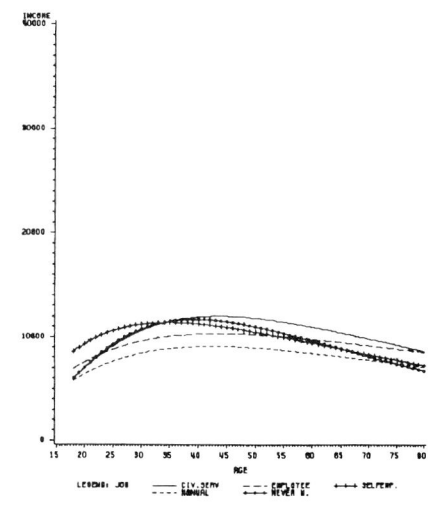

Figure 10.8.d

Age-μ profiles, United Kingdom
non-working, job

Chapter 11
EMPIRICAL RESULTS: POVERTY LINES AND POVERTY DETERMINANTS

Given the explanation of the welfare parameter µ and the income functions for different household types, we may now, following the procedure described in chapter 5, derive poverty lines and poverty determinants, both for different household types within a country and for some average household in each country.

This chapter is structured as follows. First we present, in section 11.1, poverty lines for each household type for all countries, applying the results for µ of chapter 10. Section 11.2 compares poverty lines over countries. Section 11.3 gives some special attention to the cost of children and child benefits. Section 11.4 compares one- and two-earner families. In section 11.5 the probability of being poor is calculated for households with different socio-economic characteristics.

## 11.1 Poverty lines, differentiated according to household type

In chapter 5 it was described how poverty lines, differentiated according to socio-economic characteristics, may be derived once the equation for µ, and possibly for σ as well, has been estimated. Before applying this procedure, the choice of the socio-economic characteristics that are used for differentiation and the choice of a welfare level has to be made. As to the socio-economic characteristics, we have maintained the elements that our different household types were composed of, i.e. the number of adults in a household, the number of children in a household, and the number of people working in a household. Of all other socio-economic characteristics that influence µ we have taken the weighted average in the population. As was described in chapter 1, this is a political choice by nature. We have chosen the 0.5 welfare level to be the poverty threshold. This is the level between the verbal descriptions "sufficient" and "insufficient", which is an appealing borderline between poor and non-poor. For comparison with other research we will also present poverty lines at other levels, in section 11.2. Hence, in this section poverty lines are derived at the 0.5 level for different household types. They are presented in table 11.1.

Table 11.1 Poverty lines for $\delta = 0.5$, differentiated according to household type, in Dutch guilders per annum[1]

| | BEL | DEN | FRA | GER | IRE | ITA | NET | UK |
|---|---|---|---|---|---|---|---|---|
| single person, working | 15,667 | 12,902 | 19,346 | 12,648 | 10,712 | 12,594 | 14,690 | 10,948 |
| single person, not working | 13,916 | 12,510 | 17,842 | 12,302 | 10,774 | 12,217 | 14,498 | 10,467 |
| one-parent family, working | 16,624 | 14,073 | 20,745 | 14,854 | 13,814 | 14,338 | 15,935 | 11,714 |
| one-parent family, not working | 14,766 | 13,646 | 19,132 | 14,447 | 13,893 | 13,909 | 15,727 | 11,199 |
| couple, two working | 17,704 | 19,916 | 22,182 | 12,590 | 12,760 | 14,441 | 17,862 | 13,781 |
| couple, one working | 17,347 | 16,694 | 21,509 | 13,217 | 12,448 | 15,013 | 18,338 | 13,997 |
| couple, not working | 15,408 | 16,188 | 19,837 | 12,855 | 12,519 | 14,563 | 18,098 | 13,382 |
| family, two working | 18,785 | 21,724 | 23,786 | 14,786 | 16,455 | 16,441 | 19,376 | 14,745 |
| family, one working | 18,406 | 18,210 | 23,064 | 15,522 | 16,053 | 17,092 | 19,892 | 14,976 |
| family, not working | 16,349 | 17,657 | 21,271 | 15,097 | 16,145 | 16,580 | 19,362 | 14,317 |
| extended family, two working | 20,418 | 17,707 | 25,056 | 15,027 | 15,020 | 13,909 | 21,486 | 13,999 |
| extended family, one working | 20,006 | 14,842 | 24,296 | 15,776 | 14,653 | 14,460 | 22,059 | 14,218 |
| extended family, not working | 17,770 | 14,392 | 22,407 | 15,343 | 14,737 | 14,027 | 21,771 | 13,593 |

It is seen that large differences are found in the levels of these poverty lines, both between countries and between household types within countries. In this section we concentrate on the latter; the differences between countries are discussed in the next section.

Looking at the figures for household types we see that the poverty line of one household type is lowest for all countries, viz. a single person who is not working (a minor exception is found in Ireland; however, the difference between working and non-working single persons in Ireland is not significantly different from zero). Families or extended families have highest poverty lines, while couples and one-parent families are somewhere in between. In general, households where no one is working have lower poverty lines than those where at least one person is working; the ratio varies (for a single person) from 88 % of the income of a working person in Belgium to 99 % in the Netherlands.[2] This implies that the differences in perceived needs between working and non-working households are not very large. In the Netherlands the figures are consistent with the present situation in the social security system where the minimum wage is virtually equal to the social assistance level. A similar pattern is found for couples and families; the differences between working and non-working families are not very large in most countries. For families the lowest ratio (of 81 %) is found in Denmark. It implies that differences in needs resulting from, e.g., the absence of household production in a family where two persons are working are, at this welfare level, not very large. Recent research on Dutch data [Homan, Van Praag and Hagenaars (1984)] shows that the value of this household production probably varies according to welfare level, and although possibly insignificant at the poverty line level, there are indications that it is a non-negligible source of income in kind for higher welfare levels.

Finally, we note that differences between household types are small for Germany, Italy and the United Kingdom, whereas in the other countries large differences are found. Ireland has relatively the largest differences; the highest poverty line is 54 % higher than the lowest. However, differences may be even larger, in other countries as well, due to the effect of children. In this table the average number of children is used for comparison. The effect of children is discussed in more detail in section 11.4.

## 11.2 Poverty lines in different countries

As we have seen in table 11.1, the differences between countries are very large. Rather than discussing these differences for various household types, geometric mean poverty lines per country are given in table 11.2. We have presented these for three welfare levels, 0.4, 0.5 and 0.6; in each poverty line the average value of σ per country was used.[3]

If we first look at the 0.5 levels, it is seen that the United Kingdom and Germany have lowest poverty lines, followed by Ireland and Italy. With higher poverty lines Belgium, Denmark and the Netherlands follow, but an absolute top is found in France. With two exceptions, this sequence is what one might expect. The exceptions are obviously Germany and France. One would rather think that Germany would have a poverty line not dissimilar to Belgium and the Netherlands, and it is certainly surprising to find the highest poverty line in France.

Table 11.2  Geometric mean poverty lines for δ = 0.4, 0.5 and 0.6

|  | BEL | DEN | FRA | GER | IRE | ITA | NET | UK |
|---|---|---|---|---|---|---|---|---|
| 0.4 | 13,946 | 13,750 | 17,123 | 10,937 | 11,854 | 12,300 | 15,320 | 11,262 |
| 0.5 | 16,911 | 17,366 | 21,277 | 13,876 | 14,465 | 15,573 | 18,131 | 13,640 |
| 0.6 | 20,506 | 21,933 | 26,438 | 17,604 | 17,652 | 19,718 | 21,459 | 16,520 |
| $\exp(\mu_y)$ | 28.640 | 21.270 | 22.970 | 25.562 | 17.023 | 23.503 | 26.014 | 20.408 |
| $\sigma_y$ | 0.314 | 0.347 | 0.354 | 0.271 | 0.295 | 0.279 | 0.179 | 0.248 |

For comparison, two parameters of the income distribution in each country are presented, median income $\exp(\mu_y)$, and the standard deviation of log incomes $\sigma_y$. We see that Belgium has highest median income, followed by the Netherlands and Germany. Lowest median income is found in Ireland, followed by the United Kingdom. The other countries are in between. Income inequality, as reflected by $\sigma_y$, is highest in France, followed by Denmark and Belgium. The Netherlands has by far the lowest inequality, followed by the United Kingdom. The high income inequality in France, combined with its high poverty line leads to the hypothesis that the poverty line may perhaps be influenced by the degree of income inequality in a country. In fact, this is the consequence of equation (10.1) in chapter 10, where μ was seen to be significantly influenced both by median income and income inequality. If we substitute in that equation the equality $\ln y_{0.5} = \mu =$

ln y, the poverty line at the 0.5 level is equal to

(11.1) $\quad \ln y^*_{0.5} = \frac{1}{1-0.574} [1.410 + 0.224 \mu_y + 0.712 \sigma_y + 0.085 \ln fs]$

We see that the elasticity of the poverty line with respect to median income equals

$$\frac{d\ln y^*_{0.5}}{d\mu_y} = \frac{0.224}{1-0.574} = 0.526$$

Hence the relativity of the poverty line is halfway on the scale between completely absolute and completely relative. If median income increases with 10 %, the poverty line increases with 5 %. This result, interesting as it is, should be interpreted with caution: it is based on a cross-section at one point in time, and does not necessarily yield the result that time series would give. A panel, containing international data over time is needed to provide the elasticity per country over time.

As is seen from (11.1), income inequality also increases the poverty line. An increase in income inequality of 10 % yields an increase in the poverty line of $\frac{0.712}{1-0.574} \sigma_y 10 \% = 0.167 \sigma_y$. With $\sigma_y$ varying between 0.179 and 0.354, this effect varies between 3 % and 6 %. Again, these figures do not necessarily predict changes over time.

This finding partly explains the high poverty line in France. It may also explain the fact that Ireland has a higher average poverty line than the United Kingdom; income inequality is higher in Ireland. (Another aspect contributing to this latter difference is the frequency of families with children: families with children have higher poverty lines in Ireland, and more families with children are found in Ireland. If we compare household types, other differences are found, as shown in table 11.1.)

Although the differences in income inequality partially explain the low German line as well, we think this is not a full explanation yet. However, as poverty, especially subjective poverty, is determined by many factors, it may very well be that a country's culture and history, that cannot be expressed in simple figures denoting income inequality or median income, will influence the level of the poverty line as well. Finally, we note that the real welfare value of a cash poverty line depends on the non-cash benefits that are available in a country. It is possible that the difference in poverty lines between, e.g., France and Germany is the result of a larger non-cash part of government expenditures in Germany, in the form of health care, education, public transport, et cetera.

We conclude this section by looking at two other welfare levels, 0.4 and 0.6. The differences in ordering of the countries at those levels are due to differences in the welfare sensitivity. We see, e.g., that at the 0.6 welfare level the German poverty line is higher than the British, and almost equal to the Irish. At the 0.4 level, however, the German line is definitely lowest. The French poverty line is highest at all welfare levels.

The policy implications of the results of this chapter will be discussed in chapter 13.

## 11.3 The effect of children

We will now discuss the effect of the number of children in a family on the poverty line. The poverty lines differentiated according to the number of children are presented in table 11.3. When discussing the regression equation for $\mu$ in chapter 10, we already mentioned that in some countries the welfare needs do not increase monotonously with the number of children. This effect, of course, shows in table 11.3 as well. The largest effect of children is found in Italy; hardly any effect at all is found in France, the U.K. and Denmark. The fact that children not necessarily increase welfare needs has been remarked upon by Kapteyn and Van Praag (1976). Apart from economies of scale, this is due to the fact that children may be seen as consumption goods, that are partly substitutes for leisure, holidays, et cetera.

If we want to compare these welfare differences with the actual family allowances in different countries, both tax differences and child benefits have to be taken into account. The effect of taxes is included in the income equation, discussed in chapter 9.1, if we compare after-tax net income of couples without children and families with children.[4] This amount, calculated at the 0.5 welfare level, is also given in table 11.3. As regards child benefits we have chosen to calculate the average amount that was reported by all households of a specific composition as the benefits received by that household type, rather than giving a summary of official regulations. By giving an average, we ignore problems arising in

Table 11.3 Poverty lines at the 0.5 welfare level, for one-earner families with different family sizes, and actual tax and child benefits regulations

|  | BEL | DEN | FRA | GER | IRE | ITA | NET | UK |
|---|---|---|---|---|---|---|---|---|
| one child | 17,541 | 18,056 | 22,397 | 14,770 | 14,576 | 16,144 | 19,733 | 15,157 |
| two children | 18,237 | 18,362 | 23,010 | 15,470 | 15,315 | 17,301 | 19,622 | 14,490 |
| three children | 18,372 | 17,955 | 22,055 | 16,931 | 16,060 | 17,566 | 20,721 | 15,964 |
| four children | 20,342 | 18,621 | 22,877 | 18,403 | 16,842 | 20,869 | 18,933 | 15,052 |
| couple | 17,347 | 16,694 | 21,509 | 13,217 | 12,448 | 15,013 | 18,338 | 13,997 |
| tax advantage compared to couple | 2828 | 2432 | 2913 | 1274 | 3536 | 2535 | 540 | 1318 |
| average child benefits |  |  |  |  |  |  |  |  |
| one child | 1437 | 873 | 2740 | 778 | 195 | 584 | 971 | 911 |
| two children | 3359 | 1167 | 2278 | 1858 | 475 | 829 | 2487 | 1583 |
| three children | 6475 | 1574 | 5290 | 3317 | 646 | 1077 | 3947 | 2305 |
| four children | 8009 | 1830 | 6486 | 4854 | 842 | 1579 | 5460 | 2747 |

some countries, where the official regulations depend, apart from age, on the question whether the children are studying, or have an income of their own. We see that the reported child benefits vary widely over countries; Ireland has lowest amounts, both absolutely and relatively, and Belgium has highest. However, in Ireland the tax advantage for families with children is highest for all countries; the lowest tax advantage is found in the Netherlands. If tax advantage and children allowances are added up, the Netherlands is least generous for families with one or two children, while France is most generous. For larger families, the United Kingdom is least generous and Belgium is most generous.

If these total income additions for different household types are compared to the extra welfare needs, it appears that almost always the cost of children is over-compensated. The only exceptions are found in Ireland and Italy where families with three or more children have higher extra needs than compensation. In general, the conclusions of Kapteyn and Van Praag still hold: if one bases child benefits on the cost of children only, large families tend to be over-compensated, as children have a positive effect on welfare that is neglected in such a procedure.[5]

## 11.4 Comparison of one- and two-earner households

Although the main interest of this book is in the description and explanation of poverty, which is rarely found in households where two persons are working, we present some figures on the effect of a working partner both on the poverty line and on household income. As we have seen in chapter 5, the partner's income may be seen as an addition to the main breadwinner's income:

$$(11.2) \quad y_m + y_p = y_m(1 + \frac{y_p}{y_m}) = y_m(1 + \alpha)$$

where the decision of the partner to participate in the labour market may depend on the presence of children, education, age, and the income of the main breadwinner. By calculating $\alpha$ we assess the additional income as a percentage of the main income. However, the main income may also be influenced by the working of the partner: as we have seen in section 9.1, the income of a man whose partner is working is lower, <u>ceteris paribus</u>, than of a single breadwinner. If we calculate this factor, that may be the result of taxes or decreasing hours of work, as a percentage of the income of a single breadwinner, we have:

(11.3)    $y_m$(partner working) = $y_m$(partner not working)$(1-\gamma)$

Combining (11.2) and (11.3) we write

$$y_m + y_p = (1+\alpha)(1-\gamma)y_m(\text{partner not working})$$

The product $(1+\alpha)(1-\gamma)$ represents the multiplicative factor needed to compare the income of a household where two persons are working with the same household where only one breadwinner is working. On the other hand the poverty line of a household where two persons are working may be different from a one-working household. This was allowed for in the equation for $\mu$ by the inclusion of dummy variables representing the number of adults working. This effect may also be written as a multiplicative factor, to be applied to a one-working household:

$$y^*_{0.5}(\text{partner working}) = y^*_{0.5}(\text{partner not working})(1+\varepsilon)$$

where  $\varepsilon = \exp \dfrac{(\beta_{\text{two adults working}} - \beta_{\text{one adult working}})}{1 - \beta_y}$

and $\beta$ represent the respective coefficients of the dummy variables from the $\mu$-equation. These effects of the partner's working, both on the poverty line and on income, have been tabulated in table 11.4.

Table 11.4  The effect of the partner's working on income and the poverty line at the 0.5 welfare level

|  | BEL | DEN | FRA | GER | IRE | ITA | NET | UK |
|---|---|---|---|---|---|---|---|---|
| extra income $(1+\alpha)$ | 1.274 | 1.476 | 1.891 | 1.233 | 1.202 | 1.746 | 1.235 | 1.310 |
| effect of taxes on $y_m$ | 0.895 | 0.865 | 0.937 | 0.987 | 0.827 | 0.885 | 0.965 | 0.951 |
| total effect on income $(1+\alpha)(1-\gamma)$ | 1.140 | 1.277 | 1.772 | 1.217 | 0.994 | 1.545 | 1.192 | 1.246 |
| total effect on poverty line $(1+\varepsilon)$ | 0.957 | 1.193 | 1.031 | 0.953 | 1.025 | 0.955 | 0.974 | 1.077 |

The table shows that the partner's contribution to the household income varies from 20 % to 89 % of the income of the main breadwinner. The contribution is low in Ireland, Germany and the Netherlands, and is high in Italy and France. The negative effect on the main breadwinner's income, through taxes, is only minor in Germany and the Netherlands,[6] but considerable in Denmark and Ireland. These two effects combined yield a total effect on income, which is shown in the third row in table 11.4. It appears that the total contribution of the partner's working on the household income varies from 14 % to 77 %, except in Ireland, where it is almost equal to zero. This implies that in Ireland total household income in two-earner households is not higher than the one-earner income. Countries where the total contribution of the partner to the household's income is lowest are Belgium, the Netherlands and Germany. The contribution is highest in France and Italy. This may be because in these latter two countries it is still common to have grandparents taking care of children, and thereby enabling full-time work of the partner. In, for example, the Netherlands and Germany this is less frequently found.

Comparing, finally, the extra addition to the main breadwinner's income with the extra effect on the poverty line for two-earner families, it is seen that in all countries except Ireland the extra income is more than sufficient to cover the extra cost. In Ireland the extra costs are slightly higher than the total extra income.

We conclude that families where the partner is working are less poverty prone than families where the partner is not working, except in Ireland.

## 11.5 The probability of being poor

Once we have estimated the effects of socio-economic characteristics both on income and on $\mu$, we may combine them to assess their effect on the probability that someone is poor, i.e. has an income lower than his poverty line at a certain welfare level. If we again choose the welfare level $\delta = 0.5$, the general formula describing the probability that someone is poor equals (see formula (5.9) of chapter 5)

$$(11.4) \quad PPOV = \Phi \left[ \frac{X_m \beta_m + X_0 \beta_0 - X_m \gamma_m (1-\beta_y)}{1 - \beta_y} ; \; 0, \sigma_{11} + \frac{\sigma_{22}}{(1-\beta_y)^2} - \frac{2\sigma_{12}}{1 - \beta_y} \right]$$

The variance of this normal variate consists, apart from the residual variance of the μ and ln y equation respectively, of a covariance term between the error terms $e_1$ and $e_2$. We may estimate this covariance by combining both regression equations (5.1) and (5.2) in a simultaneous linear system, that may be estimated using, e.g., the LISREL program [Jöreskog (1978)]. The combined system reads

$$(11.5) \quad [\ln y \; \mu] \begin{bmatrix} 1 & -\beta_y \\ 0 & 1 \end{bmatrix} = [X_m \; X_0] \begin{bmatrix} \gamma_m & \beta_m \\ 0 & \beta_0 \end{bmatrix} + [e_1 \; e_2]$$

with $E(e_1 e_2') = \sigma_{12} I_N$, $E(e_1 e_1') = \sigma_{11} I_N$ and $E(e_2 e_2') = \sigma_{22} I_N$.

We have estimated this system by LISREL using zero-restrictions on elements of $\beta_m$ to ensure identification of the model, but the covariance between the two error terms did not appear to be significantly different from zero. When $\sigma_{12} = 0$, the model is recursive, and may be estimated by ordinary least squares on each equation separately. We have therefore maintained our OLS estimates, and have put $\sigma_{12} = 0$ by assumption in (11.4). The resulting probability, PPOV, equals 0.5 for people who are on the borderline, i.e. who evaluate their actual income as 0.5. For people with a higher probability of being poor, we have PPOV > 0.5, for people with a lower probability we have PPOV < 0.5.

We will now calculate this poverty probability for various socio-economic types. The effect of education and occupation will be analysed first, in subsection 11.5.1. The effect of age will be described in subsection 11.5.2. Other socio-economic characteristics are discussed in subsection 11.5.3, while subsection 11.5.4 concludes.

## 11.5.1 The effect of education and occupation

We have calculated these probabilities first for people with different occupational and educational background. As both income and the poverty line are influenced by the fact whether one is working or not, these probabilities are presented both for working households and for non-working households. With respect to other characteristics, that have not been differentiated, we have calculated the average value within the relevant social type. Thus the poverty probability for manual workers is calculated by the comparison of the income of manual workers with the poverty line of manual workers, where the average value of education, urbanization, etc. for manual workers is used. These probabilities, firstly calculated at the age of 40, are presented in table 11.5. In later sections we discuss the effects of age, other socio-economic characteristics, children, and income of the partner.

Table 11.5  Poverty probabilities for working families at the age of 40, according to occupation and education

|  |  | BEL | DEN | FRA | GER | IRE | ITA | NET | UK |
|---|---|---|---|---|---|---|---|---|---|
| education level | 1 | 0.335 | 0.380 | 0.557 | 0.147 | 0.472 | 0.422 | 0.204 | 0.242 |
|  | 2 | 0.263 | 0.371 | 0.471 | 0.109 | 0.426 | 0.330 | 0.158 | 0.251 |
|  | 3 | 0.230 | 0.365 | 0.502 | 0.082 | 0.399 | 0.269 | 0.193 | 0.254 |
|  | 4 | 0.223 | 0.360 | 0.430 | 0.069 | 0.366 | 0.217 | 0.135 | 0.257 |
|  | 5 | 0.169 | 0.354 | 0.365 | 0.060 | 0.344 | 0.162 | 0.118 | 0.259 |
| manual worker |  | 0.255 | 0.420 | 0.612 | 0.114 | 0.493 | 0.283 | 0.231 | 0.303 |
| employee |  | 0.212 | 0.378 | 0.290 | 0.086 | }0.469 | 0.247 | 0.166 | 0.205 |
| civil servant |  | 0.289 | 0.490 | 0.468 | 0.116 |  | 0.384 | 0.157 | 0.248 |
| self-employed |  | 0.207 | 0.374 | 0.458 | 0.032 | 0.382 | 0.286 | 0.133 | 0.262 |
| farmer |  | - | 0.261 | 0.457 | 0.000 | 0.403 | 0.234 | 0.152 | - |
| overall |  | 0.273 | 0.384 | 0.530 | 0.109 | 0.457 | 0.300 | 0.186 | 0.247 |

We see that for almost all types the probability of being in poverty is below 0.5. The only types within this household type with one income earner that may be said to be poverty prone are manual workers and people with low education in France. Within each country, the probability of being in poverty is lower for people with higher education. It is seen that although farmers have in general low monetary incomes, their lower needs as a result of their non-cash income imply that the probability of a farmer being poor is not in general higher than that of other occupations. With respect to the overall probability of being poor for this household type, it is highest in France, followed by Ireland and Denmark, and lowest in Germany, followed by the Netherlands. Only France has an overall probability higher than 0.5 for this household type.

If we look at the poverty probabilities for non-working families, a completely different picture is found. Table 11.6 gives these poverty probabilities for the same educational and occupational groups, including an extra category "never worked".

Table 11.6 Poverty probabilities for non-working families at the age of 40, according to occupation and education

|  | BEL | DEN | FRA | GER | IRE | ITA | NET | UK |
|---|---|---|---|---|---|---|---|---|
| education level 1 | 0.595 | 0.625 | 0.873 | 0.449 | 0.835 | 0.636 | 0.673 | 0.875 |
| 2 | 0.598 | 0.633 | 0.854 | 0.356 | 0.802 | 0.545 | 0.613 | 0.861 |
| 3 | 0.383 | 0.638 | 0.777 | 0.282 | 0.781 | 0.477 | 0.518 | 0.855 |
| 4 | 0.599 | 0.642 | 0.843 | 0.238 | 0.753 | 0.416 | 0.576 | 0.848 |
| 5 | 0.602 | 0.646 | 0.826 | 0.209 | 0.733 | 0.340 | 0.547 | 0.841 |
| manual worker | 0.523 | 0.658 | 0.849 | 0.313 | 0.838 | 0.459 | 0.549 | 0.856 |
| employee | 0.516 | 0.688 | 0.646 | 0.274 | 0.841 | 0.398 | 0.488 | 0.784 |
| civil servant | 0.355 | 0.506 | 0.685 | 0.230 | }0.845 | 0.539 | 0.624 | 0.720 |
| self-employed | 0.661 | 0.614 | 0.891 | 0.306 |  | 0.522 | 0.507 | 0.630 |
| farmer | - | 0.362 | 0.780 | 0.000 | 0.790 | 0.274 | 0.501 | - |
| never worked | 1.000 | 0.674 | 0.744 | 0.472 | 0.878 | 0.604 | 0.604 | 0.976 |
| overall | 0.553 | 0.627 | 0.848 | 0.364 | 0.813 | 0.522 | 0.542 | 0.867 |

In the category non-working families almost all households are poverty prone. With the exception of Germany, in all countries an overall probability of being poor larger than 0.5 is found. The probability of being poor for non-working households is largest in the United Kingdom, followed by France and Ireland. There still is a tendency for the poverty probability to decline with increasing education, but even at the highest educational levels the poverty probability is in most countries larger than 0.5. The largest probabilities of being poor are found in the United Kingdom and Belgium for people who have never worked.

### 11.5.2 The effect of age on the poverty probability

In the previous subsection the probabilities have been calculated at the age of 40. In this section, a table is compiled where the overall probabilities of being poor are given for different ages. Moreover, the average probability over different ages is given as well. This probability is calculated as:

$$\text{PPOVPERM} = P \left[ \int_{c_0}^{c_1} \ln y^*_\delta (X_m, \text{age}) \, d\,\text{age} < \int_{c_0}^{c_1} \ln y (X_m, \text{age}) \, d\,\text{age} \right]$$

$$= P \left[ \int_{c_0}^{c_1} \{\ln y^*_\delta (X_m, \text{age}) - \ln y (X_m, \text{age})\} \, d\,\text{age} < 0 \right]$$

where $c_0$ and $c_1$ denote respectively the lower and upper limit of lifetime. As a result of our specification of $\mu$ and ln y, we may write

$$\ln y_\delta^* (X_m, \text{age}) = a_0(X_m) + a_1(X_m)\ln \text{age} + a_2(X_m)\ln^2\text{age} + \frac{e_2}{1-\beta}$$

and

$$\ln y (X_m, \text{age}) = b_0(X_m) + b_1(X_m)\ln \text{age} + b_2(X_m)\ln^2\text{age} + e_1$$

The intercepts $a_0$ and $b_0$ depend on $X_m$ via the dummies for socio-economic characteristics and the coefficients of ln age and $\ln^2$age may depend on socio-economic type, viz. education or occupation. The vectors a and b may hence be calculated for each socio-economic type; we will omit the functional relation with $X_m$ in the remainder.

We have

$$\text{PPOVPERM} = P\left[\int_{c_0}^{c_1} \{a_0 - b_0 + (a_1-b_1)\ln \text{age} + (a_2-b_2)\ln^2\text{age} + \frac{e_2}{1-\beta} - e_1\} \, d\,\text{age} < 0\right]$$

$$P[(a_0-b_0)(c_1-c_0) + (a_1-b_1)\{c_1(\ln c_1 - 1) - c_0(\ln c_0 - 1)\}$$

$$- (a_2-b_2)\{2c_1(\ln c_1 - 1) - 2c_0(\ln c_0 - 1) - c_1 \ln^2 c_1$$

$$+ c_0 \ln^2 c_0\} + (\frac{e_2}{1-\beta} - e_1)(c_1-c_0) < 0]$$

$$= N(v, 0, \frac{\sigma_{22}}{(1-\beta)^2} + \sigma_1 - \frac{2}{1-\beta}\sigma_{12})$$

where $v = (b_0-a_0) + \dfrac{b_1-a_1}{c_1-c_0} \{c_1(\ln c_1 - 1) + c_0(\ln c_0 - 1)\}$

$$- \frac{(b_2-a_2)}{c_1-c_0} \{2c_1(\ln c_1 - 1) - 2c_0(\ln c_0 - 1) - c_1 \ln^2 c_1 + c_0 \ln^2 c_0\}$$

Once $c_0$ and $c_1$ are chosen, this probability may be calculated for each socio-economic type. In table 11.7 the probability is presented for the average socio-economic type during working life ($c_1$ = 65 and $c_0$ = 20). Again it is assumed that $\sigma_{12}$ = 0.

It is seen that the average poverty probability for working households is almost equal to the overall poverty probability at 40 years of age, that we presented in table 11.5. Only France has an average probability of being poor which is higher than 0.5. The lowest poverty probabilities are found for Germany and the Netherlands; the highest for France and Ireland. In all countries, the probability of being poor is highest for relatively young working people; in general the probability decreases with age, although it sometimes increases slightly at the years before retirement.

Table 11.7 Poverty probabilities for working and non-working families, at different ages, and on average over age

|  | BEL | DEN | FRA | GER | IRE | ITA | NET | UK |
|---|---|---|---|---|---|---|---|---|
| **Working** | | | | | | | | |
| age = 30 | 0.325 | 0.438 | 0.589 | 0.140 | 0.491 | 0.358 | 0.205 | 0.232 |
| 40 | 0.273 | 0.384 | 0.530 | 0.109 | 0.457 | 0.300 | 0.186 | 0.247 |
| 50 | 0.241 | 0.371 | 0.490 | 0.106 | 0.430 | 0.258 | 0.167 | 0.225 |
| 60 | 0.219 | 0.379 | 0.462 | 0.118 | 0.408 | 0.226 | 0.150 | 0.187 |
| PPOVPERM | 0.277 | 0.410 | 0.535 | 0.128 | 0.455 | 0.298 | 0.181 | 0.215 |
| **Non-working** | | | | | | | | |
| age = 30 | 0.661 | 0.670 | 0.884 | 0.535 | 0.884 | 0.227 | 0.599 | 0.854 |
| 40 | 0.553 | 0.627 | 0.848 | 0.364 | 0.813 | 0.522 | 0.542 | 0.867 |
| 50 | 0.480 | 0.574 | 0.812 | 0.284 | 0.780 | 0.642 | 0.479 | 0.838 |
| 60 | 0.431 | 0.535 | 0.777 | 0.250 | 0.775 | 0.658 | 0.415 | 0.779 |
| PPOVPERM | 0.563 | 0.684 | 0.844 | 0.401 | 0.841 | 0.410 | 0.522 | 0.828 |

For people who are not working, the overall view was seen to be rather sombre. France, Ireland and the United Kingdom have highest poverty probabilities, but in all countries non-working households are poverty prone at certain periods in life. The only countries where the average poverty probability is lower than 0.5 are Germany and Italy. The latter is the result of integration over the rather peculiar age-income profile; in fact all households with a main breadwinner of 40 years or older are poverty prone in Italy. Again, the probability of being poor is in general highest for young people, who have not yet built up pension rights or social security rights. In Belgium, Germany and the Netherlands non-working households above 50 years of age are not poverty prone, while younger households are. The old-aged, though poverty prone in five countries, do not have the highest poverty probability of all non-working households. It should be borne in mind, however, that for these poverty probabilities no differentiation is made in the poverty line for people who are not working because of unemployment, retirement or other reasons. As we have seen in table 9.13, the effect of these characteristics on income varies over countries. In countries where old-age pensioners have a significantly lower income than unemployed (Denmark and Italy), the actual poverty probability of this group is higher than table 11.7 suggest. The same holds for unemployed in countries where they have a lower income than old-age pensioners and others; this holds for Belgium, Germany, Ireland, the Netherlands, and the United Kingdom. In these countries, the probabilities given in table 11.7 are underestimates for the unemployed.

The striking differences in poverty probabilities between working and non-working families, which has appeared throughout this section, may be further illustrated by the comparison of average age-income profiles and poverty lines differentiated according to age for working and non-working families. These are presented in figures 11.1 to 11.8 in the appendix.
The dotted line represents the poverty line (averaged over all characteristics and household types). The continuous line represents income of the main breadwinner, again averaged over all socio-economic characteristics. The first of each two figures is the poverty line for working families, the second for non-working families. Looking at the working families first, it is seen that average working families are above the poverty line at all ages in Belgium, Germany, Italy, the Netherlands, and the United Kingdom. In Denmark, people younger than 23 are on average below the poverty line, while in France this holds for people younger than 35. In Ireland the age below which working people are poor is about 30; it is also seen that in Ireland the working families are only slightly above the poverty line at all ages.
If we look at non-working households, a dramatically different picture arises. In France, Ireland, the United Kingdom, and Denmark non-working families are below the poverty line at all ages. The overall income shortfall is very large in France and Ireland; in Denmark, the shortfall is largest for young families, while in the United Kingdom this holds for

families between 35 and 40.

In all countries, certain age groups of non-working households are under the poverty line on average. In Belgium and the Netherlands people younger than 45, in Germany people younger than 30, and in Italy people older than 37. With the exception of Italy, this again shows that for non-working households the poverty probability is relatively high for young families.

The figures presented also show large differences between the extent of poverty between countries in the sense of income shortfall. This severity of poverty, also reflected by large poverty probabilities for certain socio-economic types, may be used as an indicator for the poverty gap in a country. We will return to this problem of measuring the extent of poverty in the next chapter.

## 11.5.3 The effect of other socio-economic characteristics on the poverty probability

We have discussed the effects of education, occupation, age, and work on the probability of being poor. In the equations explaining income and $\mu$ we have included other variables as well. In this subsection we indicate for all these variables whether their effect is to increase or to decrease the poverty probability. This is done by comparing their effect on income with their effect on the poverty line: if the former is larger than the latter, the characteristic decreases the probability of being poor, and vice versa.

The net effect, denoted by + if it increases PPOV, and by - if it decreases PPOV, is given in table 11.8.

Table 11.8 The effect of other socio-economic characteristics on the probability of being poor

|  | BEL | DEN | FRA | GER | IRE | ITA | NET | UK |
|---|---|---|---|---|---|---|---|---|
| **Working** | | | | | | | | |
| small town | + | + | - | - | + | - | + | + |
| large town | ++ | ++ | 0 | -- | - | + | ++ | ++ |
| small fluctuations | - | + | - | - | - | - | - | - |
| large fluctuations | + | ++ | + | + | - | -- | + | -- |
| income has increased | - | - | 0 | 0 | 0 | - | - | - |
| income has decreased | + | + | + | + | + | + | + | + |
| female | + |  | + | + | + | + | + | + |
| **Not working** | | | | | | | | |
| small town | - | - | - | - | -- | - | - | + |
| large town | -- | + | + | -- | - | -- | + | 0 |
| small fluctuations | - | -- | - | -- | - | ++ | - | - |
| large fluctuations | + | - | + | - | -- | - | - | -- |
| income has increased | - | - | 0 | 0 | 0 | - | - | - |
| income has decreased | + | + | + | + | + | + | + | + |
| female | + | + | + | + | + | - | + | + |

If, in case of two dummy variables, one has a stronger effect than the other, the strongest of the two is denoted by ++ or --. It is seen that for working families, the probability of being poor is larger if one is living in a larger town in Belgium, Denmark, the Netherlands, and the United Kingdom. In the other countries the effect is not very systematic, except in Germany where the probability of being poor decreases with the degree of urbanization.

The effect of fluctuations in income also varies rather unsystematically over countries; in Ireland, Italy and the United Kingdom the probability of being poor decreases if one has large fluctuations in income; in Denmark it increases. In almost all countries people who are experiencing an increase in income have a lower probability of feeling poor, because there is a lag in the adaptation of needs. The reverse holds for people with decreasing incomes.

In non-working households the probability of being poor decreases with degree of urbanization, except in the Netherlands, Denmark and France. No systematic effects of fluctuations in income are found, and the effect of decreases or increases in income are similar to the effects described for working households. Female heads of non-working households, finally, have a higher probability of being poor.

### 11.5.4 The probability of being poor: conclusion

In the subsections above the effects of various socio-economic characteristics on the probability of being poor have been described. For all countries holds that families who are not working, have a low education, have experienced a decrease in income, and have female heads of household are poverty prone. These effects have been analysed *ceteris paribus*; of course, a cumulation of poverty determinants will result in an ever larger probability of being poor. Apart from these characteristics that hold for each country, some characteristics will have a country specific effect on the poverty probability. By taking these into account as well we can derive which socio-economic type has the largest probability of being poor in each country; this is, for example, in the United Kingdom a female head of household who has never worked, has the lowest level of education, is about 40 years of age, and is living in a small town.

What percentage of people in a country are poor depends on the incidence of these poverty increasing characteristics in that country. As non-working families are poverty prone in all countries, the unemployment percentage in a country will be a major determinant of poverty, as well as the percentage of old-aged. In France, however, poverty is also found among working households, so the poverty incidence in France will be higher than in other countries.

This brings us to the next chapter, where an index will be calculated that measures the extent of poverty in a certain country.

## NOTES TO CHAPTER 11

[1] See also footnote 3 in chapter 8 for exchange rates and purchasing power parities used.

[2] This may also be derived from tables 10.1 to 10.8, by calculating $\exp(\frac{\beta_{\text{one adult working}}}{1-\beta_y})$. For Belgium, for instance, this yields 1.125, which implies that a one-earner household has <u>ceteris paribus</u> a poverty line that is 12.5 % higher than the poverty line of a non-working household.

[3] As we have described in 10.2, the poverty lines at the 0.4 and 0.6 levels are not, in fact, correctly calculated by the formula $\ln y^*_\delta = \mu + \bar\sigma u_\delta$ with constant $\bar\sigma$; however, in order to make our results comparable with other poverty research using this poverty line definition, we have maintained this simple calculation method.

[4] Again it should be noted that the after-tax income advantage of families with children may, apart from taxes, also be the result of a larger working week for main breadwinners of families.

[5] However, one <u>caveat</u> should be made in this section: the effect of children is measured as far as it is included in the income evaluation question. If, as is sometimes argued, people only refer to their permanent income in answering this question, the irregular income that child benefits usually represent may not be included, however important it is as a temporary extra source of income. However, it is not known to what extent people answer the income evaluation question in such a way.

[6] This was before the change in tax system in the Netherlands according to the "Wet Tweeverdieners" that imposed higher taxes on two-earner households.

APPENDIX TO CHAPTER 11

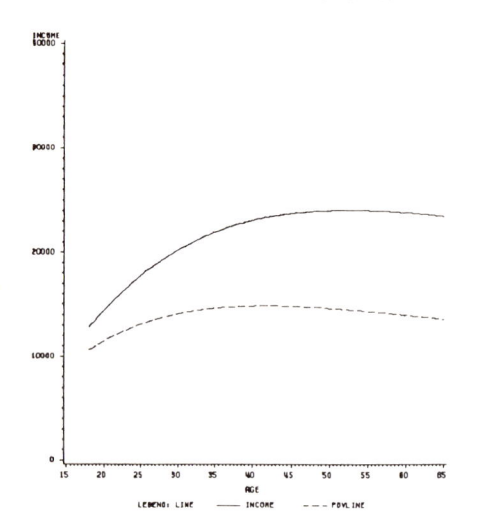

Figure 11.1.a

Poverty line and income, working Belgium

Figure 11.1.b

Poverty line and income, non-working Belgium

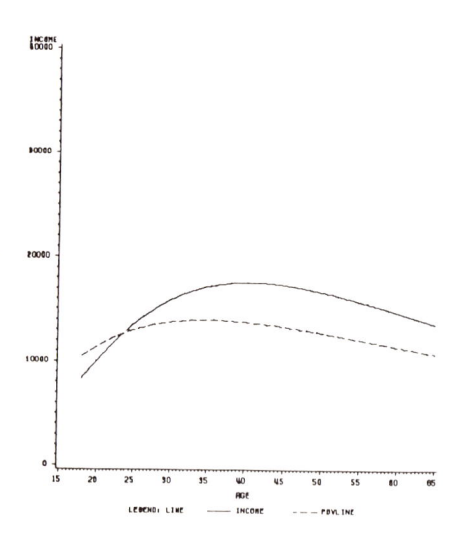

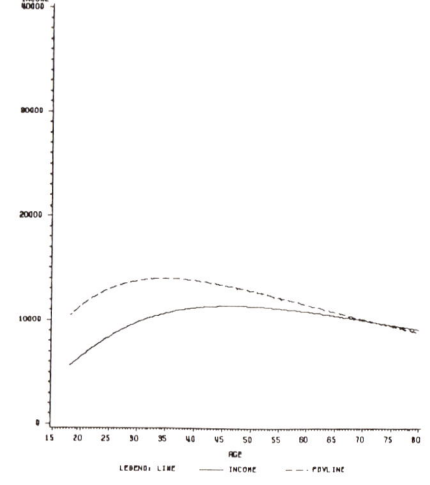

Figure 11.2.a

Poverty line and income, working Denmark

Figure 11.2.b

Poverty line and income, non-working Denmark

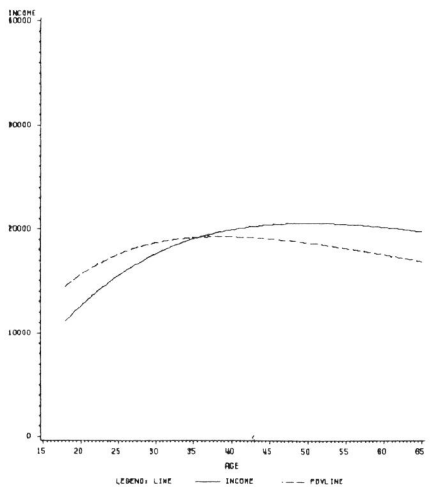

Figure 11.3.a

Poverty line and income, working France

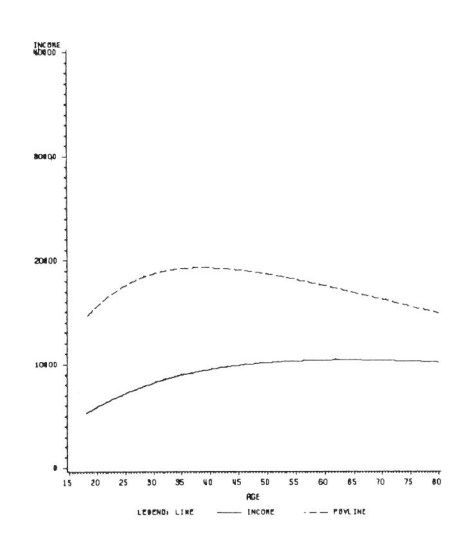

Figure 11.3.b

Poverty line and income, non-working France

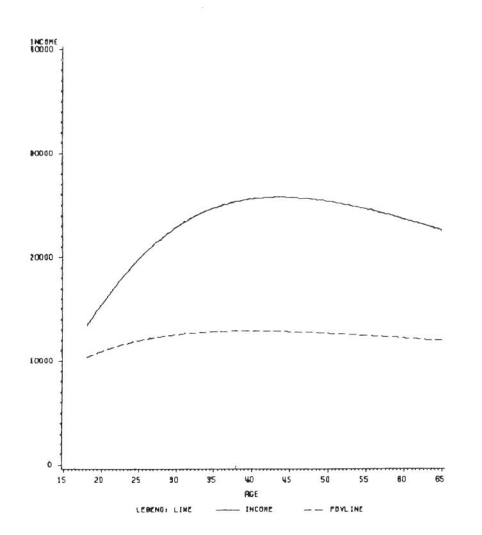

Figure 11.4.a

Poverty line and income, working Germany

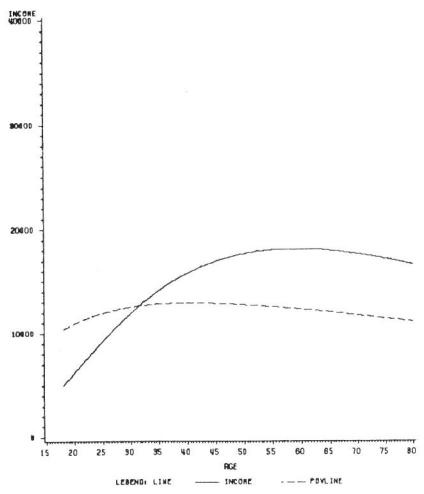

Figure 11.4.b

Poverty line and income, non-working Germany

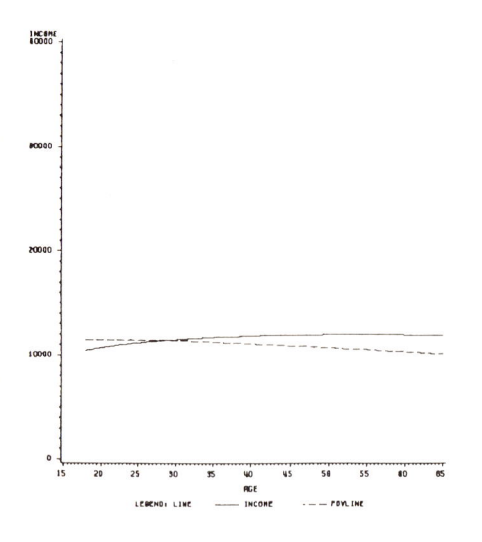

Figure 11.5.a

Poverty line and income, working Ireland

Figure 11.5.b

Poverty line and income, non-working Ireland

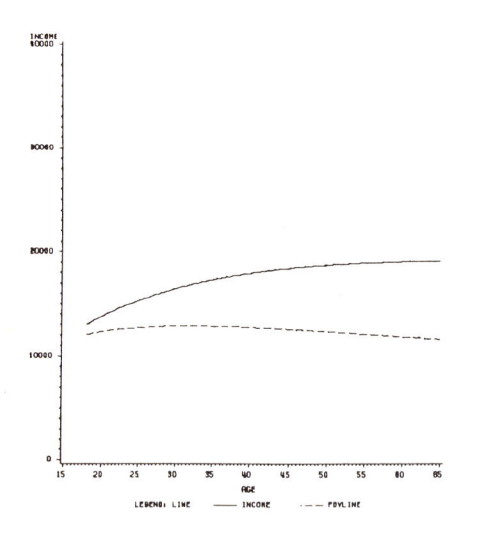

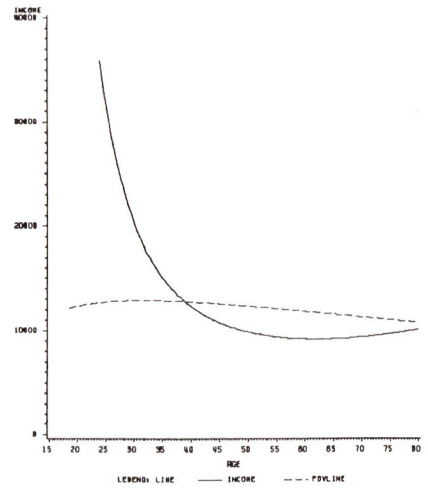

Figure 11.6.a

Poverty line and income, working Italy

Figure 11.6.b

Poverty line and income, non-working Italy

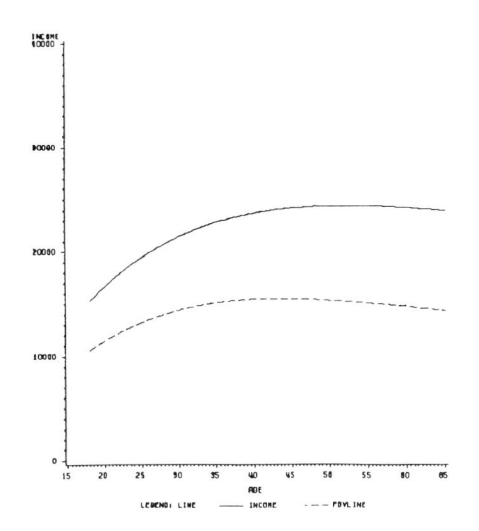

Figure 11.7.a

Poverty line and income, working
The Netherlands

Figure 11.7.b

Poverty line and income,
non-working The Netherlands

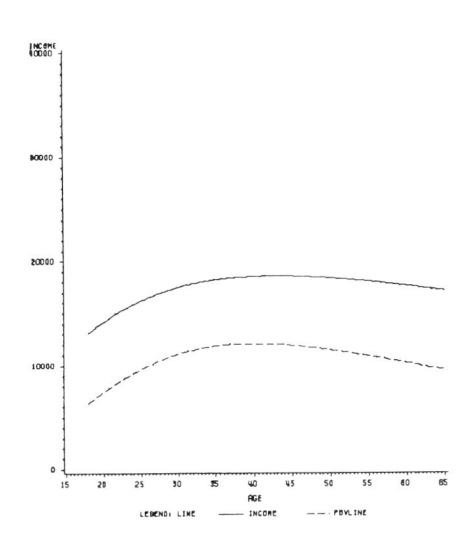

Figure 11.8.a

Poverty line and income, working
United Kingdom

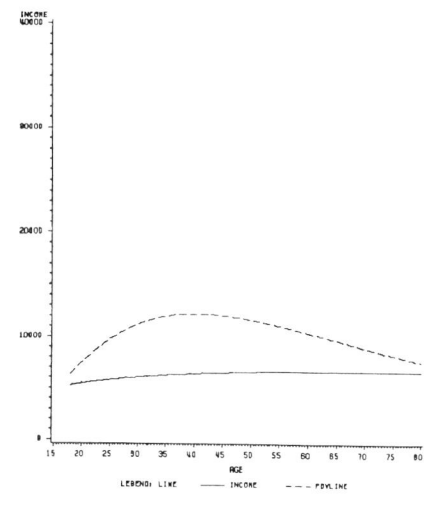

Figure 11.8.b

Poverty line and income,
non-working United Kingdom

Chapter 12
EMPIRICAL RESULTS: THE EXTENT OF POVERTY

We have calculated poverty lines, differentiated according to various characteristics for each country, and we have analysed which characteristics make people poverty prone. In this chapter we aggregate the individual information on poverty into one poverty index. As we have seen in chapter 12, the properties of such an index depend on the choice of a utility function. We calculate the poverty index for several concave utility functions in section 12.1. In section 12.2, we apply the class of poverty indices to the welfare function of income, both for the countries as a whole and for different household types within a country. We conclude by some predictions with respect to the effect of economic and demographic changes on the extent of poverty.

## 12.1 The poverty index for concave utility functions

In section 6.5 of chapter 6, a member of the Atkinson class was proposed based on a logarithmic utility function. In table 12.1 this poverty index $P_8$ is calculated for all countries as well as CHU's $P_5$ for $\beta=-1$. These poverty indices are calculated for two different levels of the poverty line for each country: in the first two columns of the table the Leyden poverty line, calculated at 0.5 is used for each country separately; in the last two columns one poverty line is used for all countries, viz. the Irish poverty line at 0.5, which is lowest of all countries. The latter poverty line may hence be seen to provide some absolute point of reference for the calculation of poverty indices.

The table shows that both for relative poverty and for absolute poverty all countries are ordered in the same way by $P_5$ and $P_8$. With respect to the relative indices, we see that France is highest, followed by Ireland. Next come the United Kingdom, Denmark, and Italy, followed by Belgium and the Netherlands, while Germany is lowest.
If we look at the absolute indices, the picture changes: Ireland is lonely at the top of the poverty list, followed by the United Kingdom. France, Italy and Denmark follow. Down at the bottom we have again Belgium, the Netherlands and Germany.

Table 12.1 Poverty indices

| | relative poverty | | | | absolute poverty | | | |
|---|---|---|---|---|---|---|---|---|
| | poverty line (0.5) | poverty index | | | poverty line | poverty index | | |
| | | $P_5$ ($\beta=-1$) | $P_8$ | H | (Ireland) | $P_5$ ($\beta=-1$) | $P_8$ | H |
| Belgium | ƒ 18.210,- | 0.032 | 0.027 | 0.138 | 14.540 | 0.009 | 0.008 | 0.040 |
| Denmark | ƒ 19.336,- | 0.114 | 0.093 | 0.294 | 14.540 | 0.041 | 0.034 | 0.155 |
| France | ƒ 21.761,- | 0.212 | 0.162 | 0.417 | 14.540 | 0.080 | 0.060 | 0.180 |
| Germany | ƒ 14.804,- | 0.024 | 0.018 | 0.057 | 14.540 | 0.023 | 0.017 | 0.056 |
| Ireland | ƒ 14.540,- | 0.169 | 0.133 | 0.371 | 14.540 | 0.169 | 0.133 | 0.371 |
| Italy | ƒ 16.523,- | 0.067 | 0.052 | 0.173 | 14.540 | 0.044 | 0.034 | 0.121 |
| the Netherlands | ƒ 18.953,- | 0.037 | 0.030 | 0.161 | 14.540 | 0.010 | 0.008 | 0.036 |
| the United Kingdom | ƒ 15.649,- | 0.119 | 0.097 | 0.284 | 14.540 | 0.096 | 0.079 | 0.249 |

It is obvious that the high relative index of France is due to the high poverty line found in this country. Apart from France, the countries can be ordered both with respect to relative poverty and with respect to absolute poverty in three groups: countries with a large extent of poverty (Ireland, United Kingdom), a moderate extent of poverty (Denmark, Italy), and a low extent of poverty (Germany, Belgium, the Netherlands). France is included in the first group according to the relative index and in the second group according to the absolute index.

In table 12.3 we have completed this summary with the head-count ratio H. Although this index does not meet the requirements that we have made to a poverty index, it gives information on a certain aspect of poverty that one usually is interested in per se, namely the relative number of poor. The highest percentage of poor, 41.7 %, for the relative poverty line is found in France. Ireland, as before, is second with 37.1 %, but the third is Denmark (29.4 %) before the United Kingdom with 28.4 %. Next come Italy, the Netherlands, Belgium, and finally Germany with the lowest percentage of 5.7 %.

If we look at the absolute figures, almost the same pattern arises that we found for $P_5$ and $P_8$: Ireland has highest absolute poverty with 37.1 %. The United Kingdom follows with 24.9 %, France has 18 % poor and Denmark 15.5 %, while in Italy 12.1 % poor are found. The other three countries have a small percentage of poor, viz. 5.6 %, 4 % and 3.6 % for Germany, Belgium and the Netherlands respectively .

We conclude that according to all indices a division in three groups can be made, a first group with severe poverty, consisting of Ireland and the United Kingdom with respect to all criteria, and France with respect to the relative poverty line; a second group with moderate poverty, consisting of Denmark and Italy (and France with respect to the absolute poverty line); and a third group where poverty is lowest, consisting of Belgium, Germany and the Netherlands.

It should be noted, however, that even in the third group the relative poverty percentages indicating the percentage of people that are poor according to their own standards, is 16 % in the Netherlands and 13.8 % in Belgium, which is still a considerable percentage.

## 12.2 The poverty index with the welfare function of income

We now turn to the calculation of the poverty index if the utility function is chosen to be the welfare function of income, which is estimated for each respondent in the sample. The advantage of this approach is that, rather than assuming a certain functional form, the functional form is observed directly.

We first discuss the general results over countries, and then the decomposition of the poverty index in subgroups per country. In table 12.2 the resulting Dalton index is given at the welfare level 0.5, as well as the average welfare level of the poor.

Table 12.2 The Dalton poverty index based on the individual welfare function of income

|  | BEL | DEN | FRA | GER | IRE | ITA | NET | UK |
|---|---|---|---|---|---|---|---|---|
| $\overline{U(y^*)}$ | 0.466 | 0.439 | 0.407 | 0.474 | 0.412 | 0.462 | 0.465 | 0.440 |
| $D_p^{WFI}$ | 0.067 | 0.123 | 0.185 | 0.052 | 0.175 | 0.076 | 0.069 | 0.120 |

The ordering of countries does not vary much from the one found before: Germany, Belgium and the Netherlands are lowest, France and Ireland are highest, which was the ordering found before for "relative poverty". It is seen, however, that the difference between France and Ireland is much smaller than it was for the other poverty indices.

We may now turn to the decomposition of this poverty index in different subgroups. In table 12.3 the poverty indices are presented for different household types, as well as the relative frequency of the types in the sample (between parentheses).

This table shows that the poverty index is highest for non-working one-parent families in Denmark, Germany, the Netherlands and the United Kingdom, for single persons who are not working in Belgium, France and Italy, and for non-working families with children in Ireland. Lowest poverty indices are found for couples or families where two persons are working. It is seen that within each country vast differences in poverty are found. In the Netherlands, for instance, the general poverty index is small

Table 12.3  Decomposition of the poverty index $D_p^{WFI}$ in household types

|  | BEL | DEN | FRA | GER | IRE | ITA | NET | UK |
|---|---|---|---|---|---|---|---|---|
| overall | 0.067 | 0.123 | 0.185 | 0.052 | 0.175 | 0.076 | 0.069 | 0.120 |
| single person, working | 0.082 (2.67 %) | 0.146 (9.39 %) | 0.234 (13.66 %) | 0.042 (7.63 %) | 0.118 (1.79 %) | 0.100 (4.11 %) | 0.069 (5.82 %) | 0.146 (2.46 %) |
| single person, not working | 0.186 (4.89 %) | 0.211 (10.00 %) | 0.351 (7.53 %) | 0.103 (8.21 %) | 0.347 (4.73 %) | 0.217 (4.52 %) | 0.085 (7.72 %) | 0.312 (1.08 %) |
| one-parent family, working | 0.051 (2.84 %) | 0.183 (3.63 %) | 0.179 (5.22 %) | 0.064 (3.69 %) | 0.194 (8.94 %) | 0.072 (6.19 %) | 0.124 (1.96 %) | 0.056 (2.39 %) |
| one-parent family, not working | 0.100 (2.68 %) | 0.392 (1.67 %) | 0.291 (2.01 %) | 0.222 (1.84 %) | 0.369 (5.14 %) | 0.183 (1.82 %) | 0.239 (2.86 %) | 0.394 (1.01 %) |
| couple, two working, no children | 0.020 (4.81 %) | 0.085 (14.44 %) | 0.077 (7.79 %) | 0.022 (9.22 %) | 0.026 (1.38 %) | 0.015 (4.73 %) | 0.014 (9.47 %) | 0.026 (12.44 %) |
| couple, one working, no children | 0.058 (6.23 %) | 0.110 (8.53 %) | 0.204 (8.48 %) | 0.017 (8.21 %) | 0.133 (4.04 %) | 0.085 (7.02 %) | 0.033 (6.35 %) | 0.077 (6.29 %) |
| couple, not working, no children | 0.030 (5.12 %) | 0.158 (6.56 %) | 0.202 (6.76 %) | 0.042 (6.17 %) | 0.353 (5.31 %) | 0.143 (7.95 %) | 0.068 (8.89 %) | 0.178 (4.99 %) |
| family, two working, children | 0.022 (21.75 %) | 0.074 (30.59 %) | 0.074 (18.28 %) | 0.009 (15.46 %) | 0.034 (4.50 %) | 0.018 (16.22 %) | 0.017 (12.59 %) | 0.034 (28.92 %) |
| family, one working, children | 0.029 (43.74 %) | 0.093 (13.48 %) | 0.135 (25.04 %) | 0.022 (34.22 %) | 0.117 (46.52 %) | 0.068 (36.59 %) | 0.053 (38.68 %) | 0.082 (35.79 %) |
| family, not working, children | 0.054 (1.97 %) | 0.299 (0.76 %) | 0.268 (3.00 %) | 0.127 (2.48 %) | 0.372 (6.92 %) | 0.110 (3.95 %) | 0.145 (4.39 %) | 0.126 (2.31 %) |
| extended families | 0.045 (3.31 %) | 0.087 (0.96 %) | 0.223 (2.23 %) | 0.018 (2.86 %) | 0.148 (10.73 %) | 0.033 (6.91 %) | 0.010 (1.27 %) | 0.096 (2.31 %) |

(0.069), but the largest poverty index found is as large as 0.239 for the non-working one-parent family.

Again our conclusion is that non-working is the main characteristic of the poor, and we may add that single persons and one-parent families are in most countries especially vulnerable. The extent to which the poverty of the poorest group is reflected in the overall poverty index of a country depends upon their relative frequency in the population. As non-working one-parent families form in most countries a relatively small group, their high degree of poverty does not make a large contribution to the overall poverty index.

However, it is especially this decomposition into social subgroups that will serve policy purposes better than the overall index; it is revealing that even in Germany, the country with lowest overall poverty, certain subgroups are found that have as large a degree of poverty as the poorest in Italy. These decompositions do, however, confirm the fact that the largest extent of poverty is found in Ireland and France; the non-working families in Ireland, non-working one-parent families and non-working couples in Ireland are all poorer than any group in France. The fact that Ireland has an overall poverty index which is slightly lower than France results from the relatively better position of the working Irish.

The largest overall poverty index, finally, is found in the United Kingdom for non-working one-parent families. Again, their relatively small number implies that this does not weigh heavily in the total index.

The decomposition given aboven also enables us to predict the effect of certain economic or demographical changes on the extent of poverty; if another 10 % of all working households gets unemployed, the poverty index will increase drastically in all countries. The precise effect if 10 % of the total population will find themselves non-working families with children rather than one-working families with children is illustrated for the Netherlands, assuming that both poverty lines and incomes for working and non-working households will follow the structure found in our sample:

$$D_p^{WFI}(\dot{u} = 10\ \%, \text{Netherlands}) = 0.069 + 10\ \%(0.145) - 10\ \%(0.053)$$

$$= 0.078,$$

which is an increase of 13 % in the poverty index.

Analogously, we may predict the effect of demographic changes, like an increase of one-parent households, as a result of increasing numbers of divorces and separations; as in all countries one-parent households have a high poverty index, this will increase total poverty per country. This latter effect is not so easily calculated, however, as the splitting up of families implies that the size of the total population of households changes as well. For the Netherlands, however, it may be illustrated if we assume that a family where one person is working splits up into a non-working one-parent family and a single person who is working; for the last category, the poverty index happens to be equal to the average poverty index, and we merely have to calculate the effect of the additional one-parent families:

$$D_p^{WFI}(10 \text{ \% more divorces, Netherlands})$$

$$= 0.069 + 10 \text{ \%}(0.239) - 10 \text{ \%}(0.053) = 0.088$$

which is an increase of 27 % in the poverty index.

The assumptions made in both predictions are rather severe: the poverty lines do not change, while it is to be expected that a lower median income as a result of 10 % more unemployment will eventually decrease perceived needs as well, and hence the poverty line. The other assumptions are that incomes remain unchanged. This is not necessarily true; if unemployment increases, social pressure may promote larger unemployment benefits, but on the other hand more unemployed will be a larger burden for the social security system and government expenditure, which may have the opposite effect to reduce benefits. The net effect cannot be predicted.

The consequences of these findings for social policy will be discussed in the next and final chapter.

Chapter 13
CONCLUSIONS

The purpose of this book has been threefold: we intended to derive poverty lines for a set of European countries; we wanted to identify socio-economic characteristics that make people poverty prone, and, thirdly, we wanted to measure the extent of poverty in different countries and in different household types. For each of these objects we will now summarize the results obtained.

## 13.1 Derivation of poverty lines

We have derived poverty lines for different household types and different countries. With respect to the first differentiation, welfare neutral poverty lines are in general slightly lower for non-working households than for working households. They furthermore increase with the number of family members in a household. The exact household equivalence scales vary per country.

Comparing poverty lines between countries, large differences are found. These differences may be partly explained by differences in the income distribution between countries, represented by median income and income inequality. The poverty line is found to have an elasticity with respect to median income of about 0.5. It is, moreover, found to be increasing with income inequality. This implies that both economic growth and reduction of income inequality may be successful means of reducing poverty. If one, for instance, aims at reducing the poverty percentage to a certain "optimal" value, one may derive a set of combinations of median income and income inequality at which this optimum is reached. If, for instance, the income distribution may be described by a lognormal distribution function, the relation between median income and income inequality at which this optimum is found may be derived as:

$$(13.1) \quad \int_{-\infty}^{\ln z} \Phi(x; \mu_y, \sigma_y^2) = P_{opt},$$

where $P_{opt}$ is the optimal poverty percentage.
If the poverty line is specified, given the results in chapter 11, as

(13.2)    $\ln z = \ln z_0 + 0.526 \mu_y + 1.671 \sigma_y$

with $\ln z_0$ as a constant, equations (13.1) and (13.2) may be combined to give

(13.3)    $\Phi[\dfrac{\ln z_0 + (0.526-1) \mu_y + 1.671 \sigma_y}{\sigma_y}; 0,1] = P_{opt}$

or    $\mu_y = \dfrac{1}{1-0.526} [\ln z_0 + \sigma_y \{1.671 - \Phi^{-1}(P_{opt}; 0,1)\}]$

for all optimal poverty percentages smaller than 45 % ($\Phi^{-1}(0.45;0,1) = 1.67$) this is an increasing linear function of $\sigma_y$; if income inequality is high, a higher median income is needed to reach the desired poverty percentage.

However, not all differences in poverty lines are explained by these differences in income inequality; exceptional high poverty lines in France and low poverty lines in Germany are not completely accounted for. These different poverty lines in different countries may give rise to differences between socio-economic policy per country and in a European context. Per country the poverty lines estimated indicate what is needed for a welfare evaluation of income between "sufficient" and "insufficient". A social and economic objective may be to arrive at a social security structure such as to guarantee this national poverty line; the different poverty lines for different household types may further specify this objective. As to a European policy, however, one may object to international transfers according to these national welfare evaluations. If income transfers are needed, one is usually interested in alleviating the problems of the poorest first; hence, before alleviating relative poverty, one wants to be sure that absolute poverty is abolished. Hence, for European policy these levels may be considered as guidelines for a stepwise reduction of poverty, where the lowest poverty line should be guaranteed in all countries firstly, the one-but-lowest poverty line secondly, et cetera.

The elasticity of the poverty line of 0.526, that is found in this sample, might with some caution be interpreted optimistically; it looks as if poverty at least in theory may be solved by an appropriate mixture of economic policies. The caution is due, however, to the fact that this elasticity is based on a cross-sectional survey of eight countries at one point in time; a more reliable estimate of this extremely relevant parameter may be found when panel data of several countries are available. Collecting data of this type seems to be the next step in improving our knowledge. Even more caution is due in interpreting these results as guidelines for social policy because of the divergence between scientifically derived optimal policies and actual policy practice. The analysis in this book is basically static and descriptive, and does not go into historical and structural causes of the situations found.

Pessimistically, one might say that it thus confirms the status quo, in which situation the analysis is made, rather than aiming at some ultimate goal beyond the present socio-economic structure. We admit that no sociological, historical or economical explanation is given for the existence and persistence of poverty, in terms of social and economic structure, like any of the theories summarized in Townsend (1980) or George and Lawson (1980). Instead we have tried to present figures that have some use for actual present-day policy with regards to practical problems, like the assessment of social benefit levels. As these levels by their nature depend on the present social situation, the limited framework does not hamper us in reaching this objective. Finally, however, a last warning is in order as regards the value judgement whether or not the figures presented should be used in social policy. In the derivation of any poverty line definition, various assumptions and hypotheses have to be made. Ours is no exception. We have tried to be as explicit as possible about the assumptions made and value judgements implied. They amount to the following definition of the poverty line:

> The poverty line is the income level in between "sufficient" and "not sufficient", as defined by people who have that income themselves.[1]

This definition provides a poverty line that divides society into poor and non-poor according to their own perception of sufficiency. Such a "democratic" definition has some advantages, but does not necessarily have to be the one used for social policy. One may have other objectives in mind in determining minimum wages and social benefits, like the reduction of income inequality, or establishing social justice. These concepts do not have to result in a poverty line as defined above. On the other hand, one does not want minimum wages or social benefits to be such that the labour market stops functioning, or such that government expenditures double or triple. All these considerations may result in a social policy different from the one following from our study; no scientific study can replace political decisions. In all these decisions, however, information on the subject is invaluable, and it is that kind of information the poverty lines presented here supply.

## 13.2 Poverty characteristics

The second aim of our study was to assess which socio-economic characteristics make people poverty prone. This is done by comparison of the determinants of income with the determinants of the poverty line: if certain socio-economic characteristics result in a high poverty line but low income, they are said to be poverty determinants: someone with these characteristics will have a relatively high probability of being poor. These poverty probabilities have been calculated for various socio-economic characteristics, like age, occupation, education, employment. The conclusion is that one characteristic is of overwhelming importance in deciding whether someone is poor or not, viz. the fact whether one is working or not. In almost all countries people who are not working are poor, whatever age, education or occupation they have, and people who are working are generally non-poor. This holds for all European countries included in the survey, and implies that it is the unemployed, unabled and retired that should get most attention in programs reducing poverty. Neither manual workers, nor farmers, nor large families are found to be in general a category that is poor, although they are incidentally found to be so (France, Ireland).
Another general finding is that the probability of being poor is larger for young people than for old people. This holds both for working and for non-working households. Even in working families, the youngest age classes are below the poverty line in some countries. In non-working families one is either poor in all age classes, or in the younger age classes only.
With respect to other characteristics, it is seen that families who have experienced a decrease in income are more likely to be poor than people whose income has remained constant or has increased. This implies that people who have recently become unemployed or retired, or have otherwise

suffered an income decrease find it more difficult to cope with this situation than people who have been used to it. This is an argument in favour of gradual adaptation procedures in social security benefits or old-age pensions.

Finally, it is seen that female breadwinners have a higher probability of being poor. Their earnings are considerably lower than the incomes of working men. The same holds for female heads of non-working families.

All these effects have been derived ceteris paribus. It is clear that a cumulation of characteristics with a high poverty probability will result in an increased poverty probability. A combination that makes people very poverty prone is that of a female breadwinner who is not working, and younger than say 40 years of age. This includes both single women, one-parent families, and other families.

Summarizing, the poor are found amongst the non-working, the young, and female heads of household. These three groups have significantly lower incomes than the working, middle-aged and males respectively. Although especially for the non-working their poverty line is lower as well, the difference in needs is smaller than the difference in income.

As both the number of unemployed and the number of one-parent households has increased considerably over the last years, and is still increasing in most countries, this implies that the number of poor is increasing rapidly.

## 13.3 The extent of poverty

Our third and last aim was to develop means of measuring the extent of poverty. Most existing poverty indices choose a combination of three elements: the percentage of poor, the average income shortfall of the poor, and the income inequality of the poor.

In this book an axiomatic approach is given to evaluate these different indices. It appeared that two indices meet the requirements that follow from these axioms. One of these two, that is based on a social welfare framework, is generalized into a class of poverty indices, that may be used to evaluate the extent of poverty at different places or different moments in time. For the application of this class of indices to our dataset we have to make a further choice; we have to decide whether we will measure absolute or relative poverty. In the former case, one poverty line should be used to evaluate all countries; in the latter case each country is given its own national poverty line. We have calculated the extent of poverty according to both criteria. The conclusion is that according to absolute poverty, the European countries may be divided into three groups: one group with severe poverty, found in Ireland and the United Kingdom, a middle group, consisting of Italy, France and Denmark, and a third group with low poverty, found in the Netherlands, Belgium and Germany.

If relative poverty is our main interest, the same order is roughly found, but France is now the poorest country. We conclude that alleviating poverty in the U.K. and in Ireland ought to have priority according to both absolute and relative criteria, while France should be given even higher priority if one is concerned with relative poverty.

The poverty index has been decomposed into poverty indices in different subgroups, from which decomposition the extent of poverty within each subgroup can be found, as well as the contribution of this subgroup to the total poverty index. This decomposition confirms the main results from the analysis of poverty determinants: the highest poverty indices are found for non-working single persons and one-parent households. These groups are on average in considerable poverty, even in countries like the Netherlands, Belgium and Germany where on the whole poverty is lowest of all countries. The decomposition also enables us to predict changes in the poverty index as a result of certain changes in economic or demographic variables. For example, the effect of an increase in unemployment is a more than proportional increase in poverty. An increase in the number of non-working one-parent households on the poverty index is even larger. As both unemployment and divorces have augmented over the last years, and appear to be still increasing, this result suggests that poverty is growing to be more and more of a problem.

13.4 Recent developments

The survey on which the figures in this book are based has been carried out in October 1979. Some of the findings presented may have changed in the past five years. We briefly mention some developments that may have an impact on the conclusions of our research.

Firstly, it ought to be mentioned that the worldwide economic recession has left its traces in the European countries that we have studied. Table 13.1 gives a review of the changes in unemployment rates in the eight countries.

Table 13.1  Unemployment rates in eight European countries

|                    | 1979 | 1984 |
|--------------------|------|------|
| Belgium            | 8.4  | 14.5 |
| Denmark            | 6.1  | 10.5 |
| France             | 5.9  | 9.5  |
| Germany            | 3.2  | 8.0  |
| Ireland            | 6.1  | 16.8 |
| Italy              | 7.5  | 10.0 |
| the Netherlands    | 4.1  | 15.5 |
| the United Kingdom | 5.6  | 11.5 |

Source: OECD Economic Outlook (1983, 1984).

These figures, combined with our finding that people without work tend to have a much higher poverty probability than people with work, do not make one optimistic. The poverty estimates given in this book will certainly be underestimates of the present situation because of this higher unemployment.

Moreover, in some countries social security benefits and unemployment benefits have also decreased in real terms over the last few years, yielding a higher degree of poverty.

This effect is even stronger because of the asymmetry in the reaction of people's needs to changes in income: in chapter 10 it appeared that decreases in income tend to have a stronger, and probably larger effect on the feelings of (decreased) welfare than increases in income; it is easier to adapt one's needs to a higher income than to a lower income.

In short, the economic crisis has made the poverty problems that Europe is confronted with at the moment even larger than the figures in our study suggest. An attempt to solve these problems should be based on recent and accurate measurement of the extent of poverty, the determinants of poverty, and the level of poverty lines. In this book a method has been described that enables these three aspects to be measured, based on the answers to the so-called income evaluation question that is included in a representative survey. By carrying out such a survey on a regular basis in all EC countries, e.g. by Eurostat, one might update the information provided in this book and eventually check the effect of certain policy measures undertaken to diminish poverty. As the proper diagnosis and measurement of a problem is the first step towards solving it, an instrument for measurement is extremely important. We hope that this research has provided instruments and information that will eventually have an effect in the struggle against poverty.

NOTES TO CHAPTER 13

[1] This verbal description of the poverty line definition both applies to the definition used throughout this book and to the definition as used by Deleeck et al. (1984). The distinction between these two is in the method used to identify the households that are on the poverty line; see chapter 1 on these different methods.

# BIBLIOGRAPHY

Abel-Smith, B., and P. Townsend (1965), The poor and the poorest, Occasional Papers on Social Administration, No.17, Bell & Sons, London.
Afifi, A.A., and R.M. Elashoff (1966), "Missing observations in multivariate statistics, I. Review of the literature", Journal of the American Statistical Association, Vol.61, pp.595-605.
Ahluwalia, M.S. (1978), "Rural Poverty and Agricultural Performance in India", Journal of Development Studies, Vol.14, No.3, pp.298-323.
Aitchison, J., and J.A.C. Brown (1957), The Lognormal Distribution, Cambridge University Press, Cambridge.
Atkinson, A.B. (1970), "On the Measurement of Inequality", Journal of Economic Theory, Vol.2, pp.244-263.
Atkinson, A.B. (1972), Unequal Shares: Wealth in Britain, Allen Lane, London.
Atkinson, A.B. (1974), "Poverty and Income Inequality in Britain", in: D. Wedderburn (ed.), Poverty, Inequality and Class Structure, Cambridge University Press, London.
Atrostic, B.K. (1982), "The Demand for Leisure and Nonpecuniary Job Characteristics", American Economic Review, Vol.72, pp.428-441.
Beale, E.M.L., and R.J.A. Little (1975), "Missing values in multivariate analysis", Journal of the Royal Statistical Society, Ser.B, Vol.37, pp.129-145.
Becker, G.S. (1965), "A Theory of the Allocation of Time", The Economic Journal, Vol.75, pp.493-517.
Becker, G.S. (1975), Human Capital, National Bureau of Economic Research, Columbia University Press, New York.
Bentham, J. (1823), "An introduction to the principles of morals and legislation", in: A.N. Page (1968), Utility Theory, A Book of Readings, John Wiley and Sons, New York.
Bergson, A. (1938), "A Reformulation of Certain Aspects of Welfare Economics", Quarterly Journal of Economics, reprinted in: A.N. Page (1968), Utility Theory : a Book of Readings.
Blackorby, Ch., and D. Donaldson (1977), "Measures of relative equality and their meaning in terms of social welfare", Journal of Economic Theory, Vol.18, pp.59-80.
Blackorby, Ch., and D. Donaldson (1980), "Ethical indices for the measurement of poverty", Econometrica, Vol.48, No.4.
Blaug, M. (1968), Economic Theory in Retrospect, Heinemann, London, 2nd edition.
Blum, Z.D., and P.H. Rossi (1969), Social Class Research and Images of the Poor: A Bibliographic Review", in: D.P. Moynihan (ed.), On Understanding Poverty, Basic Books, New York.
Booth, C. (1892), Life and Labour of the People in London, MacMillan, London.
Bouma, N., B.M.S. van Praag and J. Tinbergen (1976), "Testing and Applying a Theory of Utility", European Economic Review, Vol.8, pp.181-191.
Bradford, D.F., and H.H. Kelejian (1973), "An Econometric Model of the Flight to the Suburbs", Journal of Political Economy, Vol.81, No.1, pp.566-589.
Bressler, B. (1969), "Relative Poverty, Absolute Poverty, and Policy Implications", Quarterly Review of Economics and Business, Vol.9, pp. 65-76.

Bressler, B. (1974), "Income Distribution, Relative Poverty and Family Size", Quarterly Review of Economics and Business, Vol.14, pp.27-37.
Bross, I.D.J. (1958), "How to use Ridit Analysis", Biometrics, Vol.19, pp.18-38.
Brown, J.A.C. (1954), "The Consumption of Food in Relation to Household Composition and Income", Econometrica, Vol.22, No.3, pp.444-460.
Brown, R.S., M. Moon, and B.S. Zoloth (1980), "Incorporating Occupational Attainment in Studies of Male-Female Earnings Differentials", Journal of Human Resources, Vol.15, No.1, pp.3-28.
Buyze, J. (1982), "The Estimation of Welfare Levels of a Cardinal Utility Function", European Economic Review, Vol.17, pp.325-332.
Cain, G.G. (1976), "The Challenge of Segmented Labor Market Theories to Orthodox Theory: A Survey", Journal of Economic Literature, Vol.14, pp.1215-1257.
Caplovitz, D. (1963), "The Poor Pay More", The Free Press, New York.
Cartwright, D., and A. Zander (eds.) (1968), Group Dynamics, Research and Theory, 3rd edition, Harper and Row, New York.
Central Bureau of Statistics (1980), Monthly Statistic of Prices, March 1980, Voorburg.
Chiswick, B.R., and J.A. O'Neill (1977), Human Resources and Income Distribution, Norton & Co., New York.
Clark, S., R. Hemming and D. Ulph (1981), "On Indices for the Measurement of Poverty", The Economic Journal, Vol.91, pp.515-526.
Colasanto, D., A. Kapteyn, and J. van der Gaag (1984), "Two Subjective Definitions of Poverty: Results from the Wisconsin Basic Needs Study", Journal of Human Resources, Vol.19, pp.127-137.
Cooter, R. and P. Rappoport (1984), "Were the Ordinalists Wrong About Welfare Economics?", Journal of Economic Literature, Vol.22, pp. 507-531.
Council of Economic Advisers (1965), "The Problem of Poverty in America", in: B.A. Weisbrod (ed.), The Economics of Poverty, Prentice-Hall, New Jersey.
Council of Economic Advisers (1965), "Some Economic Tasks of the Great Society", in: B.A. Weisbrod (ed.), The Economics of Poverty, Prentice-Hall, New Jersey.
Cowell, F.A. (1984), "The Structure of American Income Inequality", Review of Income and Wealth, Vol.30, pp.351-375.
Cramer, J.S. (1969), Empirical Econometrics, North Holland Publishing Company, Amsterdam.
Dagenais, M.G. (1973), "The use of incomplete observations in multiple regression analysis", Journal of Econometrics, Vol.1, pp.317-328.
Dalton, H. (1920), "The Measurement of the Inequality of Incomes", Economic Journal, Vol.91, pp.348-361.
Danziger, S., R. Haveman, and R. Plotnick (1981), "How Income Transfer Programs Affect Work, Savings, and the Income Distribution: A Critical Review", Journal of Economic Literature, Vol.19, pp.975-1028.
Danziger, S., and M. Taussig (1979), "The Income Unit and the Anatomy of Income Distribution", The Review of Income and Wealth, Vol.25, pp. 365-375.
Danziger, S., J. van der Gaag, M.K. Taussig, and E. Smolensky (1984), "The Direct Measurement of Welfare Levels; How Much Does it Cost to Make Ends Meet?", Review of Economics and Statistics, Vol.66, pp.500-505.
Dasgupta, P., A. Sen, and D. Starrett (1973), "Notes on the measurement of Inequality", Journal of Economic Theory, Vol.6, pp.180-187.

Datta, G., and J. Meerman (1980), "Household Income or Household Income per capita in Welfare Comparisons", Review of Income and Wealth, Vol.26, pp.401-418.
Deaton, A. and J. Muellbauer (1980), Economics and Consumer Behavior, Cambridge University Press, Cambridge.
Deleeck, H. (1977), "Bestaanszekerheid en het sociale zekerheidsstelsel in België - 1974", Belgisch tijdschrift voor Sociale Zekerheid, Vol.19, pp.1-23.
Deleeck, H., J. Berghman, P. van Heddegem, and L. Vereycken (1980), De sociale zekerheid tussen droom en daad. Theorie - onderzoek - beleid, Van Loghum Slaterus, Deventer/Antwerpen.
Deleeck, H., J. Berghman, and P. Janssens (1984), "Sociale Zekerheid: Inkomensverdeling en doelmatigheid anno 1982", De Gids op Maatschappelijk Gebied, Vol.75, pp.595-623.
Deming, W.E., and F.F. Stephan (1940), "On a Least-Squares Adjustment of a Sampled Frequency Table when the Expected Marginal Totals are Known", Annals of Mathematical Statistics, Vol.11, pp.427-444.
Dennett, J., E. James, G. Room, Ph. Watson (1982), Europe Against Poverty, Bedford Square Press, London.
Diamond, P., and M. Rothchild (1978), Uncertainty in Economics, Academic Press, New York.
Doeringer, P.B., and M.J. Piore (1971), Internal Labor Markets and Manpower Analysis, Heath Lexington Books.
Douglas, M. and B. Isherwood (1979), The World of Goods, Basic Books, Inc., New York.
Drewnowski, J. (1976), The Definition and Measurement of Poverty, Institute of Social Studies, The Hague.
Dubnoff, S. (1982), A method for the validation of equivalence scales, presented at the American Association of Public Opinion Research.
Duesenberry, J.S. (1949), Income, Saving and the Theory of Consumer Behavior, Princeton University Press, Princeton.
Engel, E. (1883), "Der Werth des Menschen. I. Teil: Der Kostenwerth des Menschen", Volkswirtschaftliche Zeitfragen, Vol.37-38, pp.1-74.
ESPOIR Report (1980), "Europe Against Poverty: Evaluation Report of the European Programme of Pilot Schemes and Studies to Combat Poverty", Report to the Commission of the European Communities.
Fase, M.M.G. (1969), An Econometric Model of Age-Income Profiles, Universitaire Pers Rotterdam.
Fiegehen, G.C., and P.S. Lansley (1976), "The Measurement of Poverty: a Note on Household Size and Income Units", Journal of the Royal Statistical Society, Series A, Vol.139, pp.508-518.
Fiegehen, G.C., P.S. Lansley, and A.D. Smith (1977), Poverty and Progress in Britain 1953-1973, Cambridge University Press, London.
Field, F. (1975), "What is Poverty?", New Society, Vol.33, No.677, pp. 688-691.
Field, M., and Ch. Pond (1977), To Him Who Hath, A Study of Poverty and Taxation, Penquin Books, Harmondsworth, Middlesex, England, pp.204-228.
Fields, G.S. (1980), Poverty, Inequality and Development, Cambridge University Press, Cambridge.
Fishman, L. (1966), Poverty amid Affluence, Yale University Press, New Haven.
Foster, J., J. Greer and E. Thorbecke (1984), "A Class of Decomposable Poverty Measures", Econometrica, Vol.52, pp.761-767.

Frey, W.H. (1980), "Status Selective White Flight and Central City Population Change", Journal of Regional Science, Vol.20, No.1, pp.71-89.
Friedman, M. (1953), "Choice, Chance, and the Personal Distribution of Income", Journal of Political Economy, Vol.61, pp.277-290.
Friedman, R.D. (1965), Poverty: Definition and Perspective, American Enterprise Institute for Public Policy Research, Washington D.C.
Fuchs, V. (1967), "Redefining Poverty and Redistributing Income", Public Interest, Summer, pp.88-95.
Galbraith, J.K. (1960), The Affluent Society, Hamilton, London.
Garfinkel, I., and R.H. Haveman (1977), "Earnings Capacity, Economic Status, and Poverty", Journal of Human Resources, Vol.12, pp.40-70.
Garfinkel, I., and R.H. Haveman (1977), Earnings Capacity, Poverty and Inequality, Academic Press, New York.
George, V., and R. Lawson (1980), Poverty and Inequality in Common Market Countries, London and Boston, Routledge and Kegan Paul, 1980.
Ghez, G.R., and G.S. Becker (1975), The Allocation of Time and Goods over the Life Cycle, National Bureau of Economic Research, Columbia University Press, New York.
Gibrat, R. (1931), Les Inégalités Economiques, Recueil Sirey, Paris.
Ginsburg, H. (ed.) (1972), Poverty, Economics and Society, Little Brown and Company, Boston.
Goedhart, Th., V. Halberstadt, A. Kapteyn, and B.M.S. van Praag (1977), "The Poverty Line: Concept and Measurement", The Journal of Human Resources, Vol.12, pp.503 520.
Griliches, Z. (1977), "Estimating the Returns to Schooling: Some Econometric Problems", Econometrica, Vol.45, pp.1-22.
Grootaerts, C. (1981), "The Conceptual Basis of Measures of Household Welfare and their Implied Survey Data Requirements", paper presented at the 17th General Conference of the Association for Research in Income and Wealth, Gouvieux (France), August 16-22.
Hagenaars, A.J.M. and B.M.S. van Praag (1985), "A Synthesis of Poverty Line Definitions", Review of Income and Wealth, Vol.31, pp.139-153.
Hamilton, D. (1968), The Economics of Poverty, Random House, New York.
Harrington, M. (1962), The Other America, Macmillan Company, New York.
Hart, P.E. (1976), "The Comparative Statistics and Dynamics of Income Distributions", Journal of the Royal Statistical Society, Series A, Vol.139, pp.108-125.
Hartley, M.J., and N.S. Revankar (1974), "On the Estimation of the Pareto-Law from Underreported Data", Journal of Econometrics, Vol.2, pp.327-341.
Hartog, J. (1980), Personal Income Distribution: A Multicapability Theory, Martinus Nijhoff, Boston.
Hartog, J., and J.G. Veenbergen (1978), "Long-run Changes in Personal Income Distribution", De Economist, Vol.126, pp.521-549.
Hausman, J.A. (1980), "The Effect of Wages, Taxes and Fixed Costs on Women's Labor Force Participation", Journal of Public Economics, Vol. 14, pp.161-194.
Hauver, J.H., J.A. Goodman, and M.A. Grainer (1981), "The Federal Poverty Threshold: Appearance and Reality", Journal of Consumer Research, Vol.8, pp.1-10.
Haveman, R.H., (1985), Does the Welfare State Increase Welfare?, Stenfert Kroese BV, Leyden.
Heckman, J., and S. Polachek (1972), The Functional Form of the Income-Schooling Relationship, National Bureau for Economic Research, New York.

Heckman, J. (1974), "Shadow Prices, Market Wages and Labor Supply", Econometrica, Vol.42, pp.679-694.
Heckman, J. (1976), "The Common Structure of Statistical Models of Truncation, Sample Selection and Limited Dependent Variables and a Simple Estimator for Such Models", Annals of Economic and Social Measurement, Vol.5, pp.475-492.
Heckmann, J.J., and Th.E. Macurdy (1980), "A Life Cycle Model of Female Labour Supply", Review of Economic Studies, Vol.47, pp.47-74.
Hill, T.P. (1959), "An Analysis of the Distribution of Wages and Salaries in Great Britain", Econometrica, Vol.27.
Hobsbawm, E.J. (1968), "Poverty", International Encyclopaedia of the Social Sciences, New York.
Holman, R. (1978), Poverty, Explanations of Social Deprivation, Martin Robertson, London.
Homan, M.E., B.M.S. van Praag and A.J.M. Hagenaars (1984), "The Female Participation Decision, Household Cost Functions, and the Shadow Price of Household Production", Center for Research in Public Economics, Report 84.08, Leyden University.
Hyman, H.H. (1942), "The Psychology of Status", Archives of Psychology, No.269, pp.5-38,80-86, reprinted in: Hyman and Singer (1968), pp. 147-165.
Hyman, H.H. and E. Singer (1968), Readings in Reference Group Theory and Research, The Free Press, New York.
Jackson, D. (1972), Poverty, McMillan Studies in Economics.
Jevons, W.S. (1871), The Theory of Political Economy, MacMillan, London.
Johnson, N.L., and S. Kotz (1970), Distribution in Statistics, Continuous Univariate Distributions - 2, Wiley & Sons, New York.
Joint Economic Committee, United States Congress (1967), "Report on the January 1964 Economic Report of the President", in: B.A. Weisbrod (ed.), The Economics of Poverty, Prentice-Hall, New Jersey.
Joreskog, K.G., and W. Sörbom (1978), Lisrel V, Estimation of Linear Structural Equations Systems by Maximum Likelihood Methods: a FORTRAN IV Program, International Educational Services, Chicago.
Kakwani, N. (1980), "On a Class of Poverty Measures", Econometrica, Vol. 48, No.2, pp.437-446.
Kapteyn, A., and B.M.S. van Praag (1976), "A New Approach to the Construction of Family Equivalence Scales", European Economic Review, Vol.7, pp.313-335.
Kapteyn, A. (1977), A Theory of Preference Formation, Ph.D. thesis, Leyden University, Leyden.
Kapteyn, A., B.S.M. van Praag, and F.G. van Herwaarden (1978), "Individual Welfare Functions and Social Reference Spaces", Economics Letters, Vol.1, pp.173-178.
Kapteyn, A., T.J. Wansbeek, and J. Buyze (1978), "The Dynamics of Preference Formation", Economics Letters, Vol.1, pp.93-97.
Kapteyn, A., and V. Halberstadt (1980), "Il Concetto di Reddito Minimo. Definizioni Misure e Politiche nella Comunità Europea", Rivista Internazionale di Scienze Sociali, No.2, pp.183-219.
Kapteyn, A., and B.M.S. van Praag (1980), "Family Composition and Family Welfare", in: J. Simon, and J. DaVanzo (eds.), Research in Population Economics, II, JAI-Press, Greenwich, pp.77-97.
Kapteyn, A., and T.J. Wansbeek (1982), "Empirical Evidence on Preference Formation", Journal of Economic Psychology, Vol.3, pp.137-149.

Kapteyn, A., and T.J. Wansbeek (1982), "The Individual Welfare Function: Measurement, Explanation and Policy Applications", Statistical Studies, Vol.32, Staatsuitgeverij, The Hague.

Kiker, B.F. (1966), "The Historical Roots of the Concept of Human Capital", Journal of Political Economy, Vol.74, pp.481-499.

Kilpatrick, R.W. (1973), "The Income Elasticity of the Poverty Line", The Review of Economics and Statistics, Vol.55, pp.327-332.

Klein, L.R. (1974), A textbook of econometrics, Prentice-Hall, Inc., New Jersey, 2nd edition.

Kmenta, J. (1978), "On the Problem of Missing Measurements in the Estimation of Economic Relationships", Report R-102, Center for Research on Economic and Social Theory, University of Michigan.

Kondor, Y. (1975), "Value Judgement implied by the Use of Various Measures of Income Inequality", Journal of Income and Wealth, Vol.21, pp.309-321.

Kundu, A. and T.E. Smith (1983), "An Impossibility Theorem on Poverty Indices", International Economic Review, Vol.24, pp.423-434.

Kuznets, S.S. (1976), "Demographic Aspects of the Size Distribution of Income: An Exploratory Essay", Economic Development and Cultural Change, Vol.25, pp.1-94.

Lamale, H. (1958), "Changes in Concepts of Income Adequacy in the Last Century", American Economic Review, Vol.48, Supplement, pp.291-299.

Lampman, R.J. (1971), Ends and Means of Reducing Income Poverty, Institute for Research in Poverty Monograph Series, Markham Publishing Company, Chicago.

Lansley, S. (1979), "What Hope for the Poor?", Lloyds Bank Review, No. 132, April.

Lansley, S. (1980), "Changes in Inequality and Poverty in the U.K., 1971-1976", Oxford Economic Papers, Vol.32, No.1, pp.134-151.

Layard, R. (1980), "Human and Satisfaction and Public Policy", The Economic Journal, Vol.9, pp.737-750.

Leigh, D.E. (1979), An Analysis of the Determinants of Occupational Upgrading, Academic Press, New York.

Locke Anderson, W.H. (1964), "Trickling down: The Relationship between Economic Growth and the Extent of Poverty among American Families", Quarterly Journal of Economics, Vol.78, pp.511-524.

Love, R., and G. Oja (1975), Low Income in Canada, Paper presented at the 14th General Conference of the International Association for Research in Income and Wealth.

Lydall, H.F. (1968), The Structure of Earnings, Clarendon Press, Oxford.

Maddala, G.S. (1977), Econometrics, McGraw-Hill, New York.

Maddala, G.S. (1983), Limited-dependent and Qualitative Variables in Econometrics, Cambridge University Press, Cambridge.

Manning, S.L., and E.L. Vatter (1964), Financial Management Practices of Families with Steady or Fluctuating Incomes, Publication of the New York State College of Home Economics.

Marshall, A. [1890] (1920), Principles of Economics, 8th ed., McMillan, London.

Mayhew, H. (1851), "London Labour and the London Poor", The London Street-Folk, Vol.1, Woodfall and Son, London.

Meade, J.E. (1964), Efficiency, Equality and the Ownership of Property, Allen and Unwin, London.

Miller, H.P. (1965), "The Dimension of Poverty", in: B. Seligman (ed.), Poverty as a Public Issue, The Free Press, New York.

Miller, S.M., and M. Rein (1965), "The War on Poverty: Perspectives and Prospects", in: B. Seligman (ed.), Poverty as a Public Issue, The Free Press, New York.
Miller, S.M., M. Rein, P. Roby, and B. Gross (1967), "Poverty, Inequality and Conflict", The Annals, No.373, pp.16-52.
Miller, S.M., and P. Roby (1970), The Future of Inequality, Basic Books, New York.
Miller, S.M., and P. Roby (1974), "Poverty: Changing Social Stratification", in: P. Townsend (ed.), The Concept of Poverty, Heinemann, London.
Miller, W. (1969), "The Elimination of the American Lower Class as a National Policy: A Critique of the Ideology of the Poverty Movement of the 1960s", in: D.P. Moynihan (ed.), On Understanding Poverty, Basic Books Inc., New York.
Mincer, J. (1958), "Investment in Human Capital and Personal Income Distribution", Journal of Political Economy, Vol.66, pp.281-303.
Mincer, J. (1970), "The Distribution of Labor Incomes: A Survey", Journal of Economic Literature, Vol.8, pp.1-26.
Mincer, J. (1974), Schooling, Experience and Earnings, National Bureau of Economic Research, Columbia University Press, New York.
Mirer, Th.W. (1977), Aspects of the variability of Family Income, in: M.L. Moon, and E. Smolensky (eds.), Improving Measures of Economic Well-Being, Institute for Research on Poverty, Madison, Wisconsin.
Moon, M.L. (1977), "The Economic Welfare of the Aged and Income Security Programs", in: M.L. Moon and E. Smolensky (1977) (eds.), Improving Measures of Economic Well-Being.
Moon, M. and E. Smolensky (1977) (eds.), Improving Measures of Economic Well-Being", The Academic Press, New York.
Morgan, J.N., et al. (1962), Income and Welfare in the United States, McGraw-Hill, New York.
Morgan, J.N., and J.D. Smith (1969), "Measures of economic well-offness and their correlates", American Economic Review, Vol.59, pp.450-462.
Moynihan, D.P. (ed.) (1969), On Understanding Poverty, Basic Books Inc., New York.
Moynihan, D. (1973), The Politics of a Guaranteed Income, Vintage Books, New York.
Muellbauer, J. (1980), "The Estimation of the Prais-Houthakker Model of Equivalent Scales", Econometrica, Vol.48, No.1, pp.153-176.
Nerlove, M. (1974), "Household and Economy Toward A New Theory of Population and Economic Growth", Journal of Political Economy, Vol.82, pp.S200-218.
Ng., Y-K. (1981), "Welfarism: A Defence against Sen's Attack", The Economic Journal, Vol.91, pp.527-530.
OECD (1976), Public Expenditures on Income Maintenance Programs, Studies in Resource Allocation, Vol.3, Paris.
OECD (1983, 1984), Economic Outlook, Paris.
Ornati, O. (1972), "What is Poverty?", in: H. Ginsberg (ed.), Poverty, Economics and Society, Little Brown and Company, Boston.
Orshansky, M. (1965), "Counting the Poor: Another Look at the Poverty Profile", Social Security Bulletin, Vol.28.
Orshansky, M. (1968), "The shape of poverty in 1966", Social Security Bulletin, Vol.31, pp.3-31.
Page, A.N. (1968), Utility Theory: A Book of Readings, John Wiley and Sons, New York.

Pareto, V. (1927), "Manuel d'Economie Politique", in: Page (1968), pp.168-183.
Pen, J. (1971), Income Distribution, Allen Lane The Penguin Press London.
Pigou, A.C. [1920] (1932), The Economics of Welfare, MacMillan, London.
Plotnick, R.D., and F. Skidmore (1975), "The measurement of Poverty", in: Progress against Poverty, Academic Press, New York, pp.31-46.
Plotnick, R.D., and F. Skidmore (1975) (eds.), Progress Against Poverty: A Review of the 1964-1974 Decade, Academic Press, New York.
Pond, Ch. (1978), "How Poverty gets Taped", New Society, Vol.43, No.798, pp.129-130.
Pratt, J.W. (1964), "Risk Aversion in the Small and in the Large", Econometrica, Vol.32, pp.122-136.
Projector, D.S., and G.W. Weiss (1969), "Income-Net Worth Measures of Economic Welfare", Social Security Bulletin, Vol.32, pp.14-17.
Pyatt, G. (1980), Poverty and Welfare Measures based on the Lorenz Curve, Paper presented at the World Conference of the Econometric Society, Aix-en Provence.
Rainwater, L. (1969), "The Lower-Class Culture and Poverty-War Strategy", in: D.P. Moynihan (ed.), On Understanding Poverty, Basic Books, New York.
Rainwater, L. (1974), What Money Buys: Inequality and the Social Meanings of Income, Basic Books, New York.
Rein, M. (1974), "Problems in the Definition and Measurement of Poverty", in: P. Townsend (ed.), The Concept of Poverty, Heinemann, London.
Ritzen, J.M.M. (1977), Education, Economic Growth and Income Distribution, North-Holland Publishing Company, Amsterdam.
Robbins, L. (1932), An Essay on the Nature and Significance of Economic Science, MacMillan, London.
Rosenthal, G. (1969), "Identifying the Poor: Economic Measures of Poverty", in: D.P. Moynihan (ed.), On Understanding Poverty, Basic Books Inc., New York.
Rothenberg Pack, J. (1973), "Determinants of Migration to central cities", Journal of Regional Science, Vol.13, No.12, pp.249-260.
Rowntree, B.S. (1901), Poverty: A Study of Town Life, MacMillan, London.
Rowntree, B.S. (1901), The Poverty Live: a Reply to Mrs. Bosanquet, Longmans, London.
Rowntree, B.S. (1941), Poverty and Progress: a Second Social Survey of York, Longmans, London.
Rowntree, B.S. (1951), Poverty and the Welfare State: a Third Social Survey of York dealing also with Economic Questions, Longmans, London.
Runciman, W.G. (1966), Relative Deprivation and Social Justice, Routledge & Kegan Paul, London.
Sahota, G.S. (1978), "Theories of Personal Income Distribution: A Survey", Journal of Economic Literature, Vol.16, pp.1-55.
Samuelson, P.A. (1953), "The Foundation of Economic Analysis", reprinted in: A.N. Page (1968), Utility Theory: A Book of Readings, pp.317-363.
Sarpellon, G. (1984) (ed.), Understanding Poverty, Angeli, Milano.
Sawyer, M.C. (1975), Poverty in some developed countries, 14th General Conference of the International Association for Research in Income and Wealth, Finland.
Scase, R. (1974), "Relative Deprivation: a Comparison of English and Swedish Manual Workers", in: D. Wedderburn (ed.), Poverty, Inequality and Class Structure, Cambridge University Press, London.

Seligman, B. (ed.) (1965), Poverty as a Public Issue, The Free Press, New York.
Sen, A.K. (1970), Collective Choice and Social Welfare, North-Holland Publishing Company, Amsterdam.
Sen, A.K. (1973), On Economic Inequality, Oxford University Press, London.
Sen, A.K. (1974), "Informational Bases of Alternative Welfare Approaches", Journal of Public Economics, Vol.3, pp.387-403.
Sen, A.K. (1976), "Poverty: an ordinal approach to measurement", Econometrica, Vol.44, pp.219-231.
Sen, A.K. (1979), "Issues in the Measurement of Poverty", Scandinavian Journal of Economics, Vol.81, pp.285-307.
Sen, A.K. (1982), Poverty and Famines, Oxford University Press, London.
Sen, A.K. (1983), "Poor, Relatively Speaking", Oxford Economic Papers, Vol.35, pp.153-170.
Sharma, B.D. (1983), "Measuring Poverty and Equalitarian Trends", North Eastern Hill University Journal of Social Sciences and Humanities, Vol.1, pp.1-10.
Shorrocks, A.F. (1975), "On Stochastic Models of Size Distributions", Review of Economic Studies, Vol.42, pp.631-641.
Slutsky, E.E. (1915), "Sulla teoria del bilancio del consumatore", Giornale degli Economisti, Vol.3, pp.1-26.
Smeeding, T.M. (1977), "The Economic Well-Being of Low Income Households, Implications for Income Inequality and Poverty", in: M. Moon and E. Smolensky (eds.), Improving Measures of Economic Well-Being, Institute for Research on Poverty, Madison, Wisconsin.
Smeeding, T.M. (1977), The Trend toward Equality in the Distribution of Net Income: A Reexamination of Data and Methodology", Discussion Paper, Institute for Research on Poverty, University of Wisconsin, Madison.
Smith, A. [1776] (1979), The Wealth of Nations, Penguin Books Ltd., Harmondsworth.
Smolensky, E. (1973), "Poverty, Propinquity and Policy", Annals of the American Academy of Political and Social Science, Income Inequality, pp.120-125.
Sociaal en Cultureel Planbureau (1977), Profijt van de Overheid, Staatsuitgeverij, 's-Gravenhage.
Social Science Research Council (1968), Research on Poverty, Heinemann, London.
Somermeyer, W.H., and R. Bannink (1966), Determinanten van de individuele consumptiedrang: een econometrische analyse van de resultaten der CBS-spaarenquête 1960, W. de Haan N.V., Hilversum.
Spence, A.M. (1973), "Job Market Signalling", Quarterly Journal of Economics, Vol.87, pp.355-374.
Staehle, H. (1943), "Ability, Wages and Income, Review of Economics and Statistics, Vol.25, pp.77-87.
Stigler, G.J. (1950), "The Development of Utility Theory", in: A.N. Page (1968), Utility Theory: A Book of Readings, pp.55-123.
Stiglitz, J.E. (1975), "The Theory of Screening, Education and the Distribution of Income", American Economic Review, Vol.65, No.3, pp.283-300.
Stouffer, S.A., et al. (1949), The American Soldier, Princeton.
Strumpel, B. (ed.) (1974), Subjective Elements of Well-Being, OECD, Paris.
Takayama, N. (1979), "Poverty, Income Inequality, and their Measures: Professor Sen's Axiomatic Approach Reconsidered", Econometrica, Vol.47, No.3.

Taubman, P. (1975), <u>Sources of Inequality in Earnings</u>, North-Holland Publishing Company, Amsterdam.
Taubman, P., and T. Wales (1974), <u>Higher Education and Earnings</u>, National Bureau of Economic Research, McGraw-Hill, New York.
Thon, D. (1979), "On Measuring Poverty", <u>Review of Income and Wealth</u>, Vol.25, pp.429-439.
Thon, D. (1981), "A Poverty Measure", Mimeo, The Norwegian School of Economics and Business Administration.
Thon, D. (1981), "Income Inequality and Poverty, Some Problems", <u>Review of Income and Wealth</u>, Vol.27, No.2.
Thon, D. (1982), "An Axiomatization of the Gini Coefficient", <u>Mathematical Social Sciences</u>, Vol.2, pp.131-143.
Thon, D. (1983), "A Note on a Troublesome Axiom for Poverty Indices", <u>The Economic Journal</u>, Vol.93, pp.199-201.
Thurow, L.C. (1969), <u>Poverty and Discrimination</u>, The Brookings Institution, Washington D.C.
Thurow, L.C. (1975), <u>Generating Inequality</u>, Basic Books, Inc., New York.
Tinbergen, J. (1975), <u>Income Distribution</u>, North Holland Publishing Company, Amsterdam.
Titmuss, R.M. (1965), <u>Income Distribution and Social Change</u>, Unwin University Books, London.
Townsend, P. (1954), "Measuring Poverty", <u>British Journal of Sociology</u>, Vol.5, pp.130-138.
Townsend, P. (1962), "The Meaning of Poverty", <u>British Journal of Sociology</u>, Vol.13, pp.210-227.
Townsend, P. (1974), <u>The Concept of Poverty</u>, Heinemann, London.
Townsend, P. (1974), "Poverty as Relative Deprivation: Resources and Style of Living", in: D. Wedderburn (ed.), <u>Poverty, Inequality and Class Structure</u>, Cambridge University Press, London.
Townsend, P. (1979), <u>Poverty in the United Kingdom</u>, Penquin Books, Middlesex.
United Nations (1979), <u>Statistical Yearbook 1978</u>, New York.
Van de Stadt, H., A. Kapteyn, and S.A. van de Geer (1982), "The Relativity of Utility: Evidence from Panel Data", Report 82.12, Center for Research in Public Economics, Leyden University, Leyden.
Van Herwaarden, F.G., and A. Kapteyn (1981), "Empirical Comparison of the Shape of Welfare Functions", <u>European Economic Review</u>, Vol.15, pp. 261-286.
Van Neuman, and Morgenstern (1953),
Van Praag, B.M.S. (1968), <u>Individual Welfare Functions and Consumer Behavior</u>, North Holland Publishing Company, Amsterdam.
Van Praag, B.M.S. (1971), "The Welfare Function of Income in Belgium: An Empirical Investigation", <u>European Economic Review</u>, Vol.2, pp.337-369.
Van Praag, B.M.S. (1978), "The Perception of Income Inequality", in: A. Shorrocks and W. Krelle (eds.), <u>Personal Income Distribution</u>, North Holland Publishing Company, Amsterdam.
Van Praag, B.M.S. (1978), "The Perception of Welfare Inequality", <u>European Economic Review</u>, Vol.10, pp.189-207.
Van Praag, B.M.S. (1980), "A Social Filter Approach to the Individual Welfare Function", Report 80.12, Center for Research in Public Economics, Leyden University, Leyden.

Van Praag, B.M.S. (1981), "Reflections on the Theory of Individual Welfare Functions", Report 81.14, Center for Research in Public Economics, Leyden University, Leyden, published in the Proceedings of the American Statistical Association, Detroit.
Van Praag, B.M.S. (1982), "Objective and Subjective Definitions of Poverty", paper presented at the Venice Conference on Poverty, published in: G. Sarpellon (1984), Understanding Poverty.
Van Praag, B.M.S. (1984), "Household Cost Functions and Equivalence Scales. An Alternative Approach", Report 84.04, Center for Research in Public Economics, Leyden University.
Van Praag, B.M.S., T.K. Dijkstra, and J.H.C.M. van Velzen (1985), "Least-Squares Theory based on General Distributional Assumptions with an Application to the Incomplete Observations Problem", Psychometrika, Vol.50, forthcoming.
Van Praag, B.M.S., T. Goedhart, and A. Kapteyn (1980), "The Poverty Line. A Pilot Survey in Europe", The Review of Economics and Statistics, Vol.62, pp.461-465.
Van Praag, B.M.S., A.J.M. Hagenaars, and W.J. van Eck (1983), "The Influence of Classification and Observation on Errors the Measurement of Income Inequality", Econometrica, Vol.51, pp.1093-1108.
Van Praag, B.M.S., A.J.M. Hagenaars, and J. van Weeren (1982), "Poverty in Europe", The Review of Income and Wealth, Vol.28, pp.345-359.
Van Praag, B.M.S., and A. Kapteyn (1973), "Further Evidence on the Individual Welfare Function of Income: An Empirical Investigation in The Netherlands", European Economic Review, Vol.4, pp.33-62.
Van Praag, B.M.S., A. Kapteyn, and F.G. van Herwaarden (1979), "The Definition and Measurement of Social Reference Spaces", The Netherlands Journal of Sociology, Vol.15, pp.13-25.
Van Praag, B.M.S., and J.S. Spit (1982), "The Social Filter Process and Income Evaluation - An Empirical Study in the Social Reference Mechanism", Report 82.08, Center for Research in Public Economics, Leyden University, Leyden.
Van Praag, B.M.S., J.S. Spit, and H. van de Stadt (1982), "A Comparison between the Foodratio Poverty Line and the Leyden Poverty Line", Review of Economics and Statistics, Vol.64, No.4, pp.691-694.
Van Praag, B.M.S. and H. van Weeren (1983), "Some Panel Evidence on the Time Discounting Mechanism in the Formation of Value Judgements on Income with Applications to Social Security and Income Policy", Center for Research in Public Economics, Report 83.22, Leyden University.
Van Praag, B.M.S., and B. Wesselman (1984), "The Hot-Deck Method; an Analytical and Empirical Evaluation", Computational Statistics Quarterly, Vol.1, pp.205-233.
Vietorisz, Th., and B. Harrison (1973), "Labor Market Segmentation: Positive Feedback and Divergent Developments", American Economic Review, Papers and Proceedings, Vol.63 (II), pp.366-376.
Wansbeek, T.J., and A. Kapteyn (1983), "Tackling Hard Questions by Means of Soft Methods: The Use of Individual Welfare Functions in Socio-Economic Policy", Kyklos, Vol.36, pp.249-269.
Ward, S. (1976), "On the Poverty Line", New Society, Vol.37, No.724, pp.399-400.
Watts, H. (1968), "An Economic Definition of Poverty", in: D.P. Moynihan, On Understanding Poverty, Basic Books, Inc., New York, pp.316-329.

Watts, H.W. (1967), "The Iso-Prop Index: An Approach to the Determination of Differential Poverty Income Thresholds", The Journal of Human Resources, Vol.2, pp.3-18.
Wedderburn, D.C. (1962), "Poverty in Britain Today: The Evidence", Sociological Review, Vol.10, pp.257-280.
Wedderburn, D.C. (ed.) (1974), Poverty, Inequality and Class Structure, Cambridge University Press, Cambridge.
Weisbrod, B.A. (1965), The Economics of Poverty, Prentice-Hall, New Jersey.
Weisbrod, B.A., and W.L. Hansen (1968), "An Income Net-Worth Approach to Measuring Economic Welfare", American Economic Review, Vol.58, pp. 1315-1329.
Welch, F. (1975), "Human Capital Theory: Education, Discrimination, and Life Cycles", American Economic Review, Vol.75, No.2, pp.63-73.
White, D. (1975), "What is a Luxury?", New Society, Vol.33, No.677, pp. 686-688.
Will, R.E., and H.G. Vatter (eds.) (1965), Poverty in Affluence: The Social, Political and Economic Dimensions of Poverty in the United States, Harcourt, New York.
Withey, S.B. (1974), "Values and Social Change", in: B. Strumpel (ed.), Subjective Elements of Well-Being, OECD, Paris.

## AUTHOR INDEX

Abel-Smith  26, 28
Afifi  160
Aitchison  112
Atkinson  120, 128, 129, 131, 132, 133, 137, 138
Atrostic  73
Atwater  17, 18
Bannink  72
Beale  160
Becker  9, 71, 72, 77
Bentham  2, 4, 41
Bergson  5
Bernoulli  1
Blackorby  119, 120, 126, 135
Blaug  1
Booth  15
Bouma  73
Bradford  82
Bross  84
Brown, J.A.C.  21, 112
Brown, R.S.  75
Buyze  65
Cain  76
Cartwright  87
Chiswick  68
Clark  120, 126
Colasanto  42
Cooter  4, 41
Cowell  69
Cramer  66
Dagenais  160
Dalton  6, 128, 129, 132, 134, 135, 136, 137, 138, 139, 141
Danziger  41, 42, 69, 76
Datta  69

Deaton  24
Deleeck  31, 32, 45, 279
Deming  154, 160
Doeringer  75
Donaldson  119, 120, 126, 135
Douglas  16
Drewnowski  1
Duesenberry  65
Dunlop  17, 18
Dijkstra  160
Elashoff  160
Engel  20
Fase  74, 75
Fechner  3
Fields  39, 41
Foster  120, 126, 137, 138
Frey  82
Friedman, M.  47, 72
Friedman, R.D.  22, 57, 64
Fuchs  26
Galbraith  i
Garfinkel  9, 41, 68, 110
George  273
Ghez  77
Gibrat  74
Goedhart  31, 32, 42, 65
Gossen  3
Greer  120, 126, 137, 138
Griliches  77
Grootaerts  24
Hagenaars  12, 42, 44, 55, 65, 66, 97, 159, 231
Halberstadt  29, 65
Hansen  89
Harrison  75

Hartley  159
Hartog  74, 77, 82
Hausman  80
Haveman  9, 41, 68, 76, 77, 110
Heckman  80, 81, 200
Hemming  120, 126
Homan  97
Hyman  66
Isherwood  16
Jevons  2, 3
Johnson  81
Kakwani  119, 126
Kapteyn  5, 7, 28, 29, 42, 47, 65, 66, 87, 89, 91, 92, 97, 100
Kelejian  82
Kiker  72
Kilpatrick  12, 30, 42
Kmenta  160
Kotz  81
Kundu  120, 124, 127, 133
Kuznets  69
Lampman  1, 21, 28, 41
Lansley  26, 27
Lavers  20
Lawson  273
Layard  65
Leigh  77
Little  160
Love  24
Lydall  76
Maddala  81
Manning  96
Marshall  2, 16
Marx  17
Meade  74
Meerman  69
Menger  2

Mill  81
Miller  27, 28, 41
Mincer  71, 72, 74, 82
Mirer  9
Moon  9, 41
Morgan  9, 41
Morgenstern  47
Muellbauer  24
Nerlove  72
OECD  26, 27, 30, 76
Oja  24
O'Neill  68
Orshansky  10, 20, 21, 22, 23, 56, 62, 64
Page  2
Pareto  4
Pen  82
Pigou  1, 3, 6
Piore  75
Plotnick  28, 29, 76
Projector  41
Rainwater  26, 30, 41, 42
Rappoport  4
Rein  18, 26, 41
Revankar  159
Ritzen  77
Robbins  2, 4, 7
Roby  27, 28, 41
Rosenthal  24
Rothenberg Pack  75
Rowntree  15, 17, 18, 19, 20, 56, 64
Runciman  25
Sahota  71, 82
Samuelson  5
Savage  47
Sawyer  26

Sen  5, 6, 11, 17, 41, 69, 119, 122, 126, 135, 136, 139
Sharma  125
Shorrocks  75
Skidmore  28, 29
Slutsky  4
Smeeding  9, 68, 159
Smith, A.  73
Smith, T.E.  120, 124, 127, 133
Smolensky  41
Sociaal en Cultureel Planbureau  82
Somermeyer  72
Spence  72, 76
Spit  24, 42, 62, 63, 65, 66, 89
Staehle  82
Stephan  154, 160
Stigler  4, 6, 41
Stouffer  25
Takayama  119, 120, 122, 126, 135
Taubman  77
Taussig  9, 69
Thon  120, 122, 123, 124, 126, 127, 128, 135
Thurow  11, 28, 29, 76
Thorbecke  120, 126, 137, 138
Tinbergen  73, 76
Townsend  17, 18, 25, 26, 27, 28, 34, 35, 36, 41, 138, 273
Ulph  120, 126
Van de Geer  89
Van der Gaag  42
Van de Stadt  24, 42, 62, 63, 66, 89, 91
Van Eck  159
Van Herwaarden  47, 65
Van Neumann  47

Van Praag  5, 6, 7, 12, 24, 42, 44, 47, 55, 62, 63, 65, 66, 73, 87, 88, 89, 91, 92, 97, 102, 141, 149, 159, 160, 231
Van Velsen  160
Van Weeren  42, 65, 66, 88, 89, 102
Vatter  96
Veenbergen  82
Vietorisz  75
Wales  77
Wansbeek  65, 89
Watts  8, 14, 19, 24, 41, 42, 66
Weber  3
Wedderburn  28
Weisbrod  9
Weiss  41
Wesselman  160
Withey  31
Zander  87

## SUBJECT INDEX

absolute deprivation 12, 39, 119
absolute poverty, empirical assessment of the extent of 265
absolute poverty line 11, 22, 53
age 78, 83, 99
age-income profiles 212
   Belgium 212
   Denmark 212
   France 213
   Germany 213
   Ireland 214
   Italy 214
   the Netherlands 215
   the United Kingdom 215
age-μ profiles 232
   Belgium 232
   Denmark 233
   France 234
   Germany 235
   Ireland 236
   Italy 237
   the Netherlands 238
   the United Kingdom 239
analysis of response 152
anthropology of consumption 16
Atkinson inequality index 129, 131
Atkinson poverty index 129, 131, 264, 265
average welfare level in society 168
axiomatic requirements to a poverty index 121
basic needs 7, 15, 16, 17, 19, 56, 57, 64
bias 80, 158
budget restriction 8
budget survey 61
caloric estimates 18
cardinal utility 1, 5, 46-50
censored income distribution 119, 127
chance 72, 74

changes in financial situation 96, 100
child benefits 113
children, the effect on welfare of 49
children, the empirical effect of children on the poverty line 254
chi-square statistic 153
choice of differentiating characteristics 15, 107
circular definition 14, 19, 25
command over resources 3, 9, 10, 50
compensating differentials 71, 72, 76
concave utility functions 130
conditions of living survey 149
convolution theorem 112
cost of clothing 19
cost effects 95
cost of food 15, 16, 17, 19, 20, 21, 56
Dalton inequality index 128, 129
Dalton poverty index 129, 267
decomposition of poverty indices 120, 138, 268
definition of economics 2
definition of poverty 10
definition of poverty line 10, 15-40
democratic process 15, 108
deprivation index 36
determinants of income 67, 180
   empirical 180
   theoretical 67
determinants of poverty 67, 105
   empirical 240
   theoretical 67, 105, 109

determinants of welfare parameter μ
    empirical   216
        Belgium   216
        Denmark   219
        France   220
        Germany   221
        Ireland   221
        Italy   222
        the Netherlands   222
        the United Kingdom   223
    theoretical   86
determinants of welfare parameter σ
    empirical   227
    theoretical   100
differentiation of the poverty line   14, 33, 43, 52
discrimination   75
dispersion parameter σ   47
dual labour market theory   76
earnings capacity   9, 11, 95
economic growth   1, 3
economic status   9, 10, 11, 68
economies of scale   23
education   78, 84, 99, 100, 195
elasticity of the poverty line
    empirical   244
    theoretical   12, 54, 55, 56, 57, 59
Engel coefficient   20, 21, 57
Engel function, estimates of the   56
equally distributed equivalent income   119, 120, 127
equal quantile assumption   46, 47
equivalence scales   10, 12, 22, 27, 50
equivalent adult   27, 91
exchange rates   174
expectations on the future   14
explanation of welfare parameter μ
    Belgium   216
    Denmark   219
    France   220
    Germany   221
    Ireland   221
    Italy   222

the Netherlands   222
the United Kingdom   223
extent of poverty
    empirical   264
    theoretical   119
family size   86, 97
    the effect on income   245
    the effect on μ   50, 86
family size elasticity   50
farmers   13, 50, 67
fluctuations in income   9, 78, 85, 96, 100, 195
food ratio   24, 57, 64
full income   9
full wealth   9
Gallup poll   30
Gini social welfare function   134
head-count ratio   119, 135
health   13, 14
heteroskedasticity   158
home production   9
household, as unit for welfare measurement   69
household size   50
household type   117, 168, 240
human capital   69, 71
hungerline   125
hypotheses on income   77
hypotheses on μ   95
hypotheses on poverty determinants   115
hypotheses on σ   100
impossibility theorem   120
incidence of poverty   119
income definition   67
income evaluation question   44, 45
income functions for female breadwinners   196

income functions for non-working
    households  204
    Belgium  204
    Denmark  206
    France  206
    Germany  207
    Ireland  207
    Italy  208
    the Netherlands  208
    the United Kingdom  209
income functions for partners  198
income functions for working men
    180
    Belgium  181
    Denmark  184
    France  185
    Germany  187
    Ireland  188
    Italy  190
    the Netherlands  191
    the United Kingdom  193
income functions for working women
    196
income inequality  27, 55, 90
income inequality of the poor  119
income gap of the poor  119, 135
income redistribution  3
income stability  90
indicators of style of living  34
indifference curves
    individual  8
    social  130
individual choice  71
inheritance  71, 74
international comparison of income
    functions
    for working men  194
    for non-working households  209
international comparison of µ-functions  224
interpersonal comparison  1, 5
interview  150, 151
leisure  9, 14
Leyden Income Evaluation Project
    44, 49, 64

Leyden poverty line definition  30-34, 43-63
life-cycle  69, 71, 72
location parameter $\mu$  47, 49
lognormal distribution function  47
luxuries  8
marginal utility  3, 6
market imperfections  71, 75
material welfare  2
material welfare school  1
mean income, poverty line defined
    as a percentage of  25, 58, 64
meaning of words  6, 45
measurability of utility  2
measurement errors  159
median income, effect on the poverty line  53, 244
median income, poverty line defined
    as a percentage of  25, 58, 64
Mill's ratio  81
minimum income question  30, 31
minimum welfare level  63
missing observations  158
monotonicity axiom  121, 142, 145
multicapability theory  74
natural unit of income  49
necessities  8
needs, satisfaction of  1, 7
non-cash income  50, 68
non-cash transfers  9
non-competitiveness  75
normal distribution function  47, 59
normalization  84
number of poor  119
nutritional needs  17
objective definition of poverty  13, 23, 28
Occam's razor  4

occupation 78, 85, 98, 100, 196
official definitions of poverty 21
ordinal utility 4
panel data 62, 89, 273
partial interpersonal comparison 5, 6
participation in communal activities 11, 34
participation in the labour market 79, 80
partner, the empirical effect of the partner's working on the poverty line 247
percentage of mean income, poverty line defined as 25, 58, 64
percentage of median income, poverty line defined as 25, 58, 64
percentile of income distribution 27, 59, 64
permanent income 68
physical efficiency 17
Pigou-Dalton transfer 6
population frequencies 154, 161
population symmetry axiom 121, 143, 147
poverty, definition of 1
poverty determinants 67, 105, 109, 240
poverty index
   empirical 264
   theoretical 119
poverty line, definition of 10, 52, 64
poverty lines, empirical
   according to household type 240
   average per country 243
poverty probability, theoretical 109
poverty probability, empirical 249
   the effect of age on 252, 260-263
   the effect of education on 250
   the effect of occupation on 250
   the effect of other socio-economic characteristics on 256
poverty threshold, definition of 10, 52, 167
preference drift 50, 54, 87, 95
proportion of poor axiom 121, 144, 148
public income redistribution 71, 76
purchasing power parities 174
questionnaire, design of 150
quota sampling 150
random sampling 150
ranked relative deprivation 122
RAS technique 154
reference drift 50, 54, 87, 95
relative deprivation 12, 25, 27, 34, 39, 119
relative poverty, empirical 265
relative poverty line, theoretical 12, 22, 53
representativeness 153
response rate 152
risk preference 47
sample frequencies 154, 161
sampling method 150
segmented labour market theory 75
sex of the main breadwinner 78, 98
social filter 87
social indicator 30, 34
social reference group 50, 53, 87, 88, 92
social welfare 2
social welfare function 5, 119, 120, 128, 129
specification error 90
standard deviation of log incomes 55

occupation 78, 85, 98, 100, 196
official definitions of poverty 21
ordinal utility 4
panel data 62, 89, 273
partial interpersonal comparison 5, 6
participation in communal activities 11, 34
participation in the labour market 79, 80
partner, the empirical effect of the partner's working on the poverty line 247
percentage of mean income, poverty line defined as 25, 58, 64
percentage of median income, poverty line defined as 25, 58, 64
percentile of income distribution 27, 59, 64
permanent income 68
physical efficiency 17
Pigou-Dalton transfer 6
population frequencies 154, 161
population symmetry axiom 121, 143, 147
poverty, definition of 1
poverty determinants 67, 105, 109, 240
poverty index
    empirical 264
    theoretical 119
poverty line, definition of 10, 52, 64
poverty lines, empirical
    according to household type 240
    average per country 243
poverty probability, theoretical 109
poverty probability, empirical 249
    the effect of age on 252, 260-263
    the effect of education on 250
    the effect of occupation on 250
    the effect of other socio-economic characteristics on 256
poverty threshold, definition of 10, 52, 167
preference drift 50, 54, 87, 95
proportion of poor axiom 121, 144, 148
public income redistribution 71, 76
purchasing power parities 174
questionnaire, design of 150
quota sampling 150
random sampling 150
ranked relative deprivation 122
RAS technique 154
reference drift 50, 54, 87, 95
relative deprivation 12, 25, 27, 34, 39, 119
relative poverty, empirical 265
relative poverty line, theoretical 12, 22, 53
representativeness 153
response rate 152
risk preference 47
sample frequencies 154, 161
sampling method 150
segmented labour market theory 75
sex of the main breadwinner 78, 98
social filter 87
social indicator 30, 34
social reference group 50, 53, 87, 88, 92
social welfare 2
social welfare function 5, 119, 120, 128, 129
specification error 90
standard deviation of log incomes 55